HARVARD ECONOMIC STUDIES

I. The English Patents of Monopoly. By William H. Price. 8vo.

II. The Lodging House Problem in Boston. By Albert B. Wolfe. 8vo.

III. The Stannaries: A Study of the English Tin Miner. By George R. Lewis. 8vo.

IV. Railroad Reorganization. By Stuart Daggett. 8vo.

V. Wool-Growing and the Tariff. By Chester W. Wright. 8vo.

VI. Public Ownership of Telephones on the Continent of Europe. By Arthur N. Holcombe. 8vo.

VII. The History of the British Post Office. By J. C. Hemmeon. 8vo.

VIII. The Cotton Manufacturing Industry of the United States. By M. T. Copeland. 8vo.

IX. The History of the Grain Trade in France. By Abbott Payson Usher. 8vo.

X. Corporate Promotions and Reorganizations. By A. S. Dewing. 8vo.

XI. The Anthracite Coal Combination in the United States. By Eliot Jones. 8vo.

XII. Some Aspects of the Tariff Question. By F. W. Taussig. 8vo.

XIII. The Evolution of the English Corn Market from the Twelfth to the Eighteenth Century. By N. S. B. Gras. 8vo.

XIV. Social Adaptation: A Study in the Development of the Doctrine of Adaptation as a Theory of Social Progress. By L. M. Bristol. 8vo.

XV. The Financial History of Boston, from May 1, 1822, to January 31, 1909. By C. P. Huse. 8vo.

XVI. Essays in the Earlier History of American Corporations. By J. S. Davis. 8vo. 2 volumes.

XVII. The State Tax Commission. By H. L. Lutz. 8vo.

XVIII. The Early English Customs System. By N. S. B. Gras. 8vo.

XIX. Trade and Navigation between Spain and the Indies in the time of the Hapsburgs. By C. H. Haring. 8vo.

XX. The Italian Emigration of Our Times By R. F. Foerster. 8vo.

XXI. The Mesta: A Study in Spanish Economic History, 1273–1836. By Julius Klein. 8vo.

XXII. Argentine International Trade under Inconvertible Paper Money: 1880–1900. By J. H. Williams. 8vo.

XXIII. The Organization of the Boot and Shoe Industry in Massachusetts before 1875. By Blanche E. Hazard. 8vo.

XXIV. Economic Motives. By Zenas C. Dickinson. 8vo.

XXV. Monetary Theory before Adam Smith. By Arthur E. Monroe. 8vo.

XXVI. Canada's Balance of International Indebtedness, 1900–1913. By Jacob Viner. 8vo.

XXVII. The History of the United States Post Office to the Year 1829. By W. E. Rich. 8vo.

XXVIII. The Theory of International Prices. By James W. Angell. 8vo.

XXIX. Forests and Sea Power. By Robert G. Albion. 8vo.

XXX. Banking Theories in the United States before 1860. By Harry E. Miller. 8vo.

XXXI. Karl Marx's Interpretation of History. By Mandell Morton Bober. 8vo.

XXXII. Grain Growers' Coöperation in Western Canada. By Harald S. Patton. 8vo.

XXXIII. The Assignats. By S. E. Harris. 8vo.

XXXIV. The Economic and Social History of an English Village. By N. S. B. Gras and E. C. Gras. 8vo.

XXXV. Direct Taxation in Austria. By John V. Van Sickle. 8vo.

XXXVI. The Greenbacks and Resumption of Specie Payments, 1862–1879. By Don C. Barrett. 8vo.

XXXVII. The Street Railway in Massachusetts. By Edward S. Mason. 8vo.

XXXVIII. The Theory of Monopolistic Competition. By Edward Chamberlin. 8vo.

XXXIX. Interregional and International Trade. By Bertil Ohlin. 8vo.

XL. The French International Accounts, 1880–1913. By Harry D. White. 8vo.

XLI. Twenty Years of Federal Reserve Policy. By S. E. Harris. 2 vols. 8vo.

HARVARD UNIVERSITY PRESS

CAMBRIDGE, MASS., U.S.A.

HARVARD ECONOMIC STUDIES

VOLUME XL

AWARDED THE DAVID A. WELLS PRIZE FOR THE YEAR 1931–32 AND PUBLISHED FROM THE INCOME OF THE DAVID A. WELLS FUND. THIS PRIZE IS OFFERED ANNUALLY, IN A COMPETITION OPEN TO SENIORS OF HARVARD COLLEGE AND GRADUATES OF ANY DEPARTMENT OF HARVARD UNIVERSITY OF NOT MORE THAN THREE YEARS STANDING, FOR THE BEST ESSAY IN CERTAIN SPECIFIED FIELDS OF ECONOMICS

LONDON : HUMPHREY MILFORD
OXFORD UNIVERSITY PRESS

The French International Accounts 1880–1913

BY

HARRY D. WHITE

ASSOCIATE PROFESSOR OF ECONOMICS, LAWRENCE COLLEGE
FORMERLY INSTRUCTOR IN ECONOMICS, AND TUTOR IN THE DIVISION OF HISTORY, GOVERNMENT, AND ECONOMICS, HARVARD UNIVERSITY

CAMBRIDGE
HARVARD UNIVERSITY PRESS
1933

PRINTED AT THE HARVARD UNIVERSITY PRESS
CAMBRIDGE, MASS., U. S. A.

To

F. W. TAUSSIG

PREFACE

This study is another in the series of inductive studies the purpose of which is to test and verify the doctrines of the orthodox theory of international trade. The study was undertaken because the French situation presents problems of special interest to the student of international trade: gold played a very important rôle in the monetary and banking system, and capital exports formed a large part of her international accounts. Not only this, but the question of the ultimate gain or loss from foreign investment presents itself with special emphasis. The fact that France invested abroad so large a portion of her savings was a source of considerable controversy in pre-war France. In recent years that general question has received considerable attention in England and the United States as well. Some attempt is therefore made to evaluate the effect of her huge foreign investments upon the welfare of France.

The years 1880 to 1913 were selected in order to avoid the confusion caused by the wars of 1870 and 1914 and the complications of bimetallism.

The statistical material pertaining to the subject was found to be much poorer than had been expected. Where original data existed, there had been little attempt to compile, or to analyze, or to put into useful shape. Price series of the kind needed were lacking and had to be constructed; monetary and banking statistics, tho more plentiful, were in no sense adequate for all the years. Some of the source material is wholly trustworthy; some is less accurate than it ought to be for an inductive study of this kind. It is hoped that the reader will bear in mind that the probable error in many of the estimates and statistical series is greater than would be found in studies of England, Canada, the United States, or for a later period in France; the conclusions, therefore, are to be accepted with greater caution.

Tho the study is largely in the nature of a test of the theory of international trade, the analysis of pertinent statistics bearing on the French foreign trade and monetary and banking practices will not be without interest for the student of French economic history.

The study is divided into two parts. Part I is devoted to a construction of a balance sheet of international accounts and to an analysis of the important items with the view of tracing the mechanism of adjustment. Part II deals first with the French monetary and banking movements in their relation to the movements of commodities and of capital exports. Following this the terms of trade at which France exchanged her exports for her imports are considered. Finally an attempt is made to evaluate the effects of French capital exports on the well-being of France.

I am glad to express my thanks to Professor F. W. Taussig, under whose direction this study was carried on, for most helpful criticism and advice. I am indebted also to my colleague, Professor M. M. Bober, and to Dr. L. B. Currie of Harvard University for their careful reading of the manuscript and for many suggestions. My discussions with Dr. A. G. Silverman of the National Bureau of Economic Research have been very helpful in clarifying certain aspects of the theory of international trade.

The Bureau of International Research of Harvard University and Radcliffe College, thru its liberal grant of funds for research, made it possible to gather information from French sources which would otherwise have been unavailable. To the Harvard Committee on Economic Research I am indebted for financial assistance in the final preparation of the manuscript.

My wife has given me invaluable aid at every stage of the work.

H. D. W.

Appleton, Wisconsin
November, 1932

CONTENTS

LIST OF CHARTS

LIST OF TABLES

THE FRENCH INTERNATIONAL ACCOUNTS

CHAPTER I

INTRODUCTION

THE theory of international trade has at no time remained undisputed. Altho its tenets have been for more than a century widely accepted both in England and in the United States, criticism has always been directed towards one or other of its aspects. Before the war it came chiefly from the Continent, where there existed neither great interest in nor thoro understanding of the orthodox theory. The contemporary attack, stimulated in large part by interest in problems arising from the war, — reparations, dislocated exchanges, heightened tariff schedules, shifts in international trade, huge foreign investments, — comes from economists well schooled in the classical doctrine and thoroly versed in its tenets. The effect of the concentrated criticism, especially as regards that part of the theory which purports to explain the mechanism of adjustment, has been to render dubious an explanation which only a generation ago was regarded as impregnable.

Just how the mechanism of adjustment functions is a matter of no small importance. Upon a correct explanation rests in large part the establishment of a wise policy with regard to international gold flows, reparations payments, tariff schedules, control of central bank discount rates, and — what is of increasing moment — capital exports. The absence of any settled and sustained policy in these important economic matters has in part been caused by uncertainty as to the manner in which international accounts are adjusted. A theory that correctly explains the mechanism of the exchange of goods and services between countries, the factors that influence the terms at which those exchanges are made, and the effects of international loans on the borrowing and lending countries will go a long way toward bringing about some measure of intelligent control of international trade and finance.

Such a theory can scarcely be arrived at thru deductive reasoning alone; it needs the support of verification. As Professor

Taussig has said, "Until we test and verify the hypothesis, we have no theory of international trade; we have no more than prolegomena to a theory." Inductive studies of certain aspects of the international trade of the United States, Argentina, Canada, China, Great Britain, and Germany have already been made. The present study of the international accounts of France attempts to supply another link in the verification or confutation of the theory.

Before proceeding to the detailed narrative and analysis of the French situation it is necessary to make a preliminary statement of the theory and of the apparent or real conflicts in it. We shall devote no time to tracing the historical development of the theory of international trade from its crude beginnings in the seventeenth century to its carefully refined formulation in the twentieth. It has been admirably traced by Professor Angell.[1] To review that development here can serve no useful purpose; the crudities which encumbered the theory at its various stages of development, and the refinements and corrections contributed by Thornton, Ricardo, Mill, Goschen, Cairnes, Edgeworth, Marshall, Bastable, and others, are of considerable interest in the history of economic thought; but for our purpose we need to restate only that formulation of the theory of international trade which has been most carefully worked out. There is little to be gained by tilting at the windmills of the well recognized errors and omissions of the earlier explanations.

For the statement of this, the neo-classical formulation, we draw chiefly on Professor Taussig's recent book International Trade,[2] an exposition of the orthodox theory, amplified, refined, and carefully modified to meet modern monetary and banking practice. The theory purports to explain (*a*) what causes some goods rather than others to be imported or exported, (*b*) the terms under which the exchanges take place and the factors which influence those terms, and (*c*) the mechanism of adjustment of international accounts. It is with the last part of the theory, the mechanism of adjustment, that we are here primarily concerned.

[1] J. W. Angell, The Theory of International Prices (Cambridge, 1926).

[2] New York, 1927.

The neo-classical explanation of the sequence of forces correcting a disturbed equilibrium in a country on a gold standard is as follows:

(1) A sustained increase on the debit side of the international accounts (caused by an increase in imports, or increased lending, or payment of indemnities, or tourist expenditures abroad, etc.) operates to increase the demand for foreign bills needed for remittance abroad. The increase in the demand for exchange causes the price of exchange to rise. The rise will continue until the gold export point is reached unless checked by an adequate increase in the supply induced by the rising price of exchange. The increased supply would be induced by the heightened rate if one or more of the following situations resulted:

(*a*) An increased excess of merchandise exports resulting from the lowered price of exchange to foreign importers and an increased price to domestic importers; that is, exports become less expensive in terms of foreign currency and imports more expensive in terms of domestic currency, tho no change in price occurs in terms of the exporting countries' currencies.

(*b*) An increased expenditure by foreigners on services rendered by the home country, and decreased expenditure by that country on foreign services. This occurs, as in the case of merchandise exports, because with the lowered exchange rates services in the home country cost less in terms of foreign currency, while foreign services are more expensive in terms of the home country's currency.

(*c*) An increase in long-term investments in the home country by foreigners, the increase occurring because of the slightly lowered cost of securities in terms of foreign exchange. For the same reason foreign securities become slightly higher in price to the home country (in which the price of exchange is rising), and therefore the rate of lending or investing abroad is reduced.

(*d*) Speculative sales of exchange by exchange dealers or banks against their foreign balances in anticipation of a reverse movement in the near future. These foreign balances may be permitted to decline until the other half of the speculative transaction — the *purchase* of bills — is completed, or they may be maintained by short-term foreign borrowing.

Situations (*b*) and (*c*) as possible sources of an increase in the supply of exchange are generally recognized to be negligible. The demand for foreign services and long-term investments [1] is not sufficiently elastic to be much affected by a rise or fall of one per cent or so in price.[2] With regard to (*a*) there is no such unanimity of opinion. By some writers it is held to be important, perhaps sufficient in itself to prevent the exchange rate from rising to the gold export point. By others it is held that the increase in the supply of bills is usually too small to accomplish this result.[3] The second check — speculative transactions — may, and doubtless does, help to correct minor disequilibrium. Obviously, however, speculative sales will hardly be undertaken unless there is an expectation of a not too distant increase in the supply of exchange. If undertaken, the completion of the transaction — the purchase of the bills — will again cause the rates to rise, unless in the interim something has happened to create an increased supply of exchange. Nothing, however, aside from accidental factors, factors in no way connected with the newly created disequilibrium in the balance of payments, does occur; therefore the rise in exchange rates will be checked only temporarily.

When the movement of exchange rates fails to cause a relative increase in the supply of exchange by increasing (relatively) exports or the import of capital (long-term investments), the sustained increased demand for bills cannot be satisfied, and the exchange rate must rise to the gold export point.

(2) It then becomes profitable for bankers to export gold to provide the needed supply of bills. This gold usually comes from bank reserves. When the amount of gold in circulation is to a

[1] The distinction made in this connection between short- and long-term investments is important. It is based solely on the intent of the investor, and not on the kind of security or commercial paper purchased or sold. If foreign securities are sold with the intent of buying them back when the rate of exchange drops, the transaction is in reality a short-time investment and falls into the category of speculative sales considered under (*c*).

[2] It is to be borne in mind that we are speaking here solely of exchange between countries on a gold standard.

[3] The matter will be considered in some detail in Chapter 7.

large extent controllable by banks — as, for example, in the United States, where gold certificates, rather than gold coins, circulate — the gold may actually come from hand-to-hand circulation rather than bank reserves. That is, the gold may be taken from the stock of gold in the treasury which is not counted as reserves.[1] In such case the sensitivity of the banking system to specie movements is lessened. When, however, the gold in circulation is in the form of coin, the gold cannot be withdrawn from circulation without causing an equivalent reduction in the gold reserves.[2]

(3) The reduction of gold reserves in the gold exporting country and the increase of reserves in the gold receiving country lead to a relative expansion of loans (deposits) in the gold receiving country and cause discount rates to rise relatively in the gold losing country. The change in relative discount rates may not occur at once. Each bank tries to increase its earning assets (loans) as much as feasible, and an increase of reserves makes the increases possible. If business in the gold receiving country is buoyant, with entrepreneurs eager to borrow, the loans will be expanded as soon as reserves are augmented, and the increase in gold reserves will serve to postpone or to check rising discount rates. If, on the other hand, the period is one of depression, of business pessimism, the banks may be unwilling to expand their portfolios, notwithstanding increasing reserves, because of the adoption of a more cautious lending policy. Or they may be unable to expand their loans even tho equipped and eager to do so because desirable borrowers may at such a time be disinclined to increase their borrowing. The rising reserve ratio, bringing with it declining bank profits, will in time cause banks to adopt a more liberal lending policy and they will tempt increased borrowing by lowering the discount rates. A year or even more may elapse before the increased reserves in the gold receiving country result

[1] This is possible because the people normally have no preference, and the banks can therefore replace at will gold certificates with other forms of paper currency.

[2] Gold coin circulates either because the people have a preference for gold coin, or because paper currency in small denominations is not available. In either circumstance the banks are normally unable to substitute paper currency for gold coins.

in increased demand liabilities. In the gold losing country the opposite tendency is in effect; a rise in discount rates occurs in order that the reserve ratio may be prevented from reaching a level considered dangerously low. The rise in discount rates may not occur at once. Gold reserves may be so high as to permit a considerable decline without approaching the danger point, or business activity may be on the decline and deposit liabilities decreasing at a rate fast enough to offset the loss in gold reserves. In the gold losing country as in the gold receiving country a long period may thus elapse before the increased or decreased gold reserves would affect discount rates or the volume of bank loans.

The cyclical movement of business activity is obviously an important factor in retarding or hastening the influence of increased gold reserves on bank loans, but it is not the only factor. The nature of the banking system and the tenor of economic life are other elements which cause differences in the sensitivity of bank deposits to bank reserves. In countries where, as in England, deposit banking is an all-important part of the banking and monetary system, the reaction of deposits and discount rates to gold flows will be more rapid and more dominating than in a country such as pre-war France, where deposit banking was relatively in its infancy. Notwithstanding the varying degrees of sensitivity of banking systems to bank reserves and the modifying effects of the cyclical movements of business activity, a sustained flow of gold out of the country eventually calls forth a rise in discount rates in the gold losing country, and a fall (relatively) in the gold receiving countries.

(4) The rising discount rate in the gold losing country tends to attract short-term funds from abroad and to discourage their outward movement. The unfavorable position of exchange (in the gold losing country) serves to enhance the attraction of short-term funds from abroad, since it increases the possibility of gain to the lenders of such funds from movements of exchange rates. The effect is to check the loss of gold.[1] The rise in discount rates also

[1] It may even reverse the flow if the difference in discount rates becomes great enough to offset the probable loss that results, in the case of a reverse flow, from the movement of exchange rates. The flow tends to be self-discouraging because of

tends to reduce the price of fixed income yielding securities and to make more attractive to foreign operators their purchase for speculative purposes. These movements of short-term funds to the gold losing country serve to check the outflow of gold and may cause it to cease entirely. But they are essentially no more than short-term movements and serve merely to postpone the outflow. If — to repeat what was said above regarding speculative exchange dealings — during the postponement *new* forces were introduced which would cause the supply of bills in the gold losing country to increase, the short-time funds could flow back to their place of origin without the aid of gold movements. The equilibrium would thus have been restored without the movement of much gold or without any change in sectional price levels. This accidental correction of equilibrium doubtless does frequently happen. But the factor establishing the equilibrium in such case is not part of the mechanism; it has not been called into being by the previous disequilibrium, and is therefore no link in the causal sequence. The situation would be that of two independent forces negating each other. One circumstance supplies bills of exchange and the other creates a demand for them, so that the original equilibrium in the balance of payments is not disturbed, or if disturbed by one of the forces, is subsequently restored by the operation of the other. Needless to point out, when this happens, no mechanism of adjustment is brought into play. Only those independent changes that do not offset each other call for a means of adjusting the resulting disequilibrium. Short-time movements in funds or speculation in exchange can only *postpone* the operation of adjustment of such disequilibrium; they do not constitute a means of adjustment.

(5) If the basic disequilibrium is not small enough to be corrected by the increased supply of bills provided exclusively from

the probability of loss from movements of exchange rates. Just as an unfavorable exchange rate (unfavorable to the gold losing country) makes likely a gain from exchange to lenders of short-term funds to the gold losing country, so does a favorable rate (i.e. exchange at the gold import point in the country where discount rates are rising) make likely a loss (from the movement of exchanges) to the foreign lenders of short-time funds. The probable gain or loss in both cases occurs, of course, when the short-time funds are subsequently withdrawn.

shipments of gold, the efflux of gold continues until the volume of credit in either or both countries is affected. After a lapse of a short or a long time, as pointed out above, bank demand deposits expand in the gold receiving country because of the augmented reserves, and decline in the gold losing country because of declining reserves.

(6) Expansion in the gold receiving country (relative to the gold losing country) is accompanied by rising prices and incomes. Goods produced for domestic consumption and for export increase in price and the volume of exports tends to decline. The relative decline in the price of imports stimulates their increase. In the gold losing country, on the other hand, prices and incomes are falling. Their exports consequently increase and their imports decline in quantity until the value of the exports is so much greater than the value of the imports as to supply the additional bills of exchange necessary to establish equilibrium in the balance of payments.

Such, in brief outline, is the neo-classical explanation of the mechanism of adjustment for international accounts. The criticism to which this explanation is being subjected is based primarily on the ground that the theory does not conform to the facts. It is claimed that the role ascribed to gold flows is much too important; that specie movements between countries on a gold standard are compensatory in nature; that they serve to help establish equilibrium only in so far as they directly increase the supply of exchange; and that sectional price levels are insensitive to gold flows, such changes as do occur being the cause, not the result, of specie movements. Some writers go so far as to deny the existence of any automatic or self-regulating mechanism, and claim that equilibrium in the international accounts is achieved either accidentally or thru positive steps taken by the government to modify exchange rates, gold flows, and trade.

Inductive studies are, of course, the one means of ascertaining whether or not the theory conforms to the facts. The results of such studies, however, have not been conclusive. Professor Viner in his study of Canada[1] believes that the evidence

[1] J. Viner, Canada's Balance of International Indebtedness (Cambridge, 1924).

supplied by the pertinent statistical data of Canada's international trade and credit and price movements verifies the classical doctrine. He found that the heavy increase in Canadian foreign borrowing after 1900 was accompanied by a shift in Canada's trade balance from an excess of exports to a marked excess of imports. The movements of specie, bank reserves, bank liabilities, and sectional price levels were, he believes, wholly in accord with the classical reasoning. The increased borrowings had led in Canada to a drop in exchange rates to the gold import point. The ensuing influx of gold went to increase Canadian bank reserves, and credit expansion occurred on a scale that would hardly have been possible had the gold reserves not been augmented by the new supply. The price of Canadian exports rose more rapidly than the price of imported goods (tho not so rapidly as the price of domestic goods not entering into international trade). Finally, imports increased more rapidly than exports until the excess of imports was large enough to reestablish equilibrium in the balance of payments.

Certain of the conclusions which Professor Viner draws from his study of the Canadian balance of payments are challenged by Professors Angell and Carr. Angell believes that Viner's data "warrant the inference — despite the opposite conclusion which he himself draws — that the classical theory is erroneous with respect to the role of gold flows, under modern conditions. The correction of the maladjustment in trade produced by loans did not come from the effects of the gold flows, or of the changes in the outside bank balances. It came from the effects of the original (and prior) increase in Canadian bank deposits." [1]

The objection on the score of chronological sequence is, however, not serious. True, Professor Viner's findings differ from the orthodox explanation in that credit expansion instead of *following* the increases in bank reserves appears to have preceded them. But the difference in chronological sequence need not, as Professor Taussig has pointed out, be held as inconsistent with the orthodox reasoning, because Canadian banks regarded their newly acquired claims on foreign specie as equivalent to an increase in

[1] J. W. Angell, op. cit., p. 174.

their reserves.[1] Instead of drawing on their foreign balances (created by the loans) and thus increasing their gold reserves, they loaned a good part of the funds in the New York call market and kept the remainder largely in New York banks. Both the funds loaned on call and those in the New York banks they regarded as secondary reserves. They could draw at will on these reserves and thus augment the gold reserves in their own vaults; but they did so only after increasing their domestic demand liabilities. Canadian banks presumably would not have increased their demand liabilities if their secondary reserves had been inadequate. Thus the fact that specie movements into Canadian vaults followed rather than preceded credit expansion hardly constitutes an inconsistency with the orthodox explanation; it represents merely a modification arising from modern banking practice. The significant thing is that the expansion in Canada could not have been so large had the secondary reserves not been augmented by the loans. The credit expansion within Canada from 1909 to 1913 proceeded at so rapid a rate as to cause the ratio of combined cash and outside reserves to decline impressively. The marked decline in the ratio of reserves from 1909 to 1913 would seem to indicate that credit was being extended to the utmost. If so, the orthodox analysis would seem, for those years at least, to be substantiated.

Professor Carr's criticism appears to be no more serious than Angell's.[2] Carr fails to find in Viner's statistical data any verification of the classical sequence in the mechanism of adjustment. The rise in Canadian prices relative to world prices, Carr maintains, *preceded* increases in capital imports and increases in bank deposits, and could not, therefore, have been initiated by credit expansion based on increased reserves. Had this actually been the case, then price movements could not have been caused by the expansion of credit brought about by capital imports. It were well to note, however, that the lags in question are not very clearly

[1] See Taussig, op. cit., Chap. 19, for a detailed discussion of the relation of gold flow to expansion in Canada.

[2] R. M. Carr, The Role of Price in the International Trade Mechanism, Quar. Jour. of Econ., August, 1931.

defined.[1] They must be interpreted with caution, particularly since the price curve used in the time comparison represents the difference between Canadian prices and world prices, both of which were moving in the same direction.

But even if we grant the existence of a lag, Carr's conclusion about Viner's findings can hardly be so destructive to the classical theory as Carr believes. It is quite true that capital imports may be stimulated by a rise in domestic prices, but in evaluating the role of gold flows the important thing is not always, as has been pointed out above, the order of sequence; what signifies is whether or not the additional gold reserves accompanying the capital imports were essential to the sustained rise in prices. As Professor Taussig writes with regard to a borrowing country that is expanding, — a situation similar to that of Canada from 1900 to 1913, — "During the years of the upswing period, the import of specie into a borrowing country may seem to be due at each several date to the higher prices and the higher money rates to follow these, not precede them. But these higher prices could not be maintained, much less could move still higher, unless the flow of specie came to the rescue, so to speak. And it could not be a supporting factor for the persisting expansion unless there were some other force at work, such as an international loan." [2]

Nor can Carr's interpretation of the spread between Canadian and world prices be considered damaging to the classical theory. He states: "Instead of finding that the foreign borrowing inflated prices and thereby automatically set in motion a chain of sequences tending to establish an equilibrium in international prices, one finds that the rise in prices stimulated borrowing and that international prices were farther from equilibrium at the end of the period than at any time during it." [3] The larger spread

[1] For illustration, Carr accepts Angell's claim that the balance of trade has "a characteristic tendency to a lag of about a year" behind the movements in deposits. Examination of the data shows that if any such tendency is present, it certainly is not marked. In seven of the twelve years both movements are in the same direction, and in two of the remaining years, tho the direction is not the same, there is hardly enough amplitude in either movement to make the lag significant. It is only in 1907, 1910, and 1912 that there is a definite lag.

[2] Op. cit., p. 209.

[3] Op. cit., p. 719.

which Carr finds at the end as compared with the beginning of the borrowing period is not an indication that international prices [1] "were further from equilibrium." Indeed, in the case of a country whose rate of foreign borrowing is increasing a growing spread may be indicative not of growing disequilibrium, but of approaching equilibrium. *Equilibrium* is not to be confused with *equality*.[2] Disequilibrium between price structures (of countries on a gold standard) exists only when major gold flows are occurring. In the case of Canada net gold imports in 1913 were smaller than in several prior years, indicating the possibility that disequilibrium was less, not greater, than in previous years. They were not so small as at the beginning of the period, but in view of the fact that the volume of borrowing had been increasing greatly there is no

[1] I presume Carr means by the term "international prices" the relation of the Canadian price structures to the price structures of other countries.

[2] The term *equilibrium* as applied to the relationship between the price structures of two or more countries on the gold standard has never been clearly defined. Tho the word is constantly used, writers are not always agreed as to its meaning, nor always consistent in their own usage. I employ the term here to describe such a relationship between the price structures of two or more countries as gives rise to no major gold flows. This appears to be the meaning of the term as used by Ricardo, perhaps the first economist of importance to employ the word in this connection (see Principles of Political Economy, Chap. VII), and many others. It is true that gold movements may arise from causes other than a disturbed equilibrium in the price relationship, but when this occurs, the flow of gold serves to modify an existing relationship. Therefore it may logically be held that the mere existence of net gold movements of any significant size indicates a state of disequilibrium, and a cessation of gold flows a state of equilibrium. A reduction in gold flows would thus be a sign of approaching equilibrium, the correction of disequilibrium being in progress either because the disturbing force is diminishing or because the corrective force is becoming more potent.

The refusal of certain economists to regard gold flows as an indication of disequilibrium between price structures is puzzling in the absence of any clear statement on their part as to the meaning they give the term. Unwillingness to accept gold flows as an indication of disequilibrium in international accounts is even more strange, for in this connection the term equilibrium is not vague. It has been clearly defined as existing only in the absence of net gold movements (see, for example, J. S. Mill, Bk. III, Chap. 21), and has been so used by most writers. There may be grounds for desiring that the definition of equilibrium in international accounts be changed because the word has connotations which are too complex to permit its use in any such simple manner, but unless the definition is changed, it is illogical to deny that gold flows are an indication of disequilibrium in international accounts.

reason why they should have been, for an increase in the rate of borrowing tends to counteract the approach to equilibrium induced by previous gold flows.[1]

The criticism of Professors Angell and Carr serves to emphasize the variations possible in the sequence of changes in the adjustment process, but it does not eliminate gold flows as an essential link in that sequence. Whether capital imports in the Canadian instance were stimulated by rising Canadian prices, and whether they occurred before, after, or concomitantly with the expansion of Canadian deposits is of interest, but does not touch the essential question to which Viner was seeking the answer.

Professor Taussig's inductive study of the international trade of Great Britain between the years 1880 and 1913 also appears to support the neo-classical analysis, but here again the evidence is not conclusive.[2] Professor Taussig found that the merchandise balances moved in accordance with the major fluctuations in capital exports, and that they did so without the lag observed in the Canadian instance. The net movements of capital in and out of Great Britain were effected quickly thru merchandise movements. Import and export prices were, on the whole, such as the classical reasoning would presuppose: the increase in capital exports was accompanied by a rise in the price of imports relative to exports. Somewhat different results in the matter of Great Britain's price

[1] Carr finds also "embarrassing to the classical analysis" the "fact that according to Viner's estimates all but 1.6 per cent of the capital imports (for the period as a whole) was absorbed by commodities and services." 1.6 per cent is much too small an amount, Carr holds, to have provided Canada with the increase in purchasing power requisite for carrying on a growing domestic trade at the sustained higher price level. It is easy to dispose of this criticism, resting as it does on an error in the interpretation of Viner's data. In attempting to account for the increase in Canada's purchasing power, Carr quite overlooks the 120 millions of net specie imports which are included with merchandise under the head of commodity balance (90 millions unrecorded and 30 millions recorded). This amount of specie, on the basis of the approximate 10 per cent reserve ratio then prevailing in Canada, could have sustained an expansion of purchasing power of over 1 billion dollars. The importance of this billion may be judged from the fact that the total demand liabilities in Canada rose by no more than 800 millions, i.e. from 340 millions in 1900 to 1.14 billions in 1913. Thus instead of "embarrassing" the classical analysis, Viner's data on this point offer a bit of supporting evidence.

[2] F. W. Taussig, op. cit., Chaps. 20–21.

movements were obtained by Dr. Silverman. On the basis of a monthly price series which he constructed especially for his study, he found evidence that for most of the period 1880 to 1913 there was an inverse correlation between the annual variations in the net barter terms of trade (import prices divided by export prices) and capital exports; that is, the net barter terms of trade became more, not less, favorable as capital exports increased.[1] These results, however, are not strictly comparable with those of Professor Taussig, who was concerned with trends rather than with annual variations. A comparison of trends shows greater similarity. The trend obtained by Dr. Silverman displays a less marked downward movement from 1880 to 1900, but the direction is the same. Nevertheless, the results yielded by Dr. Silverman's careful investigation of the monthly movements of import and export prices must incline us to question the weight of the evidence supplied in Taussig's study of the British instance.

The evidence in Professor Taussig's study of the international trade of the United States during post-war years is puzzling, and serves neither as verification nor as refutation of the classical doctrine.[2] The net capital exports during those years and the merchandise balance of trade moved closely together, but apparently the relationship was maintained quite without the specie-flow-price mechanism. The large gold movements of that period did not affect the price level; as Professor Taussig points out, the monetary system was very insensitive to specie movements. How explain, then, the rapid adjustment of the balance of payments? How account for the remarkably close correlation between capital and merchandise movements notwithstanding abrupt changes in the principal items of the international account?

Professor Taussig holds the adjustment to have been accidental, that "things just *happened* so. . . . From the movements of gold, prices, and merchandise . . . one can make out nothing in the nature of an ordered sequence, of conformity to rule or to reason." Professor Angell, after examining the data, came to

[1] A. G. Silverman, Some International Trade Factors for Great Britain, The Review of Economic Statistics, August, 1931.

[2] F. W. Taussig, op. cit., Chap. 25.

much the same conclusion.[1] The movements of capital and of goods were largely independent of each other. They were "directly or indirectly the common results of a common antecedent condition, the fluctuating state of economic affairs in Europe. . . . Neither item had to adapt itself to the other's fluctuations, for the two sets of fluctuations were roughly coincident and compensating by their very origin." Angell concludes that this explanation "is intellectually rather unsatisfactory. . . . But it is apparently the only way of accounting for the almost total absence of a discernible connection between the movements of the net balance of payments and the movements of internal credit and prices; and for the absence of any clear lag or precedence between the changes in the net capital items and net commodity items of the balance itself."

Notwithstanding the agreement of two eminent authorities, it is difficult to attribute such synchronization of independent movements over so long a period to "accident." It is expected, to be sure, that the economic conditions which give rise to increased foreign borrowing will also stimulate trade. But is there any reason why the amplitude of the two movements should be so nearly the same? So close a relationship suggests something more than accident; it strongly suggests a causal sequence. Is the causal factor to be found perhaps in the changes of demand schedules in both the borrowing and the lending countries, changes which inevitably accompany movements of capital? Is this shift in demand schedules the important instrument of adjustment? If it is, then the neo-classical sequence, which was found to be absent in the case of the United States and also perhaps of Canada, may not be essential to the adjustment of disequilibrium in the balance of payments. The rapidity also with which the adjustment was found to have taken place in the instance of Great Britain and the United States might be readily explained if changes in demand schedules were the effective mechanism.

The mechanism, perhaps best termed the changes-in-demand-schedules mechanism, may be presumed to operate in the follow-

[1] J. W. Angell, Equilibrium in International Trade: The United States 1919–26, Quar. Jour. of Econ., May, 1928.

ing manner. The transfer of funds out of the lending country causes the demand schedules for all commodities to shift to the left (in varying degrees, depending upon what has been called "flexibility" of demand as distinct from elasticity of demand, i.e. changes in demand induced by changes in *income*, not in *prices*). Imported commodities feel the effects of the change in demand, and imports decline. A reduction in the amount of goods purchased from the borrowing country accounts for part of the decrease in imports; that is, the borrowing country's exports to the lending country decline. The converse occurs in the borrowing country. There the newly acquired purchasing power causes demand schedules to move to the right. Imports into this loan receiving country increase as a result of the general increase in demand schedules. Some of the increase in imports is purchased in the lending country, thereby increasing its (the lending country's) exports. The new situation in the lending country is a decline in imports and an increase in exports; in the borrowing country an increase in imports and a decrease in exports. The lending country will develop an excess of exports and the borrowing country an excess of imports, *all of which can occur without the agency of the classical specie-flow-price sequence.*

Adjustment of the balance of payments partly thru this means was first suggested by Bastable, tho it received only his passing notice. In 1889 he wrote, "The inhabitants of the former country [a creditor country which had claims on the debtor country] having larger money incomes will purchase more *at the same price* and then bring about the necessary excess of imports over exports."[1] Notwithstanding the italics, and his familiarity with Nicholson's views, in his Theory of International Trade[2] he made, curiously enough, no mention of the point.[3] Writing a few years after Bastable's article was published, but before the third and fourth edition of his (Bastable's) International Trade, Nicholson gave the matter more notice. In a discussion of the way in

[1] On Some Applications of the Theory of International Trade, Quar. Jour. of Econ., October, 1889, p. 16.

[2] Published before the second and subsequent editions of his book.

[3] See Bastable's 4th edition, Appendix C.

which the payment of a tribute takes the form of goods, he wrote: "There will be partly a lessened demand for imports and partly an excess of home commodities available for exports. At the same time the receiving country — when money is sent to it — will have so much more to spend and can take more imports and also consume things formerly exported. In this way an excess of exports from the paying country equivalent to the tribute can be brought about without any change in general prices." [1]

Altho stated so clearly, the idea was apparently lost sight of for over twenty years. It was not mentioned again until 1918 in a paper by Professor Taussig,[2] who held that a loan would increase the demand schedules in the borrowing country but would cause imports to increase only a little because part of the funds borrowed would be spent at home on domestic goods and services; and that in any event changes in price levels consequent upon the gold flows supplied the only visible mechanism whereby the export excess would exactly equal the borrowings. Professor Wicksell in an answering paper stated very briefly that even if the funds were spent at home, the effect would be the same as tho they were spent abroad, since the increased demand for domestic goods would leave fewer goods available for export.[3] Professor Viner, reviewing the discussion, stated his agreement with Taussig. He went on to show that "In the absence of special circumstances, such as the requirement that the proceeds of the loan be immediately used in making purchases in the lending country, and in the absence of price changes, there is no reason why borrowing abroad should disturb the proportions in which the total purchasing power in the borrowing country, including that derived from the loan, is used in buying domestic and foreign commodities. Without a disturbance in these proportions the loan cannot wholly enter in the form of commodities." [4]

[1] J. S. Nicholson, Principles of Political Economy, Vol. II, Bk. III, Sec. 14, p. 290.

[2] International Trade and Depreciated Paper, Quar. Jour. of Econ., Vol. 31, p. 39.

[3] K. Wicksell, International Freights and Prices, Quar. Jour. of Econ., 1918, Vol. 32, p. 404.

[4] J. Viner, Canada's Balance of International Indebtedness, pp. 203 ff.

It appears to me that Professor Viner's conclusions on this point are not valid. There is every reason to believe, on the contrary, that borrowings abroad would disturb the proportions. Increased borrowings are to a country what a loan is to an individual. The additional purchasing power provided by the loan will not be allocated to all items in the budget in the proportions occurring in the original income. Indeed it would be surprising if it were, especially if the funds be borrowed for a specific purpose — the usual case in foreign borrowing. An illustration may serve to make the point clear. A foreign loan is made by Colombia for the construction of an electric railway. Most of the material needed for the construction must be purchased abroad. Suppose half the loan to be expended at home on labor and materials and half on imported material. According to the statement of Professor Viner such a division of expenditure would be expected to occur only if the country normally spent half its income on imports. Clearly that need not be so. There need be no close relationship between the proportion of a country's income spent on imports and the proportion of a loan so expended. Using Professor Viner's illustrative figures, it is quite reasonable to come to other conclusions than those he draws.

The example is of a country with the following economic program:

Domestic production	$10,000,000
Exports	1,000,000
Goods similar to exports consumed at home	1,000,000
Imports	1,000,000

The country borrows abroad $1,000,000. According to Viner only 10 per cent (the proportion of domestic expenditures on imports) of this sum will be spent on additional imports; i.e. the million dollar loan would result (because of the shift in demand schedules) in increased imports to the amount of $100,000 and decreased exports to the amount of another $100,000. But there is much more likelihood that the money will be expended in a different proportion. The amount of the loan expended directly on imports might range from $100,000 to $800,000, depending entirely on the purposes for which the loan was made and the pattern of the national economy; that expended on goods normally exported might increase from $100,000 to $500,000. In other words, there are no *a priori* grounds for expecting the division of expenditures to remain the same with income increased by foreign borrowing. Just as an individual unconsciously readjusts the *proportions* of his total expenditures as the result of a loan, so does a country. The readjusted expenditures may bear more heavily on imported commodities, or on domestic commodities normally exported, or on domestic services.

Countries that borrow abroad are often predominantly agricultural. They usually borrow for the extension of public works, or for the expansion of industry. In either case large portions of the loan will be spent directly on imported equipment and material, even tho imports may constitute a small percentage of the total domestic expenditures. It is thus reasonable to expect a borrowing country to spend a *much larger* proportion of the loan directly on imports than that indicated by the ratio of domestic expenditures to imports. Moreover, when the lending country happens to be highly industrialized, a large proportion of the proceeds of the loan is likely to be spent directly in the lending country. When a semi-industrialized country — France, for instance — is the lender, direct export sales are less likely to occur. When, also, the borrowing is for the purpose of balancing budgets, or for funding short-time loans held within the country, the direct expenditure on imports will be much less. Nevertheless, because the borrowing country is often industrially undeveloped, and because funds are very frequently raised for plant expansion, railroad building, the purchase of military equipment, electrification programs, and so forth, the probability that a goodly portion of the loan will be immediately spent on imports is by no means a small one.

It can hardly be denied that changes in demand schedules brought about by loans cause movements in imports and exports to take place (frequently to a significant extent) in the lending and the borrowing country. But can these changes in demand schedules unaided bring about merchandise movements of *suffi-*

cient amplitude to correct the disequilibrium? This is a much more difficult question to answer. The claim advanced by Professor Taussig and concurred in by Professor Viner is that without price changes there is no visible mechanism to bring about *equality* between capital exports and merchandise movements. It seems to me that this view may be questioned; equality between capital exports and merchandise movements may quite possibly be brought about by the changes in demand induced by movements of capital. The reasoning which suggests such a possibility is as follows:

The purchasing power of the borrowing country is augmented, that of the lending country decreased, by at least the amount of the loan. The increase and decrease may be greater than the actual amount of the loan, for an increase of foreign balances will be regarded by banks in the borrowing country as equivalent to an increase in cash holdings and may consequently permit an expansion of deposits in the domestic banking system in excess of the quantity of increased "reserves." On the other hand, in the lending country the transfer of deposits from domestic to foreign account may be regarded as a weakening factor calling for the maintenance of a higher reserve ratio, and may cause a decline in deposits on domestic account in excess of the loan.[1] The effect on merchandise movements is thus greater than it would be if the credit expansion and contraction could not exceed the actual gain or loss in gold. To illustrate, if 10 per cent of the additional purchasing power resulting from the loan should be spent on imports, the increase in imports might equal not 10 but 20 or more per cent of the amount of the loan. Similarly in the lending country if 10 per cent of the loss in domestic purchasing power impinges on imports, the decrease in imports might equal 20 or more per cent of the amount of the loan. Just as in the classical analysis a movement of gold would affect prices thru its expanding or contracting effect on credit, so the effect of a loan on demand schedules would

[1] A movement of gold may, of course, occur. When it does, the increase of cash reserves in the loan (and gold) receiving country (and the loss of gold in the lending country) permits increases in excess of the gold movement (and favors decreases in the gold losing countries).

be enhanced thru the expansion or contraction of demand deposits.[1]

If the country spends the entire loan on imports, and if these additional imports are all obtained from the lending country, then, clearly, the loan is translated into merchandise movements without any specie-flow-price mechanism. But it is extremely unlikely that all the additional funds will be spent on imports (unless the conditions of the loan demand it); and it is even less likely that all the additional imports purchased will be obtained from the lending country. What actually will happen in any given situation depends entirely upon the importance of imports and of exports in the economy of both the lending and the borrowing countries; the economic conditions in the lending and the borrowing countries; and the nature of the goods produced, exported, and imported in each country. Variations in any one of these conditions will change the proportion of the loan spent directly on imports from the lending country.

Obviously it is impossible to estimate the probable proportions in any given instance without knowing something about each of the conditions enumerated. Yet for the purpose of theoretical analysis we may proceed on the basis of a likely assumption.

The following conditions would be reasonable to presuppose: A portion of the loan will be spent by the borrowing country on the imports of several countries, including goods of the lending country; the remainder will be spent on domestic goods and services. In the lending country, as a result of the loss in purchasing power, there will occur a decline in imports — to the extent of a small proportion of the loan — and a decline in domestic purchases of domestic goods and services — to the extent of the re-

[1] Tho the establishment of an import balance in the borrowing country (and export balance in the lending country) will be hastened by the possibility mentioned above with respect to the gain (and loss) of purchasing power via credit expansion (or contraction) in excess of the amount of the loan, it is clear that the gain in purchasing power in excess of the loan will decline rapidly as adjustment proceeds. It will disappear when adjustment is reached because in the borrowing country the increase in the foreign balance resulting from the loan has been employed to pay for the import excess. In the lending country the development of an export excess has transferred the balances owned by the foreign countries back to domestic ownership.

mainder of the loan. In such case, the capital movements will be equal to the merchandise movements if one further assumption — an important one — be made; namely, that in the borrowing country (as a result of the increased purchasing power) there be a rough equalization between the increase in the purchase of domestic goods and the decline in exports; and in the lending country (as a result of the loss in purchasing power) there be a rough equalization between the decline in domestic purchases and the increase in exports. This is equivalent to saying that (1) the borrowing country employs her total loan either on imports or on goods that otherwise would have been exported, and (2) the lending country exports those domestic commodities it would have consumed had the loan not been made.

The question is, can such an assumption reasonably be made? If it can, then we may conclude, first, that the specie-flow-price mechanism is sometimes unimportant as a means of adjustment in the balancing of international accounts, and, secondly, that changes in demand schedules caused by transfers of purchasing power may play a principal role in the adjustment. If it cannot, then changes in demand schedules constitute only one of two or more channels necessary to establish equilibrium; some other mechanism must play the important role in bringing about the equalization of capital and merchandise movements. Let us see, then, whether the foregoing assumption has any basis.

What are the possible effects of changes in the volume of domestic expenditure (caused by transfer of purchasing power) on the exports of the lending and of the borrowing country? First as to the borrowing country. If the supply of domestic goods (and services) cannot be increased, then additional domestic purchases can come only from goods that would normally be exported, or — what amounts to the same thing — from the diversion of some of the factors of production from export goods into the production of goods for domestic consumption. But it is hardly reasonable to assume that the only means of increasing the supply of domestic goods and services is to reduce the amount available for export. *Some* increase in domestic production can take place. Excess plant capacity and slightly obsolete machinery may be utilized;

more land can be called into use; the supply of credit can be expanded; and the supply of labor except, perhaps, when near the peak of a boom period can be augmented.[1]

How much of an increase can take place depends upon the state of business activity at the time of borrowing. During a period of slackening business activity, or during the early period of recovery from a depression, the supply of domestic commodities and services can increase much more than during a period of rapid expansion. Since during a period of increased foreign borrowing a country is more likely to be passing thru an upward phase of business activity than thru any other phase of the cycle, the effect of increased domestic purchases is apt to be a significant curtailment of exports. The decrease in exports will be somewhat diminished by the rise in domestic prices consequent upon the increase in demand, because the rise itself will absorb part of the newly acquired purchasing power. The volume of goods available for export in the borrowing country will thus in any case decline less in total value than the part of the loan spent at home.[2] The relationship between the two, however, if not close, need not necessarily during a period of expansion be remote.

In the lending country the relationship between curtailed domestic purchases and increased exports is likely to be even less close. A decline in the demand for domestic goods and services leaves more goods available for export, but that does not necessarily mean that these additional export goods will be purchased by other countries; some part of the decrease in domestic demand will be felt by goods and services for which there is no foreign demand. Yet some increase in exports will doubtless occur without any change in prices *being necessary* to induce the increase, be-

[1] Even when in a given country the supply of certain commodities — e.g. agricultural crops — is fixed for several months at a time, there is some elasticity provided by the possibility of increasing the rate of withdrawal from warehouses.

[2] The increase in the demand for domestic goods and services consequent upon the increase in purchasing power cannot impinge solely on goods similar in kind to goods normally exported. Therefore an increase in the supply of certain goods can curtail the production of export goods only after sufficient time has elapsed to divert the factors of production from certain of the export industries to certain of the domestic industries.

cause the borrowing country is increasing its imports from the lending country (as has been pointed out), and because other foreign countries will also increase their imports as a result of the increased demand schedules in these countries.

This last factor, — the increase in the lending country's exports caused by increases in the total demand in other countries (the result, in turn, of their increased exports to the borrowing country),— tho it has been scarcely mentioned in the literature of international trade,[1] may warrant some attention as a contributory force in the development of an export surplus in the lending country. The operation of this force is felt (in differing degrees) in all the countries that trade with the lending and the borrowing countries. In those countries which experience an increase in exports to the loan receiving country, there occurs an increased demand either for domestic goods or for imports to fill the void left by the increase in exports. The new demand impinges in part on imports, some of which come from the lending country. Thus, thru the operation of this roundabout process, the lending country's exports are increased. A French loan to Russia will hence cause an increased Russian demand for British, German, and American products as well as French, and will subsequently increase the British, German, and American demand for French commodities among others.

The tendency toward equilibrium effected directly by these changes in demand schedules may be either strengthened or weakened by the sectional price movements which accompany such changes. The changes would be brought about in this way. In the borrowing country the additional purchasing power impinges on both purely domestic goods and imports and exports, both actual and potential, and tends to cause the prices of all three classes of goods to rise. The larger the proportion of the loan spent directly on domestic goods, the more will domestic prices

[1] The only writer who mentions this contributory channel of adjustment is Ohlin, who in a paper on the reparations problem gives it passing attention (see footnote, p. 29). The paper also considers in some detail the effects of changes in demand schedules on international trade. Professor Ohlin appears to be a strong adherent of the changes-in-demand-schedules theory of adjustment.

be affected, and the less the price of imports will rise. In such case the relative rise in the price of domestic goods will accentuate and hasten the increase in imports and the decline in exports.

If, however, the borrowing country expends the bulk of the loan on imports, the price of domestic goods will not rise (or rise much less), and exports will not be curtailed to the same extent (if at all). Thus the larger the share of the loan spent on imports, the smaller the decline in exports. But the larger the portion spent on imports, the less is the adjustment — the creation of an import surplus — dependent upon the decline in exports (from the borrowing country). It is therefore apparent that price changes act as a retarding influence on the development of an import surplus when such influence is least effective — at a time when the surplus is already large as a result of the changes in the demand schedules. On the other hand, when the import surplus does not occur directly as a result of the changes in the demand schedules, price changes hasten the development of the import surplus. They act as a supplementary force, which is potent in proportion with the need; the greater the need for the supplementary force, the more potent does it automatically become.

In the lending country similar forces are at work. If the decrease in purchasing power results in a greater drop in the demand for domestic goods than for imports, the prices of domestic goods — and therefore of exports — will tend to decline, thereby hastening the creation of an export surplus. If the full force of the decrease in purchasing power is directed towards imported commodities, the price of export goods will not decline. The relative decline in the price of imports will then tend to check the growth of the export surplus needed for the correction of the disequilibrium in the international account. But — as in the case of the exporting country — the larger the drop in purchases of imports, the less does the adjustment depend upon the increase in exports, the export surplus being created by a drop in imports.[1]

[1] No mention has been made of foreign changes in demand which operate to modify the price changes traced above. When speaking of the lending country's exports it was pointed out that the price of export commodities declines with the decline in the domestic demand for home goods. We disregarded at the time the

It is thus apparent that tho sectional price changes consequent upon shifts in demand may either favor or oppose the adjustment of disequilibrium, their effects are in the main of secondary importance; they operate in the direction of aiding adjustment when the process of adjustment is most in need of assistance, and oppose it when it is least in need of assistance.

This brief analysis of the changes in imports and exports brought about by changes in demand schedules hardly serves to answer the question posited earlier. That question, it will be remembered, was: can the assumption be reasonably made that transfers of purchasing power cause changes in demand schedules which in the borrowing country give rise to a rough equalization between the increase in the purchase of domestic goods and the decline in exports; and in the lending country between the decline in domestic purchases and the increase in exports? Our analysis suggests that there may well be some approach to such equalization. The assumption, it would seem, may therefore be made; but it remains, unless better supported, merely a reasonable assumption. If it operates at all, the medium of changes in demand as a corrective of disequilibrium has an effectiveness not possessed by the specie-flow-price mechanism. The latter causes exports from the lending country to increase because of the drop in the price of those exports, but it fails to produce an export excess unless the elasticity of the foreign demand for the lending country's goods is more than unity. The changes-in-demand mechanism causes exports to increase without a prior drop in prices being necessary. It can therefore more easily serve to develop an export surplus.

But before venturing even a tentative evaluation of this appar-

counteracting influence of an increase in the foreign demand for the lending country's exports.

If the increase in the foreign demand for the lending country's exports is greater than the decline in its demand for its own goods, the price of its exports will tend to rise rather than fall. But whenever this situation occurs, the checking effect of the rise in price on exports is of little consequence; the adjustment has been approaching consummation in direct proportion with the very decline in imports which had caused the price of exports to rise. In other words, the counteracting influence on prices is increased when the adjustment is less affected by it. The same line of reasoning must be applied to the imports and exports of the borrowing country.

ently so simple means of adjustment, one question of prime importance must be answered. We speak very glibly of the transfers of purchasing power which cause demand schedules to change, but we make no mention of the process by which these transfers are made. Are they made to the extent that we have presupposed, or are they limited to net gold movements?

The manner of transfer is the crucial point in the controversy between J. M. Keynes and Professor Ohlin regarding the payment of German reparations.[1] Keynes claims that the requisite change in Germany's balance of trade — the development of a large excess of exports — must be brought about by a relative drop in German prices. Professor Ohlin maintains the thesis that changes in demand schedules would be sufficient to effect the necessary changes in Germany's balance of trade. Keynes is noncommittal as to the general principle of the effects of changes in demand schedules in correcting disequilibrium; but in the case of Germany, he says, it can play no role because the transfer of purchasing power cannot take place. That, according to Keynes, is the kernel of the difficulty. He writes: "If Germany was in a position to export large quantities of gold, or if foreign balances in Germany were acceptable to Central Banks as a substitute for gold in their reserves, then it would be a different matter. For if Germany could set the ball rolling by exporting sufficiently large quantities of gold to have an appreciable effect on world prices, this, I agree, might help the situation by changing demand correlations." [2] Since gold could not be exported in sufficient quantities, and foreign banks did not wish to accept balances in German banks in exchange for domestic balances (balances which would have to be kept in Germany until she developed a sufficient export surplus), Keynes maintains that a discussion of the effect of change in demand conditions consequent upon transfers of pur-

[1] J. M. Keynes, The Transfer Problem, Economic Journal, March, 1929; A Reply, ibid., September, 1929. B. Ohlin, Transfer Difficulties, Real and Imagined, Economic Journal, July, 1929; A Rejoinder, ibid., September, 1929.

[2] The latter part of the quotation shows Keynes to be thinking of changes in demand in *the market sense* (apparently to be induced by the specie-flow-price mechanism) and not the kind of changes in demand with which Ohlin is concerned. Yet Keynes' opinion on that score is not pertinent to the present discussion.

chasing power is irrelevant. Professor Ohlin is vague in his reply. He explains that the transfer of purchasing power would take place thru the expansion of credit in foreign countries, the expansion to be based on the purchase of the bills on Germany by foreign central banks. Elsewhere Ohlin sets forth his views more clearly.[1] His point is that central banks in reparations receiving countries *ought* to make possible transfers of purchasing power by buying bills on Germany. The balances would be left in the Reichsbank until the mechanism of adjustment began to operate (thru changes in demand schedules). The ensuing German export surplus would supply the bills necessary to permit those foreign balances to be withdrawn.

In the light of this explanation it is clear that Keynes and Ohlin are not meeting on the issue. One maintains that transfers of purchasing power in significant quantities cannot be made because foreign banks will not coöperate; the other argues that the necessary transfers could be made *if* foreign banks would coöperate as they ought to do. The controversy thus fails to provide an answer to the question how transfers *are* made.

There are two means whereby purchasing power may be transferred without employing major *net* movements of gold: (*a*) thru the flows of gold which do not remain for any considerable length of time in the gold receiving country (or away from the gold sending country); (*b*) thru the movement of short-time foreign balances. The first means, which, curiously, has received very little attention in the literature of the subject, is not to be confused with *net* gold flows. For some purposes of analysis it is net gold flows that signify, but as a medium of the transfer of purchasing power it is *total* gold flows that are important, and these are several times greater than net gold flows. Annual gold imports of 100 millions and exports of 90 millions will leave at the end of the year a net import of only 10 millions; yet a major portion of the 100 millions may have remained within the country for many months. In the United States from 1919 to 1930 the total of gold movements, including ear marked gold, was about 6.5 billion dollars while the net total movement was only 1.2 billions. In

[1] The Reparations Problem, The Index, April, 1928.

France from 1880 to 1913 the ratio of total to net gold movements was about the same — 28 to 6.5 billions. In both countries in every calendar year large sums of both imports and exports of specie were recorded. A significant portion of the flow remained either in or away from the country for several months at a time, as indicated by the fact that, in almost all the years, for several consecutive months there was recorded either a net import or a net export of specie.[1]

Total gold flows (as distinct from net gold movements) as a means of transferring purchasing power thus assume importance. The period elapsing between the inward and outward movements of gold from any one country may be too short to permit of any appreciable effect on sectional prices, yet it may be quite long enough to influence merchandise movements thru shifts in demand schedules. Thus, if equilibrium of the international accounts of a country is disturbed by a loan, the immediate consequence may be an outflow of specie from the lending country to the amount of all or part of the loan. In the loan receiving country the added purchasing power (in form of receipts of gold) will cause demand schedules to shift to the right, increase imports, and thus bring about an outflow of gold which will leave the net imports of gold much smaller than the total imports. In the lending country the converse occurs. There the outflow of gold causes an increased merchandise export excess and brings about an inflow of gold.

The importance of such cancelling movements of gold as a means of adjusting balances is to be measured by comparing the sum of such movements not with the total of international transactions, but rather with that portion of international accounts which serves to disrupt an existing equilibrium. At all times, except during periods of extreme fluctuations caused by wars and by severe political and economic disturbances, by far the larger proportion of the total value of the transactions entering into the international accounts would continue from year to year unaffected by any changes in any of the items entering into international accounts. The economy, products, price structure, cus-

[1] See Table 49, for the monthly movements of specie into France.

toms, economic institutions of a country are relatively so fixed that only small changes occur from year to year in all items except the net movements of capital. One may perhaps refer to that significant portion of the total of international transactions as being the "marginal transactions." Just as in the determination of prices it is the little more or little less demanded or supplied — rather than the total demand and supply — that is significant, so in adjusting the international accounts it is the fluctuating portion of the transactions to which attention must be directed. Tho it is impossible to determine even roughly the proportion which these sums — the significant sums for comparison with total gold flows — bear to the total of international transaction, it is certain that the proportion is small. The importance, therefore, of total gold flows as a means of transferring purchasing power and adjusting disequilibrium is much greater than appears at first glance.

The importance of the second method of transferring purchasing power — thru movements of short-time foreign balances — is perhaps even greater, particularly in recent years. If banks in the lending country provide the foreign bills for the lenders, and by borrowing abroad secure in the borrowing country the means of payment with which to meet the borrower's claims, the transfer of purchasing power may take place without any gold flows. Or, again, the transfer may be executed without gold flows if banks in a loan receiving country purchase from the borrowers bills on the lending country and employ the foreign funds to build up their foreign balances. If, further, this transfer in purchasing power after a short time causes merchandise movements to take place, the foreign balances can be kept within reasonable limits with the aid of minor net gold flows. But is there sufficient elasticity in the movement of foreign balances to permit such changes? Apparently there is, at least in some countries.

In the United States, for illustration, during the years 1926 to 1929 the foreign deposits in American banks fluctuated between one and a half and two billion dollars, while American deposits abroad ranged between 200 and 300 million dollars.[1] Similar

[1] This was the minimum range. The figures are taken as of December 31 of each year, and it is very unlikely that the maximum and minimum for the period should have occurred on that day of the year.

changes in the short-time position of England and France were common during post-war years, and indicate that it is quite possible for the deposits in the lending country to increase (on foreign account) by the amount of several hundred millions and to remain at such heights until transferred back to domestic account thru the medium of increased commodity exports. Such meagre facts cannot, of course, serve even as partial verification of the changes-in-demand mechanism; they merely constitute evidence that the increase and the decline of foreign balances are in some countries of sufficient magnitude to provide the means of transferring purchasing power.[1]

[1] That such a sequence actually takes place cannot be tested without a record of monthly movements. No such record is available, yet evidence suggesting that the sequence occurs is furnished by certain annual data. When we compare the yearly movements of short- and long- term indebtedness with commodity balances recorded in the international accounts of the United States, we find the relationship to be such as to suggest that the transfer of purchasing power between the United States and other countries may very likely have been effected by movements of short-time balances. Examination of the table below containing the figures of these movements for the United States for the years 1922 to 1930 reveals a high inverse correlation between (*a*) the increase in the indebtedness of American banks to foreign depositors and (*b*) the difference between the commodity balance and the net export of capital.

Year	Commodity Balance of Trade	Annual Net Export of Long-Term Capital	Annual Net Export of Short-Term Capital *	Excess of Commodity Balance over Net Export of Capital (Col. 1 − Col. 2)
1922	506	753	375	−247
1923	−39	−30	3	−69
1924	646	733	216	−87
1925	705	560	−61	145
1926	202	540	359	−338
1927	737	696	...	41
1928	1137	718	−226	419
1929	528	318	13	210
1930	500	290	−443	210
			−236	284

* Increase in indebtedness of American banks to foreign depositors.

The figures for the table are computed from the United States Department of Commerce Trade Information Bulletin No. 761, The Balance of International Payments for the United States, 1930.

A possible interpretation of the inverse correlation between Col. 3 and Col. 4 is the following. Long-term foreign investments are first converted into foreign deposits in American banks (i.e. the ownership of deposits in American banks passes

No generalization can be made about the extent to which transfers of purchasing power (made thru the movement of foreign balances) can affect merchandise movements. The efficacy of this mechanism differs with the country and the period. In order that the mechanism shall operate to a significant extent, the changes in foreign balances (in either the lending or the borrowing country or both) must continue long enough for the changed demand schedules to affect merchandise movements. If, however, there is a considerable lag between changes in demand schedules and changes in merchandise movements, and if, in addition, the extent to which foreign balances are permitted to expand or contract is not large, then in such case a major and sustained disequilibrium cannot be adjusted without large gold flows.

Once large gold flows take place, it is a nice question just how the ensuing changes in merchandise movements occur. Are they brought about by shifts in demand schedules induced by changes in the volume of credit based on changes in the gold reserves, or are they caused by changes in sectional prices consequent upon shifts in the demand schedules? The answer again, it seems, would vary with the country and with the period. In some countries at certain times one mechanism may be the effective one and the other supplementary; in other countries, or at other times, the order of effectiveness may be reversed. In a country with large gold reserves, highly developed system of banking, with a sectional price level insensitive to gold holdings — conditions which characterized the United States during post-war years — the effective mechanism may likely be changes in demand schedules.

from American to foreign hands). The subsequent changes in demand schedules bring about an increase in exports roughly to the amount of the net foreign investment. When such adjustment occurs within the year, the increase in the export excess approximates the net foreign investment, and the short-term balance to the credit of foreigners in American banks is then no larger than at the beginning of the year. When, on the other hand, the adjustment does not occur before the end of the year, the difference between the two appears in the increase of net debt of American banks to foreigners.

The inverse correlation cannot, of course, be taken as *proof* of the claim that adjustment was made thru the medium of changes in demand schedules induced by movements of short-term balances, because there are other possible interpretations of the table.

Where, on the other hand — as in England — the banking system is highly sensitive to gold flows, where international trade is very important in the national economy, and where deposits of foreign banks are regarded as dangerous liabilities, the efficient mechanism is more likely to be sectional price changes. These would be supplemented by changes in demand schedules caused by credit movements, induced or permitted by changes in the gold reserves.

This brief review of the theory of the mechanism for adjustment prepares the way for an examination of the international accounts of France. Just how these accounts were balanced is a matter of peculiar interest, for the situation in pre-war France was unique: deposit banking was relatively in its infancy; gold reserves were very large and growing; the domestic banking situation was relatively insensitive to external gold movements. As compared with England, the international trade of France played a smaller role in the national economy and her industrial life was sluggish. Her foreign investments, like those of Great Britain, were large and rapidly increasing. Thru what medium, under these special conditions, was the adjustment made? Was the specie-flow-price mechanism of the classical theory the efficient force, or did some other mechanism serve to adjust the disequilibrium? In the succeeding chapters we shall examine in detail all the pertinent data and determine as best we may which forces were the effective ones in bringing about equilibrium in the French international accounts.

CHAPTER II

THE COMMODITY BALANCE OF TRADE

THE starting point for an inductive study of the theory of international trade is a balance sheet of international accounts. Such a balance sheet is a record of the annual totals of all transactions that give rise to payments from one country to another. It serves a variety of purposes: to the economic historian it reveals important economic trends; to the economist it supplies some essential data for investigations of problems in the fields of international trade and finance — monetary and banking control, tariff policies, foreign lending and borrowing; for the student of the theory of international trade it provides indispensable data for verification or confutation of the orthodox tenets.[1] In the present study, by supplying the figures for the annual movements of merchandise, specie, and international services (those which give rise to money payments), it serves as one of the important means of estimating capital exports, and constitutes one of the bases upon which much of the subsequent analysis rests.

For the period covered by this survey — 1880 to 1913 — no annual balance sheet has ever been constructed.[2] In view of the great interest in France, ever since 1870, in the amount of her

[1] Cleona Lewis (with the aid of the council and staff of the Institute of Economics), in a useful little book describing the best procedure of constructing balance sheets of international accounts, lists eight types of investigations that have already been served by such balances as follows: (1) currency regulation; (2) testing proposed tax measures; (3) ascertaining volume and trend of foreign assets; (4) shedding light on economic developments; (5) extending and improving scientific methods; (6) verifying economic theory; (7) analyzing war and reconstruction problems; (8) furnishing continuous and comparable official data. — The International Accounts (New York, 1927).

[2] Léon Say in his report on the payment of the French indemnity in 1874 gives some data on merchandise, specie flows, and capital movements for the few years preceding, but the report includes too few items to serve as a balance sheet for those years.

foreign investments, and in view of the elaborate effort to ascertain their quantitative importance,[1] it is strange that no attempt was made to approach the problem from this angle, especially as other countries had long before recognized the importance of such an approach. A statement of international accounts for the United States had appeared as early as 1853, for Great Britain as early as 1877. Even in Russia, Austria-Hungary, and Italy economists had constructed balance sheets for their respective countries as early as 1898 and 1905.[2] Yet no statement of international accounts covering any of the pre-war years appeared for France until 1916. Since that year two French writers, Pupin and Meynial, constructed statements for the year 1913, and Moulton and Lewis, in their study of the French debt problem, made a quinquennial statement for the years 1870 to 1913.[3] The balance sheets of the two French writers are of small use, since they are for one year only, while the quinquennial accounts of Moulton and Lewis, tho useful as a basis of comparison, cannot take the place of an annual statement. It was necessary, therefore, as a first step in analysis and verification to undertake the laborious task of constructing an annual balance sheet of international accounts.

In the following pages the estimates of the items entering into the balance sheet are discussed in some detail in order to provide the reader with a basis for criticism and enable him to judge

[1] See Chapter V.

[2] Annual international accounts have been carried back for the United States to 1860; for Great Britain to 1870; for Canada to 1900; for Germany to 1894; for Italy to 1905; for Austria-Hungary to 1892. References to the existing balance sheets and brief descriptions of them will be found in Lewis, op. cit. The only one apparently overlooked is the excellent report by Gruber on Austria-Hungary, Daten zur Zahlungsbilanz der österreichisch-ungarischen Monarchie, Bulletin de l'Institut International de Statistique, Vol. XV, 1906, Part 2, pp. 113–198.

It is interesting to note that tho a French economist, Neymarck, was the leading spirit of the international committee whose chief aim was to foster reports of international balances, no report of French international accounts was submitted. However, Neymarck did report frequently on direct estimates of foreign investments. These reports are considered in detail in Chapter V.

[3] R. Pupin, La richesse de la France devant la guerre (Paris, 1916); P. Meynial, Créances et dettes internationales (Paris, 1926); H. G. Moulton and C. Lewis, The French Debt Problem (New York, 1926).

their validity. The discussion is interspersed, when pertinent, with considerations of methodology.[1]

The items which are of sufficient importance to warrant inclusion in the balance sheet of France are as follows:

1. Merchandise imports and exports.
2. Specie imports and exports.
3. Shipping charges on imports and exports.
4. Maritime insurance and commission charges.
5. Transit charges due France on foreign goods transported thru France.
6. Expenditures of foreign ships in French ports and of French ships in foreign ports.
7. Tourist expenditures.
8. Funds carried in and out of France by immigrants and emigrants and by casual laborers.
9. Immigrant and emigrant remittances.

[1] A word about the terminology used in this study. Professor Viner justly calls attention to the need of distinguishing between the terms "balance of payments" and "balance of indebtedness" and to the confusion that sometimes arises from the failure to use the terms accurately. (See Canada's Balance of International Indebtedness, p. 22.) The term "balance of payments" he would apply only to "the balance of immediate (and honored) obligations," and the term "balance of indebtedness" he would apply to "the balance of all obligations, immediate and deferred." The United States Department of Commerce, the League of Nations, and most European writers do not follow this practice; hence Professor Viner's usage, tho strictly accurate, is apt, I believe, to prove somewhat confusing to non-specialists. In this study I have followed the practice of Lewis in applying the term "international accounts" to the *balance sheet* which contains *all* the credit and debit items. The term "balance of payments" is applied, as Professor Viner suggests, to the *balance* of immediate obligations. A credit *balance of payments* will exist if in the international accounts there appears an excess of gold imports (and a debit balance if there appears an excess of gold exports). The balance of payments is measured by the difference between imports and exports of gold. The term *balance of indebtedness* is used solely for international loans. A credit balance of indebtedness will exist when the sum of funds loaned abroad during the year is greater than the sum borrowed, and will be measured by the difference of those two sums. Thus the international accounts may show in the same year a credit balance of payments and a debit balance of international indebtedness (or vice versa).

For convenience, thruout this study the term "France" is used when meaning the residents of France, and the term "foreign countries" (e.g. Russia, Italy, etc.) when meaning the residents of foreign countries; when the French Government as distinct from the residents of France is involved in the transaction, it is so specified.

10. Brokerage charges.
11. Home government expenditures in Colonies.
12. Foreign loans and investments.
13. Interest and dividend payments.

The transactions listed above fall into the two classes termed "visible" and "invisible" items. Merchandise imports and exports and specie imports and exports alone constitute the visible items, and it is with the measurement of these that this chapter will be concerned.

In attempting to form an estimate of merchandise movements, we are confronted with two sets of statistical data. During the period under consideration the French official practice has been to compile two separate sets of import and export statistics, one under the head of "general commerce" and the other under the head of "special commerce." The former includes under imports all merchandise imported into France, whether for French consumption, re-export, storage, or transit, and under exports all merchandise of foreign and of domestic origin that is sent out of France. The latter (special commerce) includes under imports merchandise brought into the country for consumption only, and under exports all exported domestic products as well as foreign products which have been admitted, sold in the open market of the interior, and resold to foreign countries. Foreign merchandise imported to be worked over and then to be re-exported is not included in the totals for special commerce but is listed separately as "temporary admissions." [1]

[1] France has several times changed methods of valuation of exports and imports, but from 1880 to 1913 official values were fixed annually several months after the close of the year by the Commission Permanente des Valeurs en Douane, which operated under the direction of the Department of Commerce and Industry with the aid of various chambers of commerce. For imports the basis of value is the price of goods at the time and place of presentation to the customs office and does not include French customs duties, nor French internal taxes. For exports the value shown is the price on arrival at the French ports or frontier stations. For further details of French trade statistics practice see E. Levasseur, Histoire du commerce de la France (Paris, 1912), Vol. 2, Chap. X; U. S. Dept. of Commerce, Import and Export Schedule of France, Misc. Series 102 (Washington, 1920); G. Pallain, Les douanes françaises (Paris, 1913), Vol. II; Y. Guyot, Dictionnaire du commerce (Paris, 1906).

Since the purpose of constructing a statement of international accounts is to record only those items which give rise to sums due France from foreign countries or due foreign countries by France, the figures under general commerce are not pertinent. Goods that pass thru France, en route from Germany to Italy, for example, would appear in the figures for general commerce altho they do not give rise to sums due to or by France. To include them in the commodity balance of payments would give erroneous totals of payments to be made. They do give rise to sums due France for transportation, but such sums are included in the international accounts under the head of "shipping and transportation earnings." It is, therefore, the figures appearing under special commerce that are used for the merchandise balance of payments. To the totals of special commerce has been added the excess of exports over imports classed as temporary admissions; the excess of such admissions represents sums due from foreigners for work done on foreign goods by French industry.

Merchandise movements to and from French Colonies and Protectorates are included in the balance of trade. The colonies and protectorates are thruout this study treated as foreign countries inasmuch as their inclusion under France would serve merely to render more difficult the tracing of the mechanism of international trade. In quantity their trade is relatively unimportant, and their different economic institutions and customs, trade barriers, poor statistical data, and comparatively primitive economic and social development introduce too many elements of heterogeneity to warrant their inclusion.

Some modifications must be made in the totals of the merchandise balance as officially recorded. The French statistics of exports and imports for the period under consideration are unfortunately subject to imperfections; because of omissions and errors in evaluation they do not represent exactly movements of merchandise involving payment and receipt of money. Thus the movements of certain precious jewels are not included in the figures for foreign trade; [1] nor the movements of various agri-

[1] Guyot cites that information furnished by the President of the Chamber of Commerce of Anvers showed that in 1907 92 million francs' worth of diamonds

cultural products from lands near the frontiers; nor is allowance made for smuggling; nor for French goods in the baggage of outgoing travelers.[1] More serious are the errors in the evaluation of exports and imports. The values are seldom exact, especially as regards the exports, owing to the lesser care taken in their compilation because of their smaller fiscal importance. Commenting on the inaccuracies of the export evaluations Guyot writes:

> The commission generally accepts whatever valuation the exporter places on his merchandise. . . . Even if the business men were desirous of being exact, the French exports are so diverse as to make a detailed declaration very complicated; therefore merchants declare such value as suits their purpose. They are prone to give a lower value in France in order to decrease the ad valorem import duties in the importing country.[2]

Again, Liesse [3] in comparing the import and export statistics of France with those of various countries concludes that "export statistics do not offer, except for those commodities upon which there is a bounty, even relative security," and Coste, writing in 1888, mentions that he is well aware that exports are undervalued in the trade export statistics partly because of the custom among exporters to declare the value of the exports at the cost to them rather than at the selling price to the importer.[4] The inaccuracies in export evaluations persisted, it may also be added, in spite of the fact that after 1863 a fine of 100 francs was imposable on false

were imported and over 94 millions were exported. Neither movement appeared in the trade statistics. The same writer comparing trade statistics of the movements of goods between Belgium and France found considerable discrepancies in the statistics of both countries purporting to record the same quantities of merchandise. Y. Guyot, Le commerce et les commerçants (Paris, 1909), Book VII, Chap. 1.

For discussion of French trade statistics see also C. Legrand, Les statistiques douanières (Mons, 1908); E. Allard, La statistique douanière internationale (Paris, 1908); La statistique douanière et ses méthodes (Paris, 1911); A. Bateman and H. Fountain, The Import and Export Statistics of Various Countries, Bull. de l'Inst. Inter. de Stat., Vol. 15, p. 235; R. Giffen, The Use of Import and Export Statistics, Economic Inquiries and Studies (London, 1904); League of Nations, Vols. 1–2, Balance of Payments and Foreign Trade Balances, 1910–1923 (Geneva, 1924).

[1] Goods carried by outgoing travelers are included in the estimate of tourist expenditure.

[2] Y. Guyot, op. cit., Bk. VII, Chap. 1.

[3] A. Liesse, La statistique, les difficultés, les resultats, Chap. II.

[4] L. Coste in Journal de la Société de Statistique de Paris, Vol. 1888, p. 238.

declarations of exports; for no one paid the slightest attention to the law.[1]

Another contributory factor to error in the recorded exports is due to the undervaluation of parcel post packages. Before 1904 estimates of parcel post exports were far below their real value. All parcels were evaluated at an average price of only a few francs per package, a figure much lower than the real value because a goodly portion of the shipments consisted of silks. After 1904 a separate classification of parcel post was made for silks, but all other packages were lumped together and priced at a standard low rate per package. Since a large part of French exports aside from silks is composed of goods that are high in value but very small in bulk, the consequent undervaluation even after 1904 is not negligible.

Altho the inaccuracies of the evaluation of exports tended to decrease in the later years covered by this study because of the more widespread appreciation of the utility of accurate trade statistics, and because of the improved facilities for ascertaining those values, they remained of sufficient importance to call for modification of the official statistics. Pupin sent questionnaires to members of the Commission Permanente des Valeurs en Douane (the commission responsible for the official figures) and received responses indicating that most of the members felt that the figures for imports ought to be increased 3 per cent and those for exports from 5 to 15 per cent.[2] If 3 per cent of the imports and 10 per cent of the exports are selected as the average undervaluation over the period of this study, the debit balance of trade is reduced by 200 to 500 million francs annually. The cumulative total of the annual difference in the merchandise balance of trade that results if allowance is made for the probable underestimate mounts to almost 10 billion francs, a sum representing about one fourth of the total net capital exports during that period. Clearly, so large an item cannot be ignored without seriously distorting the balance of indebtedness. Therefore in the balance sheet both sets of figures — without and with the correction — have here been recorded for subsequent consideration.

[1] J. Schuller, La statistique douanière et ses méthodes, p. 225.

[2] R. Pupin, La richesse privée et finances françaises (Paris, 1919), Chap. V.

One further correction needs to be made in regard to exports. Ships' provisions purchased in France are included under special exports. They are divided into provisions of French ships and of foreign ships, but it is only this latter group that ought to appear under exports. Ships' provisions leaving France in French ships do not give rise to international payments but merely to transfers of funds from one group of Frenchmen — ship owners — to another group of Frenchmen — provision merchants. Therefore the sums included under ships' provisions have been deducted from the recorded value of exports in French ships.[1]

The figures for annual imports and exports for the entire period 1880 to 1913 appear on pages 44 and 45. They are the *official* figures for special commerce. These figures corrected for relative undervaluation of exports and for ships' provisions are tabulated on pages 114 ff.

The official statistics of imports and exports of gold and silver are no more free from criticism than the statistics of merchandise movements. Their accuracy has been challenged by many writers. Soetbeer in 1866 cited several instances of the inaccuracies in the specie imports and exports of several countries.[2] He compared the English and French specie movements between those two countries for the years 1871 to 1884 and found discrepancies ranging from 10 to 50 per cent.[3] "It is immaterial," he concluded,

[1] Before 1895 the trade statistics did not separate ships' provisions from other exports, and it has therefore been necessary to estimate the amounts before that date. The annual sums representing this item have been added to the excess of merchandise imports in the balance sheet.

[2] A. Soetbeer, Materials toward the Elucidation of the Economic Conditions Affecting the Precious Metals and the Question of Standards, translation by F. W. Taussig, Part IV.

	Millions of Marks
[3] Imports into England from France — British statistics	1067
Exports to England from France — French statistics	581
Excess of British over French figures	486
Imports into France from England — French statistics	1195
British statistics	1038
Excess of French over British figures	156

The French statistics would have shown a net excess of imports for that period of 614 million marks, whereas the English figures would have it be 156 million, a difference of 458 million over the whole period, or about 35 million average per year.

TABLE 1

MERCHANDISE EXPORTS OF FRANCE, 1880–1913[1]

(Millions of francs)

Year	Raw Materials	Food Stuffs	Manufactured Goods	Temporary Admissions	Total	Excess of Imports
1880	916	811	1839	133	3600	1511
1881	824	863	1874	125	3686	1248
1882	807	878	1888	136	3710	1190
1883	751	849	1850	133	3585	1291
1884	759	783	1690	119	3354	1052
1885	707	720	1631	94	3182	950
1886	773	731	1745	96	3344	910
1887	805	703	1739	105	3351	725
1888	813	726	1706	116	3362	812
1889	950	837	1925	118	3821	566
1890	897	855	2000	138	3891	629
1891	832	808	1928	153	3722	1130
1892	822	759	1878	113	3573	681
1893	784	710	1741	111	3347	568
1894	754	666	1657	139	3217	710
1895	873	591	1909	162	3535	285
1896	836	651	1913	176	3576	356
1897	944	720	1933	91	3789	325
1898	932	662	1915	148	3659	913
1899	1210	675	2267	197	4349	306
1900	1084	769	2254	201	4309	530
1901	1018	745	2249	180	4192	312
1902	1170	707	2374	186	4438	96
1903	1175	663	2413	184	4436	497
1904	1220	693	2536	189	4640	4
1905	1338	780	2748	221	5088	−137
1906	1474	711	3079	250	5515	282
1907	1507	746	3341	243	5839	556
1908	1341	746	2962	219	5269	539
1909	1693	823	3200	248	5966	472
1910	1930	858	3444	255	6488	864
1911	1830	736	3520	246	6322	1920
1912	1945	849	3918	260	6972	1442
1913	1858	838	4183	286	7166	1460

[1] These figures are taken from Statistique Générale de la France, Annuaire Statistique.

TABLE 2

MERCHANDISE IMPORTS OF FRANCE, 1880–1913 [1]

(Millions of francs)

Year	Food Stuffs	Raw Materials	Manufactured Goods	Temporary Admissions	Total
1880	1961	2472	599	78	5111
1881	1686	2493	683	71	4934
1882	1670	2376	775	79	4900
1883	1638	2397	768	72	4876
1884	1438	2208	696	63	4406
1885	1455	2022	610	44	4132
1886	1540	2082	584	46	4254
1887	1423	2014	589	50	4076
1888	1507	2021	579	67	4174
1889	1441	2303	572	71	4387
1890	1445	2372	619	63	4520
1891	1652	2447	668	84	4852
1892	1400	2172	614	67	4254
1893	1060	2228	564	62	3915
1894	1197	2104	548	77	3927
1895	1035	2100	583	100	3820
1896	1006	2173	618	134	3932
1897	1028	2318	608	58	4114
1898	1505	2348	618	100	4572
1899	951	2839	727	137	4655
1900	819	3035	843	142	4839
1901	783	2813	772	135	4504
1902	818	2798	777	140	4534
1903	961	3020	819	132	4933
1904	817	2853	832	142	4644
1905	822	3087	868	172	4951
1906	940	3687	999	170	5797
1907	1038	4013	1171	172	6395
1908	934	3589	1116	168	5808
1909	952	4113	1180	192	6438
1910	1413	4345	1414	179	7352
1911	2020	4525	1520	177	8242
1912	1803	4813	1614	184	8414
1913	1817	4945	1658	205	8626

[1] Same as Table 1.

"that for some years the figures tally more or less closely. This must be ascribed to accident, in face of the enormous discrepancies in other years. Moreover, there seems to be no general tendency in the variations from which one could reach any conclusion as to their causes." [1] Compared to these discrepancies between French and British figures it is significant to note that the British and United States statistics of specie exports and imports of gold (between the United States and Great Britain) are in close agreement. This suggests that the errors are probably in the French statistics rather than in the English.

A further indication of the probable error in the recorded trade movements of specie appears in the findings of Léon Say, who concluded from a comparison of the recorded trade figures for specie flow with figures compiled on the basis of information gained from Paris banks that the exports of specie, particularly of gold, were underestimated in French statistics.[2] Again, Giffen, commenting on the same inaccuracies, mentions the practice of sending gold from one place to another under the description of silver for the sake of evading the higher freight charges.[3] A similar source of error in the practice of shipping gold by parcel post is described by Roulleau, a former assistant director of economic research of the Bank of France. He is of the opinion that this practice was fairly common across the frontiers, and resulted in considerable underestimates, since parcel post shipments were valued at only a few francs per package. It is his belief that from 1901 to 1910 the imports of gold bullion alone were underestimated at least 200 million francs and exports 330 millions because of parcel post statistics. By checking up from all available sources of information Roulleau found that in cases of long distance transportation

[1] A. Soetbeer, ibid., p. 534.

Guyot in Le commerce et les commerçants cites an instance of a shipment of millions of roubles by a Paris concern to St. Petersburg in 1900, and not the least mention of it appears in French statistics. Ferrais gives several illustrations of errors in statistics of international movements of specie. C. Ferrais, Examen des difficultés particulières que rencontre la statistique du mouvement des metaux précieux dans le commerce international," Bull. de l'Inst. Inter. de Stat., Vol. II, p. 235.

[2] L. Say, Rapport sur le paiement de l'indemnité de guerre (Paris, 1874), p. 62.

[3] R. Giffen, Statistics (London, 1913), p. 85.

the import and export statistics are fairly reliable; nevertheless, he concluded that "the movements of coined gold escape investigation by customs officials with an ease deplorable for the statistician." [1]

The inacurracies of specie statistics are amplified by the omission of specie carried by travelers, an item which completely escapes recording.[2] Travelers, foreign casual laborers, and immigrants passing between France and the neighboring countries were undoubtedly carriers of quantities of gold and silver coin. Italians, Belgians, Spaniards, and Swiss were accustomed to using 10 and 20 franc gold pieces and 5 franc silver pieces — current coin in France as well as in their respective countries — and carried them when traveling, much as an American would carry several ten dollar bills when journeying from one state to another. Indeed, the foreign casual laborers and visitors to France from Belgium, Italy, and Switzerland were more apt to carry their funds in the form of gold than in letters of credit or travelers' checks, because they were not accustomed, as were Americans and English, to that type of credit instrument.[3]

[1] G. Roulleau, La production et les mouvements internationaux des metaux précieux au début du XXe siècle, Jour. de la Soc. de Stat. de Paris (1912), Vol. 53, p. 70.

[2] A peculiar situation which arose in regard to the movement of 5 franc silver pieces (*écus*) between France and Belgium, and France and Switzerland points to the inaccuracies such omissions may create. The price of Belgian exchange frequently prevailing in France from 1901 to 1909 allowed a small profit to be made by buying Belgian exchange in a border French town — at a slight discount — crossing the frontier with the bills purchased, and cashing them at par, demanding and receiving écus, which were carried back to France. Altho the gross profit on the transaction was very small — less than ½ of 1 per cent exclusive of expenses involved — it was enough to cause a movement estimated at over 500 million francs from Belgium to France between 1901 and 1910, and at least 200 million from Switzerland during the same period. This movement would be of no significance for this study but for the fact that the Banks of Belgium and of Switzerland purchased from the Bank of France the écus necessary to replace their depleting reserves of écus, and these purchases doubtless appear in the specie export statistics, whereas the return movement taking place by parcel post or carried across the frontier was probably not included in the import statistics. This would result in a relative underestimate of imports.

[3] Even the Portuguese returning from California, where they had become accustomed to the use of gold coin as the medium of hand to hand circulation, as late as 1913 carried much of their funds in gold coin.

Such movements of specie do not, however, belong in the balance of international accounts. They do not give rise to any demand or supply of foreign bills, nor do they directly affect the recorded international movement of goods. They are of significance, as will be seen, when estimating tourist expenditures or immigrant remittances, and estimates of these sums will be attempted when those items are being considered.

With the exception of these estimates, the official figures of specie movements are the only ones appearing in the balance sheet of international accounts. Further change is scarcely warranted in the absence of definite information as to the extent of inaccuracy in the recorded statistics of specie flows. However, it must be noted that these figures include movements of silver bullion. There is no reason for such inclusion under specie rather than under merchandise since thruout the whole period there was no free coinage of silver in France. Silver bullion differed in no respect from other merchandise, and to include it with gold bullion and gold and silver money serves only to defeat the purpose of separating specie movements from merchandise movements. From 1880 to 1913 the total value of silver bullion imported was 1600 million francs, and of silver bullion exported 490 millions. The net excess of 1110 million francs constitutes almost one-fifth of the total excess of specie imports, a sufficient proportion to justify its not being included under the classification of specie imports. Wherever this distinction is of importance — as in the comparison of merchandise with specie movements and in the consideration of the specie-flow-price mechanism — deduction for silver bullion movements is made.

The figures for the annual imports and exports of gold and silver bullion and money are tabulated on the following pages. They are the figures contained in the annual reports to the French Minister of Finance. In many cases these figures differ somewhat from those recorded in other sources, but the discrepancies are not large.

TABLE 3

SPECIE EXPORTS OF FRANCE, 1880–1913 [1]

(Millions of francs)

Year	Gold			Silver		
	Bullion	Money	Total	Bullion	Money	Total
1880	44	364	408	12	50	62
1881	3	220	223	5	74	79
1882	16	176	192	26	131	157
1883	45	89	134	18	78	96
1884	10	72	82	11	35	46
1885	36	165	201	17	121	138
1886	77	122	199	10	124	134
1887	111	147	258	10	129	139
1888	32	161	193	3	106	109
1889	16	113	129	11	92	103
1890	92	159	351	15	94	109
1891	31	204	235	14	132	146
1892	17	94	111	21	81	102
1893	9	108	117	14	112	126
1894	7	101	108	7	102	109
1895	20	224	244	8	71	79
1896	24	287	311	6	195	201
1897	20	112	132	9	183	192
1898	44	269	313	52	136	188
1899	21	141	162	8	211	219
1900	3	123	126	7	199	206
1901	21	124	145	12	129	141
1902	7	120	127	10	107	117
1903	7	127	134	15	90	105
1904	14	110	124	12	114	126
1905	29	103	132	15	86	101
1906	36	129	165	19	152	171
1907	9	145	154	15	187	202
1908	2	20	22	20	155	175
1909	37	173	200	27	104	131
1910	7	166	173	15	200	215
1911	5	134	139	9	135	144
1912	1	34	35	17	265	282
1913	12	62	74	68	347	360
Total	867	4795	5662	483	4527	5010

[1] These figures are compiled from the annual Rapport au Ministre des Finances, Administration des Monnaies et Médailles.

TABLE 4

SPECIE IMPORTS OF FRANCE, 1880–1913 [1]

(Millions of francs)

	Gold			Silver		
Year	Bullion	Money	Total	Bullion	Money	Total
1880	31	163	194	18	83	101
1881	37	197	234	37	933	130
1882	31	253	284	34	94	128
1883	26	38	64	23	59	82
1884	58	69	127	22	79	101
1885	26	217	243	24	212	236
1886	107	154	261	24	160	184
1887	31	62	93	24	154	178
1888	36	66	102	21	143	164
1889	194	144	338	17	93	110
1890	56	61	117	24	115	139
1891	119	243	362	36	140	176
1892	85	302	387	19	101	120
1893	55	250	305	21	138	159
1894	227	234	461	25	64	89
1895	80	173	253	47	93	140
1896	142	159	301	71	107	178
1897	149	142	291	71	100	171
1898	109	91	200	73	118	191
1899	144	175	319	45	143	188
1900	155	304	459	57	89	146
1901	277	152	429	40	57	97
1902	327	114	441	36	61	97
1903	249	79	328	63	69	132
1904	557	98	655	41	56	97
1905	505	274	779	47	57	104
1906	321	115	436	60	96	156
1907	344	148	492	87	95	182
1908	796	217	1013	89	84	173
1909	314	78	392	67	81	148
1910	128	102	230	49	122	171
1911	161	104	265	61	136	197
1912	160	93	253	62	213	274
1913	602	62	664	66	323	389
Total	6639	5133	11772	1600	3828	5428

[1] Same as Table 3.

TABLE 5

SPECIE IMPORTS AND EXPORTS OF FRANCE, 1880–1913

(Millions of francs)

Year	Imports	Exports	Excess of Imports	Cumulative Excess
1880	296	470	−174	−174
1881	364	302	62	−92
1882	411	359	52	−40
1883	146	235	−89	−129
1884	229	128	101	−28
1885	479	339	140	112
1886	445	333	112	224
1887	271	397	−126	98
1888	266	301	−35	63
1889	448	232	216	279
1890	256	359	−103	176
1891	539	381	158	324
1892	508	214	294	618
1893	464	243	221	839
1894	552	217	335	1174
1895	395	325	72	1246
1896	479	513	−33	1213
1897	462	323	139	1352
1898	391	502	−111	1241
1899	506	382	124	1365
1900	605	333	272	1637
1901	526	286	241	1878
1902	538	243	295	2173
1903	441	238	204	2377
1904	754	234	520	2897
1905	885	232	653	3550
1906	601	337	264	3814
1907	805	370	436	4250
1908	1173	183	990	5240
1909	539	359	180	5420
1910	406	390	16	5436
1911	462	285	177	5613
1912	527	317	210	5823
1913	1053	434	619	6442

CHAPTER III

TRANSPORTATION EARNINGS

We proceed now to a consideration of the non-commodity or the "invisible" items in the French international accounts. Payments arising out of services in transportation — shipping, transit, and maritime insurance — will be estimated in this chapter.

The French practice during the period under survey was to record all imports at their c. i. f. values and all exports at their f. o. b. values. Thus shipping charges due foreigners already appear on the debit side of the international accounts under merchandise imports. But imports carried in French ships are also included as a debit item, altho obviously they represent merely a payment due from one group of Frenchmen to another. On the other hand, exports carried in French ships presumably give rise to payments due France; yet these payments are not included under merchandise exports. To arrive, therefore, at a correct balance of payments it is necessary to deduct from the debit side the French shipping earnings on imports and to add to the credit side French earnings on exports.[1] The net effect is the same if no deductions are made from the debit side and all the earnings of French shipping — whether on imports, exports, or shipments between foreign ports — are placed on the credit side. The latter, which is the only feasible method in view of the paucity of shipping data, is the one employed here.

The total of shipping earnings can be estimated in several ways. The procedure most commonly used is to deduct the total world exports from the total world imports — the latter being

[1] This assumes that the importer paid transportation charges from the point of embarkation. Such, however, was not always the case. The practice differed with the country and the seller. Yet the French customs requirement was that imports be valued c. i. f. at port of entry and exports f. o. b. at the point of departure from the country. Whenever a French exporter quoted goods at c. i. f. prices, he was required to record the f. o. b. (point of departure from country) value of the exports, that is at the quoted price — c. i. f. in this instance — minus transportation charges from the point of departure from the country.

valued c. i. f. and the former f. o. b. — and to regard the remainder as a rough measure of the difference in value due to the cost of world shipping. The shipping earnings of a particular country are then determined by the ratio of that country's shipping to world shipping.[1] In the case of France, lacking statistics of the tonnage of freight carried by French ships, the results that could be obtained by this method would be too crude to warrant its use. A direct estimate of shipping earnings is also not feasible. For such an estimate, statistics of the tonnage of freight carried by French ships, of shipping rates, and other pertinent data — lacking for the period of this survey — are necessary.

Estimates of French shipping earnings have been made by Meynial and by Pupin [2] who constructed international accounts for certain years, but neither their estimates nor their method are dependable. Meynial reached an estimate in the following manner. He first compared the total of French ship tonnage entering and leaving France in cargo with the total of foreign ship tonnage. The proportion so derived he applied to the known tonnage of total imports and exports, thereby obtaining what he assumed to be an estimate of the tonnage of freight carried by French ships. This tonnage he then multiplied by an "average" freight rate on an assumed average distance and arrived at the result of 400 million francs, to which he added 80 million francs for passenger service and 20 million francs for expenditures of foreign ships in France. This method of estimating shipping receipts is not valid in the case of France because an "average" freight rate is employed in the computation. An average freight rate may be of significance for certain purposes, but when such an average is employed, it is one that has been obtained by dividing total freight receipts by ton-miles carried. Here the total freight receipts are an unknown quantity, the very one we are seeking to

[1] In the use of this method, however, allowance has to be made for the practice of certain countries — United States, Canada, Mexico, and several others — which record imports f. o. b. instead of c. i. f. Both Giffen and Hobson use this method in estimating British shipping earnings. See C. K. Hobson, The Measurement of the Balance of Trade, Economica, Vol. 2, p. 133, for a description of this and other methods of estimating shipping earnings.

[2] P. Meynial, op. cit., p. 15; R. Pupin, op. cit., p. 24.

discover. How then could this "average" have been determined? Shipping freight rates per mile differ according to weight, bulk, value, perishability of cargo, distance carried, port of loading and unloading, season of year, kind of ship, and direction of voyage. It is, of course, simple to calculate, once you have the freight rates, an arithmetic mean of the freight rates of a ton-mile of coal on a coal barge, of beef on a fast refrigerator steamer, of oil on a tanker, and of silk gowns on a passenger steamer; but after the average is obtained it is quite without meaning. Its use as a base for estimating freight revenue renders the estimate untrustworthy.

Meynial's method, again, is open to criticism in that it assumes that every French ship entering or leaving port carries not only the same proportion of a full cargo that foreign ships do — since the comparison is based on records of ships leaving in ballast and those leaving with cargo — but also the same proportion of the same kind of goods. If English ships enter laden with coal, and French ships with raw silk or raw wool, a comparison of tonnage as a basis for earnings is subject to great error. Nor is every outgoing ship classed in the official records as being under "ballast" empty, nor every ship not so classed full. Moreover, Meynial apparently draws no distinction between sailing vessels and steam vessels, thus assuming that a ton of sailing ship is as effective as a ton of steamship. Since the French mercantile marine contained a larger proportion of sailing ships to steamships entering and leaving French ports, the earnings of French ships would be exaggerated. Further, his method excludes earnings of French tramp ships in carrying cargo between foreign ports. In view of all these possible sources of error, his estimate of 500 million francs for 1913 cannot be given much weight.

Pupin's estimate in his balance of payments for 1913 is even less dependable than that of Meynial. Pupin recorded shipping costs as a net *debit* item to the extent of 345 million francs on the basis of 23 million tons imported under foreign flags at 15 francs per ton. How the figure of 15 francs per ton was derived, he did not explain, and he also overlooked the fact that imports are recorded c. i. f. and that adding shipping costs as a *debit* item is to count them twice, an error further exaggerated by not counting French shipping earnings on exports. That such crude errors of logic in the construction of international accounts could be made by an economist is indicative of the general indifference of French economists before the war toward the theory of international accounts.

The most practical method for estimating shipping earnings, in view of the inadequacy of French statistics, appears to be to accept as a base Hobson's estimate of annual British shipping earnings, and to modify it to fit French conditions by making allowance for the relative tonnage and efficiency of ships. His estimate was arrived at in the following manner. He first determined the earnings of British ships engaged in foreign commerce for the year 1907 by three independent methods:[1] (1) The total world shipping cost on international freight was estimated and multiplied by the ratio of net tonnage of British shipping engaged in foreign commerce to world tonnage so engaged. From the result was deducted one-third, which was estimated as the proportion of receipts expended in foreign ports on provisions, bunker coal, unloading, sailors' expenditures, and so forth. (2) The expenses of British shipping, including interest and dividends on capital invested, depreciation, and operating costs, were computed. In other words, the individual items making up the cost were estimated and the profit added, the result being the total receipts. (3) Books of certain shipping companies were analyzed to determine the average receipts per gross ton, and then this sum was multiplied by the total British tonnage. From this were deducted the expenses abroad as in the previous methods.

From a comparison of the results of these three methods Hobson concluded that an estimate of "£90 million is the figure that may perhaps be taken as the amount to be credited to the United Kingdom in 1907 for shipping services of every kind." Having thus ascertained the earnings for 1907, Hobson constructed an index of freight rates, with the aid of the Board of Trade index for the years 1870 to 1913. Then he constructed another index of the efficiency of British shipping and applied it to the total

[1] The Export of Capital (London, 1914), Chap. VII.

British tonnage. Using these two indices with the year 1907 as the base year he arrived at the annual British shipping earnings.

In order to employ Hobson's results as a basis for estimating French shipping earnings, some modifications and some further assumptions have to be made. His index of freight rates can be accepted as roughly representative of the movements of French freight rates because French and British ships competed within narrow limits.[1] But a factor tending to introduce error into estimates of shipping earnings based on this index is the difference in the weights of exports compared to imports in the French and British carrying trade, and the fact that Hobson's index is a mean between indices of outgoing and incoming freight rates. Besides, the index of outgoing freight is based wholly on rates on coal and iron — reasonably so for England since the weight of her exports consisted largely of coal and iron — which were of little importance in French exports. Nor can the inward and outward freight rate indices, the mean of which Hobson adopts, be applied separately to French shipping since British outward freight rates were not the French outward freight rates. The inward freight rates — based largely on shipping charges on foodstuffs — apply only to a relatively small portion of the French volume of imports, while exports from ports of France were rather in a class by themselves owing to their relatively light weight.

The great differences in weights between the French imports and exports is shown in Table 6, page 57. In 1880, it will be noted, imports weighed about five times as much as exports. This difference decreased slowly, but in 1900 it was still almost four times as great, and in 1913 twice as great. Nor is that all. These figures are for *total* imports and exports and include merchandise moved by rail. When shipping alone is considered, the discrepancy is even greater. For example, the weights of total imports and exports in 1913 were 44 million tons as against 22 million tons, — that is, two to one, — whereas the weights of imports and exports carried on ships were 30 million tons as against 9.8 million tons, or more than three to one. Furthermore, these

[1] Effects of the War upon French Economic Life, Carnegie Endowment of International Peace, p. 20.

TABLE 6

ANNUAL MOVEMENTS OF THE WEIGHTS OF FRENCH EXPORTS AND IMPORTS (SPECIAL COMMERCE), 1880–1913

Year	Imports (Millions of tons)	Relatives (1900 = 100)	Exports (Millions of tons)	Relatives (1900 = 100)
1880	21.8	77	4.5	52
1881	21.0	74	4.7	54
1882	22.4	79	4.6	53
1883	23.2	82	4.7	54
1884	22.9	81	4.7	54
1885	20.9	73	4.6	54
1886	20.3	71	4.8	53
1887	20.7	73	5.3	55
1888	21.5	76	5.4	61
1889	21.0	76	6.5	62
1890	22.7	80	6.7	75
1891	24.2	85	6.8	77
1892	22.5	79	6.7	79
1893	22.5	79	6.4	77
1894	23.4	82	6.6	74
1895	21.8	77	7.0	76
1896	22.6	79	7.3	80
1897	24.0	86	7.9	84
1898	25.9	91	7.8	91
1899	25.3	90	8.4	90
1900	28.3	100	8.6	100
1901	27.0	95	8.1	94
1902	26.5	94	8.6	100
1903	27.3	96	9.3	108
1904	27.3	94	10.4	121
1905	26.6	91	11.7	134
1906	32.3	114	11.6	134
1907	33.7	119	12.8	148
1908	33.1	117	12.8	148
1909	34.1	120	14.3	166
1910	35.7	126	15.5	180
1911	40.4	143	16.9	196
1912	39.7	140	20.3	236
1913	44.2	156	22.1	257

figures are for special commerce and do not include the movement of Swiss imports and exports. The Swiss trade, a goodly proportion of which passed thru French ports, was even more expensive as to exports and more bulky as to imports.[1]

These discrepancies in weights of imports and exports are due not to differences in the total values of each, but to the differing nature of their constituents. France imported a large quantity of heavy merchandise: coal from England and from Rotterdam; petroleum and copper from the United States; phosphates from Algeria; iron from Spain; sulphur from Italy; nitrates from Chile; tin from India. Her exports, on the other hand, were relatively light in weight and small in bulk: jewelry, clothes, fine silks, laces, fancy leather goods, clocks, and, more recently, electrical appliances. The result of this discrepancy in the weight of imports and of exports was to render very keen the competition for the export carrying trade. A large proportion of ships entering French ports laden with freight had to leave in ballast. For example, in 1880 8.4 million tons of foreign shipping (net tonnage) arrived with cargo, and 3.5 million tons left with cargo, the remainder presumably leaving empty. The movements of export freight rates, therefore, are not apt to have been in accord with those of England. Nevertheless, the difference between import and export quantities did not differ very much from year to year, and the *relative* movement of freight rates — which is what we are seeking — was not affected seriously. The disagreement between the British and the French incoming and outgoing freight rates is doubtless a source of error, but in the absence of an index of French freight rates, the British are used.

In using the British shipping earnings as a base of comparison, the difference in the efficiency between French and British shipping must be taken into consideration. A comparison of the relative efficiency ton for ton of French as against British shipping would probably find England the more favorably situated. Shipping is there conducted on a larger scale and plays a much more important part in the country's economy. England, too, has a longer and broader experience in foreign transportation and pos-

[1] M. Lujon, Le fret d'exportation (Montpellier, 1923).

sesses more improved port facilities. On geographic and historic grounds it would be expected that England would lead France in efficiency of ocean transportation. The fact that England converted her sailing ships into steamships at a much faster rate than did France — even as late as 1913 sailing ships formed 38 per cent of French mercantile marine and only 7 per cent of the British — suggests that the former was the more progressive in the conduct of her ocean transportation. The efficiency of French shipping is therefore estimated at 10 per cent less during the base year of 1907. The efficiency of other years differs. Hobson estimated that the increase in efficiency in British shipping between 1870 and 1912 was not less than 70 to 80 per cent. To permit a somewhat lesser rate of increase of efficiency for French shipping as against British appears reasonable. This increase in efficiency doubtless did not take place at the same rate of speed as the index would indicate; but it is impossible to correct for this factor with the data available.

Hobson further modified his estimate of British shipping earnings for 1907 by deducting one-third of the earnings to cover expenditures of British ships in foreign ports. This estimate, which was arrived at after an analysis of the accounts of several shipping companies, is in accord with an investigation made by Walsh of the cost of 600 double voyages.[1] But French shipping engaged in tramp carrying far less than did British shipping, and therefore it is to be expected that a smaller proportion of gross receipts was spent abroad by French shipping than by British. French crews also probably spent less abroad than British crews because the former consisted almost wholly of Frenchmen, whereas the number of foreigners in British shipping was large. On the other hand, British ships coal at home whenever possible; French ships do not. To allow for this difference in foreign expenditures the French earnings are increased by 15 per cent.[2] The tables on the follow-

[1] R. Walsh, Industrial Economy, cited by Hobson.

[2] An increase of 15 per cent represents a 33 per cent decrease in the estimate of French shipping expenditures abroad compared with British shipping expenditures abroad.

Moulton and Lewis in their study The French Debt Problem estimated shipping earnings for France for five year periods using Hobson's estimate as a base. The

ing pages give the pertinent figures for French and British shipping and freight rate indices with the estimated figures of annual shipping earnings.

There remain to be considered under shipping earnings the expenditures of foreign ships in France. Ship supplies — coal and provisions — purchased by foreign ships are included in the figures of special exports and ought not, therefore, to be recorded again here. There are, nevertheless, port, pilot, and unloading expenditures that are not included in the exports, and these must be placed in the international accounts. The expenditures of a 3100 ton steamship in 1907 on these items alone ranged from 1000 to 10,000 francs, depending upon the port, cargo, and length of stay.[1] An average, therefore, of one franc per ton after 1900 and three-fourths franc per ton before 1900 seems a very conservative estimate. To this must be added the expenditures of the crews of foreign ships in French ports. In 1880 sailors on foreign ships entering French ports numbered 365,000; in 1890 375,000; in 1898 430,000; in 1911 801,000.

An allowance of 10 francs per man is considered a conservative estimate of their expenditures in France. In Table 9, on page 64, are listed the annual estimates of such expenditures. The expenditures of foreign shipping in France exclusive of ships' stores appear as a separate item on the credit side of the balance sheet.

The earnings of French railroads and canals on all foreign merchandise transported from one frontier to another also give rise to sums due from foreigners. In 1913 837,000 tons of merchandise were so transported. The average railroad freight rate

results they obtained differ somewhat from those made for the present study because they did not go into such refinements. Their estimated shipping earnings are as follows:

Average per Year
(Millions of francs)

1881–1885	170 millions	1897–1902.......	138 millions
1886–1890	155 millions	1903–1908.......	1660 millions
1891–1896	1285 millions	1909–1913.......	215 millions

[1] C. K. Hobson, Export of Capital, Appendix C.

TABLE 7

EFFECTIVE MERCHANT MARINE OF FRANCE AND OF THE UNITED KINGDOM, 1880–1913

(Thousands of tons)

	France			United Kingdom			
Year	Sail [1]	Steam [1]	Reduced to Steam Tonnage [2]	Sail [3]	Steam [3]	Reduced to Steam Tonnage [2]	Ratio of French to British Tonnage (%)
1880	641	277	388	3850	2723	4000	9.7
1881	602	311	511	3680	3003	4203	12.1
1882	566	416	604	3621	3335	4537	13.3
1883	536	467	645	3513	3728	4898	13.0
1884	522	511	685	3460	3944	5090	13.4
1885	507	492	661	3456	3973	5128	12.9
1886	492	500	664	3397	3965	5102	13.0
1887	465	506	661	3249	4085	5117	12.9
1888	451	509	659	3114	4349	5387	12.5
1889	440	492	638	3041	4717	5730	11.1
1890	444	499	647	2936	5042	6020	10.7
1891	426	521	653	2972	5307	6297	10.3
1892	407	498	633	3080	5560	6586	9.6
1893	396	498	630	3038	5740	6750	9.3
1894	398	491	623	2987	5970	6965	8.9
1895	386	500	628	2866	6120	7075	8.9
1896	390	503	633	2735	6280	7192	8.8
1897	421	499	639	2590	6360	7223	8.6
1898	414	485	623	2380	6610	7400	8.4
1899	450	507	657	2240	6917	7663	8.5
1900	510	527	697	2096	7207	7905	8.0
1901	564	546	734	1990	7617	8380	8.7
1902	668	548	771	1950	8104	8784	8.7
1903	650	585	802	1860	8400	9000	8.8
1904	653	696	913	1802	8751	9351	9.7
1905	676	711	936	1670	9064	9620	9.7
1906	677	723	948	1550	9612	10128	9.4
1907	662	739	960	1460	10023	10509	9.1
1908	648	808	1024	1400	10138	10604	9.5
1909	638	806	1018	1300	10284	10717	9.5
1910	636	815	1027	1112	10440	10818	9.4
1911	624	838	1046	980	10710	11036	9.4
1912	614	904	1109	902	10990	11240	9.8
1913	601	980	1180	846	11270	11552	10.1

1 Source: Annuaire Statisque de la France.
2 Reduced at the rate of 3 sail tonnage = 1 steam.
3 Source: Statistical Abstract of United Kingdom.

TABLE 8

FRENCH SHIPPING EARNINGS, 1880–1913

Year	1 French[1] Tonnage (Millions of tons)	2 Freight[2] Index 1900=100	3 Shipping Efficiency	Product of Cols. 1, 2, & 3	Shipping[3] Earnings 1907 = 186 (Millions of francs)
1880	388	153	100	593	100
1881	511	137	102	714	121
1882	604	134	104	841	143
1883	645	132	106	902	153
1884	685	116	108	858	146
1885	661	104	110	756	128
1886	664	101	112	750	127
1887	661	100	114	753	127
1888	659	110	116	841	142
1889	638	122	118	919	156
1890	647	106	120	823	140
1891	653	100	122	803	136
1892	633	87	124	683	116
1893	630	84	126	666	113
1894	623	80	128	638	108
1895	628	75	130	598	101
1896	633	79	132	660	107
1897	639	83	134	710	120
1898	623	93	136	788	135
1899	657	88	138	798	136
1900	697	100	140	976	166
1901	734	75	142	782	132
1902	771	71	144	788	133
1903	802	73	146	855	145
1904	913	71	148	959	171
1905	936	76	150	1067	182
1906	948	84	152	1209	206
1907	960	85	154	1256	213
1908	1204	73	156	1166	197
1909	1018	75	158	1206	205
1910	1027	85	160	1496	254
1911	1046	95	162	1609	273
1912	1109	131	164	2378	350
1913	1180	...	166	...	250

[1] Reduced to steam tonnage at rate of 3 sailing tons = 1 steam ton.
[2] British freight index compiled by C. K. Hobson in The Export of Capital, p. 187.
[3] Includes addition of 15 per cent for difference in foreign expenditure abroad. See p. 59.

per kilometer-ton was in that year 4.2 centimes.[1] The rate on canals and rivers was less. A good part of the merchandise must have traveled part of the way by water and therefore a rate of 3.5 is more reasonable. The average number of kilometers per ton is a matter of conjecture. It could hardly have been less than 350 or more than 800 kilometers, and therefore an average of 500 kilometers is assumed. This would make the cost of transporting 837,000 tons about 17 million francs.[2] The earnings for the years from 1880 to 1913, arrived at in a similar fashion, are tabulated on page 65. The results are entered on the credit side of the balance sheet under transit earnings.

Maritime insurance and commissions are another source of revenue to France. As in the case of shipping charges, these charges on imports are already included in the import statistics, where, it will be remembered, imports are valued c. i. f. The total earnings from this source whether on imports or exports should therefore be recorded on the credit side of the international accounts. Giffen estimated these earnings for Great Britain at 2 per cent of the entire British foreign trade; Hobson made it 2½ per cent. This percentage includes ¾ per cent for insurance, ¼ per cent for bankers' commissions on bills of exchange, and 1½ per cent for all other charges including "cost of services performed in London by which British capital operating abroad is directed and controlled."[3] France, however, did not play nearly so important a rôle in that type of finance as England, and the major portion of the 2½ per cent estimated by Hobson as earned by Great Britain would not apply in the case of France.

Partly in recognition of this and partly because France carries only 30 per cent of her sea borne freight, Moulton and Lewis estimated French earnings from this source at 1 per cent. This seems too high because only about 60 per cent of French foreign trade is sea borne and also because it assumes that France secures in-

[1] This average, published annually, is arrived at by dividing total freight receipts by ton-miles.

[2] Meynial estimated revenue from this source at 30 millions for 1913, but does not give the basis of his computation.

[3] C. K. Hobson, op. cit., p. 189.

TABLE 9

EXPENDITURES OF SHIPS AND CREWS IN FRENCH PORTS, NOT INCLUDING SHIPS' STORES, 1880–1913

Year	Foreign Ships Entering French Ports with Cargo		(Millions of francs)		
	Number (Thousands)	Tons (Millions)	Docking, Pilotage, and Unloading Costs	Expenditures of Crews	Total Expenditures
1880	26	8	6	3	9
1881	25	8	6	3	9
1882	25	8	6	3	9
1883	25	9	6	3	9
1884	22	8	6	3	9
1885	20	8	6	3	9
1886	20	8	6	3	10
1887	20	8	6	3	10
1888	20	9	6	4	10
1889	18	8	6	4	10
1890	19	9	7	4	11
1891	20	10	7	4	11
1892	18	9	7	4	11
1893	18	9	7	4	12
1894	18	9	7	4	12
1895	17	9	7	5	12
1896	17	10	7	5	12
1897	18	10	8	5	13
1898	19	11	9	5	14
1899	19	12	10	5	15
1900	19	14	13	5	18
1901	18	13	13	5	18
1902	17	13	13	5	18
1903	18	14	14	5	19
1904	17	14	14	6	20
1905	17	15	15	6	21
1906	19	18	18	6	24
1907	20	20	20	6	26
1908	20	21	20	7	27
1909	20	21	21	7	28
1910	20	22	22	7	29
1911	21	23	23	8	31
1912	21	23	23	8	31
1913	22	26	26	8	34

TABLE 10

FRENCH TRANSIT EARNINGS, 1880–1913

Year	Tonnage of Mdse. Carried by Land[1] (Millions of tons)	"Average" R. R. Rate per Ton Km. (Centimes)	Transit Earnings (Millions of francs)
1880	264	595	6
1881	280	588	6
1882	240	589	6
1883	310	573	7
1884	200	590	5
1885	190	594	5
1886	190	594	5
1887	290	580	7
1888	320	566	7
1889	400	555	8
1890	450	546	9
1891	500	536	10
1892	430	536	9
1893	550	525	11
1894	520	520	10
1895	510	516	11
1896	530	512	12
1897	600	500	12
1898	600	492	12
1899	631	478	12
1900	649	469	12
1901	641	471	13
1902	610	471	12
1903	710	463	13
1904	736	460	13
1905	759	452	13
1906	774	453	14
1907	831	437	14
1908	731	429	13
1909	795	426	14
1910	724	427	13
1911	868	419	14
1912	775	420	14
1913	837	420	14

[1] Shipments originating and ending outside of France.

surance premiums on all imports and exports. Hobson's justification for estimating the British earnings at 2½ per cent of both imports and exports was that a great deal of the trade of foreign countries is financed thru England. This was hardly true of France. It consequently seems that an estimate of 1 per cent of the recorded exports alone is more nearly in accord with the French situation. It is upon this basis that the earnings from maritime insurance and commissions have been estimated. They are entered on the credit side of the balance sheet, page 114.

CHAPTER IV

TOURIST EXPENDITURES, IMMIGRANT REMITTANCES, HOME GOVERNMENT EXPENDITURES IN COLONIES

THE remaining items in the statement of international accounts are tourist expenditures, immigrant remittances, home government expenditures in colonies, and loans and interest. We turn our consideration first to tourist expenditures. These in the case of France constitute a very important item on the credit side of the balance sheet, exceeded, indeed, only by revenue from foreign investments. Here, again, accurate estimates are impossible. Several have been attempted for isolated years, but none is free from criticism.

For the years before 1870 Say estimated annual tourist expenditures to have been 200 to 300 million francs.[1] For the period 1881 to 1897 Pougnet estimated that the expenditure of tourists in France exceeded that of French tourists abroad by a sum of two billion francs, or an average of 120 million francs per year. This estimate is much lower than Say's would lead us to expect, even allowing generously for French tourist expenditures abroad, there being every reason to believe that tourist expenditure in France was greater in the decades following the war of 1870 than in the decade preceding. This is borne out by Gide. He states that in the years preceding 1900 there were from 400,000 to 500,000 foreigners registered in Paris hotels and pensions alone and that in 1900, the year of the exposition, the number increased to 550,000.[2] It may be safely assumed that in addition there were 50,000 foreigners in cities other than Paris. He further estimated that foreigners spent in France an average of more than 500 francs. This would bring the total expenditures of foreigners in

[1] Cited by Moulton and Lewis in The French Debt Problem, p. 341.

[2] C. Gide, Principes d'économie politique (Paris, 1910), p. 375, note.

France for the year 1900 up to 300 million francs, a figure which tallies exactly with the estimate of Masse for the same year.[1]

Some estimates for later years show that in the twentieth century tourist expenditure in France was much greater. Paish estimated that in 1908 American tourists abroad spent, in addition to passage money, 1036 million francs,[2] and Moulton and Lewis in their study estimated that one-fourth of this sum was spent in France. Together with the expenditures of other nationals they estimated the tourist expenditures in France for 1908 at 550 to 600 million francs. Pupin's estimate is very much higher. According to his figures in the years preceding the Great War there were from 800,000 to 900,000 foreigners visiting France each year and that the sum left in France by them was two billion francs.[3] The estimate is unquestionably too high. It would make the per capita expenditure 2000 francs; whereas the greater part of visitors to France were English, Germans, and Italians, many of whom remained only a week or two and spent very much less than 2000 francs.[4] Meynial's tourist estimates also indicate that

[1] R. Masse, La production des richesses (Paris, 1925), p. 666. Masse incidentally stated that in 1889 400,000 foreigners visited French watering places, leaving in those resorts at least 150 million francs. This, however, was the exceptional year of the World Fair during which, Neymarck estimated, 1,500,000 foreigners visited France, and therefore the figure cannot be used as the basis of estimate for other years. Neymarck's estimate is found in Finances contemporaines, Vol. III, p. 434. The 1½ million visitors consisted of the following groups: 225,000 Belgians; 380,000 English; 160,000 Germans; 52,000 Swiss; 56,000 Spaniards; 38,000 Italians; 90,000 North Americans; 25,000 South Americans; 32,000 Austrians; 7,000 Russians. He estimated that the average expenditure was 500 francs.

[2] In 1913 277,000 tourists left the United States via seaports, some of them going to the West Indies and to Middle and South America. In 1920 about 30 per cent went to ports other than European, a percentage which was probably smaller than in 1913 because of prohibition and the increasing popularity of the West Indies. It would therefore appear that the number of 220,000 tourists bound for Europe in 1908 is not too low. If American tourists in 1913 spent abroad on the average 700 francs exclusive of passenger fares (see p. 70), they very probably spent less rather than more in 1908. Hence Paish's estimate of 1036 million francs appears about 300 million francs too high.

[3] Soc. de Stat. de Paris, 1916.

[4] Pupin in La richesse privée et finances françaises, p. 26, estimated tourist expenditures in 1912 as 1937 millions and for 1913 1830 millions, but his method of arriving at that estimate deserves no consideration. On the ground that there is no method of estimating tourist expenditures directly, he subtracted his estimated

Pupin's figure is too high. He says that of the 600,000 foreigners entering France via her seaports at least 300,000 remained in France.[1] This does not include the bulk of Belgians, Italians, Spaniards, and Germans who crossed the frontiers. He also estimated the amount spent in France by those who arrived by boat at 2000 francs each, making a total of 600 million francs spent by foreigners other than the French neighbors enumerated above.

Estimates of per capita expenditures of visitors in France vary from 500 to 2000 francs, but none appears to be based on any published or objective data. The only attempt at an estimate based on adequate facts is the investigation of tourist expenditures by the Finance and Investment Division of the United States Department of Commerce in preparation for their annual balance of international accounts for the years 1928, 1929, 1930.[2] They sent questionnaires to thousands of applicants for passports, asking in these questionnaires for detailed information regarding expenditures abroad. Altho only one-third of the number of applicants replied, they were considered fair sampling. The results of the investigation are given below. The number of American passengers to Europe in 1928 was made up as follows:

		Arithmetic Average Expenditure
Third Class	65,903	$517
Tourist and Student Classes	57,691	705
Second Class	45,995	982
Cabin Class	63,266	1171
First Class	70,145	1985
Total	303,000	$1270

The gross expenditures of the 303,000 at the average rate derived from the questionnaire was found to be $336,000, i.e. about $1110 per person. That expenditure includes steamship fare, which

debits from the estimated credits and called the remainder Tourist Expenditure. He defends this method as follows: "It is in our eyes the only way in which we can be informed on this very important point, because all direct inquiries lead nowhere in this task."

[1] Créances et dettes internationales, p. 85.

[2] Department of Commerce, Bureau of Foreign and Domestic Commerce, The Balance of International Payments of the United States in 1928, by R. Hall, Trade Information Bulletin Nos. 625, 761.

probably accounts for one-third of the expenditures, leaving about $740 per person spent abroad. More accurate figures for 1930 are given by the report for that year, because several new sources of information were utilized. They show that the average expenditure of American tourists on European soil was about $700.[1]

If changes in purchasing power are allowed for, expenditure for the same quantity of services and merchandise would approximate $500 in 1913. Since real income has increased in the United States in the last 15 years, there is no reason to expect travel expenditures to play the same proportionate rôle. It would seem that smaller real incomes would leave less to be spent on luxuries such as foreign travel; larger incomes would leave more. That the average tourist expenditures may differ considerably from year to year is evident from the averages obtained in the years 1927 and 1928. The average expenditure of first class passengers was $118 more in 1928 than in 1927, that of second class passengers $146 more, and that of third class $3. The phenomenal increase in stock market values in that year may have been largely responsible for this difference, which suggests that the 1927 average is more suitable for a base of comparison with pre-war years. Another shifting factor over long periods is the changing type of tourist. European tourist travel is no longer considered the prerogative of the wealthy. From 1880 to 1913 the percentage of tourists of the smaller income groups increased. The recent development of "tourist" class accommodations on steamships is indicative of that change. These changes increase the range of probable error when the average expenditure for 1928 is used as a base for pre-war estimates. Nevertheless, it is the only objectively derived figure that has been published, and is, therefore, more reliable than guesses based on personal observation.

The estimates of tourist expenditures in the present study are guided by the results in this investigation of the United States Department of Commerce. The average per capita expenditure in Europe is first modified by averaging the expenditures of the two years investigated after allowance has been made for passage. The sum obtained, $700, when deflated becomes $450, or 2300

[1] Trade Information Bulletin, op. cit., p. 31.

francs. Changes in real income and shifts in the income class of tourists are ignored.

What part of this 2300 francs is spent in France depends on the number of American tourists in France who visit other countries as well. Many visit France only, thus spending the total 2300 francs there. Many more doubtless visit at least one country in addition to France, and leave in France anywhere from 200 to 1500 francs. It is very unlikely that any American entering France departs without leaving at least 200 francs in hotel bills, tips, landing fees, and railroad fares, while the bulk of those Americans who visit an additional country spend much more than that sum. An estimate, therefore, of 1200 francs spent in France by each American entering France in 1913 does not seem unreasonable. This is almost half the sum estimated by Meynial, but in the light of the investigation discussed above, an average expenditure of 2000 francs in France by tourists who arrive via seaports appears very unlikely. Pupin's estimate of 1000 francs per tourist, including as it does all the European visitors, who constituted by far the largest number of tourists in France, is much too high. Not only do the Europeans have a smaller income than Americans and therefore spend less on travel, but a trip to France is more unusual and much more of an event in the life of the average American tourist than it is in that of the average European tourist, to whom a trip to France frequently is a matter of a few hundred miles and a two weeks' stay. English clerks, for instance, frequently spent their fortnight vacations in Paris. The same was true of Germans, Belgians, and Italians. I am thus inclined to the opinion that the modal expenditure of the European visitors to France was under 300 francs, but that the arithmetic mean was more because of the fact that many very wealthy Europeans made Paris and Nice their rendezvous in the winter.

It would appear that Meynial's estimate of 600 million francs [1] is much closer to the facts than Pupin's estimate of two billions,

[1] Meynial estimated that 600,000 foreigners came to France via seaports. He claims that at least 300,000 remained in France, each leaving 2000 francs there, making a total of 600 million francs. His estimate of average expenditure is too high, but allowance should be made for the expenditures of tourists reaching France by rail.

or Hoschiller's estimate of 450 millions.[1] Moulton and Lewis, who have made the only estimate of tourist expenditures covering more than two years, accept figures close to 600 million.[2] Gide's estimate of 500 to 600 francs for the average per capita expenditure of tourists in France during 1900 seems a reasonable one for that year because of extra expenditures apt to be called forth during a year of international fairs, but appears too high for the years before and after.

Compromising, then, on 600 francs as the average expenditure of tourists in 1913, and estimating the number of foreign visitors to France at 800,000, we arrive at the figure of 450 millions. To this sum must be added expenditures of foreign students in France and of wealthy foreigners who maintain a permanent residence in France but who receive their incomes from abroad. Giffen,[3] writing in 1880, stated that there was an American colony of several thousands constantly resident in Europe which alone accounted for 30 to 40 million pounds annually. Considering the number of nationalities which were represented in Paris by wealthy sojourners — Paris was and is a Mecca not only for wealthy Americans but also for wealthy South Americans, Spaniards, Russians, Scandinavians, and even Asiatics — it is not unreasonable to place at 10,000 the total number of those whose expenditures before the war were well over 5000 francs per person. If one-fourth of their income was from other countries, it would mean 10 million francs spent in addition to ordinary tourist expenditures.

From the total tourist expenditures in France the amount spent abroad by Frenchmen must be deducted. Pupin estimated this at 10 per cent of the amount spent by foreigners in France

[1] Cited by Kuszynski in Die Zahlungsbilanz Frankreichs, Deutsch-Französische Wirtschaftskorrespondenz, December 28, 1925.

[2] The estimates made by Moulton and Lewis (op. cit., p. 342), based on Paish's estimate for 1908, were as follows:

AVERAGE ANNUAL EXPENDITURE

1881–1885	370 millions	1897–1902	525 millions
1886–1890	430 millions	1903–1908	585 millions
1891–1896	475 millions	1909–1913	625 millions

[3] R. Giffen, On the Use of Import and Export Statistics, p. 34.

because he considered that the proportion of French population and French wealth to those of the world justified this sum. That appears to be a liberal estimate. The French are famed neither for their traveling proclivities nor for their spending habits. Still, in the absence of more information the figure of 10 per cent will be used here. The results are tabulated on page 115. The figures are modified for years of fairs [1] and for variations in business activity.

Altho tourist expenditures form one of the largest sources of revenue, not all such expenditures are to be placed on the credit side of the balance sheet. Some of the tourists carry coin instead of credit instruments and therefore their expenditures do not give rise to any sums due France. To include them under tourist expenditures would exaggerate the supposed supply of foreign bills in France. Coin taken into France to be spent there has no effect on the balance of payments, tho it may be of interest when considering monetary changes. The sums so carried should be deducted from the estimated tourist expenditures; the result, of course, is the same if they are merely placed on the debit side. The latter procedure, which is the one followed here, has a slight advantage in that it records these gold movements. For monetary problems such records are helpful.

The sum in which we are interested is not the sum of gold and silver coin carried in, but the excess of that sum over the sum carried out. Since there are more Belgians, Italians, Swiss, and Germans who visit France each year than there are Frenchmen who visit those countries, it is reasonable to assume that there is more gold and silver coin entering France in the pockets of tourists than there is leaving by that route. Assuming an average expenditure in France of 250 francs per European tourist, and further assuming that 25 per cent of those funds are in specie, we get a figure of about 35 millions. Allowing further a movement of 5 millions the other way, we arrive at an estimate of 30 millions or 5 per cent of total tourist expenditure in 1913. The annual sums obtained on that basis are listed in Table 20.

[1] The world fairs of 1879, 1889, and 1900 were visited by 218,000, 1,500,000, and 447,000 foreigners respectively.

The funds carried into and out of France by immigrants and emigrants, and funds remitted to and from France by Frenchmen abroad also enter into the international accounts. These can be estimated only crudely. No records were kept of the amounts carried by French emigrants and immigrants. Indeed, there are even no official figures for the number of immigrants themselves, altho there are official figures for French emigrants. Special census reports, however, contain periodic estimates of immigration arrived at by comparing population figures of successive census reports.[1] After allowance is made for the known births and deaths during the period, the net increase or decrease in population is ascribed to immigration or emigration. The results of such compilation appear below:

Years	Excess of Immigration	Excess of Emigration
1881–1886	170,000	37,000
1887–1891	...	37,000
1892–1896	132,000	...
1897–1901	224,000	...
1902–1906	...	35,000

The Annuaire Statistique of 1914 contains other estimates, apparently obtained in a similar manner but covering different periods, as follows:

Years	Excess of Immigration	Excess of Emigration
1881–1890	161,000	...
1891–1900	379,000	...
1901–1906	...	35,000
1907–1911	248,000	...

Estimates so secured include all the errors made in census reports. Moreover, when converted into annual figures, the probable error for any one year is great. For our purpose it is better to separate the immigration and emigration totals. The separate figures can be roughly obtained by adding the annual emigration figures to the estimated annual excesses. The result is tabulated on page 77.

The number of immigrants (exclusive of casual laborers) is of little importance in any one year, and the funds they carry are so

[1] Résultats statistiques du recensement (1906), Vol. 14.

small that the errors can be only of minor significance. I have been unable to find any estimates of the amount of funds carried into France by immigrants, but such an estimate has been made by Paish [1] for funds carried into the United States by immigrants from continental Europe. His estimate is $50 each. Coats [2] estimated the average at only $25. Immigrants to France certainly did not carry more than immigrants to America, and there is reason to expect that they carried less. The bulk of immigrants into France came from neighboring countries, and to them the risk involved probably appeared small. Therefore people with very small capital, who would hesitate to cross the Atlantic, would dare to settle in a neighboring town. This supposition receives some support from the fact that most of the immigrants to France settled in border towns.[3] The sums carried by poor immigrants are augmented by the much greater per capita sums carried into France by wealthy émigrés. The large wealthy foreign colonies in Paris and Nice serve to increase what otherwise would probably be a very low average of funds brought in by immigrants.

It would seem that an average of 100 francs per person up to 1899, and 150 francs since then, is a conservative estimate. This is pure guesswork, but the total involved is so small compared to estimates of service items and capital exports that the probable error is not a serious consideration. Table 11, on page 77, contains the annual estimates of these funds carried by French immigrants. The totals entered are in most cases so small that even to include them in the international accounts is to give the balance sheet a specious appearance of accuracy. Some of the years, however, involve movements of over 5 million francs, and for this reason the whole table is included.

Placing immigrant funds on the credit side of the balance sheet and emigrant funds on the debit side, as does Professor Viner in

[1] G. Paish, The Trade Balance of the United States, United States National Monetary Commission (1910), p. 182.

[2] R. H. Coats, Board of Inquiry into Cost of Living, Report of Board, Vol. II, p. 902.

[3] Rapport du directeur de la Statistique Générale de la France sur le nombre des Français à l'étranger, Bull. Stat. Gén. de la France, Vol. LV, p. 121.

his Canadian Balance of Indebtedness, and as is the practice of the United States Department of Commerce,[1] assumes that the funds brought in by the immigrants were in the form of letters of credit, or travelers' checks, or other credit instruments which would call for subsequent collection. In so far as these funds took the form of gold, they should not be included in the international account any more than they were in the case of tourist expenditures. To repeat, it is of interest to record them because of their effect on the metallic stock of the country. Consequently the total funds carried in are placed on the credit side and the amount of gold and silver coin carried in on the debit side. The amount carried in coin was doubtless large, as most French immigrants are from neighboring countries where the same gold and silver coins are current. The proportion of funds carried by French immigrants in the form of gold and silver coin is estimated at 75 per cent. The results are tabulated on the following page.

So much for funds carried in by immigrants. We turn now to funds carried out by emigrants. The emigration figures published by France in the Annuaire Statistique are those of persons leaving via French ports. In these figures residents of foreign countries are not separated from French emigrants and it is the latter that are significant for the international accounts. One study of European emigration, made in 1906, does contain figures purporting to be those of French emigration for the years 1884 to 1893,[2] but the estimates are approximately one-third of those contained in the Annuaire, and compared with the total of French supposed to reside abroad, they appear to be rather low. In 1911, according to a report by the Director of Statistique Générale de la France,[3] there were living abroad 850,000 Frenchmen in the Colonies and 600,000 in foreign countries. This figure does not include foreigners leaving France after a stay of a few years or more. The total of persons leaving French ports from 1860 to 1913 was less than a million. If one-third were French emigrants,

[1] See The Balance of International Payments of the United States in 1928, Trade Information Bulletin No. 625, p. 20.

[2] R. Gonnard, L'Emigration européen au XIXe siècle (Paris, 1906), p. 290.

[3] Bull. Stat. Gén. de la France, Vol. IV, op. cit.

TABLE 11

Funds Brought into France by Immigrants, 1880–1913

Year	Estimated Excess of Immigration (Thousands)	Estimated Emigration (Thousands)	Immigration (Thousands)	Funds Carried by Immigrants (Millions of francs)	Gold & Silver Carried by Immigrants (Millions of francs)
1880	20	5	25	2	1
1881	20	5	25	2	1
1882	30	5	25	2	1
1883	30	5	35	3	2
1884	20	5	25	2	1
1885	20	5	25	2	1
1886	20	10	30	3	2
1887	20	15	35	3	2
1888	0	25	5	0	0
1889	0	40	0	0	0
1890	0	20	10	11	0
1891	0	5	5	0	0
1892	0	5	5	0	0
1893	40	5	45	4	3
1894	40	5	45	4	3
1895	35	5	40	4	3
1896	30	5	35	3	2
1897	35	5	40	4	3
1898	40	5	45	6	4
1899	40	5	45	6	4
1900	50	5	55	10	7
1901	55	5	60	10	7
1902	0	10	0	0	0
1903	0	5	0	0	0
1904	0	5	0	0	0
1905	0	10	0	0	0
1906	0	5	0	0	0
1907	50	10	60	10	0
1908	60	5	65	10	7
1909	40	5	45	7	5
1910	50	5	55	10	7
1911	30	5	35	5	5
1912	40	5	45	7	7
1913	50	5	55	10	7

it is difficult to account for 1,400,000 French abroad, since a great many French emigrants returned to France, particularly from the Colonies.[1] Even allowing for a high birth rate, the estimate of 325,000 seems too low. However, the sums involved are again so small that the lower figure can be used without distorting the balance. The average of funds carried by French emigrants to the Americas and to the Colonies is probably higher [2] than that of the immigrants entering France from Italy, Belgium, and Spain. It would seem that an allowance of 150 francs from 1880 to 1897 and 200 from 1898 to 1913 is not too high an estimate of funds taken by French emigrants. The proportion of credit instruments before 1898 was probably approximately one-half of the total funds. As explained previously, the total outgoing funds are placed on the debit side and outgoing gold on the credit side. The only years which involve sums of more than one million francs are 1888, 1889, and 1890. Figures for the other years are too small to be included. The estimates are recorded on the following page.

More important than the capital carried in and out of France by immigrants and emigrants are sums annually sent by them to their home country and sums taken from France by foreign workers who remain in France during the harvesting season only, or who live across the boundary and work in France. Pupin [3] estimated that foreign workers in France in 1913 sent home 100 million francs, while Meynial [4] estimated this item at only 30 million francs for the same year. Pupin's estimate was based on his assumption that there were 800,000 to 900,000 foreign workers in France earning about one billion in wages, and that 10 per cent of these wages, mostly from Italians, were sent home. The total foreign population in 1911 was only 1,130,000; so the figure of 800,000 to 900,000 laborers sending a part of their wages home seems much too high.

In making an estimate of these remittances a distinction must be drawn between funds remitted to their native country by foreigners residing in France and foreigners commuting to and

[1] Y. Guyot, Lettres sur la politique coloniale (Paris, 1885).

[2] O. Asselin, Emigration from Belgium and France to Canada (Ottawa, 1911).

[3] Op. cit., p. 26. [4] Op. cit., p. 86.

TABLE 12

FUNDS TAKEN OUT OF FRANCE BY EMIGRANTS, 1880–1913

Year	Number Leaving French Ports (Thousands)	Estimated Emigration (Thousands)	Funds Taken by Emigrants (Millions of francs)	Gold & Silver Carried by Emigrants (Millions of francs)
1880	12	5	0	0
1881	12	5	0	0
1882	13	5	0	0
1883	11	5	0	0
1884	16	5	0	0
1885	16	5	0	0
1886	19	10	1	0
1887	29	15	2	1
1888	61	25	4	2
1889	82	35	5	2
1890	54	20	3	1
1891	16	5	0	0
1892	14	5	0	0
1893	15	5	0	0
1894	11	5	0	0
1895	12	5	0	0
1896	12	5	0	0
1897	12	5	0	0
1898	10	5	1	0
1899	9	5	1	0
1900	14	5	1	0
1901	12	5	1	0
1902	11	5	1	0
1903	16	10	2	1
1904	14	5	1	0
1905	12	5	1	0
1906	15	5	1	0
1907	20	10	2	1
1908	12	5	1	0
1909	12	5	1	0
1910	12	5	1	0
1911	13	5	1	0
1912	13	5	1	0
1913	12	5	1	0

from France. The former funds are sent in the form of credit instruments and should appear as a debit item in the international accounts. Most of the latter are probably carried out in the form of coin and should not be included in the balance sheet, or, if included, should be offset by a credit item for the coin so taken out. The importance of these funds may be judged from the number of Belgians working in France who commuted daily. In 1906 it was estimated that 25,000 Belgian workers passed the frontier to work, and it was said that they spent practically all their wages in Belgium.[1] That item alone would account for at least 24 million francs a year. During the summer season thousands of Belgians, Italians, Spaniards, and — after 1910 — Poles migrated to France to help with the harvesting. These workers returned in the late fall with a good part of their wages in their pockets.[2] In view of these large sums withdrawn by foreign workers, Meynial's estimate, which presumably includes gold coin carried out by the workers, is not high enough. An estimate of 60 millions for the year 1913 with reasonable modification for earlier years of prosperity and depression appears more reasonable. An annual estimate on this basis is contained in Table 17, page 115. Of these sums it is estimated that 25 per cent were taken out of France in the form of specie. This estimate, like others of the proportion of specie carried, is not based on any evidence, and all that can be said for it is that it is better than no estimate at all.

From the figure thus reached, funds sent to France by Frenchmen living abroad must be deducted. Comparatively few French workers commute to neighboring countries. France's stable population, coupled with the movement of population from rural districts to the large French cities, stimulates a demand for foreign workers rather than creates a supply of French workers who seek employment in Belgium or Italy. The wages accepted by Bel-

[1] G. Pirou, La main d'oeuvre étrangère en France (Paris, 1916). In Hallum, Belgium, out of a working population of 10,000, more than 6000 Belgian workers in France do not live in France. Merne, a small Belgian village of 12,000, sends 4000 workers to France, and Mouscron, three kilometers from Tourçong, one of the textile manufacturing centres, has 5000 inhabitants earning a living in France. See J. Nozelk, Une taxe sur la main d'oeuvre étrangère, Rev. Pol. et Parl., February, 1911.

[2] E. Payen, op. cit.

gians and Italians were too low to attract many French workers, while the foreigner was attracted to France because of higher pay.[1] Altho the total of French emigrants was smaller than the total of immigrants, the former went largely to French colonies; the proportionate total of remittances to France ought, then, to be at least half of that sent out of France. These emigrant remittances were practically all in the form of credit instruments, and estimates of these sums are recorded in Table 12.

French Colonies, it will be remembered, are here considered as foreign countries, and therefore Colonial expenditures and receipts by the French home government appear as foreign transactions. Thruout the period under consideration French Colonial ventures necessitated a net outflow of money for Colonial administration, public works, and for military expenditures. This last was an item leading to heavy debit charges in the payments because the bulk of military expenditures occasioned by the frequent military campaigns and the maintenance of French troops abroad was paid by the home government. It was not until 1893 that the French Government imposed a tax on her Colonies to share Colonial expenses, and not until 1900 did she acquire the right to impose the cost of troops on each Colony. Even after that the Colonies contributed only a small part of those expenses. In 1901 military expenditures on account of the Colonies were 91 million francs, and only 10 millions of this sum were contributed by them; in 1906 the Colonies contributed 16 of the 96 millions, and in 1910 of 101 millions only 15 were recovered from them.[2] The Moroccan occupation alone from 1907 to 1913 entailed extra military expenditures totaling 273 millions.[3] In an unpublished

[1] J. Nozelk, op. cit. [2] G. Jeze, Science des finances, 4th ed. (Paris, 1912), p. 45.

[3] Expenses Occasioned by the Occupation of Morocco from August 5, 1907, to December 31, 1912, Bull. de Stat. et de Leg. Comparée, Vol. 75, p. 184.

Year	Army	Navy	Foreign Affairs	Total
1907	6.3	4.4	.7	11.5
1908	31.6	7.3	.6	39.5
1909	13.0	2.5	.7	16.2
1910	9.8	1.7	1.0	12.6
1911	54.7	3.1	1.0	58.8
1912	130.7	3.1	1.2	135.1

study of French Colonial policy by Constant Southworth [1] it was estimated that the annual excess of expenditures over receipts from the Colonies averaged over 100 million francs from 1880 to 1890, and a little less from 1890 to 1910. These estimates are in excess of figures for Colonial expenditures as recorded in the statistics of the French budget, but the distinction between Colonial and domestic expenditures is not clearly made in French finance.

Before 1886 Colonial expenses were included in those of the Navy. Altho for those years there are no separate figures, we know that Colonial expenditures were heavy.[2] During the first year of separate Colonial budget (exclusive of Algeria) expenditures of 43 million francs are recorded. By 1903 this item had reached 103 millions, where it remained until 1914. These figures do not include expenses of Algeria, by far the most important of French colonial possessions, whose expenditures from 1881 to 1892 were treated as domestic expenditures of the respective departments. Yet the importance of Algerian expenditures during those years is indicated by the analysis of French expenditures of 1885 by De Foville, who found that the revenue from Algeria was 37 millions while the expenditures on her account 114 millions.[3] A similar analysis by Vignon in 1891 showed the revenue from Algeria to have been 40 millions and expenditures 125 millions.[4]

Even if the distinction between expenditures on domestic and Colonial accounts were made, there would still remain the more difficult problem of estimating what portion of expenditures charged to the Colonies can be considered as sums due abroad. Colonial expenditures consist of sums spent in the home country as well as in the Colonies and therefore these expenditures cannot be placed on the debit side of the balance of international ac-

[1] Cited by Moulton and Lewis, op. cit., p. 49.

[2] In 1881 30,000 troops were sent to Tunis on a punitive expedition, and tribal revolts in Algeria kept expeditionary forces busy from 1881 to 1884. Colonial expenditures for the insignificant colony of Tonkin alone reached 70 million francs in 1884. — F. Faure, Les budgets de la France depuis vingt ans, 1868–1887.

[3] La France économique, p. 456.

[4] L. Vignon, La France en Algérie (Paris, 1893), Chap. X.

counts. Indeed, it is possible that so much of the Colonial expenditure is made at home as to render the item of little importance in the international accounts. The fact of mere excess of Colonial expenditure over Colonial revenue in itself gives no indication of the amount spent abroad in excess of sums received from abroad. It is essential to know how the funds charged to Colonial account were spent.

Expenditures on military affairs, on public works, and administration make up the expense side of the budget. Of these the first was in the case of France the most important.[1] Among the items under military expenditure the principal ones are transportation, soldiers' pay, and cost of war material, of equipment, and of subsistence. Most of the soldiers' equipment and war material is purchased in France or manufactured in government plants and transported either in Navy vessels or in ships of the French merchant marines. Clearly these expenditures, then, ought not to be included in sums due abroad. They involve only payments by the French Government to French industrialists, or inter-departmental transfers of sums.[2] Still there are two items among military expenditures which do give rise to payments due abroad from France: soldiers' pay and subsistence. That portion of pay which soldiers spend abroad and of subsistence which is purchased abroad may constitute debit items in the international accounts. A detailed investigation of the records of the Quarter-

[1] From 1830 to 1891 of 5.3 billion francs spent on Colonies, 3.5 consisted of military expenses and 1.7 of public works. During this period the total receipts were only 1.3 billions. — L. Vignon, op. cit., p. 286.

Of the 114 millions of expenditure in Algeria in 1885, 56 were for the army and 56 for civil service. — De Foville, op. cit., p. 450.

In 1901 military expenditures alone were 91 millions; in 1910 of 101 millions of expenditure 83 were military. — Levasseur, op. cit., Chap. VIII.

[2] If the supplies are furnished by private industry and sent to the Colonies, they are apt to appear as exports. But this merchandise exported and paid for by the French home government should not be recorded in the international accounts since it gives rise to no international payments or debts. The import figures for Algeria give no indication of exports received on military account. In 1911 there were 305,000 French troops in Algeria, most of whom had arrived during that year, and imports into Algeria increased from 543 millions to 611 millions, while exports increased only 4 millions; whereas in 1912 the number of troops decreased but imports leaped to 722 millions.

master Corps, and an acquaintance with the spending habits of French troops abroad would doubtless yield the necessary information on these points. The labor involved has precluded any such investigation; instead a crude estimate is here resorted to.

A number of factors enter into the basis of this estimate. First there are the military expenses. France rarely kept less than 30,000 French troops abroad, and during years of military activity the number quickly increased. In 1911 there were more than 350,000 French troops abroad. Some of the food for these troops was purchased locally; part of the pay was also spent locally.[1] It is quite probable that at least 20 per cent of the soldiers' pay was so spent. As for subsistence, the portion obtained locally depends on the colony and the prevailing political condition. French colonies import little foodstuff from France. Algeria, Tunis, and French Indo-China, the principal colonies, are food exporters, and much of the subsistence in those countries must have been obtained locally, particularly in times of peace.

Expenditures on public works are another element in the estimate of sums due abroad on Colonial account. The greater part of the expenditures on this item were made in the Colonies. Wages, always an important element in public works, went almost entirely to residents of the Colonies, and part of the bulky raw material was purchased locally. Additional raw material must have been imported directly from foreign countries, since France herself is a large importer of raw materials. It may be assumed, then, that most of the expenditures on public works — in so far as they are in excess of domestic revenue — are to be included on the debit side under Colonial expenditures.

Administrative expenses, another item, consist largely of salaries, and as such constitute expenditures in the Colonies. Altho administrative expenses are not so important as the other two, they represent amounts spent mostly in the Colonies. Part of the administrative expense and of public works was covered by revenue from the Colonies, but only part. The portion of these

[1] Guyot in Lettres sur la politique coloniale (Paris, 1885), p. 45, commenting on the growth of exports to the Colonies, said, "Our own soldiers paid by France are the ones who buy French imports."

expenses not met by Colonial revenue, together with the portion of military expenses spent in the Colonies or in foreign countries, amounted to between one-third and one-half of the excess of expenditure over receipts. The other half or two-thirds was used in France for material and equipment sent to the Colonies and for the part of the soldiers' pay sent home. The estimates of Colonial expenditures based on the foregoing proportions appear on the debit side of the balance of international accounts, page 118.

A number of small items grouped under the one head "Miscellaneous" have also been included in the balance sheet. These are life insurance, fire insurance, and brokerage commissions on discounted foreign bills. French insurance companies obtain much of the insurance business placed in French Colonies. French companies audit and assist in the conduct of Colonial companies, and a goodly share of Colonial bills is discounted in France. This income is estimated to have been about 5 million francs in 1880 and to have reached 15 millions in 1913. The annual estimates are in Column 12, Table 18, page 116.

CHAPTER V

FOREIGN INVESTMENTS

THE most important of the invisible items in the international accounts of France is the export of capital. By this term is meant the transfer of purchasing power, whether in terms of goods, services, or specie, made by the residents of one country to residents of another country, when such transfers result in *no immediate* return payments, and when they are made with the intent of receiving in return adequate payment at some time in the future. The term capital exports is frequently applied also to transfer of *title* to purchasing power under the assumption that eventually the claims will be exercised and goods or services will be transferred. This transfer of title to purchasing power constitutes in almost all cases of capital movements the necessary first step. It is eliminated only where goods are sold abroad on long-term credit, or in those rare cases where imports of goods are financed by permanent loans after the goods are shipped. In all other instances of capital movements the transfer of title may not be converted into a transfer of goods or services until weeks, months, or even years have passed. A large part of the total of transfers of title is, indeed, never converted into transfers of goods or services; instead many of the transfers of title are used to offset one another. It is only the surplus of claims — i.e. title — that *must* eventually be converted into transfers of goods or services.[1]

Just when this surplus of claims will be converted into a movement of goods or services depends partly upon the cause of the transfers of title and partly upon the prevailing economic conditions in the countries concerned. For illustration, Italy may borrow funds in France and use a portion of them to increase Italian balances in French banks, thereby indefinitely postponing conversion of newly acquired claims into transfers of goods; or Italy

[1] Other claims may or may not represent transfers of title to goods and services. Obviously imports and exports of merchandise give rise to such claims.

may exchange her newly acquired title to French purchasing power for claims to purchasing power in Germany and exercise those claims to German purchasing power by importing goods from Germany. No change in this instance will appear in the international accounts of France until Germany exercises her newly acquired claim to purchasing power in France. Germany might elect to keep that purchasing power in France in anticipation of indemnity payments due France. We should then have a French loan to Italy resulting in the creation of a German deposit in France by way of German exports to Italy, in return for which France would obtain a future claim on purchasing power in Italy; in such case the transaction would in no way affect the French balance sheet until and only if the future claims on Italian goods or services were exercised.

It is apparent that any number of combinations of transfers could and do take place, and it should be equally clear that the surplus (or deficit) of claims to foreign purchasing power that is recorded as obtained in any one year need not — one might say ought not — be equal to the surplus of imports (or exports) of goods and services for that same year. In measuring the amount of capital exports, a distinction should, therefore, be drawn between transfers of title to purchasing power and transfers of goods. The measure of each must be obtained by a different method.

To obtain figures of transfers of goods (and services) a balance of international accounts must be constructed. Given the annual total imports and exports of goods, specie, and services, the difference between the totals of imports and of exports — assuming no error in the data — can be explained as transfers of merchandise and services for which there has been no payment during that year. If from this sum are deducted the amounts transferred as immigrant remittances, gifts, and indemnity payments, the remainder must represent net capital exports (or capital imports) plus interest and amortization payments; that is, the remainder represents *goods* and *services* transferred in exchange for some future claim or transferred in part or in whole settlement of debts previously created. This remainder includes sums due on account of interest, dividends, and amortization payments. Deduction for these items being made, there is left a sum which measures the annual export of capital — using the term to mean transfer of goods and services.

To obtain a measure of the total transfers of title to purchasing power it is necessary to make a *direct* estimate of all such transfers from or to France. These transfers include loans made to foreign governments, municipalities, corporations, or individuals; investments made in foreign countries by France or in France by foreign countries thru purchase of stock; deposits kept in foreign banks; funds employed for the establishment of foreign branch enterprises for the exploitation of foreign resources and for the purchase of foreign immovable property from foreigners.

The first method, to repeat, measures the actual transfer during the year of goods, specie, and services, whereas the second measures only the transfer of title during that year. The two methods should give similar results year by year only if the time lag between transfer of title and transfer of goods was always short. It must be remembered that the first, or indirect method, which depends upon the construction of an annual statement of international accounts, includes all the errors of omission and commission to which such balances are subject. That this is a disadvantage of no mean proportions in the case of France from 1880 to 1913 is apparent from the discussion in the preceding chapters as to the difficulty of estimating these items. The obstacles in the way of a correct estimate of capital exports by the second or direct method are, as will be apparent in the pages following, at least as great.

In this study both methods are employed. The measurement of capital exports by the indirect method is at this point almost finished. Only the figures for revenue due to and from France are lacking for the completion of the balance sheet. These figures, however, cannot be obtained without first securing figures of the annual export of capital by the direct method. It is thus apparent that the two methods as employed here are not wholly independent. Yet there is no alternative, for there exist no data of the total interest and dividends received by France from her foreign investments.[1] We proceed, therefore, to the estimate of capital exports by the direct method.

The largest item in capital exports consists of loans either to foreign governments or to foreign corporations. A correct estimate of these is of paramount importance. But the net movement of securities in any one year, or even for a series of years, is elusive. It is extremely difficult — one may say impossible — to ascertain with any high degree of exactness the international movement of securities after they have been once absorbed. It is true that a portion of any issue remains in the hands of the original purchasers and a larger portion usually remains in the country where they were originally sold. But there is a considerable volume of securities internationally marketable which constantly shifts from one financial market to another. In the hands of bankers and large investment brokers these securities supply the means for arbitrage transactions and also form an important international medium of exchange with which credits are established abroad. Sometimes issues once sold are repurchased in large quantities by the original borrowers — the absorption by France in the 70's of her rentes originally purchased by foreigners is an illustration of this type of movement, as are the instances of Spain and Italy, who in the 90's purchased in increasing amounts their securities originally held by the French.[2] There is also a continuous stream of amortization payments and redemptions of loans which must be taken into account.

Fortunately there are several sources of information that are of help in tracing the movements of securities and also of measuring the amount of foreign securities originally issued in France. None of them is sufficient in itself to yield the desired information, but each can be used to supplement the others, to fill in the gaps, and to serve as a partial check.

[1] See p. 105.

[2] In the latter case political events encouraged the movement. The growing antagonism between Italy and France caused in part by tariff controversies and the increasing friendliness between Russia and France led to a considerable substitution in France of Russian for Italian securities. According to reports of the Italian treasury, the coupon payments in Paris represented, in 1885, 23 per cent of foreign bond holders; the proportion fell steadily, reaching less than 5 per cent by 1906. — E. Becque, L'Internationalisation des capitaux (Montpellier, 1912), p. 47.

First are the scattered statistics of issues, of conversions, and of listings. For the years after 1895 annual statistics purporting to represent new capital issues are available; however, the amounts recorded are in reality not the amounts sold, but those admitted to listing at the Bourse and issued on the Curb. These sums bear only a distant relation to the amount of securities sold in any one year. The amounts listed on the Paris Bourse alone, for example, are double the total foreign holdings in the French portfolio. Yet these figures are useful in that they throw some light on major changes in annual flotations.

Secondly, there are taxation data. In France all foreign securities other than foreign government bonds were subject to a triple tax.[1] Foreign government securities, which form the major portion of French foreign holdings, were exempt from these annual taxes,[2] but were subject to a stamp duty at time of issue. All taxation data are available. Had there been no tax evasion, it would be comparatively simple to ascertain from treasury reports on the revenue tax the amount of foreign securities other than government bonds that circulated in France. But so great was the amount of tax evasion on foreign securities that the utility of taxation data is much diminished. The financial literature of the period contains many allusions to the very common practice and ease of evading taxes on foreign securities.[3] M. Théry estimated that one-third of foreign securities subject to taxes evaded them.[4] One writer estimated in 1903 that only half the foreign securities

[1] Revenue from all foreign securities except government bonds was subject to a tax of 3 per cent (raised in 1890 to 4 per cent). These securities were subject also to a transfer tax on the market value of the securities, but the recorded figures include an annual tax on bearer securities and a tax on other securities only if and when a transfer is made. This renders useless the transfer tax data as a reliable source of information of the amount of securities in circulation. The third tax is a stamp tax at time of issue on the nominal value of the securities.

[2] After the War of 1870, in order to help regain for Paris its pre-war position as a financial centre and to avoid retaliation on the part of foreign governments, it was decided to exempt foreign government securities from annual taxes.

[3] See especially E. Guilmard, L'Evasion fiscale (Paris, 1908); Lescoeur, Pourquoi et comment on fraude le fisc, 6th ed.; Renou, Les valeurs étrangères (Paris, 1907); Casteignau-Caumont, Le régime fiscale des valeurs mobilières (Bordeaux, 1910).

[4] Cited by M. Arboux, Les valeurs mobilières étrangères sur le marché français (Paris, 1913), p. 57.

subject to the tax paid it.[1] Caillaux in explaining the budget of 1909 stated that the Administration of Registration evaluated the annual loss to the treasury from evasion at 40 million francs, a sum which represents an investment of about 20 billion francs.[2]

The extent of evasion is further indicated by a comparison of the totals of the taxed revenue derived from domestic securities and from foreign securities (Table 13). Foreign holdings represent approximately one-third of the French portfolio, that is, one-half of the domestic holdings. About one-half of these foreign securities are government bonds not subject to tax on revenue, but one-third of the domestic holdings, being French rentes, are also not subject to the tax on revenue. We should then expect, *if there were no evasion*, the amount of foreign securities subject to the revenue tax to equal about one-third of domestic securities so taxed. A comparison of Columns 4 and 7 shows, however, the amount of foreign securities taxed before 1904 to be less than 10 per cent. This indicates evasions in the case of foreign securities of 60 per cent or more. Strenuous measures to reduce such wholesale evasion were made in subsequent years, and, judging from the increasing proportion of taxes received from foreign securities, with some success, but the amount of evasion continued to be serious up to the war. Notwithstanding the large proportion of evasions, the figures of revenue taxed are useful in indicating year to year changes in holdings of private securities, for, with the exception of the decade before the war when more stringent measures were constantly sought, there is no reason to expect the proportion of evasion to have fluctuated greatly from year to year.

As for foreign government securities, which are subject to the single stamp tax, the taxation data indicate the annual amount of those securities listed for the first time in France, but throw little light on the amount that remained in the country after they had

[1] N. Cemental in Rev. Pol. et Parl., 1903, p. 475.

[2] Banks in neighboring countries, soliciting deposits from Frenchmen, went so far as to suggest in circulars methods of tax evasion made possible by depositing securities in foreign banks or in foreign branches of French banks. — Neymarck, Finances contemporaines, Vol. 6, p. 131; also E. Becque, op. cit., p. 216.

been once sold.[1] Another difficulty in the use of this information is the fact that the tax figures include partial payments from all securities in circulation when the tax rate was increased. Nevertheless, these figures also are helpful in depicting important fluctuations.

A third source of information is contained in the studies of bank portfolios and private accounts in banks, in analyses of property left at death, and in examination of marriage contracts. Several such studies have been made, and their findings will be referred to later.

A fourth source is the reports of direct investigations of the amount of capital invested in each country. The most important of such investigations was made by various economists and financial writers for the International Congress of Securities held in Paris in 1900 under the auspices of the French Government. The reports submitted to this Congress fill several volumes,[2] and the information contained in some of them has been very useful in estimating foreign investments for this study. Since 1900 reports have been sporadically made by representatives of various States to the Institute Internationale de Statistique embodying estimates of securities issued and absorbed. In 1902 the French Government ordered a survey to be made by its consular and diplomatic agents abroad of the amount of French foreign investments. An imposing report was submitted, which, however, cannot be given much weight because of its inaccuracies.[3] Nevertheless, because of its detailed nature it does indicate the relative geographical distribution of investments.

Another source of information of the movements of foreign holdings is the accounts rendered by some of France's more important debtors. Sums invested in government bonds of Italy,

[1] The amount issued is not to be taken as the amount sold, but the discrepancy is reduced by the necessity of paying taxes on the nominal value of the securities issued.

[2] Les valeurs mobilières, International Congress (Paris, 1900), 5 vols.

[3] The report is published in the Bull. de Stat. de Lég. Comp., 1902, Vol. II, p. 450. In commenting on the report both De Foville and Leroy-Beaulieu claimed that there was hardly an error that could have been committed that was not. — De Foville, La fortune française à l'étranger, Rev. Pol. et Parl., November 10, 1902; Leroy-Beaulieu, Économiste Français, 1902, Vol. II, p. 449.

Russia, Spain, and Turkey may be ascertained with a fair degree of accuracy because those governments gave each year an account of sums paid to Paris on their debts.

A final source of information is the monographs on French foreign investments. Partly because of its quantitative importance and partly because of the repeated attempts of the French Government to increase taxes on foreign securities, the subject of French foreign investments has attracted a deal of attention in France. Considering the amount of printed matter on the subject, it is disappointing how little there is of scientific value. Scores of books and articles whose titles promise much prove to contain quantitative estimates of the most superficial nature and hardly repay reading. The theoretical analyses, with which most of the writings are concerned, frequently suggest either a naive understanding of the problems of international trade or a point of view little short of crude mercantilism. In respect to quantity treatment there are some noteworthy exceptions, Alfred Neymarck being the outstanding one.[1] His frequent reports on the growth of French foreign investments were found to be very helpful in ascertaining annual movements. Others who have contributed to quantitative estimates are Raffolovich, editor of the annual Le Marché Financier; P. Leroy-Beaulieu, editor of the Économiste Français; E. Théry, editor of Économiste Européen; Y. Guyot, editor of Journal des Économistes; and A. Coste. Moulton and Lewis in their discussion of the French debt problem have carefully compiled a quinquennial estimate of capital exports.

All the sources of information of French foreign investments which have been outlined in the previous pages have been em-

[1] As editor of the Rentier for 30 years, and as a very active contributor to the Société de Statistique de Paris and the Institut International de Statistique, he devoted much time to studies of French investments. In his first report on investments in 1888 (Soc. de Stat. de Paris, May, 1888, Les valeurs mobilières en France) he urged the formation of a standing committee which would make periodic reports relative to the quantity and kind of capital imports and exports. Such a committee was formed in 1891, and altho the reports were sporadic they contain much useful information. Neymarck himself submitted several reports which merit considerable dependence because of the care and time spent in their preparation. Most of his articles are gathered in his seven volumes of Finances contemporaines.

ployed in the attempt to determine the annual export of capital for this survey. Some of the necessary information for an accurate estimate it has been, nevertheless, impossible to obtain. As Leroy-Beaulieu, writing in 1902, stated, "Personne, absolument personne, ne peut savoir, avec une approximation même lointaine, ce que contiennent les portefeuilles français." [1] Still, enough information has been available, particularly since 1900, to make a fairly reliable basis for an annual estimate. Fortunately, also, the sums dealt with are so large that errors that bulk large in absolute amounts are comparatively of not too great significance.

The first step in making the estimate has been to ascertain the amount of foreign investments in the French portfolio in the opening year of this survey — 1880. The only estimate before 1880 that merits consideration is one for the year 1869 made by Leon Say in his report of 1874 on indemnity payments to Germany.[2] Supplementing information regarding foreign holdings gained during indemnity operations with a questionnaire sent to the larger banks apropos of foreign coupons paid thru the banks, he concluded that the revenue of France from foreign holdings was in 1869 at least 600–700 million francs. From this estimate of Say, Neymarck, by capitalizing the mean of 600–700 million francs by 5 per cent, which was the average yield of foreign investments at prices current in 1869, estimated foreign investments to be 13 billions. Théry without any explanation estimated them at 10 billions. In view of the calibre of Say's work, and in the absence of any other reliable source of information regarding the amount of French foreign investments at that time, his estimate of revenue received is accepted as a workable one. But Neymarck's estimate of 13 billions, based on Say's estimate of revenue, needs to be modified because it is based on the yield current in 1869. In that year the market values of foreign securities were higher than in the years when the bulk of those foreign investments was made. Since it is the amount of capital exported

[1] Économiste français, 1902, p. 449.

[2] Rapport sur le paiement de l'indemnité de guerre (Paris, 1874), p. 70.

that is here significant and not the market value of those investments, the revenue ought to be capitalized at the average of the rates of yield for foreign investments prevailing at the time of investment. For the decades of the 50's and the 60's the rate of 5 per cent is too low. From 1850 to 1865 the average yield of French rentes was 4½ per cent, and first class French railway bonds yielded 6 per cent. With such yields from sound domestic investments it is hardly to be expected that money would be loaned to foreigners at 5 per cent. Indeed, during this period Russian, Austrian, and Italian government bonds sold at yields of 6, 7, and 8 per cent.[1] It would seem that a capitalization rate of 6 per cent ought, then, to be used. This gives a sum of 11 billion francs invested abroad by the outbreak of the War of 1870.

From 1870 to 1880 the French portfolio experienced wide fluctuations. The war and indemnity payments resulted in the sale of two billions of foreign securities, which French investors turned over to the French Government in exchange for the new issue of French rentes, and the sale of 2.9 billions of French rentes at from 82.5 to 84. By 1873 there were 9 billions of foreign securities in the French portfolio, while the foreign holdings of French rentes had increased approximately 2.3 billions. The net French foreign investments — excess of French foreign investments over foreign investments in France — had by 1873 dropped over 4 billion francs. In the next two years almost all the French rentes were repurchased, at considerably higher prices,[2] and a strong demand for foreign investments set in. Fear of domestic insecurity and of political instability contributed in part to this overturn,[3] but the low yield of the French rentes was also no small factor. By far the most popular form of foreign investment was the foreign government bond. The number of foreign securities listed by 1880 had increased from 109 to 137 and of the increase 27 were government bonds. The stamp tax data show that from 1873 to

[1] Neymarck, Une nouvelle évaluation (Paris, 1893), p. 243.

[2] Prices of French rentes increased as follows: issued in 1871 and 1872 at 82.5 and 84.5, they reached 93.4 in 1873, 100.5 in 1874, 106.4 in 1875, 107.2 in 1876, 108.7 in 1877, 115.9 in 1878, 118 in 1879, and 120 in 1880. In eight years the yield dropped 33 per cent.

[3] Neymarck, in Jour. de Soc. de la Stat. de Paris, Vol. 1888, p. 242.

1880 six billions of foreign government bonds were issued, half of them being new issues.

By 1880, the first year covered by this study, French foreign holdings had passed the pre-war mark. In that year Leroy-Beaulieu estimated the amount of French foreign investments to be 12 to 15 billions.[1] There is no indication as to how he arrived at that figure, and it deserves mention only because of his familiarity with the investment market. A very lengthy report by Théry, which utilizes all available sources of information, is more helpful.[2] He estimated the total of securities in the French portfolio to be 56 billions, consisting of 15 foreign and 41 domestic securities. This estimate of foreign securities appears too high. As was pointed out, the amount of capital exported by 1869 was probably 11 billions. In the next few years foreigners had purchased 2 billions back as well as 2 billions of French rentes. If, as Théry estimated, France had 15 billions of foreign securities, in addition to the 2.3 billions of French rentes, which she had purchased from abroad, she must have purchased 6 billions of foreign securities. That represents a total export of capital of about 9 billions (allowing for the increased price of French rentes) in the short space of seven years, and this notwithstanding an unusually large domestic investment. The number of domestic issues from 1869 to 1880 increased from 298 to 466, a change representing an increase in nominal capital of 17 billion francs. If an estimate of 15 billions is accepted for 1880, the total of new foreign and domestic investments would have totalled 24 billions in practically seven years! So large an investment for France in those years is out of the question. The quantity of domestic issues outstanding is easily obtained; so the error must be in the amount of foreign securities supposed to have been purchased. On the basis of the foregoing, the amount of capital exported by 1880 is assumed to have been 13 billions rather than 15. The discrepancy between this estimate and Théry's estimate of 15 billions is lessened when the following is taken into consideration.

[1] Économiste français, October 23, 1880.

[2] Les valeurs mobilières en France, Congrès des valeurs mobilières, 1900, Vol. 2, No. 42.

TABLE 13

TAXATION OF REVENUE FROM FRENCH FOREIGN AND DOMESTIC SECURITIES, 1880–1913[1]

(Millions of francs)

Year	Proceeds of Tax on Revenue[2]	Revenue subject to taxation: Foreign Stocks	Foreign Bonds	Foreign Total[3]	Domestic Stocks	Domestic Bonds	Domestic Total
1880	39	20	50	71	544	618	1221
1881	44	40	52	92	711	607	1383
1882	48	65	64	130	752	626	1458
1883	48	63	61	125	708	687	1467
1884	46.8	65	58	124	603	734	1430
1885	45.9	61	59	122	562	753	1396
1886	47.2	42	62	106	580	767	1458
1887	48.9	43	62	106	605	819	1512
1888	50.4	50	62	112	624	837	1557
1889	49.1	61	65	126	602	810	1500
1890	50.8	60	70	131	636	814	1544
1891	70.4	70	85	156	672	843	1610
1892	70	80	70	151	654	838	1588
1893	67	57	72	130	613	818	1529
1894	66.2	47	70	118	601	854	1522
1895	65.6	46	70	117	604	817	1508
1896	62.9	49	71	121	628	742	1435
1897	68.5	51	75	128	636	854	1565
1898	70.2	55	70	127	663	873	1610
1899	74.3	75	76	153	727	877	1683
1900	79	86	78	156	823	873	1780
1901	82	85	78	164	839	914	1844
1902	79.8	84	88	173	769	927	1785
1903	80.1	85	91	176	770	922	1780
1904	84.4	110	103	213	821	951	1855
1905	85.8	114	98	214	859	946	1876
1906	91.4	139	123	263	936	957	1973
1907	101.1	187	127	314	1108	964	2160
1908	100	193	132	326	1038	999	2124
1909	102.5	190	162	353	1038	1036	2156
1910	107.9	208	175	380	1112	1059	2236
1911	115.6	233	210	444	1202	1100	2371
1912	126	244	217	461	1260	1250	2605
1913	138	317	267	584	1396	1302	2792

[1] Source: Ministère des finances, Bull. de Stat. et de Lég. Comp.

[2] Tax of 3 per cent increased to 4 per cent in 1890. Government securities, both foreign and domestic, are not subject to this tax.

[3] Does not include tax on revenue of foreign corporations having property in France.

Théry's estimate was at market prices. But from 1860 to 1880 the price of French securities had risen greatly. The market price of bonds had risen from 73 per cent of the nominal value to 90 per cent, and stocks had increased from 145 to 205 per cent of the nominal value.[1] These figures are measured from the prices prevailing in 1869 and not from the low prices caused by the War of 1870, and the increase is indicative of increases in the value of foreign securities. Since it is the total of capital exported that is desired, the market prices in 1880 cannot serve as basis for estimating foreign investments without correction for increases in market values of securities held in France since 1869. If allowance is made for this factor, the estimate of 13 billions is not too low.

Taxation data (tabulated on pages 97 and 99) furnish a further check on this estimate. In 1881 the amount of revenue from foreign securities subject to taxation was 92 million francs.[2] Since this sum does not include the revenue from foreign government bonds (foreign government bonds not being subject to that tax), which sold at lower yields than did corporate bonds, and since it does include dividends from foreign stocks, which contributed almost one-third of the total, a capitalization rate of 6 per cent is not excessive. On that basis the revenue taxed represents a total investment of only 1.5 billion francs. If the estimate of 13 billions is correct, then 11.5 billions of securities consist of foreign government bonds (not subject to taxation) and non-government securities which evade taxation. As previously noted, at least 50 per cent of foreign securities subject to taxation evaded them. On this basis the amount of taxable foreign securities was 3 billions, leaving 8 billions to be accounted for as foreign

[1] Totals of French domestic securities listed on the Bourse in 1869 and 1880 were as follows (in billions of francs):

	1869		1880	
	Nominal Capital	Capital at Current Prices	Nominal Capital	Capital at Current Prices
Bonds	22.0	16.0	38.0	34.4
Stocks	3.5	5.1	4.2	8.6
Total	25.5	21.1	42.2	43.0

[2] The tax on revenue would not include revenue on securities in the current year; therefore the taxation figures for 1881 are on investments outstanding in 1880.

TABLE 14

TAXATION OF FOREIGN GOVERNMENT SECURITIES, 1880–1913 [1]

(Millions of francs)

Year	Stamp Duties [2] (Thousands of francs)	Foreign Securities Taxed [3]
1880	884	....
1881	2209	....
1882	2075	....
1883	553	....
1884	1027	....
1885	1754	....
1886	968	3200 [4]
1887	1223	....
1888	2123	....
1889	3375	....
1890	2327	....
1891	2566	6688 [4]
1892	1350	....
1893	1228	....
1894	2647	....
1895	2283	....
1896	10743	5527 [4]
1897	7595	820
1898	24551	2104
1899	9972	813
1900	6384	499
1901	10667	927
1902	12107	1077
1903	20054	1845
1904	15383	1405
1905	12042	1097
1906	21271	2039
1907	23207	1740
1908	10755	471
1909	46115	2257
1910	41307	2019
1911	23798	1267
1912	11339	630
1913	....	1034

[1] Source: Annuaire statistique de la France.

[2] See p. 91.

[3] Taxed for the first time. Includes conversion. Stamp duty of .5 per 100 francs to January 1, 1896. January 1, 1899, 1 per cent; January 30, 1907, 2 per cent. But all securities in circulation in France have to pay the difference between amount stamped and the additional tax.

[4] The figures are 5-year totals.

government bonds. Did government bonds constitute so large a proportion of French foreign holdings in 1880?

The proportion of foreign government bonds to other forms of foreign securities in France is indicated by some studies that were made later. In 1897 P. d'Essars, chief of the economic division of the Bank of France, analyzed 1032 accounts selected at random [1] and found that foreign securities formed 37 per cent of the total, of which 31 per cent were foreign rentes and 6 per cent other securities. This ratio of 5 to 1 he admitted to be somewhat too high. The Bank of France attracted a larger proportion of those bonds than a fair sampling of the country's holdings would show because the Bank acted as depository for Russian government bonds free of charge. On the other hand, as has been pointed out by Neymarck and Théry, the large banks whose portfolios contained a higher proportion of foreign securities than did those of small rentiers, did not keep their securities at the Bank of France. An analysis made of all the securities listed on the Paris Bourse in 1900 showed the value of foreign government securities listed to be eight times as great as that of other foreign securities.[2] This ratio is considerably higher than the amount held by the French.[3] If allowance is made for the extra supply of Russian bonds in the Bank of France, the proportion of foreign government bonds to other foreign securities becomes closer to the ratio of 8 to 3 which was the ratio indicated above by the estimate of 13 billions.[4]

One further check on the estimate of 13 billions for 1880 is possible: a quantitative comparison of foreign with domestic holdings. The total amount of domestic securities listed in 1880 was 45.5 billions (market value). The amount held by foreigners was estimated at 10 per cent, leaving 41 billion francs of domestic

[1] Soc. de la Stat. de Paris, March 3, 1897.

[2] Decoudu, Les valeurs mobilières admises à la cote officielle de la Bourse de Paris, Congrès des valeurs mobilières, Vol. 2, No. 44.

[3] For example, there were 10 billion francs of Russian government bonds listed; whereas not more than 7 were held in France. Belgian rentes were listed at 3 billion francs, but there were not more than 200 million in the hands of the French.

[4] To this sum must be added cash and bill holdings kept on deposit in foreign banks and capital invested in property abroad but not represented by securities. The total of these items was doubtless less than one billion.

securities in the French portfolio. As has been noted, the investigation by P. d'Essars in 1897 showed the proportion of foreign securities in the accounts of the Bank of France to have been 37 per cent. This proportion would be decreased if allowance were made for the unusual number of Russian bonds on deposit. The allowance would bring d'Essar's findings close to the estimate by Théry,[1] who a few years later, after a correspondence with many bankers, decided that the proportion of foreign securities was 30–32 per cent.[2] The percentage for 1880 must have been somewhat lower as the percentage of foreign securities in French portfolios increased slightly with time. If, then, 30 per cent is accepted as the proportion of foreign securities, the sum of French foreign holdings again is indicated to be about 13 billions (i.e. 30 per cent of 41 billions, or 12.3 billions).

So far we have been considering only French foreign investments, but the figures needed are those of *net* capital exports. It is, therefore, necessary to deduct from this sum the amount invested in France by foreigners. Estimates of foreign investments in France are completely lacking. Neymarck in all his studies used the constant proportion of 10 per cent of French domestic securities as representing the amount invested in France by foreigners, and every other writer on the subject has adopted his estimate. Théry, in the report previously referred to, remarks, "This proportion has been admitted by the largest number of French statisticians who have studied the matter." An examination of all available literature on the subject reveals, however, that the statisticians referred to accept without comment Neymarck's estimate as authoritative. Neymarck, in turn, appears to have based his estimate on a report of the Administration of Finance made in 1895, which stated that of the 812 million francs paid out to holders of French rentes, 90 millions, or 11 per cent, went to foreigners.[3]

[1] Op. cit.

[2] This last estimate has been criticized as being too low on the ground that bankers were eager to make the proportion of foreign holdings seem as small as possible in view of the hostile attitude toward capital exports and toward tax evasions by sections of the press and government. — See Arboux, op. cit., p. 3.

[3] Rapport Général of the Commission Extra-Parlementaire de l'Impôt sur le Revenue, p. 1077, note 6.

But it is hardly to be expected that the amount of foreign capital in France should bear so constant a ratio to the amount of domestic issues. It would seem that the amount of French securities held abroad would be sensitive to changes in political or economic outlook both in France and in the countries where the securities were held. This was certainly true before 1880; much British capital entered France after the Napoleonic wars to establish textile factories and to construct railroads, the movement increasing after 1851. But in the 60's France repurchased the bulk of her railroad securities held by the British. Also, as noted above, the large foreign holdings of French rentes after 1871 was only a temporary phenomenon. Nor is it to be expected, as Neymarck assumed, that the proportion of foreign-held corporate stocks and bonds would be the same as foreign-held French rentes. Indeed, on grounds of theory the opposite would be expected. Since it is generally held that investors were less familiar with foreign stocks and bonds than with domestic, we should expect a Frenchman to offer a higher price than a foreigner for a French corporate bond. The French rente, on the other hand, secured an enviable reputation in investment circles after its phenomenal rise in the 70's the world over. A foreigner was thus much more apt to hold a French rente than a French industrial bond.

The claim of Neymarck, Théry, and others that 10 per cent of all domestic securities were owned abroad apparently receives no support from data on interest and dividend payments. A survey was made by Decoudu,[1] chief of the listing service at the Paris Bourse, of all the securities listed in 1899 and the interest and dividend payments. In addition to carefully compiling totals of all outstanding French securities, Decoudu added up all the dividends and interest paid on domestic securities for the year 1899. If we compare this total with the total of revenue taxed for that year, the result is rather surprising. It indicates that the amount of French non-government securities held abroad was negligible. The study shows that the total of interest and dividends paid in 1899 was 2075.4 million francs. From this figure we can obtain

[1] Les valeurs mobilières admises à la cote officielle de la Bourse de Paris, Congrès des valeurs mobilières, Vol. 2, No. 44.

with the aid of taxation data a check on interest and dividends received by residents of foreign countries. First there must be deducted from the 2075 million francs the interest paid in 1899 on French and Colonial government bonds — since they are not subject to the tax on revenue — and to it must be added the revenue from French securities not listed on the Bourse. The latter can be estimated for 1899 with a fair degree of accuracy because a careful study of domestic securities listed on all the bourses was made by Théry for 1897. He concluded that the securities listed on the Paris Bourse constituted 90 per cent of all domestic securities exclusive of French rentes. The yield from those securities was doubtless somewhat higher than the yield for all domestic securities listed on the Paris Bourse (because the latter contained many high priced bonds) and may be estimated at 5 per cent. Using this figure with other data recorded, we obtain the amount of domestic revenue which is subject to taxation as follows:

	Millions of francs
Total interest and dividends priced in 1899	2075
Interest paid on French and Colonial rentes	819
	1256
5 per cent of 4.2 billions of securities not listed on the Paris Bourse	210
	1466

Now if 10 per cent of these domestic securities were held abroad, as claimed by Neymarck, the amount of revenue subject to taxation in 1899 would have been 1326 million francs. But according to the Treasury reports the amount of revenue from domestic securities taxed was 1683 million. This includes revenue from prizes and redemption premiums and from "parts et commandites" that are not listed on the Bourse. If revenue from these sources were to be deducted, the revenue taxed would be about 1520 million francs. Unless there is an error either in Decoudu's compilation or in the Treasury reports or in the estimate of securities not listed, the French securities other than French rentes that were held abroad constituted a negligible quantity. The foregoing is not absolute proof that foreigners held less than 10 per cent of the French securities, but in the absence of any data to the contrary it must be given weight.

Further evidence that the amount of French securities held by others than the French was less than 10 per cent, in the years before 1914 at least, is offered by Pupin,[1] who in his study of French wealth for 1912 wrote: "According to information we have gathered, it is doubtful if foreigners possess more than 5 per cent of the French securities." Where and how Pupin gathered this information, he does not say.

In the absence of more detailed information on the subject, the amount of French securities held abroad in 1880 is estimated to have been 10 per cent of the total domestic securities outstanding in that year, and the proportion to have decreased as years went on, reaching 7 per cent in 1914. Some modifications have been introduced for the years of foreign depression and for years of extreme changes in the relative yields of high grade government bonds. The total amount of domestic securities outstanding in 1880 was 45.5 billions. If allowance is made for the considerable increase in market values in the 70's, 10 per cent of the amount of French securities (at price of purchase) is close enough to 4 billions to accept that figure as the amount of foreign capital in France in 1880. This leaves a net foreign investment for France in 1880 of 9 billions.

From 1880 on the estimates of capital exports made in this study are annual. They are computed with the aid of the various sources outlined earlier in the chapter, and with that of current financial comments in French economic weeklies and monthlies.[2] The annual estimates have been compared and checked with the numerous sporadic estimates made by various writers. A list of all the estimates relative to French foreign investments that appear to have been more or less independently arrived at will be found in the Appendix. The annual estimates finally arrived at in this study for the entire period are listed on page 122.

From these figures of the annual exports of capital, obtained by the direct method, we can now compute the annual interest and dividends due to and from France. These sums, it will be remembered, were the ones lacking for the completion of the international account.

[1] Richesse privée et finances français (Paris, 1919), p. 32.

[2] After 1895 Raffolovich's annual, Le Marché Financier, has been helpful.

In the French balance sheet the revenue from investments abroad is a very important item. How is this source of revenue to be measured? The most direct approach in ascertaining the annual income from this source would be to examine income data such as are published for England by the Commissioners of Inland Revenue. Such data unfortunately have not been gathered in France during the years covered by this study. With the exception of taxation reports, no statistical material which would make possible a direct approach is available. The information furnished by these tax reports does not include the income from foreign government bonds, the most important item of French foreign holdings; and, moreover, as has been pointed out, the utility of taxation data on foreign investments is seriously reduced by wholesale tax evasions.

The only other method of estimating the revenue from foreign investments is to ascertain the average rate of yield on those investments, and to apply it to the estimated foreign investments. The amount involved is so large that accuracy in estimating the rate of interest to be used in computing the revenue is especially important. A difference of one per cent in the interest rate means a difference in the annual income of France (after 1900) of from 200 to 300 million francs. In determining the revenue from foreign investment one rate of interest cannot be used for all years. In the course of the thirty-four years under consideration the rate of return from each type of security underwent considerable fluctuation: the nominal interest carried by foreign securities was as low as 3 per cent and as high as 7 per cent; the real rate of interest covered even a greater range. For illustration, from 1880 to 1897 the average yield of bonds dropped from 5 per cent to 3.3 per cent and then rose steadily from 1897 on. In addition to this fluctuation from year to year there was a wide range of yields from different kinds of investments at any given time. The yield on foreign government and municipal loans at current prices varied, according to the government report of 1902, previously referred to, from 2 to 5 per cent; on mining securities from 4 to 10 per cent; and on South American ventures it averaged 35 per cent. Further, the proportion of low yield to high yield securities was not constant thruout the period. It is clear, then, that no single rate of interest can be used for the whole period. Yet most of the writers have selected 5 per cent as the average rate of return from foreign investments. Moulton and Lewis did so in their estimate of French revenue from foreign investments, and Moulton and McGuire did likewise in the case of Germany.[1] Neither study, however, discusses in detail the basis for the decision. Meynial also accepted without discussion the rate of 5 per cent,[2] and Hobson in his Export of Capital mentions 5 per cent as the proper rate of capitalization for foreign securities. Tho it is impossible to compute accurately the yield on total foreign securities from year to year, a rough approximation can be made which is much more nearly exact than a flat rate for the whole period. An attempt has therefore been made to ascertain the average yields on French investments prevailing at different periods.

A very helpful source of information has been the report by Decoudu previously referred to. In this report he itemized and classified the interest and dividends paid during 1899 on all securities listed on the Paris Bourse. The totals of these listings in millions of francs are as follows:

	Nominal Capital	Issuing Price	Price Feb., 1900	Interest and Dividends Paid in 1899
Government				
Russian	10948	9912	10931	423.9
Other	48170	44784	42864	1633.4
	59119	54697	53795	2057.3
Corporate				
Insurance and Banks	764	767	1003	40.8
Railroad	6938	4361	4617	179.7
Other	629	644	1240	55.9
	8332	5773	6860	276.4
Total foreign securities	67451	60470	60655	2333.9
Total domestic securities	59179	48487	64307	2075.4

Converted to rates of return, the totals listed above give the results presented on page 107. These rates are computed from all securities listed, and therefore give a slightly lower rate of yield than would be the case if only those securities held by the French were considered. The reason for this is that the amount of securities listed under "foreign government" includes a greater proportion

[1] Germany's Capacity to Pay, p. 258.

[2] Op. cit., p. 87.

of first class bonds than are actually held in France. The total of foreign government securities held in 1900 was about 23 billion francs; whereas the amount listed is 48 billions. Of the 25 billions excess listed many are low yield bonds such as Belgian and English government bonds. Over 2 billions of the former and 14 billions of the latter were included in the listing; whereas France held less than 300 millions of the former and less than one-half billion of

Foreign	Rate at Nominal Capital	Rate on Issue Price	Rate at Price of Feb. 28, 1900
Russian government	3.87	4.27	3.87
Other governments	3.39	3.65	3.81
Insurance and Banks	5.35	5.34	4.07
Railroad	2.58	4.12	3.85
Other	8.88	8.67	4.51
Total foreign	3.46	3.85	3.84
Total domestic	3.54	4.28	3.23

the latter. The effect of the inclusion of these low yield bonds is obviously to reduce the average rate of return on foreign government bonds. The yield, for example, on the 13 billion English Local Loan 3 per cent 1887 at current prices was 2.7 per cent in 1899, and the yield on Belgian 3 per cent was 3.1 per cent. When allowance is made for these surpluses of low yield bonds, the rate of return rises from 3.85 to 4.19 per cent.[1]

[1] Pougnet applied rates of return at the price of the previous year, December 31, 1898, to the securities estimated to be in the French portfolio, and obtained results very close to the above returns.

	Value at Prices Dec. 31, 1898	Net Revenue Per cent	Net Revenue Francs
Russia–Finland	7. bill.	3.8	266. mill.
Spain–Cuba	3.6	4.65	167.4
Austria–Hungary	2.5	4.	100.
Italy	1.6	4.1	65.6
Belgium – Switzerland – Denmark – Holland–Sweden–Norway	1.5	3.3	49.5
England and Colonies (except Canada)	1.	2.8	28.
Germany–Roumania–Greece–Balkans	1.4	4.3	60.2
Turkey–Egypt	3.3	4.41	145.5
Portugal	.5	4.8	24.
Total European	22.4	4.05	906.2
United States–Canada	1.	3.4	34.
Central–South America	1.6	6.	96.
Total American	2.6	5.	130.
Gold Mines–Trusts–Syndicates	1.2	7.	84.
Grand total	26.2	4.28	1120.2

The estimate of 4.28 per cent is probably a little too high because the amount of Italian and Spanish securities, both carrying high yield, is overestimated.

The rate of return, however, on the *market* price of foreign securities is not to be taken as the rate of return to France from her foreign investments, since, obviously, most of the securities were not acquired in any one year. A better indication of the rate of return is the yield at prices of issue because, as was pointed out in the discussion of capital exports, altho not all securities remain in the country where issued, certainly the major part do not pass back and forth. (It need not be explained that the return on the nominal value is of no significance in this connection.) By mere coincidence the rate of return at the market price of 1899 is almost identical in the case of foreign securities with the rate of return on the price of issue. In 1910 the rate of return at market price would have been higher than on the issuing price, and in 1890 it would have been lower.

Estimates of annual revenue from foreign investments will be based on the rate of yield at the price of issue because in this study the estimates of the annual exports of capital have been based on neither the nominal nor the market value but on the purchase price of securities. Certain modifications are called for, however. First: some of the securities are purchased from other countries years after the date of issue, and, of course, the prices paid in such case are the market prices prevailing at the time of purchase. For instance, a part of the foreign securities added to the French portfolio from 1906 to 1913 are at prices yielding a greater return than those securities yielded at the time of issue, several or many years before. Similarly, some of the securities acquired from 1886 to 1895 were acquired at prices which yielded a lower rate of return than those securities did when issued.[1] The yield at which bonds were issued must then be modified to include

[1] During the 15 years from 1896 to 1911 the average yield on some British and foreign stocks was as follows:

	10 Foreign Rails	10 British Rails	British, Foreign, and Colonial Stocks	British Rail Stocks
1896	4.03	2.11	5.52	3.7
1901	3.18	3.	4.15	3.3
1906	3.19	3.5	4.13	4.1
1911	4.2	3.14	5.4	4.1

These figures represent fluctuations of 25 to 35 per cent in revenue; the extreme

those securities purchased from abroad after issue at market prices higher or lower than the issuing price.

A second modification is of greater quantitative importance. Conversions at lower rates of interest of many of the foreign bonds introduced changes in the rate of return from the foreign investments previously made. From 1889 to 1896 the prevailing rates of interest on long time investments were so low that every foreign government and corporation whose bonds were callable hastened to take advantage of the low rates and converted at the lower rate of interest as many as possible of its issues. The amount of conversions from 1889 to 1896 in government bonds alone was 25 billions (see Table 15, page 111). In one year, 1894, out of a total world issue of 17 billions, 12 billions were conversions.[1] The effect of these conversions was to reduce the yield (at price of issue) of a large part of the foreign investments in the French portfolio.

fluctuations are not included. — C. K. Hobson in The Depreciation of British Home Investments, Economic Journal, June, 1912.

The following are representative of the differences in yields of foreign bonds at current prices between 1880 and 1897.

	1880	1897
4 % Austrian	6.76	4.76
4 % Unified Egypt	7.2	3.74
3 % Holland	3.87	3.
5 % Russian	5.95	3.19
4½ % Swedish	4.36	3.
2½ % Belgian	3.75	2.56

It is noteworthy that the rate of interest had fallen so low in the early 90's that the French savings banks reduced the interest payable on deposit from 3 to 2 per cent.

[1] The decreases in nominal rates of the conversion of 1894 were as follows:

From	to	Amount (Millions of francs)
5.5 %	5. %	87
5.	4.5	565
5.	4.	3145
5.	3.5	264
5.	3.	170
4.5	4.	363
4.5	3.5	7000
4.	3.5	534
4.	3.	117
3.	2.6	375

Raffolovich, Le Marché Financier, 1894–1895, p. 698.

After modification of the rates of yield is made to allow for repurchases, conversions, and for the varying rates of yield at which additions to foreign holdings were acquired, we find that the average annual rate of return to France from all her foreign investments declined during the period from 1880 to 1902 and rose thereafter. From 1880 to 1886 the rate of return on foreign bonds held by France averaged about 5 per cent. The increased earnings from stocks increased this yield only slightly — probably to 5.5 per cent. Bonds composed more than 80 per cent of the French foreign portfolio and therefore the higher yield obtained from foreign stocks affected the average of return from all securities but little. In the 12 years following 1886 new bonds were issued at lower and lower yields. During that period about 9 billion francs of new securities besides several more billions of conversions (both together accounting for more than half the foreign securities in the French portfolio) were acquired at yields of less than 4 per cent.[1] In the few years after 1898 the rate of interest increased slightly. Neymarck estimated that in 1902 revenue on foreign bonds at the then decreased price of bonds was 4 per cent, and of stocks 4½ per cent. In 1905 and 1906 yields dropped again, but recovered in 1907 and increased steadily from then on. In 1909 Paish[2] estimated that the income from all British foreign investments at current prices was 5.2 per cent; from foreign government loans 4.75 per cent; from foreign railways 4.7 per cent; from foreign banks 13.6 per cent. Low yield Colónial and Indian government loans, forming 20 per cent of the total, helped to bring down the average return on British foreign investments. The return to the French on their foreign investments was less. The French were very cautious investors. The bulk of investing was done by the small savers who above all wished security. That is why so large a proportion of their foreign investments was in bonds. Only 35 per cent of Great Britain's portfolio consisted of bonds, of Germany's 25 per cent; whereas the proportion in France was well over 75 per cent, and

[1] A. Neymarck, op. cit., Vol. 7, p. 120, states that the average yield in 1880 on bonds was 5 per cent and in 1897 3.3 per cent.

[2] G. Paish, Great Britain's Capital Investments in Other Lands, Jour. of the Royal Stat. Soc., September, 1909. Vol. 72, p. 475.

TABLE 15

World Issues of Securities and Conversions in the World and in France,[1] 1880–1913

(Millions of francs)

Year	Total World Issue	Total World Conversions	Conversions Issued in France Domestic	Foreign	Total
1880	5500	....	....	....	....
1881	7200	....	....	....	....
1882	4500	....	....	....	....
1883	4300	....	....	....	....
1884	4900	....	....	....	....
1885	3300	....	....	....	....
1886	6700	....	....	....	....
1887	5000	....	....	....	....
1888	7900	....	....	....	....
1889	12700	....	....	....	....
1890	8100	....	....	....	....
1891	7600	....	....	....	....
1892	2500	....	490	....	....
1893	6000	....	0	178	178
1894	17800	12600	7540	3200	10746
1895	6500	1230	30	166	196
1896	16700	7590	40	122	162
1897	9600	680	425	164	589
1898	10500	1640	810	121	933
1899	11300	60	0	90	90
1900	11900	0	0	90	90
1901	9900	0	0	90	90
1902	21900	8500	6840	2053	8896
1903	18400	8740	120	6927	7059
1904	14400	1830	45	88	133
1905	19100	1670	45	425	470
1906	26500	10320	400	8254	8654
1907	15300	220	400	53	453
1908	21200	330	400	53	453
1909	24600	2450	5	800	805
1910	26500	3560	0	271	271
1911	19500	740	0	0	0
1912	20200	690	148	0	148
1913	....	....	....	....	....

[1] Source: Économiste Européen.

consisted in large part of low yielding government bonds.[1] In the last few years before the war several billions of foreign securities were acquired at prices yielding an average of approximately 5 per cent.

Taking into account the changes in the amounts of securities acquired at times of different prevailing yields together with the information of the issuing price of total securities listed, the following rates of return on the total of foreign investments were obtained and are the ones used in this study for the international accounts.

	Per cent		Per cent
1880–1885	5.5	1896–1902	4.
1886–1888	5.25	1903–1908	4.25
1889–1891	5.	1909–1911	4.5
1891–1893	4.75	1912–1914	4.75
1894–1895	4.5		

The annual revenues from foreign investments based on the above rates of return are listed in Column 2, Table 25.

Additional revenue to the lending country from foreign investments is received from amortization and redemption payments. The rate used in this study to estimate this revenue is one per cent of the total foreign holdings. This rate is based on the estimate of amortizations and redemptions by Pupin and Neymarck. The estimate of Pupin is compounded from an analysis for the years 1911, 1912, and 1913 of securities deposited in the Bank of France, which showed amortization to have amounted to 15 per cent of the revenue.[2] Neymarck stated that most loans were under obligation to make amortization payments at the rate of 1–2 per cent.[3] Redemptions Pupin estimated at 10 per cent of the revenue. The rate of 1 per cent on total foreign holdings used for this survey includes both amortizations and redemptions. Since foreign holdings include stocks upon which amortizations and redemptions are not paid, the rate of 1 per cent really amounts to about $1\frac{1}{3}$ per cent of fixed income bearing securities.

[1] A. Neymarck in Bull. de l'Inst. Int. de Stat., August, 1907. In a later study Neymarck estimated the bond holdings of France at 87 per cent.

[2] Richesse privée et finances françaises, p. 7.

[3] Les amortissements et les remboursements dans le cours du siècle, Soc. de la Stat. de Paris, April 20, 1910.

In Table 25 will be found the annual estimates of revenue from this source and also the payments by France to foreigners for the same items.

The one item left to be included in the balance sheet is revenue from brokerage fees. This revenue must be separately entered on the balance sheet since the estimates of capital exports are based on the selling price of the securities to the public and do not include underwriters' charges. Charges for floating loans vary from 2 to 6 per cent depending upon the size, security, and time of the loan.[1] The charge covers not only a net profit for the underwriters or bankers, but also the costs involved in placing the securities in the hands of the investors. Advertising, selling, printing, clerical expenses, and taxes are paid either by the underwriters or the borrowers; in either case the revenue accrues to France. According to Guyot the cost of floating securities in France was 4 to 4½ per cent as follows: expenses of the guarantee syndicate, 1¾ to 2 per cent; advertising, ½ per cent; cost of "guichet," 1½ per cent.[2] In the case of conversions the charge for underwriting was probably not so great as that on new issues inasmuch as it is usually easier to float a conversion than a new issue; yet the difference cannot have been very great. Rates in the nineteenth century were higher than in the twentieth because of the monopolistic nature of the underwriting business in France and the pressing need of some of the financially weak governments which floated loans there.

The earnings from underwriting service are in this survey estimated at 4 per cent before 1889 and 3 per cent thereafter, both on new issues and on conversions. With the recording of these earnings the construction of the international accounts is completed. The itemized balances appear in the following pages.

[1] The rate of commission paid to banks and the expense of issue of Russian loans according to official statements varied between 2½ and 3 per cent. — P. Petit, La dette publique de la Russie (Paris, 1912). Other writers claimed the commissions paid to French bankers on these loans were much higher. See p. 278.

[2] Guyot cites a Belgian loan made in England underwritten at 74, sold at 77, for which the Belgian state paid the English tax of 1 per cent, a total expense in England of slightly over 4 per cent.

TABLE 16

THE INTERNATIONAL ACCOUNTS FOR FRANCE, 1880–1913

Credit Balances

(Millions of francs)

Year	1 Excess of Merchandise Exports	2 Excess of Specie Exports	3 Shipping Earnings	4 Marine Insurance and Commissions	5 Total Commodities Imported and Exported C.I.F.
1880	...	174	100	36	310
1881	...	...	121	37	158
1882	...	...	143	37	180
1883	...	89	153	36	278
1884	...	...	146	33	179
1885	...	...	128	31	159
1886	...	...	127	33	160
1887	...	126	127	33	286
1888	...	35	142	33	210
1889	...	...	156	38	194
1890	...	103	140	39	282
1891	...	...	136	37	173
1892	...	...	116	35	151
1893	...	...	113	33	146
1894	...	...	108	32	140
1895	...	...	101	35	136
1896	...	33	107	36	176
1897	...	...	120	38	158
1898	...	111	135	36	171
1899	...	...	136	43	179
1900	...	...	166	43	209
1901	...	...	132	42	174
1902	...	...	133	44	177
1903	...	...	145	44	189
1904	...	...	171	46	217
1905	121	...	182	51	254
1906	...	...	206	55	261
1907	...	...	213	58	271
1908	...	...	197	53	250
1909	...	...	205	60	265
1910	...	...	254	65	267
1911	...	...	273	63	336
1912	...	...	350	69	419
1913	...	...	300	71	371

TABLE 17

THE INTERNATIONAL ACCOUNTS FOR FRANCE, 1880–1913

Credit Balances (continued)

(Millions of francs)

Year	6 Transit Earnings	7 Tourist Expenditure Balance due France	8 Brokerage and Underwriters' Profits due France	9 Gold Carried out by Laborers	10 Excess of Immigrant over Emigrant Funds
1880	6	300	10	3	2
1881	6	300	30	3	2
1882	6	300	15	3	2
1883	7	300	15	3	3
1884	5	325	10	3	2
1885	5	325	15	3	2
1886	5	350	15	5	2
1887	7	350	15	5	1
1888	7	350	20	5	0
1889	8	500	25	5	0
1890	9	350	20	5	0
1891	10	375	20	5	0
1892	9	375	15	5	0
1893	11	300	15	5	4
1894	10	350	15	8	4
1895	10	375	20	8	4
1896	11	375	40	8	3
1897	12	400	30	10	4
1898	12	400	60	10	5
1899	12	400	35	10	5
1900	12	450	30	10	9
1901	13	400	45	8	9
1902	12	425	55	10	0
1903	13	475	60	10	0
1904	13	425	50	10	0
1905	13	450	50	13	0
1906	14	475	65	13	0
1907	14	450	60	13	8
1908	13	525	45	10	9
1909	14	550	110	13	6
1910	13	575	120	13	9
1911	14	575	60	15	4
1912	14	550	65	18	6
1913	14	600	60	15	9

TABLE 18

THE INTERNATIONAL ACCOUNTS FOR FRANCE, 1880–1913

Credit Balances (continued)

(Millions of francs)

Year	11 Expenditure of Foreign Ships in France[1]	12 Miscellaneous Items	13 Total Invisible Credits	14 Total Credits
1880	9	5	335	645
1881	9	5	355	513
1882	9	5	340	520
1883	9	5	342	620
1884	9	5	359	538
1885	9	5	364	523
1886	10	5	392	552
1887	10	5	393	679
1888	10	5	397	607
1889	10	5	528	722
1890	11	8	403	685
1891	11	8	429	602
1892	11	8	423	674
1893	12	8	355	501
1894	12	8	407	547
1895	12	8	437	573
1896	12	8	457	633
1897	13	8	477	635
1898	14	8	499	670
1899	15	8	485	667
1900	18	10	539	748
1901	18	10	503	677
1902	18	10	530	607
1903	19	10	487	676
1904	20	10	538	755
1905	21	12	550	804
1906	24	12	603	864
1907	26	12	583	854
1908	27	12	641	891
1909	28	12	733	998
1910	29	15	774	1041
1911	31	15	714	1050
1912	31	15	699	1118
1913	34	15	747	1118

[1] Includes only docking, pilotage, and unloading charges, and expenditure of the crews of foreign ships while in French ports. Ships' provisions and coal are already included in the figures for merchandise exports.

TABLE 19

THE INTERNATIONAL ACCOUNTS FOR FRANCE, 1880–1913

Debit Balances

(Millions of francs)

Year	15 Excess of Merchandise Imports	16 Excess of Specie Imports	17 Total Commodities (Imports C. I. F.; Exports F. O. B.)
1880	1521	0	1521
1881	1258	62	1320
1882	1200	52	1252
1883	1301	0	1301
1884	1062	101	1163
1885	962	140	1102
1886	922	112	1034
1887	737	0	737
1888	824	0	824
1889	578	216	794
1890	641	0	641
1891	1145	158	1303
1892	696	294	990
1893	583	221	804
1894	725	335	1060
1895	302	72	374
1896	371	0	371
1897	341	139	480
1898	930	0	930
1899	322	124	446
1900	550	272	822
1901	330	241	571
1902	113	295	408
1903	512	204	716
1904	18	520	538
1905	0	653	653
1906	297	264	561
1907	573	436	1009
1908	556	990	1546
1909	489	180	669
1910	883	16	899
1911	1938	177	2115
1912	1463	210	1673
1913	1481	619	2100

TABLE 20

THE INTERNATIONAL ACCOUNTS FOR FRANCE, 1880–1913

Debit Balances (continued)

(Millions of francs)

Year	18 Colonial Expenditures	19 Excess of Immigrant over Emigrant Remittances	20 Gold Carried into France by Tourists	21 Excess of Gold Carried in by Immigrants over Gold Carried out by Emigrants	22 Total Invisible Items	23 Total Debits
1880	30	5	15	1	51	1572
1881	40	5	15	1	56	1376
1882	30	5	15	1	51	1303
1883	35	5	15	2	57	1358
1884	45	8	15	1	69	1232
1885	50	8	15	1	74	1176
1886	35	10	16	2	63	1097
1887	20	10	16	2	48	795
1888	20	10	17	0	47	871
1889	20	10	25	0	55	849
1890	20	10	15	0	45	686
1891	35	10	15	0	60	1363
1892	40	10	15	0	65	1055
1893	40	10	13	3	66	872
1894	40	15	15	3	73	1133
1895	40	15	15	3	73	447
1896	50	20	15	2	87	458
1897	55	15	16	3	89	579
1898	50	20	16	4	90	1020
1899	60	20	16	4	100	546
1900	60	25	20	7	112	934
1901	60	20	18	7	105	676
1902	50	20	18	0	88	496
1903	50	15	20	0	85	801
1904	50	20	21	0	91	629
1905	50	25	22	0	97	750
1906	40	25	23	0	88	649
1907	50	20	20	7	97	1108
1908	60	25	22	7	114	1660
1909	50	25	25	5	105	774
1910	50	25	28	7	110	1009
1911	60	30	30	5	125	2240
1912	80	35	28	5	148	1821
1913	60	30	30	7	127	2227

TABLE 21

The International Accounts for France, 1880–1913

Credit and Debit Balances

(Millions of francs)

	24	25		26	
	Balance of Commodity Items	Balance of Invisible Items		Balance of All Items[1]	
Year	Debit	Credit[1]	Credit[2]	Credit	Debit
1880	1211	284	794	...	927
1881	1162	299	819	...	863
1882	1072	289	849	...	783
1883	1023	285	865	...	738
1884	984	290	885	...	694
1885	943	290	905	...	653
1886	874	329	964	...	545
1887	451	345	970	...	106
1888	614	350	1010	...	264
1889	600	473	1178	...	127
1890	359	358	1048	...	0
1891	1130	369	1089	...	761
1892	839	358	1098	...	481
1893	658	289	1004	...	359
1894	920	334	1084	...	586
1895	238	364	1079	126	...
1896	195	370	1115	175	...
1897	322	388	913	66	...
1898	759	409	1109	...	350
1899	267	385	1115	118	...
1900	613	427	1197	...	186
1901	397	398	1203	0	0
1902	231	442	1292	211	...
1903	527	402	1297	...	125
1904	321	447	1472	126	...
1905	399	453	1543	54	...
1906	300	515	1670	215	...
1907	738	486	1716	252	...
1908	1296	527	1807	...	769
1909	404	628	1973	224	...
1910	632	664	2164	32	...
1911	1779	589	2179	...	1190
1912	1254	551	2181	...	703
1913	1729	620	2420	...	1109

[1] Except revenue from foreign investments.
[2] With revenue from foreign investments.

TABLE 22

THE INTERNATIONAL ACCOUNTS FOR FRANCE, 1880–1913

Credit and Debit Balances (continued)

(Millions of francs)

Year	27 Net Credit Balance (All Items)	28 Estimated Annual Export of Capital	29 Net Credit Balance with Allowance for Correction in Official Figures	30 Interest and Dividend Payments Due France	31 Net Revenue Due France from Foreign Investments
1880	−417	120	−210	710	510
1881	−343	720	−122	725	520
1882	−223	350	0	765	560
1883	−158	235	55	785	580
1884	−99	325	104	800	595
1885	−38	420	158	820	615
1886	90	505	298	845	635
1887	519	700	734	835	625
1888	396	805	609	875	660
1889	578	685	831	920	705
1890	689	590	943	910	690
1891	−41	390	186	940	720
1892	259	490	489	960	740
1893	346	695	563	935	715
1894	164	485	367	970	750
1895	841	680	1080	940	715
1896	920	865	1159	970	745
1897	591	545	846	900	675
1898	350	930	580	925	700
1899	848	810	1125	960	730
1900	584	1000	869	1000	770
1901	806	1280	1090	1040	805
1902	1061	1080	1368	1095	850
1903	770	1295	1065	1135	895
1904	1151	1440	1476	1365	1025
1905	1144	1620	1503	1325	1090
1906	1370	1790	1748	1400	1155
1907	978	1220	1369	1480	1230
1908	511	1490	843	1530	1280
1909	1569	1460	1972	1600	1345
1910	1532	1830	1960	1760	1500
1911	400	1030	785	1850	1590
1912	927	1340	1372	1895	1630
1913	691	1115	1149	2065	1800
Total ...	18766	30345	28365	37850	30070

TABLE 23

ESTIMATE OF FOREIGN INVESTMENTS IN FRANCE, 1880–1913

(Millions of francs)

Year	1 Foreign Investments in France	2 Amortization Payments Due Abroad	3 New Capital Invested in France	4 Total Foreign Investments in France (Cumulative)
1880	90	40	50	4050
1881	90	40	50	4100
1882	50	40	10	4110
1883	60	40	20	4130
1884	60	40	20	4150
1885	70	40	30	4180
1886	80	40	40	4220
1887	80	40	40	4260
1888	80	40	40	4300
1889	80	40	40	4340
1890	70	45	30	4370
1891	60	45	20	4390
1892	60	45	20	4410
1893	50	45	10	4420
1894	50	45	10	4430
1895	55	45	10	4440
1896	65	45	20	4460
1897	75	45	30	4490
1898	85	45	40	4530
1899	95	45	50	4580
1900	95	45	50	4630
1901	105	45	60	4690
1902	95	45	50	4740
1903	65	45	20	4760
1904	110	50	60	4820
1905	120	50	70	4890
1906	130	50	80	4970
1907	80	50	30	5000
1908	100	50	50	5050
1909	110	50	60	5110
1910	120	50	70	5180
1911	100	50	50	5230
1912	80	50	30	5260
1913	90	50	40	5300

TABLE 24

ESTIMATE OF FRENCH FOREIGN INVESTMENTS, 1880–1913

(Millions of francs)

Year	5 French Investments Abroad	6 Amortization and Redemption Payments Received	7 New Capital Invested Abroad	8 Total Foreign Investments in French Portfolio	9 Total Foreign Investments in France	10 Total Net Foreign Investments	11 Annual Net Export of Capital
1880 ...	300	130	170	13170	4050	9120	120
1881 ...	900	130	770	13940	4100	9840	720
1882 ...	500	140	360	14300	4110	10190	350
1883 ...	400	145	255	14555	4130	10425	235
1884 ...	500	145	255	14910	4150	10760	325
1885 ...	600	150	450	15360	4180	11180	420
1886 ...	700	155	545	15905	4220	11685	505
1887 ...	900	160	740	16645	4260	12385	700
1888 ...	1000	165	845	17490	4300	13190	805
1889 ...	900	175	725	18215	4340	13875	685
1890 ...	800	180	620	18835	4370	14465	590
1891 ...	600	190	410	19245	4390	14855	390
1892 ...	700	190	510	19755	4410	15345	490
1893 ...	900	195	705	20460	4420	16040	695
1894 ...	700	205	495	20955	4430	16525	485
1895 ...	900	210	690	21645	4440	17205	680
1896 ...	1100	215	885	22530	4460	18070	865
1897 ...	800	225	575	23105	4490	18615	545
1898 ...	1200	230	970	24075	4530	19545	930
1899 ...	1100	240	860	24935	4580	20355	810
1900 ...	1300	250	1050	25985	4630	21355	1000
1901 ...	1600	260	1340	27325	4690	22635	1280
1902 ...	1400	270	1130	28455	4740	23715	1080
1903 ...	1600	285	1315	29770	4760	25010	1295
1904 ...	1800	300	1500	31270	4820	26450	1440
1905 ...	2000	310	1690	32960	4890	28070	1620
1906 ...	2200	330	1870	34830	4970	29860	1790
1907 ...	1600	350	1250	36080	5000	31080	1220
1908 ...	1900	360	1540	37620	5050	32570	1490
1909 ...	1900	380	1520	39140	5110	34030	1460
1910 ...	2300	400	1900	41040	5180	35860	1830
1911 ...	1500	420	1080	42120	5230	36890	1030
1912 ...	1800	430	1370	43490	5260	38230	1340
1913 ...	1600	445	1155	44640	5300	39345	1115

TABLE 25

REVENUE FROM FRENCH FOREIGN INVESTMENTS, 1880–1913

(Millions of francs)

Year	Interest and Dividends Due Foreigners	Interest and Dividends Due France	Net Revenue Due France
1880	200	710	510
1881	205	725	520
1882	205	765	560
1883	205	785	580
1884	205	800	595
1885	205	820	615
1886	210	845	635
1887	210	835	625
1888	215	875	660
1889	215	920	705
1890	220	910	690
1891	220	940	720
1892	220	960	740
1893	220	935	715
1894	220	970	750
1895	225	940	715
1896	225	970	745
1897	225	900	675
1898	225	925	700
1899	230	960	730
1900	230	1000	770
1901	235	1040	805
1902	235	1095	850
1903	240	1135	895
1904	240	1265	1025
1905	245	1325	1090
1906	245	1400	1155
1907	250	1480	1230
1908	250	1530	1280
1909	255	1600	1345
1910	260	1760	1500
1911	260	1850	1590
1912	265	1895	1630
1913	265	2065	1800

PART II

ANALYSIS

CHAPTER VI

PARTIAL BALANCES. MERCHANDISE BALANCE OF TRADE

WE MAY now proceed to an analysis of the significant elements in the balance sheet. Our first concern is with the net credit balances, to ascertain which the balance sheet was primarily constructed. The item represents, it will be remembered, the net French foreign investments transmitted in the form of goods and services.

A comparison of the net credit balances and of the estimated capital exports reveals a very close approximation between the two totals, as, indeed, it ought to do, since both totals measure the same phenomena — the net foreign investments. In view of the fact that the net credit balances and the capital exports were estimated by independent methods — with the exception of revenue from foreign investments — the difference between the two totals is satisfactorily small. The total of estimated capital exports for the entire period is 30,345 millions, the total of the net credit balances 28,365 millions [1] — a difference of 7 per cent. One could hardly hope for better results. But when the estimates of annual net credits are compared year for year with the estimated annual net exports, the results are less gratifying. A glance at Chart 1, p. 128, on which the two sets of figures are plotted, reveals several large discrepancies. In 1881, 1896, 1908, and 1909 the discrepancies are from 400 to 700 million francs. During the other years differences of 200 million francs are common.

There is, however, no reason to expect the *annual* figures to agree even if all the estimates are accurate because the move-

[1] As pointed out in the discussion on import and export statistics, in the opinion of members of the commission and of many writers both sets of recorded statistics are underestimated, but in different degrees. The balance of payments ought to be modified to meet this flaw in merchandise statistics, for it involves sums large enough to distort any conclusion. The sum of 28,365 millions includes the allowance for 3 per cent underestimate of imports and 10 per cent underestimate of exports.

ments measured are not identical. The annual export of capital that appears in the direct estimate represents the international transfers of *title* to goods and services; whereas the annual sums arrived at by the indirect method measure the international transfer of the actual goods and services. The two annual sums

CHART 1

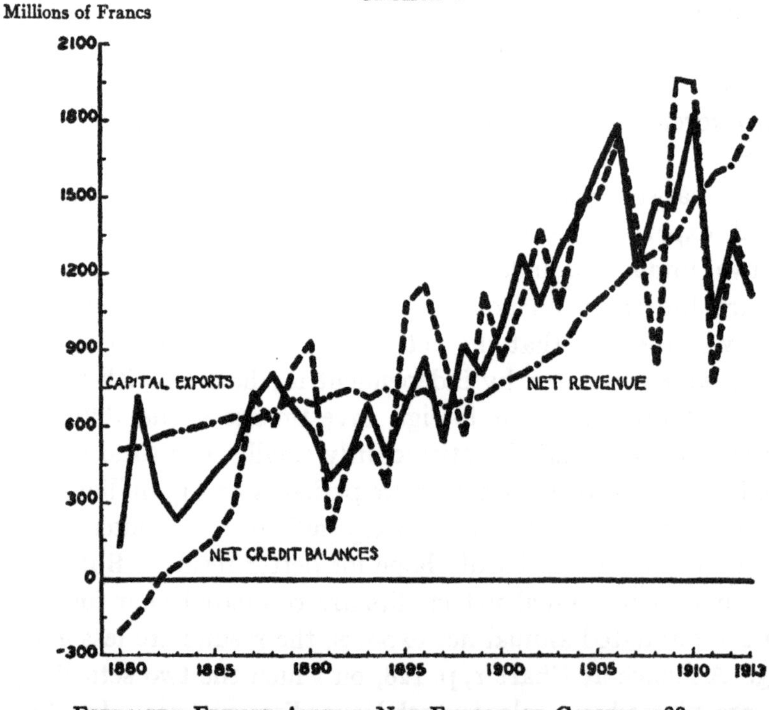

ESTIMATED FRENCH ANNUAL NET EXPORT OF CAPITAL, 1880–1913

—— Annual net export of capital (estimated).
- - - Annual net income available for new foreign investments (with correction for probable underestimate of commodity exports).
-·-· Annual net revenue from foreign investments.

can correspond only when the transfers of goods and services are made in the same years that the transfers of title are recorded. Such frequently is not the case. Even in the instances where the least delay would be expected — namely, when the foreign borrower raises the loan in order to pay for merchandise to be purchased in the lending country, and the goods needed are ordered as soon as the success of flotation is assured — even then the shipment of goods is spread over months after the transfer of title has been recorded. French foreign loans were generally of the kind not immediately spent in France by the borrowers;[1] they almost always, as will be seen later, were employed by the borrowers in making purchases in the borrowing country, or in a third country.

When a loan is made, the usual procedure is for the underwriters to place the funds to the credit of the borrowers in a bank in the lending country. Against this credit the borrower can draw at will. But the position of exchange rates or discount rates may be such that for a time the borrowers prefer to keep those funds on deposit in the lending country, or invested in bills. Even when the funds are withdrawn, the claims may be temporarily satisfied in any of several ways.[2] The banks of the lending country may permit their foreign balances to decline in the expectation of building them up at a later date; or foreign banks may prefer to let their balances in the lending country increase, regarding them as secondary reserves. Tho such measures are only temporary, they serve to cause a time lag between the recording of the loan and the transfer of purchasing power in the form of goods and services.[3] The time lag thus created need not be a regular one.

[1] See pp. 144 ff.

[2] Professor Angell has carefully worked out the details of the various ways in which an export of goods, for example, can be financed, and the immediate effects of each method on the total volume of credit in the importing and the exporting countries. The various possible results which he indicates point to the impossibility of measuring the immediate effects on the volume of purchasing power in the countries concerned without knowing many more details regarding the banks and the loan than the available pre-war French information yields. Op. cit., Quar. Jour. of Econ., May, 1928.

[3] The expectation of *any* time lag between transfer of title and transfer of goods assumes that the balance of payments is at equilibrium when the loan disturbing that equilibrium is made. The disequilibrium creates in the lending country a demand for bills on the borrowing country, which can be supplied only by increased exports or decreased imports of commodities and services. (The practice of supplying those foreign bills by the movement of foreign balances is possible [see p. 32], but is only a temporary resource; a permanent credit would be merely the offsetting of one loan by another, and equilibrium in the balance of payments would be immediately restored. We are considering here the excess of long-term lending over

The position of exchange rates, discount rates, business activity in the lending and the borrowing countries are all modifying factors. Moreover, the order of the sequence may vary. It is possible that in some of the years merchandise movements may have been the cause and not the result of subsequent capital movements. In such case the capital movements would lag behind the merchandise movements. Or, again, both movements may in some years have been dominated by movements of business activity, and for those years no lag would necessarily appear.

The time lapse between French capital exports and net credit balances may have varied in either direction from a few weeks to a year or more. The absence of any regular lag between the annual fluctuations of the curves representing these two movements does not indicate that the differences between them are due to errors in the estimates. Errors there doubtless are; but the major differences may reasonably be expected to result not from these errors, but from the nature of the mechanism which corrected the disequilibrium in the international accounts.

Turning to the figures for capital exports (page 122), we find that from 1880 to 1913 France invested abroad annually sums varying from 100 to 2000 million francs. This export of capital first took the form of transfers (from the residents of France to residents of foreign countries) of title to purchasing power in France, and sooner or later was converted into transfers of goods,

borrowing.) If, however, disequilibrium already exists, the new loan may bring about immediate equilibrium. In such case there is no delay between the time when the loan is consummated and the time when the export of goods and services takes place. It is even possible that the goods and services are transferred before the loan is made; nay, even likely when the volume of lending is fairly steady. For illustration, assume a condition of equilibrium. Large loans are contracted which sooner or later set in motion forces that tend to increase the exports and decrease the imports of the lending country. But some of the forces which affected the volume and the value of exports and imports may continue to operate in the same direction after the disequilibrium caused by the loans has been removed, and thus to set up a new disequilibrium. This last disequilibrium, however, is caused not by a loan, but by a prolongation of the increase in the excess of exports from the lending country. If, then, a new foreign loan is floated in the same country, the proceeds of that loan may not create a new disequilibrium, but they may help to reduce the existing one.

services, or specie.[1] Thru what mechanism did these transfers take place? Was it thru a diminution of imports, or an increase of exports, or both, or neither? If the transfers were made by increased French exports, what caused the increase? If neither imports nor exports were shifted to make possible the transfer, were service items or was specie the medium of transfer? Or were both capital exports and merchandise exports dependent upon and caused by a third factor such as the cyclical movement of business activity?

Before proceeding to a consideration of these questions we must note what sum was due France from the revenue on her foreign investments, for it is the difference between this sum and her foreign investments that had to be transmitted abroad. The total of net revenue estimated as due France from this source between 1880 and 1913 was 30,070 million francs. This sum is almost two billion francs more than the total of the estimated capital exports. The figures are sufficiently close to indicate that if the period as a whole is taken as the unit, France exported practically no domestic savings at all; the total addition to her foreign investment during those years (i.e. what we have termed capital exports) consisted only of the reinvested interest and dividends received from abroad. If this equality between revenue and investments for the period as a whole existed also between the *annual* movements of capital exports and revenue receipts, the answer to the questions posited above would be simple. The capital exports and the interest and dividend payments in such case would not have disturbed the equilibrium; French foreign investors would have had enough foreign bills for sale from the revenue of their foreign investments to equal the amount demanded by the new French investments abroad. The flow of gold, goods, and services would not have been affected. The transactions would have been entirely confined to the exchange

[1] Immigrant remittances and a portion of the French government expenditures in colonies are similar to capital exports in that they are not a payment for goods or services. The transfer of these sums in the form of services or commodities raises the same question as do transfers of sums on capital account, but their volume in the case of France was so small, and subject to such minor fluctuations, that these sums have been omitted from the following discussion.

market, which would have found itself with an equal increase in the demand for and the supply of foreign bills.

But the annual interest payments due France and the annual foreign investments are not equal; for any one year they differ considerably. The interest payments due France, as would be expected, fluctuated very little, while the sums invested abroad differed greatly from year to year (see Chart 1). From 1880 to 1892 the revenue from foreign investments grew slowly but fairly steadily. In the next eight years because of large conversions at lower rates and lower rates of issue on new loans, the revenue from foreign investments gained little, notwithstanding the constantly increasing total of foreign investments. From 1900 to 1913 the revenue mounted rapidly but evenly. The capital exports, on the other hand, were subject to annual fluctuations which were seldom less than 200 million francs and frequently as much as 400 million francs. And not only were the annual fluctuations in the amount of capital invested abroad of considerable volume, but also for long periods these sums were either greater or less than the revenue received from foreign investments; in the years 1882 to 1886, 1891 to 1894, and 1910 to 1913 the interest due France exceeded capital invested abroad, while during most of the remaining period the opposite was true; in only a very few years were the sums due abroad equal to the sums due France. The problem, then, of the mechanism of transfer of funds remains.

To consider the questions involved in this problem it is first necessary to break up the international accounts into the partial balances of merchandise, specie, and invisible items. When this is done, and the partial balances plotted, it is found that the curve representing the movements of the balance of invisible items in no way reflects the annual fluctuations in the curve representing capital exports. This is to have been expected. Most of the items making up the balance of invisible items are not responsive to fluctuations in foreign investments. The balance consists of revenue from foreign investments, tourist expenditures, brokerage, underwriters' profits, transit earnings, and expenditures of foreign ships. (Shipping earnings, ordinarily included in the invisible items, are here excluded for reasons to be explained presently.) Of these items we should expect to find directly responsive to changes in capital exports only brokerage earnings and, to a lesser degree, transit earnings and expenditures of foreign ships.

CHART 2

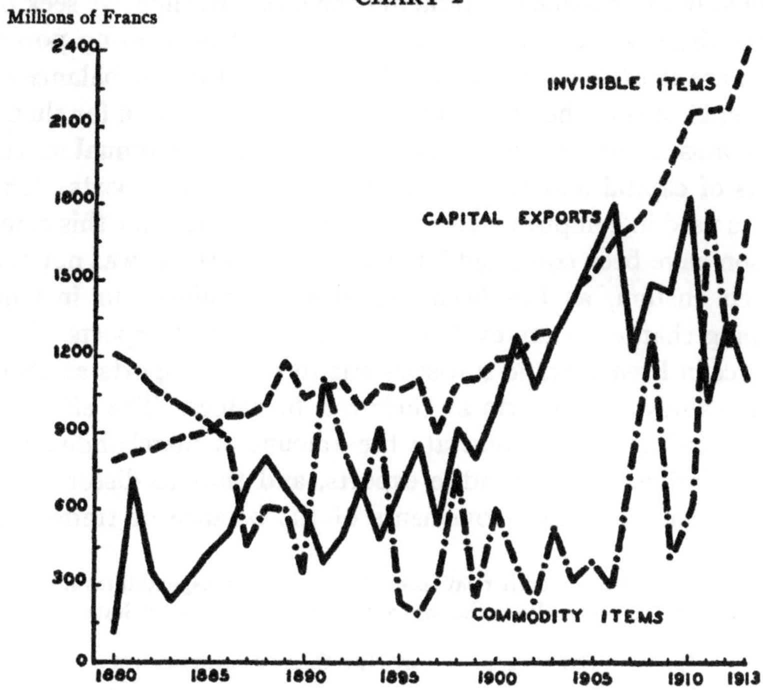

French International Accounts. Partial Balances

—— Capital exports.
- - - Invisible items.
-·-· Commodity items (excess of debits).

But these items are of little quantitative importance in the international accounts; their total reaches 100 million francs in only a few years.[1] The principal items, those of quantitative import-

[1] In 1909 and 1910 the brokerage earnings doubled previous and subsequent earnings. This was due in part to heavy new foreign issues and in part to heavy conversions of old foreign issues. In those years the foreign governments paid France for duty on their securities issued on the Paris Bourse 46 and 41 million francs. This source of income to France is included under the item of Brokerage and Underwriters' Profits.

ance, — tourist expenditures and revenue from foreign investments, — are little affected by capital exports. Interest payments, the movements of which are directly derived from capital exports, reflect, of course, only to a very slight degree movements in capital exports, while tourist expenditures are largely independent of international capital movements.[1] If, then, we seek to isolate those vehicles for the transmission of purchasing power which are most sensitive to any disequilibrium in the balance of payments, it is in the visible balance that we must look for them.

We must consider, first, the relation between the annual movements of capital and of merchandise imports and exports. The figures used in computing the merchandise balances for this comparison have been corrected for shipping charges. It was not the French custom, as has been previously explained, to include shipping charges in the evaluation of merchandise exports. The practice in French trade statistics was to record imports at their c. i. f. values and exports at their f. o. b. values. The effect of this procedure is to exaggerate the amount of merchandise imports relative to merchandise exports, and thus to distort conclusions based on the movements of the balance of trade. In

[1] The absence of any definite relationship between tourist expenditures and capital movements was found also in the case of Canada and the United States.

TOURIST EXPENDITURES AND NET CAPITAL MOVEMENTS

	United States [a]				Canada [b]		
Year	American Tourists Abroad	Foreign Tourists in U. S.	Net Capital Exports	Year	Canadian Tourists Abroad	Foreign Tourists in Canada	Net Capital Imports
1922 ...	445	87	378	1900 ...	6	7	36
1923 ...	446	104	−33	1901 ...	6	8	21
1924 ...	534	107	517	1902 ...	7	11	27
1925 ...	585	112	621	1903 ...	7	10	69
1926 ...	623	148	181	1904 ...	9	12	90
1927 ...	696	163	695	1905 ...	11	13	82
1928 ...	824	163	944	1906 ...	15	16	111
1929 ...	868	183	306	1907 ...	16	16	182
1930 ...	811	171	733	1908 ...	18	19	131
				1909 ...	19	19	159
				1910 ...	25	24	250
				1911 ...	28	26	354
				1912 ...	33	29	435
				1913 ...	37	30	414

[a] Figures taken from annual reports published by the United States Dept. of Commerce.

[b] Figures (in millions of dollars) taken from J. Viner, Canada's Balance of International Indebtedness 1900–1913, pp. 95, 106.

order to make comparable the imports and the exports, they should both be either f. o. b. or c. i. f.; otherwise shipping and insurance services are included as part of commodity imports but excluded as part of commodity exports. If all the merchandise were carried in foreign ships, there would be nothing inconsistent in including shipping charges in the cost of imports and excluding them in the cost of exports; it would be merely a case of regarding shipping services as part of the merchandise.[1]

In so far as part of transportation is done in domestic ships, however, this ceases to be true. It is therefore essential for a correct analysis of the balance of trade to record as c. i. f. only those imports carried in foreign ships and only those exports carried in domestic ships. Imports carried in domestic ships and exports carried in foreign ships ought then to be valued as f. o. b. Such procedure would give an accurate picture of international payments due from imports and exports of merchandise, and would necessarily preclude earnings from these sources as a separate item in the balance of payments. But the practice of the French Department of Commerce of recording imports c. i. f. and exports f. o. b. and the impossibility of knowing what portion of imports and of exports was carried in foreign bottoms, makes it necessary to resort to some other method of reaching comparable import and export figures.

The simplest method, as we have seen when constructing the balance sheet, was to add all the earnings of French ships engaged in international trade to the f. o. b. value of the exports. Part of these earnings represents payment from one group of Frenchmen to another group and should therefore not appear in the balance of payments since it does not give rise to any international transfer of funds or creation of international indebtedness. Imports carried on French ships fall under that category; yet they appear in

[1] There seems to be no more ground for separating transportation costs from other costs than there is for separating selling costs, or interest charges, or any other element in the total cost of merchandise. To be sure, for some purposes of analysis it is helpful to be able to break up the total cost of commodities into its various constituents of interest, labor, profits, transportation, etc., but for any analysis or understanding of the balance of trade it is quite unnecessary to treat imports on any other basis than c. i. f.

TABLE 26

EXCESS OF MERCHANDISE IMPORTS WITH CORRECTION FOR UNDERESTIMATE IN OFFICIAL FIGURES AND WITH IMPORTS C. I. F., 1880–1913

(Millions of francs)

Year	Net Excess of Imports	French Ships' Provisions	Net Increase in Merchandise Exports from Estimated Correction	Excess of Imports (Cols. 1 + Col. 2 − Col. 3)	French Shipping and Marine Insurance Earnings	Excess of Imports (Imports and Exports C. I. F.) (Col. 4 − Col. 5)
1880 ...	1511	10	207	1314	136	1178
1881 ...	1248	10	221	1037	158	879
1882 ...	1190	10	224	976	180	796
1883 ...	1291	10	213	1088	189	900
1884 ...	1052	10	203	859	179	680
1885 ...	950	12	195	767	159	608
1886 ...	910	12	208	714	160	554
1887 ...	725	12	215	522	160	362
1888 ...	812	12	213	611	175	436
1889 ...	566	12	253	325	194	131
1890 ...	629	12	254	387	179	208
1891 ...	1130	18	227	918	173	745
1892 ...	681	15	230	466	151	316
1893 ...	568	15	217	366	146	220
1894 ...	710	15	203	522	140	382
1895 ...	285	17	239	63	170	−177
1896 ...	356	15	239	132	143	−11
1897 ...	325	16	255	86	158	−72
1898 ...	913	17	230	700	171	529
1899 ...	306	16	277	45	179	−134
1900 ...	530	20	285	265	209	56
1901 ...	312	18	284	46	176	−130
1902 ...	96	17	307	194	177	−371
1903 ...	597	15	295	217	189	28
1904 ...	4	14	325	−307	217	−524
1905 ...	−137	16	359	−430	233	−713
1906 ...	282	17	378	−79	265	−344
1907 ...	556	17	391	182	271	−89
1908 ...	539	17	352	204	250	−46
1909 ...	472	17	403	86	265	−179
1910 ...	864	19	428	455	319	136
1911 ...	1920	18	385	1553	316	1237
1912 ...	1442	21	445	1018	419	599
1913 ...	1460	21	458	1023	371	652

the merchandise balance of trade as sums due foreign countries. On the other hand, exports carried on French ships give rise to sums due France; yet such sums do not appear in the balance of trade.[1] To arrive at a correct balance of trade, it is thus necessary to deduct from the debit side the French shipping earnings on

CHART 3

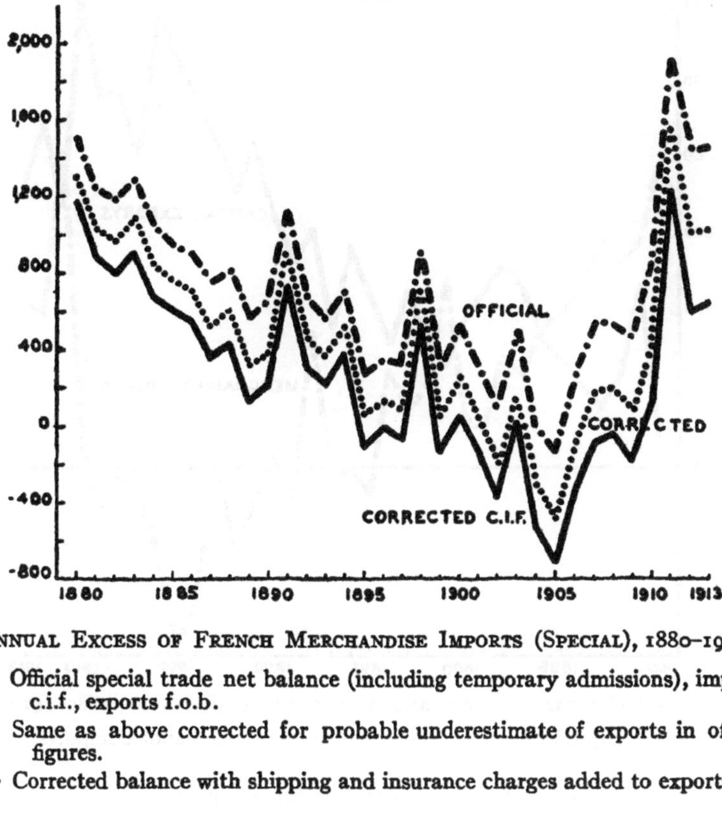

ANNUAL EXCESS OF FRENCH MERCHANDISE IMPORTS (SPECIAL), 1880–1913

-·-· Official special trade net balance (including temporary admissions), imports c.i.f., exports f.o.b.

···· Same as above corrected for probable underestimate of exports in official figures.

—— Corrected balance with shipping and insurance charges added to exports.

imports and to add to the credit side French earnings on the export carrying trade. The net effect is the same if no deductions are made from the debit side and all the earnings of French shipping — whether on imports, exports, or shipments between foreign ports — are placed on the credit side. The latter method exaggerates both the totals of imports and of exports, but the

[1] See p. 52.

difference between them, which is the important matter for the present purpose, remains the same in either case.

When the statistics of merchandise imports and exports have thus been made comparable, and when due allowance is made for the relative undervaluation of exports, the balance of merchan-

CHART 4

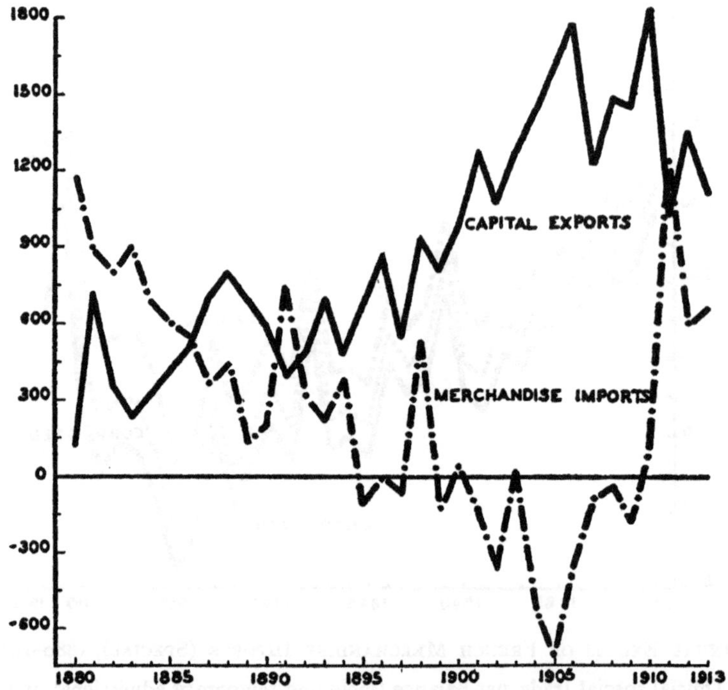

French Capital Exports and Merchandise Balances, 1880–1913

—— Capital exports. —•— Excess of merchandise imports.

dise movements presents a quite different picture from the one based on the officially recorded statistics. The figures, both the official and the corrected, for the net excess of imports are tabulated on page 136 and are plotted on the chart, page 137. It will be noted that instead of the constant excess of merchandise imports that has been generally ascribed to the revenue from her huge foreign investments, France had for twelve of the thirty-four years under survey an excess of merchandise *exports*. In several of the remaining years her import excess was practically negligible. Nevertheless, the *fluctuations* in the corrected balances remain very similar to the fluctuations in the official figures. In comparing the annual movements of merchandise balances with the movements of capital exports no significant change is introduced by using the modified figures rather than the official ones. When the curve representing the movement of capital exports is compared with the curve depicting movements of merchandise balances there appears a fairly high inverse correlation; almost every time capital exports decrease, the excess of merchandise imports increases, and when capital exports increase, the excess of merchandise imports decreases.

Some of the sharp and sudden changes in merchandise movements call for special explanation. They prove upon examination to be due principally to greatly increased food imports caused by unusually poor domestic harvests. This was true in 1891, 1894, 1898, 1903, and 1911. The only year in which there was any considerable increase in imports not due to domestic harvest conditions was 1900, when the imports of raw materials increased. This increase was due not to an increase in the physical volume of raw materials, but to the great increase that year in the cost of certain raw materials.[1] In fact, there was a decrease in the

[1] The import price of textiles and coal, both important items in French imports of raw materials, rose considerably. Coal, for example, rose from 20.6 francs per ton to 27 francs, an increase of 35 per cent. This increase in the import price of coal alone accounted for 112 millions out of the total increase of imports of 184 millions. If the same quantity of coal had been imported in 1900 as in 1899, the increase in value of coal imports would have been 86 millions, but 16.1 million tons were imported in 1900 as against 13.4 in 1899, thereby accounting for approximately 80 per cent of the increase in the value of imports in 1900. There were also considerable increases in prices and decreases in quantities of raw cotton and raw wool, both important constituents in French imports of raw materials. Below are given the imports of their quantities and prices in the years about 1900:

	Raw Cotton		Raw Wool		Coal	
	Quantity (Millions of Kgs.)	Price (Francs per Kg.)	Quantity (Millions of Kgs.)	Price (Francs per Kg.)	Quantity (Millions of Qns.)	Price (Francs per Qn.)
1898	202	.83	248	1.56	119	1.92
1899	202	.89	253	1.84	133	2.06
1900	193	1.30	189	2.25	161	2.70
1901	212	1.16	248	1.46	154	2.40
1902	213	1.20	235	1.45	151	2.03

The table above suggests that the French demand for foreign raw wool and cotton

quantity of imports for 1900. The import quantity index arrived at by the method of deflation dropped from 103 to 100 (see p. 232). On the other hand, in all other years in which there were significant increases in excess of imports, the increases were due to greater imports of foodstuffs, and in those years the increased values of imports were caused not by higher prices, but by greatly increased quantities.

The total imports in the years preceding and following those years in which sudden increases in excess of imports occurred and the imports of foodstuffs in those years were as follows:

(Millions of francs)

Year	Excess of Total Imports	Increase over Preceding Year	Excess of Imports of Foodstuffs	Increase over Preceding Year	Excess of Imports of Cereals	Increase over Preceding Year
1890 ..	149	...	590	...	345	...
1891 ..	684	535	844	254	489	144
1892 ..	259	...	641	...	427	...
1893 ..	166	...	350	...	293	...
1894 ..	320	154	531	181	349	51
1895 ..	−129	...	444	...	149	...
1897 ..	−112	...	308	...	237	...
1898 ..	484	596	843	535	606	389
1899 ..	−175	...	276	...	126	...
1902 ..	−406	...	111	...	133	...
1903 ..	−8	398	298	187	165	32
1904 ..	−561	...	120	...	98	...
1910 ..	119	...	555	...	288	...
1911 ..	1176	1057	1284	729	706	418
1912 ..	566	...	954	...	352	...

---

is much less inelastic than the demand for foreign coal. The decreased imports of raw cotton and raw wool were not due to a decreased *foreign* demand for French cotton and wool textiles. In 1900 the domestic consumption of cotton in France decreased 16 million kgs. and that of wool 63 million kgs., showing that it was the demand of the French consumer that decreased when the price rose. It is hardly likely that the price increased because of the curtailed demand. Wool and cotton are not produced under monopolistic or even quasi-monopolistic conditions, and over any one season the supply is scarcely modified by price. It is, therefore, reasonable to assume that the amount consumed declined because of the rise in price.

A glance at the table below shows that in the years when sudden increases in imports occurred, food imports constituted from one-half to the whole of the increases. These sudden changes in food imports were caused by poor domestic harvests, not by influences traceable to banking phenomena or general price changes.

	Proportion of Total Imports (per cent)	Proportion of Increase (per cent)
1891	34	47
1894	31	117
1898	33	89
1903	18	47
1911	24	69

The large excess of merchandise imports which characterized French international trade for the whole of the period from 1880 to 1888 was also probably due to non-monetary factors. Domestic crop conditions were very likely again the chief cause. The harvest in the year 1879 was very poor in all Europe and necessitated considerably increased French imports of grain in the following year. The production of wheat dropped to 75 million hectolitres, a low level matched only by the year 1891. The increase in imports of grain alone rose from 207 in 1877 to 857 in 1879 and 788 millions in 1880. In addition to bad domestic grain crops in 1879 occurred the spread of phylloxera, destroying thousands of acres of vineyard. Wine imports leaped from 29 million francs in 1877 to 314 in 1880 and remained between 300 and 400 million francs until 1893. If the wine imports caused by the destruction of domestic vineyards, and the import of foodstuffs in 1880 caused by the poor harvest of 1879, were deducted from the imports, the excess of merchandise imports from 1880 to 1888 would largely disappear, as the following table shows:

(Millions of francs)

Year	Total Excess of Imports	Imports of Wine	Year	Total Excess of Imports	Imports of Wine
1880	1098	313	1885	541	388
1881	841	364	1886	488	517
1882	722	315	1887	294	443
1883	826	376	1888	357	437
1884	586	344			

To repeat, the heights of 1891, 1894, 1898, 1903, and 1911 do not, in the main, represent any changes in the volume of imports due to causes that appear to be connected with monetary or banking phenomena. A curve representing the merchandise balance of trade with those fluctuations in food imports due to domestic crop conditions eliminated, would present a different picture than the curve of excess of imports representing the official trade statistics. Instead of a constant excess of imports, usually hovering between 1500 million and 600 million, there would probably be only a few years in which there would be any excess of imports, while the balance of merchandise movements over the whole period would show a sizeable excess of exports. The years 1881 to 1885, perhaps 1892 and 1893, and 1912 and 1913 alone would show an excess of imports, and of these in only the last two would the excess be greater than 100 to 200 million francs.

If allowance were made for the greatly increased imports in the years of poor domestic crops, the correlation between capital exports and commodity movements would be heightened. However, the increase in food imports caused by poor domestic crops cannot reasonably be eliminated from the curve unless it be certain that there exists no connection between the capital exports and the increased food imports. Of this we cannot be certain. It is true that capital movements could not have influenced to any significant extent the volume of such unusual and sudden food imports; but it is quite possible, as will be pointed out later, that the increased food imports may have affected the movements of capital exports. To eliminate, therefore, these additional food imports from the curve of merchandise movements would be unwarranted at this point in the analysis. In any case, with or without them, the correlation between merchandise movements and movements of capital exports is high enough to suggest that the mechanism of adjustment for the French international accounts should be sought among the factors which affect the flow of merchandise exports and imports.

CHAPTER VII

THE MECHANISM OF ADJUSTMENT

THE correlation noted in the previous chapter between the movement of merchandise balances and that of capital exports gives no hint as to which movement was causal. The capital exports may have induced corresponding merchandise movements, or merchandise movements may have influenced the fluctuations in capital exports. It may even be that both movements were dominated by the cyclical movement of business activity. Or — none of these sequences wholly excluding the others — there is the still further possibility that all three contributed to produce the correlation. In this chapter will be considered the first possibility — that capital exports were the causal factor.

There are four possible ways in which capital exports may bring about movements of merchandise:

(1) Thru the purchase of the lending country's products by the foreign borrowers, the purchases being made with the borrowed funds.

(2) Thru an increase in foreign purchasing power directly brought about by the loan. As the result of the increased purchasing power in the borrowing country, imported commodities share in the increase of consumption, and the lending country may participate in this increase of the borrowing country's imports. For the same reason the imports into the lending country may decrease because of the loss of domestic purchasing power.

(3) Thru an increase in foreign purchases of the lending country's commodities because the price of those commodities to the foreign purchaser has decreased solely *by virtue of the downward movement of exchange rates.* From the same cause foreign goods are less attractively priced to the lending country and its imports may be curtailed.

(4) Thru an increase in foreign purchases of the lending coun-

try's commodities caused by a relative drop in the prices of those goods for which the foreign demand is elastic, a drop in price not directly consequent upon changes in exchange rates. The relative increase in the price of foreign commodities will also serve to create an export surplus by curtailing the lending country's purchases of foreign commodities the demand for which in the lending country is elastic.

The first possibility — purchase of the lending country's products by the borrowers — can in the case of France be readily dismissed. Part of the funds borrowed from France was doubtless used by the borrowers to pay for goods purchased in France, but the portion so used was small, so small that there was repeated outcry against the practice of supplying foreign countries with funds that were not spent in France. Great pressure was brought to bear on the French Government, particularly in the decade before the war, to use its power of control over Bourse listings for the express purpose of forcing foreign borrowers to spend in France part of the sums borrowed; in fact, it became the avowed policy of the French Government in the years immediately preceding the war to demand of foreign borrowers some consideration in return for the privilege of listing their securities on the French market.[1] This policy served to secure orders for certain of the favored French industries, orders that would otherwise have gone elsewhere; but the total of such purchases was very small. Pressure could not be applied to all borrowers, and at best the requirement could be that only a part of the borrowed sums be spent in France. The pressure was used, moreover, not exclusively for the purpose of securing to French factories a portion of the expenditures; it was frequently applied to secure tariff

[1] The French Minister of Foreign Affairs stated in 1909: "In regard to applications for listings of loans to foreign governments, we endeavor to obtain satisfactions without which, usually, we refuse admission to listing on the Paris market. It is a rule to which we will not cease to conform, and which consists in according financial satisfactions only for satisfactions of a commercial and industrial order which ought to be given us in exchange." Cited in Becque, op. cit., p. 185. Becque also cites several instances of proposed loans having been refused because apparently not enough of the funds were to be spent in France. See his Chap. VI for an extended discussion of this point.

favors or to attain purely political ends.[1] The quantitative unimportance of the increase in merchandise exports due to this policy may be judged from the fact that during the period when public demand for government pressure on the foreign borrowers was at its height — 1908–1913 — almost a billion francs were invested in Spain, while the *total* exports to that country during those years of heavy borrowing were less than 800 million francs. This sum, moreover, was only 50 million francs greater than the exports to Spain in the six years preceding, when investments in Spain were slight, and this notwithstanding the rising prices of those years.

Much better evidence that the borrowers spent little of the borrowed sums on French commodities is furnished by the statistics of exports to countries in which France had made her heaviest investments. Between 1880 and 1913 over 10 billions were loaned to Russia, and yet the *total* French exports to Russia during those years were only 10 per cent of that sum; indeed, more goods were exported to Russia in the twenty years before French loans to that country began than subsequently. Loans to Austria-Hungary during that same period were over three billions; yet the total exports were less than one billion. In Turkey about three and a half billions were invested; but the entire exports to Turkey during the fifty years before 1913 did not reach that sum. In China about one billion francs were invested between 1880 and 1913; yet the total exports for those years were less than 200 millions. From 1875 to 1890 over two billions were invested in Spain, and during that period the total of French exports was little more than two billions. Between 1900 and 1913 three billions were invested in Roumania, but the total exports were less than 100 millions. In view of the fact that the total exports to the heavy debtor countries formed so small a proportion of the sums France invested in those countries, there can be no doubt that the increase in French exports caused by expenditure of the borrowed sums in France was of very slight importance.

The statement was made earlier (see p. 21) that this cause of

[1] See J. Viner's International Finance and Balance of Power Diplomacy, 1880–1914 in The Southwestern Political and Social Science Quarterly, March, 1929.

increased imports — namely, the expenditure of the borrowed sums in the lending country — is frequently of considerable importance. But it will be recalled that its importance differs with varying circumstances. When the lending country has a highly developed industrial economy and the borrower is relatively in the early stages of industrial revolution, a good part of the borrowed sums is spent directly in the borrowing country. This was the situation with British loans to her colonies and with American loans to her continental neighbors during the twentieth century. But the situation with the French loans was different. There the borrowers — Russia, Spain, Turkey, China, Austria-Hungary — were, indeed, industrially backward, but pre-war France was not highly industrialized either. The kinds of commodities that the borrowers frequently wished to purchase — railroad and mining equipment, textile and farm machinery, war materials, sheet iron, structural steel, tin plate, and so forth — did not appear in the French export trade before the turn of the century, and were negligible even up to the war. French exports were chiefly consumption goods: wines, fine textiles of silk, wool, and cotton, novelties, furs and skins, wearing apparel, jewelry, drugs. Such goods were, of course, purchased by the borrowing countries — tho in no great quantities — but they were rarely, if ever, purchased with the proceeds of the loans. When the borrowers expended the loans directly on imports, they purchased the goods not from France, but from the highly industrialized countries — England, Germany, and the United States.

We consider then the next possibility. Did the capital exports induce corresponding movements in merchandise thru the changes they brought about in the demand schedules of the borrowing and the lending countries? This possibility has been already discussed in the introductory chapter, where it was held to be in some cases a not unimportant means of adjustment. It was explained that the portion of the loan spent in the borrowing country would, by increasing incomes, cause demand schedules in that country to move to the right. Imports would share in the increase, and a portion of these would be purchased from the lending country. We do not have reference now to the portion of the loan spent by the borrowers directly on imports; we have just pointed out that the borrowers did not spend any significant portion of the loans in France. We are speaking now of the purchases made by the *residents of the borrowing countries* (as distinct from the *borrowers*). Such purchases are made as a result of increased incomes caused by the expenditure of a part of the loan in the borrowing country. The question we have to consider, then, is whether shifts in demand schedules resulted in increased imports into the borrowing country and decreased imports into the lending country. Before we can do so, however, we must ascertain whether transfers of purchasing power from France to the borrowing countries took place to a significant extent, for shifts in purchasing power could have occurred only if the transfers did take place.

As has been indicated in Chapter 1, transfers are effected either thru gold flows or thru the movement of short-term loans. Examination of the figures shows that from 1880 to 1913 during any one year the total gold movements in and out of France were much larger than the net movements. In only a few years was the movement in either direction less than 200 million francs, thus in the figures of annual net movements at least 200 millions of imports and 200 millions of exports would not appear. On the other hand to use the sum of the total flows of gold as a measure of the transfer of purchasing power is to exaggerate the importance of gold movements as a force modifying demand schedules. Some part of the inward and outward flows could have exercised no effect on demand schedules, for the movements occurred too closely together. Frequently within one week gold was imported from one country and exported to another. None the less, the figures of monthly *net* gold movements show that a large part of the flows remained in or away from France long enough to have exercised an influence on demand schedules.

To what extent did these net gold movements synchronize with the movements of capital exports? Did the increases in net monthly gold exports accompany increases in capital exports? Examination of the available data gives no conclusive answer to this question. The annual figures for capital and merchandise movements — monthly and quarterly figures for the period 1880–

1913 are non-existent — reveal no correlation, positive or negative, between gold movements and capital exports, or between gold movements and merchandise movements. In years of increased capital exports gold imports are sometimes high and sometimes low, and the same is true, tho to a lesser degree, of the relationship between gold and merchandise movements. In the years 1904–05, for example, capital and merchandise exports increased greatly, but gold imports also increased, a fact which seems to indicate that gold movements could not in those years have been the means by which capital exports were converted into merchandise exports.[1] Yet we cannot be certain of this. An examination of the monthly gold movements (see Chart 11, page 192) suggests the possibility of negative monthly correlations. In the year 1904, for example, the large gold imports were received in two spring months. It may be that the borrowings of that year were withdrawn in the summer and fall and caused the greatly reduced gold imports in those months. In 1905, again, gold imports virtually ceased in the spring and in the fall, and it is possible that during those months capital exports increased. The same may have happened in other years, for monthly movements of gold were very irregular, and we know that capital exports were also subject to wide fluctuations within the calendar year. It may be that a comparison of monthly movements would reveal an inverse relationship when a comparison of annual movements shows the opposite.

On the basis of the annual data, however, all that can be stated is that for many of the pre-war years gold movements apparently

[1] If the quantity of gold imported by other countries during those years had shown proportionately larger increases, the imports into France might have represented a decline as compared to other countries. But a glance at the following figures of the net gold imports of France, Germany, United States, and England indicate that France was receiving more than her share of the world's additional supply.

	France	England	Germany	United States
		(Millions of Francs)		
1904	490	25	425	−190
1905	600	200	200	20

In the decade preceding 1904 the United States had a net excess of gold imports of over one billion francs.

did not function as a means of transferring purchasing power from the lending to the borrowing country. That they may have performed that function in the other years is suggested by the fact that in those years gold imports declined when capital exports increased. Because of the possibly dual role of gold movements, such an interpretation is not inconceivable. Gold movements serve at times to adjust disequilibrium by compensating for the increased exports which have been engendered independently of gold flows; at other times — as when disequilibrium has been caused by capital movements — they may help to restore equilibrium by inducing merchandise movements.

Movements of short-term funds were probably of less importance as a means of transferring purchasing power than gold flows. The absence of a free gold market, with the consequent increased risks of exchange, discouraged such movements. Notwithstanding, the large commercial banks kept some funds on deposit in foreign money markets. How large these deposits were and to what extent they fluctuated it is impossible to say because no records of such movements appear in the bank statistics. Until 1900 two of the large banks published annual figures of the foreign bills discounted. They show the totals to have been fairly large, almost three billions altogether. The Bank of France did not keep any foreign bills in its portfolio until after 1909, but doubtless many of the private banking firms, aside from the two mentioned above, had foreign bills in their portfolios. The possession of a foreign bill in the portfolio indicates, however, only that the French holder would have a claim on a foreign currency when the bill matured. Whether foreign funds so obtained were called home (by selling sight drafts) or were reinvested abroad in more short-term paper would depend upon the relative interest rates and current and expected position of exchange rates. When the rate of foreign lending in France increased, causing exchange rates to become less favorable, bankers may have borrowed abroad and sold sight drafts (or permitted their foreign balances to decline by selling sight drafts against them); when the exchange rates became more favorable, the balances may have been built up again, or the loans liquidated. In such fashion a transfer of purchasing power would have taken place without the medium of gold flows. It is doubtful whether before 1900 the fluctuations in the amount of foreign net short-term holdings were very large — after 1900 they became increasingly important — but probably at no time during the thirty-four years (except for the exceptional years 1906–07) was the effect of short-term loans on demand schedules so great as the effect of gold flows.

The effect of both gold flows and short-term credits is greater than their volume would indicate because the same quantity of purchasing power can be employed many times before being finally liquidated. Thus an increase in capital exports of 10 million francs a month for ten months could be transformed into an export excess of 100 million francs by a transfer of purchasing power (in the form of gold or short-term credits) to the amount of much less than 100 millions. The loss of the first 10 million francs of purchasing power in the lending country causes an increase in exports [1] of (say) 3 million francs because of the changed demand schedules. The second monthly installment can then be transferred by the use of only 7 millions in gold or credit, the remaining three being transferred by bills of exchange created by the increased exports. The loss of the 7 millions in turn creates (say) 2 millions of additional exports. And so on. Each subsequent 10 million franc loan will be transferred with less gold or credit until the increase in exports reaches 10 million francs a month. The transaction will, of course, not be consummated with the regularity here assumed. Many months may elapse before merchandise movements are affected by the influence of gold or credit movements on demand schedules, and day-to-day fluctuations may occur in the volume of capital exports. The illustration above is used merely to point out that the modifying effect of gold and credit movements on demand schedules is enhanced by the possibility of continued re-employment before retransfer abroad.

The transfer of purchasing power having once occurred, did the increased demand schedules of the residents of the borrowing country cause their imports of French goods to increase? That

[1] All movements referred to here are relative.

this could not have been the case is readily shown by the figures of French exports which we have already examined. When, to repeat, Russia during the thirty-four years borrowed ten billion francs and spent on French imports a total of *one* billion francs, it is certain that the loans to Russia did not cause the residents of Russia to increase their purchases of French commodities to more than a negligible extent. The same was true of the other large borrowers, as the figures on page 145 indicate. Nor is there any reason to expect the debtor countries to have done otherwise. The important debtor countries normally secured only a small proportion of their imports from France: Russia less than 4 per cent; Austria-Hungary, Roumania, and China less than 2 per cent; Egypt, Turkey, and Italy less than 10 per cent; Spain alone among the borrowers more than 10 per cent.[1] With France contributing so small a share of the lending countries' imports, it is not to be expected that she would secure more than a small share of such additional imports as resulted from increased incomes.

At first thought this statement appears to contradict the claim made in the introductory chapter. There disagreement was expressed with Professor Viner's view that the borrowing country would be expected to spend directly on imports only such proportion of the newly acquired purchasing power as would be represented by the ratio of its total imports to its total domestic expenditures. But there is actually no contradiction between the foregoing disagreement with Professor Viner's view and our statement above. We are considering a different matter. The earlier discussion was concerned with the direct effect of a loan on the *total* imports of the borrowing country; we are now concerned with the indirect effect (thru increased money incomes) on imports of *that part of the loan spent in the borrowing country, and only on those imports that come from the lending country.*[2] The fact

[1] Spain obtained 15 per cent.

[2] The purpose of the loan is one of the factors determining how large a portion of it will be spent directly on imports. But we are not concerned now with the portion directly spent abroad — we have seen already that France would get a small share of that; we are concerned with the effect on French imports of that portion of the loan spent in the borrowing country. The amount spent there serves to increase the total income of the borrowing country. If the loan is employed, as many of the

that France exported so little to her debtor countries shows that such portion of the loans as was spent in the debtor countries increased the demand schedules for goods of the kind not imported from France.

None the less, French exports may have been indirectly affected by the increased demand schedules of the borrowing countries. The French loans to Russia may have increased Russia's demand for goods from England and Germany. These two countries were heavy exporters to Russia, and the increase in their sales to Russia may have led in turn to increases in the demand schedules of England and Germany, countries which were among France's chief customers. France, then, may have exported more merchandise to Germany and to England as a result of her loans to Russia without bringing into play any mechanism or influence other than shifts in demand schedules caused by the transfers of the means of payment. The point has been sufficiently developed in Chapter I.

Unfortunately no evidence of such movements can be secured. It is quite impossible to separate in the trade statistics the exports caused by shifts in demand from the exports caused by other factors. Any increase in exports to countries other than the borrowing country — increases that would be caused by changes

loans were, to correct a deficit in the budget; or to build highways, docks, stone bridges, and school-houses; or to help maintain an army, or an emperor's or sultan's court; then a good portion of the loan is spent in the borrowing country. The total of wages, salaries, profits, and perhaps rent, is then increased. Now, the question we are trying to answer at this point is what portion of this increased income will be spent on French imports. The proportions of the increase spent on food, amusement, clothing, shelter, and so forth probably would not be the same after the increase as before. There would be a change in demand schedules consequent upon the increased income, but the change would very likely be trifling. If a country normally obtained 5 per cent of its imports from France, there is little reason to expect France to receive much more than 5 per cent of any increased expenditure on imports *caused by the small increase in wages and profits*. Were the loans to result in greatly increased profits for certain groups in the borrowing country, it might well be that the increase would cause the demand schedules for imported luxuries to move to the right to a greater degree than other products. This would have been true particularly in such countries as borrowed from France. In such case France, who exported finery and knicknacks, would get a larger share than she would have, had the increased domestic expenditures resulted chiefly in increased purchasing power for workers.

in demand induced indirectly by French capital exports — would be indistinguishably merged in the movements of total exports, and it would be impossible to ascribe the fluctuations in exports solely to shifts in demand schedules, unless other factors, such as price changes, could be ruled out. Price changes, however, as we shall see when analyzing merchandise and price movements, cannot be excluded.

So far we have been speaking of the part played by French exports in the development of an export surplus. But, with equal likelihood, decreased French imports could have contributed to the development of that export surplus; the loss in domestic purchasing power consequent upon the loans may have impinged on goods imported into France. But here again we are confronted with the same difficulties in determining the changes caused by shifts in demand. Prices of imports are not stable, and it would be most unreasonable to ascribe fluctuations in French imports to changes in the French demand schedules for foreign products. An attempt to determine the influence exerted on merchandise movements by the loss in French purchasing power cannot therefore be based upon inductive analysis.

Yet some effect on imports there must have been, and if, as Professor Viner believes, the reduction takes place (if it takes place at all) in the same proportion as that borne by capital exports to the total purchasing power, the decrease in French imports can be roughly determined. We need only compare in any given year the capital exports with the total annual money income. Now in the year 1911 the total French money income from investments, from ownership of land, from wages, and from profits was estimated to have been 32 billions.[1] In that same year France exported, it is estimated, one billion francs. The proportion of capital exports to the purchasing power was, therefore, 3.1 per cent. If imports were curtailed in the same proportion as

[1] R. Pupin, La richesse de la France devant la guerre, Chap. IV. For 1906 the annual revenue was estimated by Lavergne and Henry to have been 28 billions. — La richesse de la France (Paris, 1908), Chap. III. Coste estimated it to have been 22 billions for 1890 — Étude sur les salaires des travailleurs et le revenu de la France — and Colson estimated it at 25 billions for 1895. — Cours d'économie politique, Vol. II, p. 299.

domestic expenditures, the decrease would have been 260 million francs. This decrease in imports of 260 million francs represents a transfer of merchandise — by way of an increased export excess — of one-fourth of the amount of the capital exported. This would have been a very considerable proportion. But, to repeat, there are no *a priori* grounds for believing that a decline in purchasing power should leave the proportions of domestic and foreign purchases the same. The income that goes abroad might have been spent — had it remained at home — in larger or in smaller part on imports, depending upon the alternative use to which the exported capital would have been put.

Most likely the alternative use would have been domestic investment. In France a sudden increase in foreign investments represents not so much an increase in savings as a shift from one kind of saving to another; or, to be more exact, it is a change in the direction of the flow of new savings. In other words, an investment abroad of one billion francs by French investors represents a decrease in domestic purchasing power only in the sense that the billion francs would have been spent at home if they had not been sent abroad. Each year France saves several billion francs and presumably all (except the marginal savings that would disappear if the rate of return decreased)[1] would be invested at home, provided there were no incentives to prefer foreign investments. If, then, France exported one billion francs, she spent one billion less on capital goods than she would have done had she invested that billion francs at home. The portion of this billion that in such case would have been spent on imported goods depends on the purpose for which the funds would have been borrowed. If they would have been borrowed for electrification projects, then imports of copper, rubber, and lead would have consumed a portion of the domestic loans; if, on the other hand, they would have been invested in road building, then the wages of domestic labor and transportation would have consumed the bulk of the increase. The additional income of labor would in turn have increased expenditures on coffee, cocoa, cotton, and other imported commodities as well as on domestic products.

[1] See page 291 for a discussion of this point.

Clearly, in view of the many ways in which the capital sent abroad might have been employed at home, it is impossible to determine to what extent imports were reduced by a shift to the left in the French demand schedule caused by the export of capital. Yet the reduction was probably not inconsiderable. Any decrease in the domestic expenditure on either capital or consumption goods involves necessarily a reduction in the consumption of raw materials. In the case of France the common raw materials (coal, wool, cotton, copper, chemicals, rubber, oil) formed an important part of the imports; it is reasonable to assume, therefore, that a transfer of purchasing power from France to a foreign country reduced the French imports of raw materials. When we add to this reduction in imports the increase in French exports (caused by changes in foreign demand schedules), we arrive at a net export surplus that may have formed an important part of the total export excess (or of the reduction in import excess). We may conclude, then, that changes in demand schedules played a not unimportant role in the mechanism of adjustment. But it must be emphasized that the only evidence yielded by trade statistics shows that in the case of France they did not act on exports to the borrowing countries. That they acted thru the other channels remains a likely but unverified deduction.

We now turn to changes in imports and exports caused by changes in demand in the market sense — changes in demand, that is, due to increases or decreases in prices. There are two ways in which it is possible for prices of imports and exports to be affected by an export of capital. The first to be considered is that caused by the effect on exchange rates.

Any attempt to transfer funds from one country to another is first felt on the exchange market. An increase in the demand for foreign bills without a corresponding increase in the supply drives the rate of exchange up. This increase in exchange rates makes French goods cheaper to the foreign importer and foreign goods more costly to the French importer. The change in costs presumably increases exports and decreases imports, thereby helping to increase the export excess. In the opinion of several writers the movement of exchange rates between the gold points thus acts as an important medium of adjustment. But how effective is this factor? How great a change in costs can be wrought by changes in exchange rates? [1]

[1] Professor Viner, commenting on Professor Hollander's claim that an unfavorable movement of exchanges will induce an excess of exports, writes: ". . . exchange rates cannot operate *at all* (in affecting the course of trade) except at the beginning of the period of borrowing, in the manner described by Hollander" (op. cit., p. 151 ff.). He goes on to explain that "Altho . . . a favorable rate of exchange may be expected, at the inception of borrowings, to co-operate with the effect on prices of the import of gold in stimulating imports and checking exports, variations in the exchanges exhaust their direct influence, in adjusting the balance of indebtedness to continued borrowings occurring at an even rate, at the beginnings of the borrowings, when a fall in the foreign exchanges is first a preliminary to the import of gold and then accompanies the import of gold. Once the prices in borrowing and lending countries have been adjusted to their proper relative levels, gold imports cease, and exchanges return to parity. The balance of payments is equalized, but the balance of indebtedness is not."

Viner's statement that when price levels such as will induce an excess of exports equal to the flow of foreign investments are once established, the exchange rates — in so far as foreign investments were the only factor disturbing the equilibrium — would return to parity assumes as a fact the very point questioned. The claim of Hollander and others is that an unfavorable movement of exchanges will induce an excess of exports that will in many cases be sufficient to equalize the balance of payments. They hold that this equalization may be partly or wholly attained before the gold export point is reached, depending upon the amount of the loan and the extent of short-term lending attracted by the heightened exchange rates. If gold does flow, it acts *together with* the increased export surplus, caused directly by the heightened exchange rates, to liquidate the adverse balance of payments.

The increase in the demand for bills (caused by foreign lending or increased imports) will be satisfied by an increased supply arising out of merchandise exports and gold flows. Speculative transactions, by exerting a downward pressure on exchange rates, will, if their volume is great enough, keep exchange rates from rising. But if the volume of speculative transactions should be so great as to do this, it would not only postpone the possible adjustment that would occur thru the influence of exchange rates directly on prices, but it would also prevent gold flows. If gold flows do not occur, the gold-flow-price mechanism does not operate. In short, when speculative transactions are so great as to prevent exchange rates from rising to the gold export point, they also prevent the change in price levels claimed by Viner to be the necessary link in adjustment. If, therefore, adjustment is being brought about, it must be — according to Viner — because gold flows have occurred. Since gold flows usually occur only when the exchange rate is at one of the gold points, it follows that exports become cheaper (to the foreigner) and imports more expensive (to the lending country). The ensuing merchandise and gold movements together may bring about adjustment without the assistance of changes in price levels. The fact that exchange rates are not always at one of the gold points might

The countries which traded most with France before the war were England, Germany, Belgium, and the United States. All of them being on the gold standard during the period covered by this study, the movements of the exchange rates between these countries and France were confined within the narrow limits of the gold points. But the maximum difference — the difference between the gold points — is not necessarily the measure of the difference in cost to importers resulting from an export of capital; that is, the exchange rate is not necessarily fixed at the gold import point when the capital export takes place, nor at the gold export point when capital exports decline. An examination of the exchange rates in Paris on New York, on London, and on Berlin shows that between 1880 and 1913 the changes in any one year were as follows:

Exchanges	Maximum	Minimum	Average
Dollar	1.5 %	.42 %	.8 %
Sterling	.83	.27	.55
Mark	.92	.3	.62

In only five years — 1891, 1893, 1897, 1899, 1907 — were there differences (between the high and low for the year) in dollar exchange of more than one per cent; in only four years — 1890, 1893, 1906, 1907 — were differences greater than .67 per cent in sterling exchange; and in only two years — 1901, 1905 — was the difference in mark exchange greater than .8 per cent. Records of weekly exchange rates show, moreover, that the period of extremes in rates of exchange rarely lasted more than a few months.

be held to indicate that because of the interference of short-time movements the adjustment of balances operates in spurts. It is to be remembered that the monthly flow of long-time foreign loans or of merchandise movements is not even, nor is it closely predictable, and that altho over a period of several years the net outgo of capital may be fairly steady, the weekly fluctuations are not small. Viner's qualification with regard to "continued borrowing at an even rate" (see above) hardly strengthens his position, because an even rate of borrowing rarely, if ever, occurs. Merchandise and gold movements may achieve conditions of equilibrium without the mechanism of gold flows affecting price levels. If, therefore, merchandise movements of such volume are possible, there seems to be no ground for Viner's contention that exchange movements can affect international trade only at the start of lending operations. There still remains the question: *can commodity movements of such volume be induced directly by movements of exchanges?*

In the year 1907, for illustration, — 1907 was the year of widest fluctuations for both sterling and dollar exchange in Paris from 1890 to 1909, — the high and the low for dollar exchange in Paris

TABLE 27

ANNUAL HIGH AND LOW RATES OF EXCHANGE IN PARIS ON NEW YORK, LONDON, AND BERLIN, 1890–1909 [1]

	New York			London			Berlin		
Year	High	Low	Difference	High	Low	Difference	High	Low	Difference
1890	520.	514.5	5.5	25.35	25.15	.2	124.17	123.16	1.01
1891	521.5	514.	7.5	25.31	25.18	.13	124.39	123.47	.92
1892	517.5	514.5	3.5	25.22	25.14	.08	123.76	123.09	.67
1893	520.	513.5	6.5	25.30	25.11	.19	123.84	123.02	.82
1894	517.5	514.5	3.	25.20	25.13	.07	123.56	123.08	.48
1895	515.	513.	2.	25.28	25.14	.2	123.54	123.08	.48
1896	516.	512.	4.	25.32	25.15	.17	123.56	122.74	.82
1897	517.5	517.5	4.5	25.30	25.09	.21	123.75	123.08	.67
1898	520.5	517.5	3.	25.33	25.22	.11	123.91	123.22	.69
1899	520.	514.	6.	25.34	25.17	.17	123.59	122.96	.63
1900	518.	514.	4.	25.25	25.08	.17	123.02	122.52	.50
1901	518.5	513.5	5.	25.24	25.09	.15	123.59	122.53	1.06
1902	516.5	514.	2.5	25.22	25.11	.11	123.08	122.55	.43
1903	519.5	514.	5.5	25.20	25.11	.09	123.53	122.52	1.01
1904	518.	513.5	4.5	25.26	25.10	.16	123.66	122.65	1.01
1905	518.	514.	4.	25.22	25.07	.15	123.66	122.52	1.14
1906	520.	514.5	5.5	25.28	25.09	.19	123.22	122.40	.80
1907	522.5	514.5	8.	25.3	25.12	.21	123.41	122.44	.97
1908	517.	514.7	2.2	25.20	25.09	.11	123.25	122.62	.63
1909	517.2	515.	2.2	25.24	25.10	.14	123.31	122.56	.75

[1] Sight exchange. 1890–1898 high and low of the first Monday of each month. 1899–1909 high and low of quotations on the same day of each week. Source: U. S. Nat. Monetary Commission, Senate Document No. 578, 1910.

	New York		London		Berlin	
	Francs	Per cent of Par	Francs	Per cent of Par	Francs	Per cent of Par
Average Difference ...	4.4	.8	.14	.55	.77	.62
Greatest Difference....	8.	1.5	.21	.83	1.14	.92
Smallest Difference ...	2.	.42	.07	.27	.48	.3
Highest Rate	522.5	..	25.35	..	124.39	..
Lowest Rate	512.	..	25.07	..	122.40	..
Difference	9.5	1.8	.28	1.11	1.99	1.6

was 5.225 and 5.145, but during twenty-eight weeks in the year the exchange was quoted between the narrow limits of 5.16 and 5.185. Sterling exchange likewise showed a similar tendency away from extremes. The sterling rate in that year reached 25.33 and 25.125, but during twenty-one weeks of the year exchange quo-

tations fluctuated between 25.16 and 25.24. The change of one per cent in cost of exchange referred to in the foregoing discussion operated, it is clear, only at times and only for short periods. During most of the time the differences in cost were less. On the basis of these figures one per cent would be a very liberal estimate of the changes in cost usually possible from movements of exchange rates. Any change, therefore, in French merchandise imports or exports arising from movements of the exchange rates must have been induced by a variation in cost to the importer of not more than one per cent. How potent is such a slight change in costs on the quantity of merchandise exported and imported?

Increase in French exports consequent upon a drop in the price of those exports may occur in one of two ways. There may be a substitution of French goods for goods usually purchased elsewhere. For example, a drop in exchange on Paris may cause an English importer to shift some purchases from Germany to France. Or there may be a change in the volume of foreign purchases of French articles customarily used. Thus a drop in exchange on Paris may cause an English importer to increase his purchases of Burgundy wine. At the same time (in France) the increase of one per cent in the cost of imports will cause some French goods to be substituted for foreign goods.

The expectation that a shift in purchases from one country to another may be induced by a one per cent change in cost to the importer presupposes a very unusual set of conditions: first, that the seller accepts the risks of exchange, for, if he does not, the one per cent gain to the buyer becomes uncertain, since the buyer may find that by the time the goods are shipped the exchange rate has changed, necessarily to his disadvantage;[1] secondly, that the commodity is so highly standardized, or substitutes are so close, that a difference of one per cent will make a buyer shift from a seller in one country to a seller in another; third, that the calculation of terms of credit, of cost and service in shipment, of brands, of business relations with buyers, is conducted with such nicety

[1] Since the maximum gain is one per cent, any change from that maximum must necessarily operate to make French exports cheaper to the foreign buyer by something less than one per cent.

that a difference of one per cent will make an importer shift some or all of his purchases from a British to a French exporter; and finally that the spread between the prices of competing commodities fluctuates only within and because of changes in exchange rates.

The second and third conditions make it obvious that the only commodities that can possibly be affected by fluctuations in the exchange rates within the gold points are the most highly standardized international commodities, such as silver bullion, wheat, cotton, wool, pig iron, certain chemicals, and similar homogeneous raw materials and foodstuffs. Manufactured and most semi-manufactured commodities are immediately ruled out. The differences in construction, quality, and appearance make it virtually impossible for a price difference of less than one per cent to be the determining factor in the choice of manufacturer. Foodstuffs and raw materials that differ in quality according to the country from which they come are also ruled out. There remain, at best, only the very highly standardized commodities, and of those only such as can be purchased in more than one country at the same costs, including transportation. And among these highly standardized international commodities the importance of one per cent in the cost varies with each commodity. Silver bullion, for example, is bought and sold on a very small margin of profit; here a one per cent difference in cost is a very important factor because of the relative unimportance of all factors except price. A one per cent change in the cost of pig iron or of coal, on the other hand, is not nearly so important, because of the relatively important role played by transportation costs. If Denmark, for instance, purchased silver bullion from England, a one-half per cent drop in franc exchange might be enough to induce Denmark to purchase her silver bullion in France in spite of the higher transportation cost. But that one-half per cent difference in cost would not induce Denmark to import coal from France instead of from England, because so small a change would hardly be a sufficient factor to offset transportation considerations.

Moreover, transportation cost is only one of several elements which affect the importance of the one per cent difference in cost to the importer. The moment such matters as differences in terms of purchase, significant differences in service, length of time consumed in transportation, methods of packing, port of export, reputation of exporter, have to be considered, the importance of a one per cent difference in price shrinks.[1] Again, most of these highly standardized commodities fluctuate in price almost hourly. The range covered in one day in the grain, cotton, wool markets is very frequently more than one per cent, whereas the range of fluctuation in those and other standardized commodities over a week or month is so much greater as to make the one per cent range of fluctuations in price due to exchange movements a comparatively unimportant matter.

Notwithstanding all these qualifications, it is to be admitted that there may have been some French commodities the movements of which, like those of silver bullion, were sensitive to a one per cent change in cost to the importer. What portion of French imports and exports could have been classed under this head? About 55 per cent of French exports were manufactured articles, consisting principally of textiles of silk, cotton, and wool, of jewelry, notions, artificial flowers, perfumes, and fancy articles made of leather, fur, and paper. These are the most unstandardized of all articles, unstandarized in the sense that color, design, fashion, workmanship, package, and brand are the significant factors in the articles, the very factors that permit of the least objective measurement. Certainly one could not expect these French products to have competed so closely with *foreign* substitutes that a difference of one per cent or less in cost of exchange would have made foreign importers shift to or from competing articles in other countries. The remaining 45 per cent of French exports were made up of 25 per cent raw materials and 20 per cent foodstuffs. The latter consist chiefly of wines, sugar, butter, cheese, fancy table fruits, and fish. Of

[1] Moreover, if there were commodities which satisfied the above requirements of international competition and were affected by so slight a change in price, the shift from one country to another of the foreign demand for these commodities would tend to make the spread between their prices even smaller and thereby to reduce the advantage.

these the only commodity in which taste, appearance, seasons, and brands play a minor role because of the possibility of objective standards are sugar and perhaps butter. Raw materials exported by France consist largely of skins, furs, wool, silk, lumber, and iron.[1] Curiously, every one of these commodities plays a large part in the imports as well as in the exports of France, a phenomenon easily explained by differences in transportation costs and differences in quality and type of material. Wool raised in France is not of the same quality as wool raised in Argentina or in England, and it is difficult to believe that the spread between the different grades was so close that a one per cent change would have led a textile manufacturer to use one type of wool rather than another. Similarly, it is unlikely that a Swiss importer of silk would have imported Italian silk rather than French. On the whole it would appear that the percentage of French exports that might have been sensitive to movements in exchange rates was extremely limited.

The situation as regards French imports is somewhat different. If the French importer is to decrease foreign purchases because of increase in the foreign exchange rate, he does not have a choice of substituting that commodity by similar commodities purchased from other foreign countries; he can substitute it only by domestic commodities. The principal French imports are wool, cotton, silk, coal, oil, lumber, furs, wines, coffee, metals, and chemicals, materials which are not only consumed at home, but are used in the production of finished or semi-finished exports. France's demand for these products is therefore partly determined by the foreign demand for the finished products. For many of these imports France has no close substitutes. For others domestic substitutes do exist, but a transfer of demand to these domestic substitutes would cause their price to rise and thereby reduce the incentive of both domestic and foreign purchasers to prefer French raw materials. The supply of French raw materials must be very elastic indeed to prevent an increase

[1] France produced some silver bullion, but not nearly enough for her domestic needs. Some silver bullion was exported, but the quantities were too small to have been of importance.

in demand from raising the price at least a fraction of one per cent. Certainly the domestic supply of foodstuffs in any one year is hardly so elastic, and the slightest increase in demand would react on the price and wipe out any slight advantage due to exchange rates.

But even if a decrease of one per cent in the price of franc exchange to the foreign importer may not be sufficient to induce him to buy substitutes in France, would it not be sufficient to call forth increased foreign consumption of French goods? Theoretically a decrease in price increases the demand — in the market sense — for all commodities except those for which the demand is perfectly inelastic. Theoretically, that is, a decrease in price of certain French commodities to the foreigner should lead to their increased foreign consumption, and the increase of price of foreign goods to the Frenchman should result in decreased imports. How valid is this supposition? The demand line usually drawn to depict demand schedules is continuous, but in reality it is merely a series of separated points joined together for the purpose of convenience. How far apart are the points actually? More silk stockings would be purchased at $1.25 per pair than at $1.75, but it does not follow that more would be purchased at $1.74. The demand for coal, sugar, rubber, and silk is not inelastic; yet would a factory or home use more coal if a ton cost $6.20 instead of $6.25? Or would a householder use more sugar at 20 pounds for $1.04 than at 20 pounds for $1.05? How great must the reduction in price be before the consumer reacts in the shape of increased consumption? The reduction necessary differs, to be sure, with each article, but it is hard to believe that the consumer's demand for almost any commodity is sensitive to a change of one per cent.

The claim that French merchandise movements were little affected by fluctuations in the exchange rates receives support from Professor Taussig's discussion of the effect of exchange rate fluctuations on commodity movements:

> Surely it cannot be maintained that such transactions (i.e. loans) would bring about a movement of commodities from the lending country merely thru the disturbances of foreign exchange within the limits of the gold points.

Fluctuations in exchange rates within these limits are never more than a minor factor as regards commodity exports and imports.[1]

This point of view is concurred in by Professors Viner and Angell. But the question can hardly be settled by deductive reasoning. Either large importers are influenced in their decisions as to quantity and place of buying by changes in the exchange rate or they are not. They, it seems, are the sole authority on this point. The few importers interviewed by the writer claimed that they were not, and their belief was that other importers also were not influenced by exchange rates.[2] Lacking evidence to the contrary, we are led to maintain, in accordance with the reasoning above, that the movements of French exchange rates exerted an unimportant influence on the movements of French imports and exports from and to countries on a gold standard.

In the matter of trade with countries on a paper or a gold exchange standard, however, French imports and exports may very well have been affected by fluctuations in the exchange rates. The fluctuations not being restricted within the narrow limits of the gold points become in trade with such countries a significant cause of changes in the volume of trade. Many of the heavy borrowers of French funds were in this class. Fluctuations in exchange rates of 5 to 10 per cent in any one year (during most of the period) were common, and must undoubtedly have served as an important factor in the adjustment of balances between France and those countries. Altho they bought little from France, these countries sold her much — over one-fourth of her imports came from countries not on a gold standard — and in their case the adjustment must have in part operated thru the checking or stimulating effect of widely moving exchange rates on the French imports. Just how important this influence was in the adjustment of the French balance of payments it would be impossible

[1] A Rejoinder, Quar. Jour. of Econ., 1918, Vol. XXXII, p. 694.

[2] Several large dealers in cotton and wool stated to the writer that other market factors are so much more important that movements of exchange rates within the gold points are a negligible factor. In the opinion of an officer of a very large bank, a man with thirty years' experience in the foreign bills department, exchange rates in gold standard countries play no rôle at all in the decisions of foreign or domestic wool, cotton, or grain importers.

to determine without at least separate price and quantity indices for the imports from each of the important borrowers. That it did help in the adjustment is not to be overlooked.

We now turn to the final means thru which capital exports may have affected the movements of merchandise: changes in price levels. To evaluate this influence we must examine the interrelationship of the movements of capital exports, of prices, of the physical volume of trade, and of the total value of imports and exports.

According to the orthodox explanation of the mechanism of adjustment we should expect that an increase in the exports of capital would in time cause the price of export commodities to decrease relatively to the price of imports. We should further expect that an increase in the price of imports relative to the price of exports would stimulate the sale of exports and check the purchase of imports. We should expect to find a relative increase in the physical quantities of exports to continue until the total values of exports and imports would be such as to bring about the necessary equilibrium in the balance of payments.

We find in the case of France some evidence of such a sequence. The movements of French capital exports and the movements of French import and export prices are tabulated on page 252 and plotted on the chart, page 167.[1] The price movements are represented by a single curve, obtained by dividing the import by the export price indices. A rise in the curve represents a relative increase in import prices; a drop represents a relative decrease. According to the orthodox explanation we should expect to find the price curve rising and falling with the curve of capital exports, but the correlation we do find is not very high. In the years immediately succeeding the imposition of the Meline tariff, there is an inverse correlation, possibly to be explained by the fact that the decrease in the French import price was, so far as France was concerned, purely nominal because of the imposition in 1892 of

[1] The import and export price series and the index of the physical volume of imports and exports upon which the comparisons are based are those constructed especially for this study. The construction of these series is discussed in detail in Chap. X, where they are compared with other French series.

TABLE 28

RATIO OF IMPORT DUTIES TO IMPORT VALUES OF FRANCE, 1880–1913

Year	Value of Imports	Import Duties	Percentage of Total Imports
1880	5111	331	6.4
1881	4934	327	6.6
1882	4900	328	6.7
1883	4876	329	6.7
1884	4406	333	7.5
1885	4132	368	8.9
1886	4254	324	7.6
1887	4076	334	8.1
1888	4174	381	9.1
1889	4387	355	8.1
1890	4520	361	8.
1891	4852	393	8.1
1892	4254	430	10.1
1893	3915	452	11.6
1894	3927	466	11.8
1895	3820	399	10.4
1896	3932	423	10.7
1897	4114	430	10.5
1898	4572	476	10.4
1899	4655	441	9.4
1900	4839	427	8.7
1901	4504	383	8.
1902	4534	381	8.4
1903	4933	458	9.3
1904	4644	378	8.1
1905	4951	412	8.7
1906	5797	450	8.1
1907	6395	479	7.4
1908	5808	469	8.1
1909	6438	498	7.8
1910	7352	557	7.6
1911	8242	747	9.
1912	8414	681	8.1
1913	8626	742	8.5

heavy import duties.[1] The burden of these may be judged from a comparison of the tariff receipts before and after their application (see table, page 166). In 1891 import duties were 8.1 per cent of the total value of the imports, while in 1893 they were 11.6 per cent, an increase of 30 per cent. The effect of such duties

CHART 5

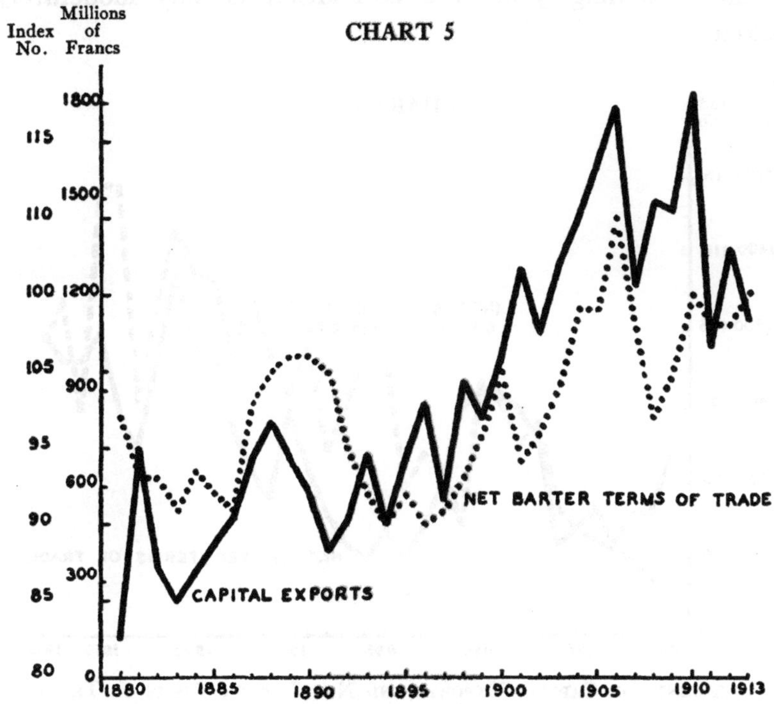

Capital Exports and Net Barter Terms of Trade of France, 1880–1913

—— Capital exports. ···· Net barter terms of trade.

would be to discourage imports; the downward movement, therefore, should not be interpreted as a stimulus to imports. For the lack of correlation in some of the other years, particularly noticeable in 1901 and 1908, I can offer no explanation. The correlation,

[1] The French tariff commission calculated that if the new schedule were applied to the commodities imported in 1889, the import duties would have been under the general tariff 212 million francs greater and under the minimum tariff 115 millions greater, an increase of 60 and 32 per cent respectively in import duties. Cited in A. Arnaune, Le commerce extérieur et les tarifs de douane (Paris, 1911), p. 330.

however, becomes somewhat more marked if instead of comparing the price series with the capital exports as measured by the direct method we compare them with capital exports as measured by the indirect method, that is with the net credit balances. The lack of correlation after the Meline tariff still remains, and for the remaining years the correlation is only moderately marked.

CHART 6

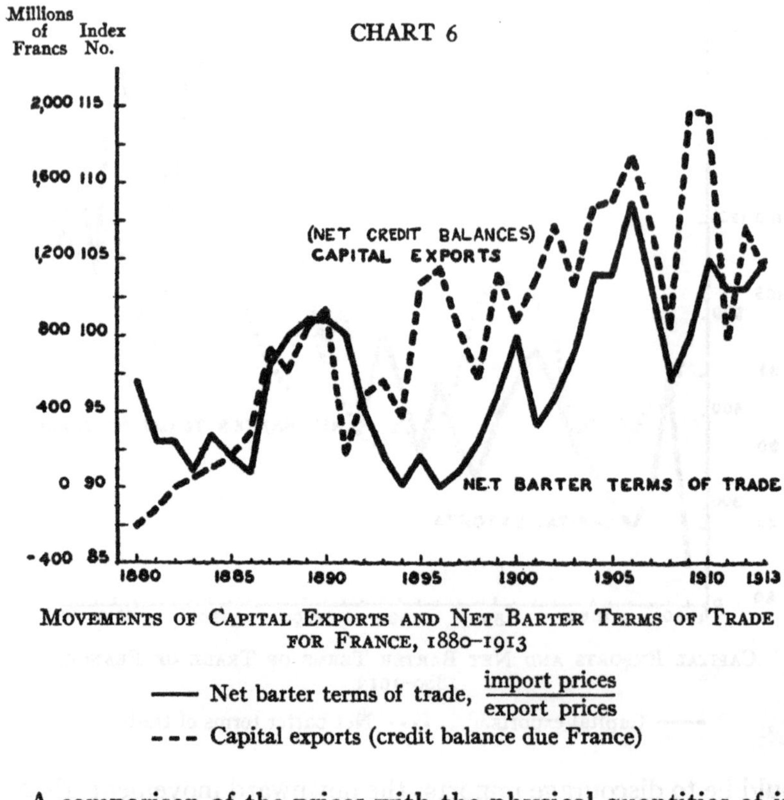

Movements of Capital Exports and Net Barter Terms of Trade for France, 1880–1913

—— Net barter terms of trade, $\frac{\text{import prices}}{\text{export prices}}$

- - - Capital exports (credit balance due France)

A comparison of the prices with the physical quantities of imports and exports shows, on the whole, the expected correspondence. The first marked change in the relative movement of import and export prices appears in 1886. From that year to 1889 the relative rise in import prices is accompanied by a relative decline in the physical quantities of imports. From 1891 to 1896 the price of imports drops sharply, but there is in those years no accompanying increase in imports except during 1894. The increase in that year, it will be remembered, was due largely to poor domestic crops. The probable reason for the lack of increase in the physical quantities of imports notwithstanding considerably decreased prices has already been suggested: import duties negated the drop in prices to the French consumer. From 1896 to 1900 import prices rise more rapidly than export prices. We find in those years a relative increase in the volume of exports, an in-

CHART 7

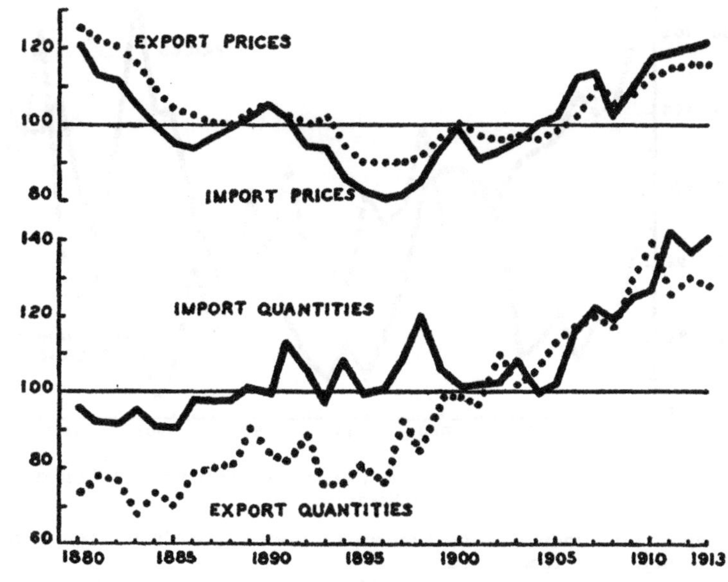

French Import and Export Prices and Quantities, 1880–1913

crease which would be even more pronounced were it not for the large imports of foodstuffs in 1896, a year of crop failure. From 1901 to 1904 the import prices again rise more rapidly and export quantities again increase. In this case, again, the relative increase would be more marked if allowance were made for the poor domestic crops. From 1908 to 1912 the movements are also in accordance with expectation. In the years 1906, 1907, and 1913, however, the reverse is true; the relative rise in export prices is accompanied by a relative rise, instead of fall, in export quantities. But with the exception of these years the inverse correlation between movements of price and movements of quantities is sufficiently strong to suggest that the movements of French import and export quantities were sensitive to price changes and moved in the expected direction.

This sensitivity, it must be remembered, is significant only when the movements of quantities are large enough to become apparent in the merchandise balance of trade and when, more-

CHART 8

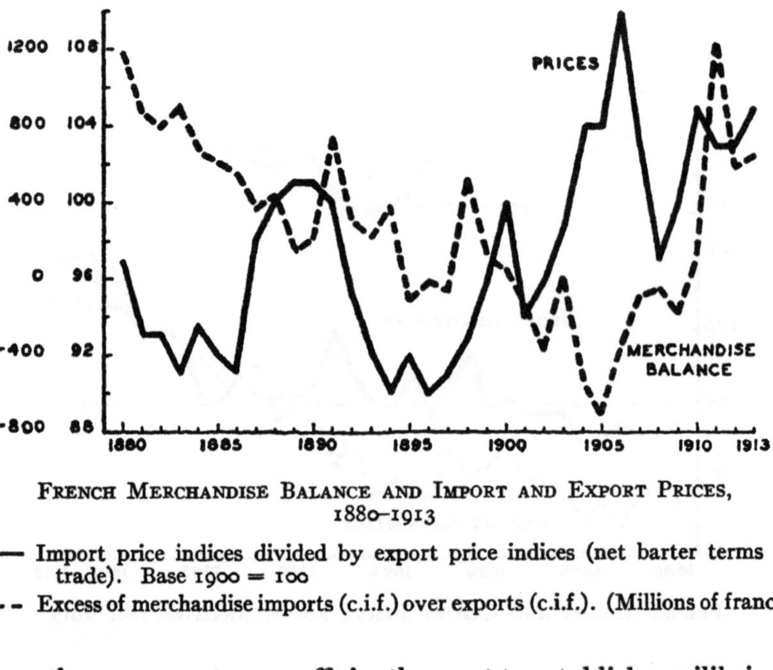

French Merchandise Balance and Import and Export Prices, 1880–1913

—— Import price indices divided by export price indices (net barter terms of trade). Base 1900 = 100

- - - Excess of merchandise imports (c.i.f.) over exports (c.i.f.). (Millions of francs)

over, the movements are sufficiently great to establish equilibrium in the balance of payments. A relative rise in the price of imports should be accompanied by a fall in the *excess* of merchandise imports.

A comparison of price movements with the movement of the excess of merchandise imports in the chart above shows this to be true in the majority of the years, but for the period as a whole the inverse correlation is certainly not high. If allowance were made for the years of bad domestic crops — 1880, 1891, 1898, 1908, 1911 — when imports would be expected to increase irrespective of price movements, a higher correlation would be discernible. The period immediately following the inauguration of the high tariff policy again forms the most marked exception in the inverse correlation; a relative decrease in the value of imports occurs notwithstanding a relative decrease in the import price level. Except for these years, price movements and the excess of merchandise imports can be considered to correlate fairly well. We have already noted that the movements of merchandise balances correlate favorably both in direction and amplitude with the movement of capital exports. (See Chart 4.)

Altogether the evidence furnished by the movements of French import and export prices, quantities, and values seems to offer some indication of a causal relationship between capital exports and movements of merchandise, yet it is not marked and in any case there is nothing in the correlations observed which offers proof that the price movements *were caused* by capital exports. Indeed, the lack of correlation noted earlier between gold movements and capital exports casts serious doubt upon the possibility. If merchandise exports increased *because* capital exports did so, thru what medium was the change in demand (in either the schedule or the market sense) brought about? It is true that in many of the years gold movements may have been the instrument; gold imports declined when capital exports increased. But why did this not occur in all the years? And what proof is there that when it did occur, gold movements served to modify sectional price levels? For evidence on this point it is necessary to examine the French banking and monetary data in all their possible connections with capital exports. Discussion of these data is undertaken in the next chapter.

CHAPTER VIII

SPECIE MOVEMENTS, BANK DISCOUNT RATE, AND BANK RESERVES

IN ATTEMPTING to find evidence of a causal relationship between capital exports and sectional prices we must examine the movements and determine the relationships of bank reserves, discount rates, note and deposit liabilities, bank portfolios, and quantity of the circulating media. We first turn to a consideration of specie movements and the reserves of the Bank of France.

We find that the Bank of France was virtually the sole depository of the specie reserve of all the French banks; specie imported into France went either into the vaults of the Bank of France or into hand to hand circulation. Thruout the period under survey specie imports were in excess of specie exports. In only five years, all before 1900, was there an annual export excess, and this was comparatively small. For the five years it totalled only 600 million francs; whereas the specie import excess during the remaining years reached the total of 5.5 billions.[1] Of the 5.5 billions received, about 1.8 billions were used for industrial purposes; the remainder went into circulation or into the reserves of the Bank of France. Banks other than the Bank of France kept in their vaults only enough cash for daily needs, relying for additional needs entirely upon their ability to rediscount commercial paper at the Bank of France. Even the savings banks thruout France kept in their vaults only a minimum of till money. The savings received were deposited, in compliance with the national law, with the Caisse des Dépôts et Consignations, a government institution, which likewise kept only a very small amount

[1] The excess recorded was 6.6 billions, but this sum included 1.1 billions of silver bullion, which was not freely coined and which could not serve as reserve against note issue. Silver bullion was a commodity that differed in no respect from other metals in its effect upon banking and monetary movements. Limited amounts of silver, legally prescribed, were used in the production of the five franc silver pieces, but the amount so used was not dependent upon the amount of silver available.

of cash on hand.[1] Cash in excess of daily needs was invested in Treasury bonds and similar short-time investments, or else deposited in either the Bank of France or the French Treasury. The latter, in turn, kept its cash in the Bank of France.

The Bank of France was thus virtually the sole depository of all cash in France except such funds as were needed by the banks for their current demands. What this amount was it is impossible to tell accurately, since none of the bank statements distinguish between cash in their own vaults and sums on deposit in the Bank of France; the reserves all appear under the one heading "cash on hand and in the Bank of France." The fluctuations in this item for the four large commercial banks (which held over three-fourths of the total commercial deposits) covered a range of from seven to twelve per cent; but the total before 1900 was less than 300 millions, and only once after 1900 did it pass 500 millions.[2] The proportion of this "cash on hand and in the Bank of France" kept in the Bank of France could conservatively be estimated at one-third. Altho the Bank of France paid no interest on such deposits, commercial banks found it expedient to keep sizeable accounts there for convenience in transfers and also because their rediscounting privilege was to some extent dependent upon the size of their deposits.[3] Of this two-thirds — estimated as the pro-

[1] With deposit liabilities of over four billions, its balance sheet in 1908 showed only one million in cash on hand. This small proportion was possible because none of its deposits were demand deposits.

[2] The holdings of other commercial banks were relatively unimportant. The Crédit Lyonnais, Société Générale, Comptoir Nationale d'Escompte, and Crédit Industriel et Commercial with their hundreds of branches covered almost every town in France. In 1907 they had over 75 per cent of the total commercial deposits, and their proportion was on the constant increase.

[3] There appears to be a difference of opinion among the French bankers as to the extent to which the discount privilege with the Bank of France depended upon the size of the account. Compare, for example, the following answers by M. Pallain, Governor of the Bank of France, and by M. Moret, manager of the Banque de Paris et des Pays Bas.

Q. Does the amount and the character of credit granted to other banks depend on the amount and the character of their accounts at the Bank of France?

A. (M. Pallain) There is no fixed rule, and although the balance of the account is not a matter of indifference, it is more especially the quality of the paper presented which fixes the extent of the credit. . . . (continued on page following)

portion of cash holdings kept in the commercial banks — probably about 15 per cent after 1900 and 20 per cent before 1900 was in the form of specie.[1] If, then, the amount of cash — specie and notes — kept as till money in all banks outside the Bank of France be generously estimated at one-half billion, the amount of *specie* in the till money was (on the basis of the percentages of specie to notes found in the monetary investigations) under 100 millions after 1900 and still less before 1900 — a sum constituting less than 5 per cent of specie holdings of the Bank of France. The reserves of the Bank of France thus remain the only important specie bank reserves in the whole of France. To trace the effect of specie *imports* on specie *reserves*, then, it is necessary to follow only the specie holdings of the Bank of France.

Q. Then you would grant discount to a bank without taking into consideration the importance of its balance with you?

A. That is not exact. And the council, when it decides discounts, has every day before it the statement of the balances of all our clients, and this examination certainly exercises an influence on the extent of credit given.

Interview with M. Moret:

Q. If you were to carry but a very small balance at the Bank of France and should go to them with a request for a very large discount, would they consider the balance that you carried with them; that is, would they say, "We cannot extend to you this amount because you are not entitled to it"?

A. No; they would not think of that. . . .

Q. The Bank of France is practically indifferent as to the amount of money you carry on deposit with them?

A. Entirely. — Monetary Interviews, pp. 207 and 271.

[1] The proportion of notes to specie was determined by the local demand. An indication of what this demand was may be obtained from the results of the government monetary inquiries. In these a detailed inventory was made of a day's receipts and, in some cases, of the total cash holdings of the Bank of France, of savings banks, and of the larger commercial banks. The composition of the money inventoried was as follows:

	Gold Coin	Silver 5 Franc Pieces	Notes
1885	22 %	10 %	67 %
1891	13	6	80
1897	11	4.5	84
1903	9.3	3.6	87
1909	8.2	2.8	87

Enquête sur la circulation monétaire et fiduciaire, September 15, 1897; October 15, 1903; October 16, 1909; Rapport au Ministre des Finances, Vols. 1898, 1904–1910.

The annual movements of specie (exclusive of silver bullion)[1] into and out of France and into and out of the Bank of France appear to fall into two distinct periods: 1880 to 1901, and 1902 to 1911. The movements are tabulated on page 176 and are plotted below. In the first period the movements of specie into France and into the reserves of the Bank of France are fairly

CHART 9

ANNUAL INCREASE OF SPECIE RESERVES OF THE BANK OF FRANCE COMPARED WITH ANNUAL SPECIE IMPORT BALANCES, 1880–1913

- - - Excess of specie imports (exclusive of silver bullion)
—— Increase of reserves in the Bank of France

close together, tho in some years the movement of reserves lags one year behind that of imports. During this first period the cumulative excess of specie imports (exclusive of silver bullion) was 1.6 billions and the increase in the Bank of France reserves 1.7 billions. Hence all the specie entering France from 1880 to 1901 found its way within a year or less into the Bank of France to remain there permanently. The reason for this flow of gold into the Bank of France reserves was not a lack of demand for more

[1] See footnote, p. 172.

TABLE 29

ANNUAL INCREASE OF THE GOLD AND SILVER RESERVES OF THE BANK OF FRANCE COMPARED WITH ANNUAL FRENCH IMPORTS AND EXPORTS OF GOLD AND SILVER, 1880–1913

(Millions of francs)

	Increase of Reserves in the Bank of France (Annual Average)			Excess of Specie Imports (Exclusive of Silver Bullion)		
Year	Gold	Silver	Total	Gold	Silver	Total
1880 ...	−239	98	−141	−213	32	−181
1881 ...	−124	−27	−150	10	17	28
1882 ...	303	80	122	91	−37	51
1883 ...	76	−94	−18	−70	−19	−89
1884 ...	38	−31	7	46	44	90
1885 ...	82	59	141	42	92	133
1886 ...	199	47	247	63	36	100
1887 ...	−113	52	−62	−165	26	−135
1888 ...	−101	40	−60	−91	38	−43
1889 ...	64	34	87	208	2	210
1890 ...	104	11	115	−133	22	−111
1891 ...	23	−2	21	127	19	146
1892 ...	268	24	282	276	20	296
1893 ...	137	−8	130	189	26	214
1894 ...	137	−8	128	354	−38	316
1895 ...	227	−19	208	9	24	33
1896 ...	−70	00	−70	−10	88	78
1897 ...	−15	−22	−37	159	−72	87
1898 ...	−88	3	−85	−114	−18	−132
1899 ...	−9	−29	−38	157	−69	88
1900 ...	237	−62	175	334	−111	223
1901 ...	207	−28	279	284	−71	213
1902 ...	138	5	143	313	−44	269
1903 ...	−56	−1	−57	194	−12	182
1904 ...	72	4	76	533	−58	481
1905 ...	290	−12	278	648	−28	620
1906 ...	−28	−53	−24	271	−55	216
1907 ...	−179	−78	−258	338	−93	245
1908 ...	245	−67	273	991	−20	920
1909 ...	578	−10	567	192	−27	165
1910 ...	−230	−32	−263	58	−88	−30
1911 ...	195	−31	−225	126	00	126
1912 ...	34	−42	−9	218	−53	165
1913 ...	103	−160	−55	590	20	610

hand to hand circulation, but a growing preference for notes as against specie. The increasing prestige of the Bank of France during the eighties and nineties and its very large gold reserves contributed greatly to this preference for the more convenient means of payment. At the same time the declining price level necessitated a smaller total volume of the means of payment.[1] Moreover, the use of checks had increased, and consequently fewer transactions had to be liquidated with specie. The result was that from 1880 to 1901 the note circulation increased from two to four billion francs, while 1.7 billions of specie flowed into the reserves.[2]

During the second period, 1901 to 1913, the situation appears to have changed radically. The movement of specie into the Bank of France reserves still parallels the movement of the import excess, — the year lag appearing in 1909 is in reality only a lag of a few months, — but the spread between the two movements becomes very large. Specie reserves of the Bank of France increased only 400 millions during this latter period, while the excess of specie imports totalled 4 billions. Of the 3.6 billions which did not go into the Bank, industry consumed about 800 millions, leaving almost 3 billions for hand to hand circulation. Note circulation in the meantime increased only 1.5 billions.

[1] In 1897 there was, according to Rist, 12 per cent less circulation than in 1878.

[2] According to the monetary investigations previously referred to, the use of specie had declined from 32 per cent in 1885 to 13 per cent in 1903.

Further evidence of this preference for notes is furnished by studies made by Des Essars and by Rist of the proportion of specie to notes used in payments and receipts of the Bank of France. The proportions at various periods are as follows:

	Specie (%)	Notes (%)	Transfers (%)	Percentage of Specie to Notes
1880	5.19	31.2	63	16
1885	3.20	36.5	60	9
1890	2.46	28.8	68	8.5
1895	2.05	23.8	74	8.5
1900	2.21	29.2	68	7.5
1905	1.98	21.6	76	9.1
1910	1.57	17.9	80	8.7

From 1880 to 1895, Des Essars, Le papier et la monnaie dans la circulation, Jour. de la Soc. Stat. de Paris, May, 1896, p. 179. From 1895 to 1910, C. Rist, La circulation monétaire française et le mouvement des prix, Rev. d'Écon. Pol., 1914, Vol. 28, p. 276.

Thus for every 100 francs in notes drawn from the Bank of France, 200 francs of gold were absorbed into circulation, a decided change from the situation of the previous twenty years, when note circulation increased two billions while specie outside the Bank of France *decreased* one billion.

I have been unable to find in the contemporary writings an explanation of this surprising change in the ratio of notes to gold. Apparently the matter caused no comment, yet it merits attention because of its possible significance in connection with the attitude of the Bank of France towards gold exports. Was the change in ratio caused by a change in money habits or by some less significant circumstance? If the greatly increased demand for specie after 1900 reflected a radical change in the money habits of the French people, then much of the elasticity claimed for the Bank of France note issue was disappearing, while the need for stimulating gold imports during the period of rising prices was becoming more urgent. A preference for gold as against notes (as a medium of exchange) in the ratio of two to one would have meant, moreover, that any expansion in the means of payment based on increased gold bank reserves was much more limited.

But there is good reason to believe that the increased use of specie after 1901 was not a reflection of a change in the money habits of the people; rather it was a change necessitated by the increased need for money combined with the peculiarities of the French monetary system. The smallest note that the Bank of France could issue was for 50 francs,[1] while checks were rarely used for payments of less than 100 francs. (See page 207.) Transactions involving smaller sums were settled in gold coins of 20 or 10 francs, or in 5 franc gold or silver pieces. There were also some 100, 50, and 40 franc gold coins in circulation, but their total was less than five per cent of the specie in circulation. From 1880 to 1896 the combination of declining prices, rapidly growing preference for notes, and increased use of checks permitted such

[1] During the War of 1870, small notes of 25, 20, and 5 francs had been issued, but the Bank of France ceased to pay them out soon after the war and destroyed those it received. By 1900 the total of such notes outstanding was less than three millions.

gold as was imported to find its way quickly and permanently to the Bank of France. By 1900 the substitution of notes for coin in settling transactions had gone as far as was possible; the amount of coin in circulation was the minimum necessary for the execution of small transactions. With the increase in prices and in business activity, the amount of coins necessarily increased. Notes increased as well, but a growing portion of the transactions formerly executed with notes was now being settled by checks and by "transfers." [1]

The only other interpretation of the increasing absorption of gold coins would be increased hoarding. But this seems very unlikely. In the first decade of the century hoarding in France was generally believed to be on the decline. The confidence of the French people in the soundness of the Bank of France and their pride in its large specie reserves was greater in the first decade of the twentieth century than at any time before. It was commonly stated that the excellent reputation of the Bank of France and the spread of carefully protected savings institutions that tapped even the smallest communities were drawing specie from the famous "bas de laine." [2] It would seem, then, that the increased use of gold after 1901 was due not to hoarding nor to a change in money habits, but rather to the need for small units of currency.

[1] The latter increased from 100 billions in 1900 to 300 billions in 1913, while the value of checks cleared at the Paris clearing house increased from 10 to 37 billions. (See Table 53.) Very few of the checks were used for transactions of less than 100 francs. Further evidence that the larger transactions were being executed preferably with checks or transfers is the rapid decrease in the proportion of total note issue formed by notes of 200 francs or over. These decreased from 75 per cent of the total note issue in 1880 to 32 per cent in 1913. From 1900 to 1913 the increase in the issue of 1000 and 500 franc notes was negligible; 100 franc notes increased from 2150 to 2970 millions; 50 franc notes from 540 to 920 millions. These figures show that the smaller units of currency were increasing more rapidly than the larger. It thus appears that the increased demand for specie (compared with the demand for notes) was due not to an increasing preference for specie, but to the growing use of checks and transfers for the larger transactions and to the greater volume of transactions of less than 50 francs.

[2] An increase in hoarding might be expected, also, to have caused the minting of the larger gold coins (50 and 100 franc pieces), but only a negligible amount of such coins was minted. By 1913 there had been minted only 85 millions in 100 franc pieces and 45 millions in 50 franc pieces.

Doubtless this was the view taken at the time by the authorities, as is evidenced by their apparently undismayed acceptance of the sharp decline in specie reserves from 90 per cent in 1909 to 70 per cent in 1913, the lowest point in thirty-five years. Moreover, the knowledge that the public would welcome the greater convenience of 20, 10, and 5 franc notes in place of coin no doubt

CHART 10

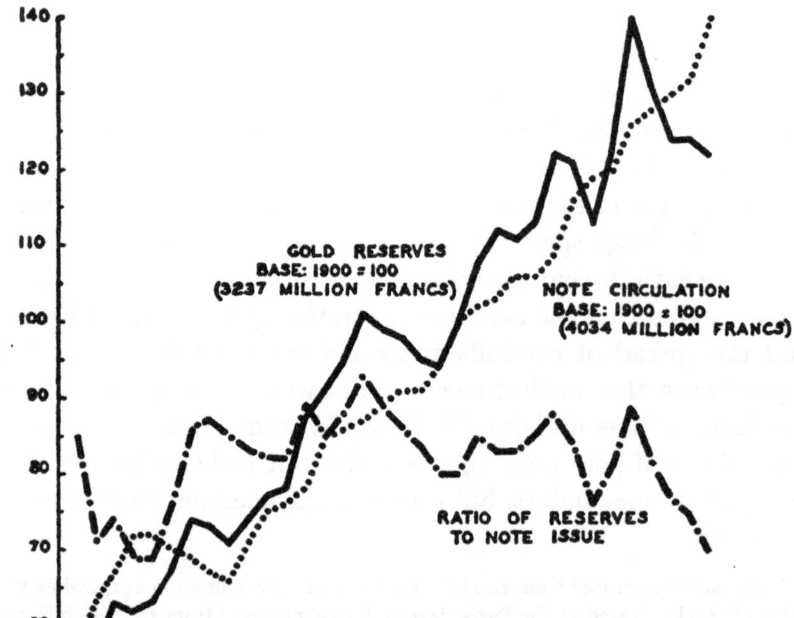

INDICES OF THE ANNUAL AVERAGES OF THE GOLD RESERVES, NOTE ISSUE, AND RATIO OF RESERVES TO NOTE ISSUE OF THE BANK OF FRANCE, 1880–1913

helped the Bank authorities to regard with equanimity the declining gold reserves so long as the gold was going into circulation instead of abroad. They felt they could, as in 1870, easily augment their gold reserves by replacing gold coins with notes of small denomination. Indeed, as soon as there was threat of war, steps were taken to issue such notes. It is reported that just before hostilities began in 1914, the Bank of France had already

TABLE 30

RELATIVE MOVEMENTS OF ANNUAL AVERAGES OF BANK OF FRANCE RESERVES TO ITS DEMAND LIABILITIES, 1880–1913

(Base 1900 = 100)

Year	Average Reserves (Millions of francs)	Index of Reserves	Average Note Circulation (Millions of francs)	Index of Circulation	Average Deposits (Millions of francs)	Index of Deposits	Index of Deposits of 4 Banks[1]
1880 ..	1974	60	2305	57	655	90	...
1881 ..	1824	56	2576	63	819	112	...
1882 ..	2046	63	2732	67	888	121	...
1883 ..	2027	62	2926	72	558	76	...
1884 ..	2035	63	2928	72	533	73	...
1885 ..	2176	67	2846	70	540	73	...
1886 ..	2422	74	2789	69	675	92	...
1887 ..	2361	73	2719	67	614	83	...
1888 ..	2301	71	2676	66	631	86	54
1889 ..	2398	74	2876	71	881	120	50
1890 ..	2513	77	3060	75	578	79	53
1891 ..	2533	78	3084	76	676	92	57
1892 ..	2826	87	3151	78	709	97	64
1893 ..	2956	91	3445	85	532	72	61
1894 ..	3083	95	3476	86	605	82	71
1895 ..	3291	100	3526	87	749	102	66
1896 ..	3222	99	2607	89	803	110	76
1897 ..	3184	98	2687	91	712	97	81
1898 ..	3100	95	3694	91	741	101	86
1899 ..	3062	94	3820	94	684	93	91
1900 ..	3237	100	4034	100	732	100	100
1901 ..	3516	108	4115	102	647	88	104
1902 ..	3659	112	4162	103	649	88	109
1903 ..	3602	111	4310	106	593	81	120
1904 ..	3678	113	4283	106	749	102	148
1905 ..	3956	122	4408	109	829	113	145
1906 ..	3931	121	4658	116	837	114	167
1907 ..	3674	113	4800	119	736	100	151
1908 ..	3956	122	4853	120	695	95	171
1909 ..	4524	140	5079	126	798	109	179
1910 ..	4261	131	5197	128	679	93	196
1911 ..	4036	124	5243	130	737	100	205
1912 ..	4027	124	5322	132	860	117	211
1913 ..	3972	122	5665	140	829	113	229

[1] Crédit Lyonnais, etc., on December 31 of each year.

prepared and distributed to all its branches a considerable stock of 20 and 5 franc notes.[1]

Before 1910 the increase in Bank of France reserves over the greater part of the thirty-four years was so large that notwithstanding a much increased note issue the ratio of reserves to notes suffered little diminution. The fluctuations of annual averages range from 93 per cent in 1895[2] to 70 per cent in 1883 and 1913, but for twenty-five years — 1886 to 1910 — only once did the ratio drop below 80 per cent. (See tables pages 181, 183.) The major fluctuations from 1888 on were due almost entirely to changes in the specie reserve, the growth of note issue continuing without marked fluctuations in the annual average.

Notwithstanding the large gold reserves, the Bank of France did not permit any drain of specie to take place without attempting to check it. The two principal methods used to prevent the drain were (*a*) an advance in the Bank of France discount rate and (*b*) an increase in the price of gold charged by the Bank of France, this latter practice generally being referred to as the gold premium policy. Advance in the discount rate was used to check both internal and external drains, increase in the gold premium for external drains only. Before 1900 the gold premium policy was employed more frequently than the discount rate as a check to gold outflows, since it was supposed to effect its purpose without disturbing domestic business. The use of a premium on gold was possible because the Bank of France could legally redeem its notes in either French gold coin or 5 franc silver pieces.[3] Since

[1] W. Felsenhardt, La Banque de France de 1897 à nos jours (Bordeaux, 1922), p. 70.

[2] During August, 1895, the notes of the Bank of France were completely covered; the reserve ratio was 100 per cent.

[3] The 5 franc silver pieces, relics of the Latin Monetary Union, have not been coined free since 1874, nor coined at all since 1878. These coins, minted by all members of the Latin Union, — France, Belgium, Switzerland, Italy, and Greece, — circulated freely between those countries as each of them in 1885 had bound herself to a policy of gold redemption of her own 5 franc pieces. In 1903 there were estimated to be over three billion francs of these coins in France, about 500 million of which were foreign coins. The Bank of France adopted a definite policy of exporting these latter whenever possible, so that from 1880 to 1913 the exports of silver coins exceeded imports by 700 million francs.

TABLE 31

RATIO OF ANNUAL AVERAGES OF RESERVES OF THE BANK OF FRANCE TO ITS ANNUAL AVERAGE DEMAND LIABILITIES, 1880–1913

Year	Ratio to Note Circulation	Ratio to Note Circulation Plus Private Deposits	Ratio to Note Circulation Plus Total Deposits[1]
1880	85	72	66
1881	71	59	53
1882	74	63	56
1883	69	60	58
1884	69	61	58
1885	76	67	64
1886	86	74	70
1887	87	76	70
1888	85	75	69
1889	83	74	63
1890	82	70	69
1891	82	72	67
1892	89	79	73
1893	85	76	74
1894	88	78	75
1895	93	80	77
1896	89	77	73
1897	86	76	72
1898	84	74	69
1899	80	71	68
1900	80	71	68
1901	85	75	75
1902	83	76	76
1903	83	76	73
1904	85	76	73
1905	88	79	75
1906	84	75	71
1907	76	69	66
1908	81	73	71
1909	89	80	77
1910	82	76	72
1911	77	70	67
1912	75	70	65
1913	70	63	61

[1] Including deposits of the French Treasury.

the value of the silver content of 5 franc pieces was much less than the nominal value of the coin, the privilege which the Bank thus possessed gave it a measure of control over its gold holdings. Whenever the Bank of France wished to discourage gold exports, it refused to redeem its notes in French gold coin. Banks in need of gold for export then had the choice of collecting gold coins from circulation or of purchasing *at a premium* foreign gold coins or bullion from the Bank of France. When the gold premium became very high, gold coin was sometimes collected from circulation and exported.[1] But it was troublesome and expensive, as many of the coins in circulation were underweight.[2]

The attempt to prevent gold exports by means of a gold premium can be successful only for short periods. It is only when the pressure on exchange rates is temporary — such as a desire on the part of short-term lenders to take advantage of more attractive discount rates in some foreign money market — that the imposition of a gold premium can operate as an effective check to gold exports. It does so by increasing the magnitude of the range between the gold import points and the gold export points. The greater the distance between these points, the greater the risk to short-term lenders of loss from exchange movements. But the immediate risk of exchange is only one of three factors which determine the volume and direction of short-term lending. The difference in discount rates in the two markets and the expected duration of this difference are factors which may promise gains large enough to offset the deterring force of the risk of exchange. When the difference is small, — one-fourth of one per cent, say, — these factors may easily prove effective enough to cause an outflow of short-term funds. When, however, the difference between the gold points is so great as one per cent, an increase in discount rates in foreign money markets loses much of its attractive force. A spread of one per cent between the gold points makes possible a loss from the movement of exchange rates sufficient to wipe out

[1] Le Marché Financier, 1899–1900, p. x.

[2] Arnauné cites an investigation showing that 40 per cent of the coins in circulation were underweight. — La monnaie, le crédit, et le change (Paris, 1894), p. 396.

the profit to be derived from a three per cent spread in interest rates (i.e. an increase of three per cent over the domestic rate) for a period of four months. The practice of the Bank of France of charging a premium on gold when a heavy outflow threatened thus constituted a formidable barrier (when the exchange rate was "unfavorable") to the outward movement of short-term funds, and rendered the French gold holdings insensitive to movements of discount rates in foreign money markets.

The efficacy of the gold premium policy as a barrier to short-term movements becomes apparent when the record of exchange movements and spreads between French and foreign discount rates is examined. We find during the thirty-four years under survey the difference between the high and low of sterling exchange in Paris to have been 1.11 per cent. This was enough, as we have seen, to have turned a gain accruing from a three per cent higher interest rate for a period of four months into a loss of .11 per cent — provided the loan was made at the gold export point and covered at the gold import point. But the difference in interest rates between Paris and London was never maintained at that level for so long a period as four months. The spread between discount rates in Paris and Berlin and Paris and New York was in several instances so high as three per cent for four month periods, but the spread between the high and low mark and dollar exchange rates (in Paris), being higher than the sterling spread, — 1.6 per cent on Berlin and 1.8 per cent on New York, — served to offset the more attractive foreign discount rates.[1]

[1] The actual range of exchange movements does not represent the full extent of the power of the gold premium policy to discourage short-term movements. The maximum range *possible* enters into the calculation of loss and gain. The gold premium is the chief factor limiting the range between the gold points, — the larger the gold premium, the greater the range, — and the height of the gold premium was limited only by the gold value of the silver 5 franc pieces. The cost of collecting gold coins from circulation was the proximate limit to the gold premium. But in the event of a premium the market price of gold would soon rise because of the increased demand, the large quantity of light weight coins in circulation, and the inconvenience of using 5 franc silver pieces in place of 20 franc gold coins. The gold value of the 5 franc silver pieces during the years of the gold premium policy was far less than the actual premium charged. Therefore in case of need the Bank of France could increase the gold premium beyond the highest point it actually employed.

The gold holdings of France were thus protected against any serious short-term drains. But when the cause of pressure on exchanges was due not to seasonal movements nor to the desire to lend abroad for a short time, but rather to the necessity of meeting an adverse balance in the international accounts arising from what might be termed permanent causes (e.g. relative increase in imports or long-term foreign investments, and so forth), the gold premium could not prevent the outflow. It could only *postpone* the loss of gold. Sooner or later the supply of drafts on foreign countries furnished by bankers and speculators who were willing to keep funds in France in the hope of a not too distant shift to more "favorable" exchange rates would be used up, while the increased demand for bills would continue. The pressure on exchanges would be augmented by the need for covering the speculative transactions. The supply of bills being presumably no greater than when the pressure first began, and the demand

In addition to the use of the gold premium, the Bank of France could, and according to one writer occasionally did, raise the export point by requiring banks which applied for gold for export to discount long-term bills many times in excess of the amount of gold demanded. (E. Kaufmann, La Banque en France [Paris, 1914], p. 75.) The Bank of France could, on the other hand, lower the gold import point by crediting importers of specie from the date of shipment rather than the date of receipt, or by accepting gold at the sea ports rather than at Paris, thus saving the shipper some of the transportation and interest costs. Both of these means were at times employed by the Bank of France, but there is no information available as to the frequency with which this form of inducement was used to encourage imports of specie. The question was asked of M. Pallain, Governor of the Bank of France, by the United States Monetary Commission, and altho his answer was not so complete as might be wished, it does state that the method was sometimes used.

Q. What measures are taken by the Bank of France if it wishes to increase its stock of gold or to stimulate the importation of gold?

A. The importation of gold does not need to be stimulated in France. It takes place naturally under the influence of the position of a creditor which France always holds toward the principal foreign markets. Certain intermediaries have sometimes asked us to facilitate their operations of arbitrage in precious metals by advancing money without interest for the time required in transportation. We have done so several times by crediting the importers from the day of shipment, but this operation, which has its limits in its own conditions, cannot be considered as a premium for importation. Such premiums, we repeat, would be useless, in consideration of the current importation which normally overabundantly supplies the French market. — Interviews on the Banking and Currency Systems of England, France, Germany, Switzerland, and Italy, Senate Document No. 405 (Washington, 1910), p. 214.

being greater than ever, gold would have to flow outward. If during the postponement of the efflux the adverse balance of payments (excluding short-term loans) disappeared because of changes in merchandise movements or in other items in the international accounts, the covering part of the speculative transactions could be consummated without causing an efflux of gold. It is in the hope or the expectation of such changes that speculators are willing to supply the bills of exchange. But, as has already been shown, when the disappearance of an adverse balance occurs thru change in the balance of trade or in the volume of long-term foreign investments, the movements of exchanges have not been the cause. Yet in such case the very postponement of an outflow is equivalent to a permanent check; the gold that in the absence of a gold premium would have left the country and later flowed back never moved at all.

To conclude, the employment of the gold premium did not operate to increase the gold holdings of France; it merely rendered them less sensitive to changes in foreign money markets and to minor shifts in the international accounts.

The gold premium policy was, according to some writers, abandoned by the new Bank administration in 1897 as a result of criticism on the part of those who needed to make payments abroad.[1] But in spite of the supposed abandonment of the gold premium policy, there is reason to believe that its use did not completely cease.[2] In fact a slight premium is recorded in 1903

[1] I. Patron, The Bank of France in Its Relation to National and International Credit, U. S. Nat. Monetary Comm. (1910), Senate Document No. 494, Chap. II.

A. Liesse, Evolution of Credit and Banks in France, U. S. Nat. Monetary Comm. (1910), Senate Document No. 522, Chap. VI.

Arnauné, writing in 1894, offered a different criticism of the gold premium system. He said, "To defend the gold reserves of the Bank to the detriment of the reserves of the country is an error the consequences of which can become fatal. The system protects the Bank reserves, but leaves the circulation without defense." — Op. cit., p. 397.

[2] From 1900 to October, 1912, according to the quotations listed in the Rapport au Ministre des Finances, there were only two months in 1901 and two in 1903 when there was any premium on gold. There is some question about the reliability of these quotations. Professor Whitaker cites several German writers who claim that "exact data concerning the premium rate cannot be secured since the official rate of premium is never made known." — Foreign Exchange, p. 566.

and 1913, but owing to the absence of any other recorded premiums after 1900 no conclusions can be drawn as to its use after that date.

The other method of checking gold exports was to raise the discount rate. This means of checking gold exports differs from the imposition of a gold premium in that a heightened discount rate may serve to check an internal as well as an external drain and to prevent a permanent as well as a temporary loss of gold. Increased domestic discount rates tend to discourage marginal domestic borrowers; hence they tend to curtail the demand for goods and services. There follows a downward pressure on prices, which in turn causes imports to decline and exports to increase. The result is an increase in the supply of bills, a movement toward more "favorable" exchanges, and a cessation of gold exports. In this sequence, since movements of short-term funds were not the cause of the cessation in gold exports, equilibrium in the balance of payments will not subsequently be disturbed by the completion of speculative transactions; there will be no speculative operations to cover. Such, at all events, are the tendencies; whether or not a discount rate heightened by one per cent — seldom was the difference in France greater in any one year — was sufficient to bring about an adjustment of the disequilibrium in the balance of payments is rather doubtful. It appears that the chief result of the increased discount rates at home was to counteract the attractiveness of increased discount rates abroad, and not to permanently augment the gold holdings in France.

The following answer by M. Pallain as late as 1909 suggests that the privilege of redeeming their notes with silver pieces was not wholly abandoned.

Q. In order to discourage the exportation of gold does the Bank of France sometimes exercise the right it possesses to refuse payment in gold and to offer to pay its notes in silver?

A. The Bank of France cannot, of course, renounce its right to redeem its notes in gold or in silver, since gold pieces and silver coins of 5 francs are equally legal tender in France. But it only uses this right with discretion and to the extent that it appears necessary in order to prevent an unjustifiable weakening of its reserves. In no case, however, whatever may have been said, have we ever charged any premium on French gold in redemption of notes. — Monetary Interviews, p. 215.

The last sentence is a little misleading. It is to be noted that the premium was not charged on French gold but on foreign gold coins. The person desiring gold for export could not secure French gold.

Checking a drain of specie by raising the discount rate was resorted to much less frequently than placing a premium on gold. The discount rate of the Bank of France was kept extraordinarily stable (see chart page 192). From 1880 to 1913 there were only thirty changes in the rate of discount as against 116 in the Reichsbank and 194 in the Bank of England rate. Moreover, the range covered by the changes was much smaller, as the following figures show. They give the high and the low points during the years 1880 to 1913:

	Low	High	Range
Bank of France	2 %	4 %	2 %
Bank of England	2	7	5
Reichsbank	3	7½	4½

The figures show that the range of fluctuation in the Bank of France rate was less than half that of either England or Germany. Stretches of three, four, and five years without a change from the 3 per cent Bank of France discount rate were common from 1880 to 1913. Stability of the discount rate was a deliberate policy on the part of the Bank of France, and one not difficult to maintain because France, unlike England, had no great superstructure of deposits built upon a narrow base of gold reserves. The system of deposit credits was relatively little developed in France, and checks formed only a small part of the circulating medium.[1] Any increase in the demand for circulating medium could be met in part by an issue of notes since there was no legal reserve requirement against note issues. There was a legal maximum, but it was only nominal; the Bank of France always obtained permission to extend the maximum whenever such action was warranted by the demand for notes.

Still, the increase in demand for hand to hand circulation could be met only in part by notes. There was always a demand for gold coin since the smallest note issued was for 50 francs. We have already noted that after 1900 the proportion of specie to notes absorbed was apparently two to one. Any attempt on the part of the Bank of France to pay out notes when coin was being demanded would have very quickly resulted in a deluge of notes

[1] See p. 207.

presented to the Bank for redemption. Thus an increase in the demand for circulating medium was not a matter of indifference to the Bank of France; yet raising the discount rate to check internal drains was resorted to only twice or possibly three times during the thirty-four years.

This stability of discount rates has generally been attributed to the great metallic reserve held by the Bank of France. The Governor of the Bank of France stated:

> It is a principle consecrated by experience that the supreme means of defense for an issue bank, to protect its metallic reserve, is to raise the rate of discount, and we never lose sight of this principle. However, the extent of our reserves allows us to contemplate without emotion important variations of our metallic stock, and we only exceptionally have recourse to a measure which is always painful for commerce and industry. The stability and the moderation of the rate of discount are considered as precious advantages, which the French market owes to the organization and traditional conduct of the Bank of France.[1]

It is doubtless true that the large specie holdings of the Bank of France decreased the importance of fluctuations in reserves, but it is also true that fluctuations in the years when the discount rate remained stable were not very great. In Germany, for example, where the position of the Reichsbank paralleled that of the Bank of France and where the conditions of reserve and of note issue were very similar, the fluctuations in specie holdings and in note issue as well as in deposit liabilities were greater.[2] The

[1] Monetary Interviews, p. 215.

[2] Below is given the difference between the annual maximum and minimum of the note issue and specie reserve in Germany and France during four consecutive years in which no unusual fluctuations took place.

(Millions of francs)

	Specie Reserves		Note Issue		Ratio of Reserves to Note Issue	
	Reichsbank	B. of F.	Reichsbank	B. of F.	Reichsbank	B. of F.
	(1)	(2)	(3)	(4)	(5)	(6)
1902	400	210	620	220	23	10
1903	240	180	500	380	20	9
1904	240	500	550	320	20	13
1905	480	330	600	330	30	11

Columns 1 and 2 give the differences between the minimum and maximum specie reserves during the year for the Reichsbank and the Bank of France. Columns 3 and 4 give the difference between minimum and maximum note issues of those banks. The increased range of fluctuations experienced by the Reichsbank

same was true of England. It would seem that the lack of fluctuation in the discount rate was due not only to the large specie reserve but also in part to the sluggishness of French industrial life. Had the industrial expansion of France kept pace with that of Germany, England, and the United States, it is doubtful whether the discount rate would have shown such stability.[1]

The policy of the Bank authorities towards external drains of specie was much more rigorous than towards internal drains. Whenever before 1900 there was a considerable movement of gold out of the country, or even a threat of such movement, the premium on gold was increased. The monthly movements of the premium on gold, of specie imports, of discount rates, of note circulation, and of Bank reserves are tabulated on pages 319 to 330 and are plotted on Chart 11, pages 192–193. It will be noted that several times the premium on gold was as high as .65 of 1 per cent, an increase which together with other costs, as we have seen, would ordinarily be enough to nullify a difference of 3 per cent between the discount rates of France and Germany or England, provided

is very marked. Columns 5 and 6 give the difference between the annual minimum and maximum ratio of reserves to note issue. The range of fluctuation in these ratios is two and three times as great as in the case of the Bank of France. It is apparent that part of this increased range of fluctuation is due to the increased range of fluctuation in note issue, tho doubtless the absolute size of French reserves is the major factor.

[1] From 1880 to 1908 the deposit liabilities in France increased from 2 to 5 billion francs, in Germany from 1 to 10 billions, and in England from 8 to 22 billions.

The following statement by the head of the largest commercial bank in France, Crédit Lyonnais, is probably representative of the extremely conservative attitude of all banks toward extending credit to business men:

"Our theory is that every merchant ought to have enough capital to go on by himself in normal times, but there are times in the busy season — say three or four months — when he will need more capital, and then he comes to us and we lend him money." — Monetary Interviews, p. 223.

Speaking of the mildness of industrial crises in France, one French writer said: "Must we attribute this result, with M. G. Pallain, to the prudence of our manufacturers, of our merchants, and congratulate ourselves upon it or should we, like certain others, call this prudence timidity, and regret that for 25 years we seem to have been sleeping close to this 'stagnant' pool of which M. W. Pareto speaks, far from the great currents which at times shatter imprudent craft, but which make fertile and alive the country that they water?" — H. Comdamain, Essai sur la conduite de la Banque de France aux époques de crise (Rennes, 1911), p. 167.

For further comment on this point see pp. 297 ff.

CHART 11

Monthly Movements of Specie Reserves, Note Issue, and Discount Rate of the Bank of France; Specie Imports and Exports of France (Exclusive of Silver Bullion); Gold Premium at Paris; Bank of England Discount Rate. 1880–1913

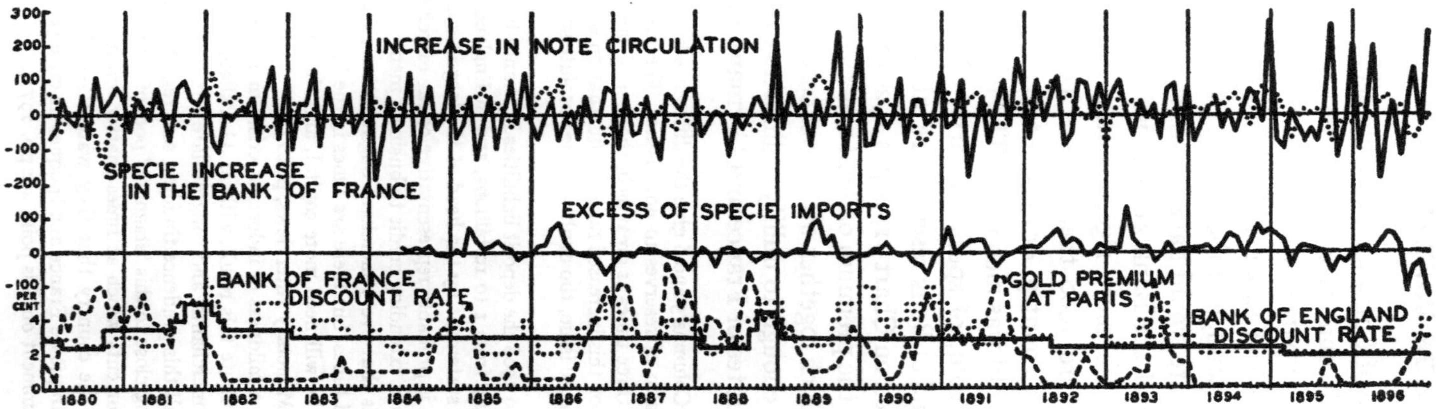

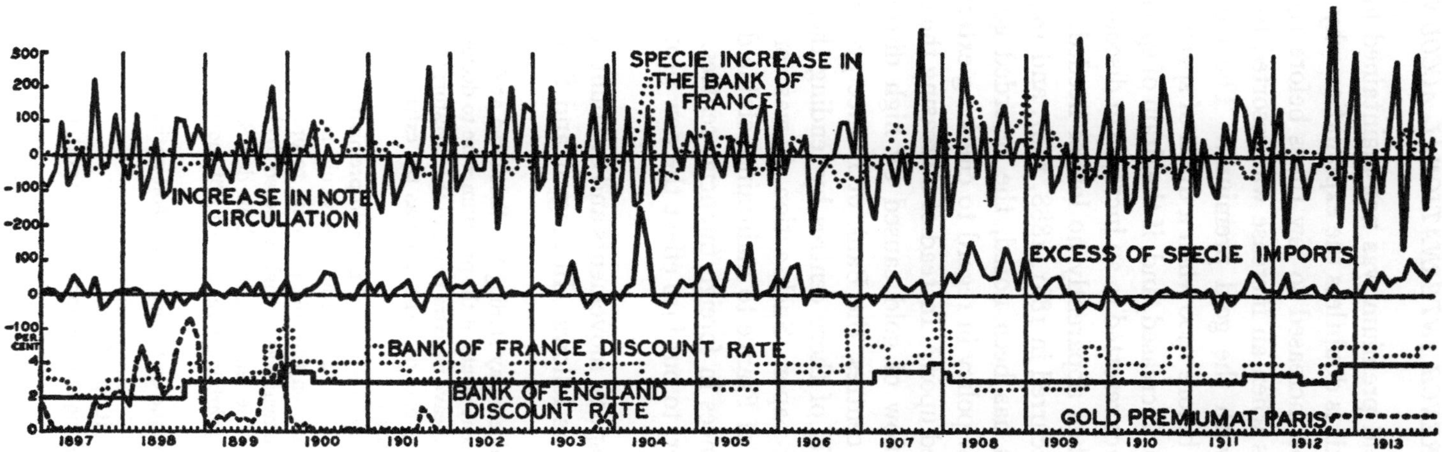

—— Upper curve: Increase in note circulation. Middle curve: Excess of specie imports (excluding silver bullion).
Lower curve: Bank of France discount rate.

- - - Gold premium at Paris (francs per thousand).

. . . . Upper curve: Increase in Bank of France specie reserve. Lower curve: Bank of England discount rate.

that the high gold premium was not maintained longer than a few months.[1] This is doubtless the explanation why the discount rate needed to be increased so few times before 1900. Even in the few instances when an increase was resorted to, it was used in conjunction with the gold premium.[2] The monthly movements show that before 1900 when a drain of specie occurred, the gold premium was increased, and, if the drain of specie continued, the Bank of France resorted to an increase in discount rates. The gold premium, then apparently no longer needed, was reduced. This sequence occurred in 1881, 1888, 1897, and 1899.

After 1900, as has been noted, the recorded gold premiums ceased, and a new policy in regard to checking external drains of specie was decided upon.[3] Instead of increasing the discount rate to check an outflow of gold caused by high discount rates in foreign financial centres, the Bank of France proposed to come directly to the aid of those centres by lending them gold or by discounting their paper. Such action, it was considered, would permit the Bank of France to maintain a stable discount rate in spite of disturbances in foreign financial centres. There was no occasion, however, to put into effect the new protective measure until 1906.

The history of specie movements and discount rates from 1900–1913 was briefly as follows. In August and September of 1901

[1] For example, a ninety-day sterling bill discounted at 6 per cent as against a domestic bill at 3 per cent would, if the premium were to decline before the expiration of the ninety days, leave no extra profit to the investor; the gain in interest for ninety days would be ¾ of 1 per cent, whereas the extra cost of exchange would have been more than that.

[2] Rosendorff, in a careful survey of the gold premium activities of the Bank of France, maintains that the Bank authorities would have preferred to rely on the discount rate rather than on the gold premium to protect the gold reserves, but that the French Government was strongly opposed to changes in the discount rate. — Dr. R. Rosendorff, Die Goldprämienpolitik der Banque de France und ihre deutschen Lobredner, Jahrbücher für Nationalökonomie und Statistik, Vol. 76, 1901, p. 632.

[3] M. Patron, La Banque de France et le crédit national et international (1908), p. 155.

H. Comdamain, op. cit., p. 163.

E. Kaufmann, La Banque en France (Paris, 1914), p. 72. Translated from the German by A. S. Sacker.

when 56 million francs of gold were exported, the gold premium reappeared. It was taken away only after exports ceased. In 1902 both specie imports and reserves increased appreciably. In 1903 specie exports appeared in September and continued thru October and December. They were slight, yet a small gold premium was in force during November and December. In 1904 the gold exports of July to September had been preceded by such heavy gold imports and such large increases in the Bank reserves that there could have been no reason to attempt to check this outflow of specie. In 1905 the imports of specie were even larger than in 1904. But in 1906 there were heavy withdrawals of gold from the London market, and in May the Bank of France loaned 40 million francs to the Bank of England in order that the latter might avoid raising the discount rate. In the following fall the loss of gold from the London market was so serious that the Bank of England rate rose in one month from 3½ to 6 per cent. The Bank of France, instead of increasing its rate of discount or setting a premium on gold as it would have done prior to 1900, came again to the assistance of the English market by discounting 75 million francs of English paper. It was virtually a loan to England without the publicity that would have accompanied such a loan. In 1907 the Bank of France reserves continued to decline and the rate was raised from 3 to 3½ per cent and kept there notwithstanding heavy imports of gold and increases in the gold reserve. In the fall of 1907 the demand for gold from the London market recurred in a more intense form, and the Bank of France forwarded 80 million francs of gold to the Bank of England and at the same time raised its rate to 4 per cent.

The next increase in the Bank rate — in 1911 — was due to an internal drain. For the first time in thirty years an internal drain of specie and notes caused the reserve ratio to drop below 78 per cent. It is possible that the Agadir incident contributed to the decline by causing an increase in hoarding. This was the first year in a decade that savings in banks declined, and in the Bank of France report of 1912 the increase in private hoarding was matter for comment. Circulation declined during the summer of 1912, but in the fall it leaped half a billion; the rate was increased to 4 per cent and kept there thruout 1913 in spite of very heavy gold imports.

From this brief review of the movement of discount rates of the Bank of France it is apparent that only once since 1900 — in 1907 — was the rate increased because of an external drain of specie. Even in that year the increase in the discount rate was put into effect not because gold was leaving the country in large quantities, but because foreign interest rates had greatly increased and there was danger that gold exports might increase. During the entire thirty-four years the discount rate was increased only three times because of declining specie reserves, and twice the cause apparently was hoarding, not an expansion of credit. It thus appears evident beyond doubt that raising and lowering the Bank discount rate was not used as a means of stimulating or checking the expansion of credit.

There is, however, the possibility that the Bank of France exerted a measure of control over credit expansion by its power to limit discounts. It was not obliged to discount all eligible paper, and in times of stress it was very cautious in its discount policy. One French writer speaks of the "implacable severity" with which bills were accepted during 1907.[1] Additional pressure thus exercised was very likely the reason why France was able to maintain a 3½ per cent rate and import gold without the aid of a gold premium while market rates in other foreign countries were double the Bank of France rate. Had this method of credit control been used frequently, the Bank rate would not be a reliable index of the Bank attitude toward the credit situation, but judging from the comments of various bankers, this practice was used only in time of stress and usually in conjunction with an increase in the Bank discount rate.

Some evidence that the power of refusing to discount eligible paper was very seldom resorted to is furnished by movements of the rate of interest charged by commercial banks on prime paper

[1] H. Comdamain, op. cit., p. 173.

According to Kaufmann the Bank of France during 1907 required banks which were withdrawing gold for export to furnish long-term paper greatly in excess of the amount of gold demanded. — Op. cit., p. 75.

— a rate usually lower than the Bank rate and referred to as the market rate.[1] Had the Bank of France curtailed discounts, the market rate would quickly have risen to the Bank rate because more than half of the discounts at the Bank of France were rediscounts.[2] The market rate, however, was as high as the Bank rate only in a few years, and in those years it will be observed the

CHART 12

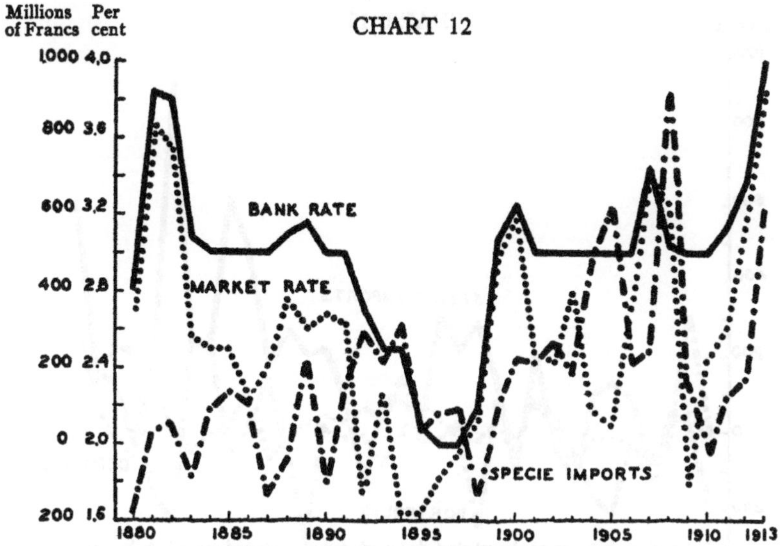

DISCOUNT RATES OF THE BANK OF FRANCE AND OF THE PARIS MARKET COMPARED WITH SPECIE IMPORTS, 1880–1913

—— Bank of France discount rate (annual average)
.... Market discount rates in Paris (annual average)
-.-. Excess of specie imports (exclusive of silver bullion)

Bank rate was increasing. It may therefore be safely assumed that the only occasions on which the Bank of France attempted to contract credit were times when the discount rate was raised.[3] Such times were rare between 1880 and 1913. The discount rate

[1] Kaufmann states that the Bank of France practice of becoming more exacting in its acceptance of paper as a means of protecting its reserves was abandoned by 1900 (op. cit., p. 74), but some comments in the annual reports of the Bank of France indicate otherwise.

[2] The Bank of France reports do not make a distinction between rediscounts and discounts, but the Governor of the Bank of France stated in 1909 that the proportion of rediscounts was over 70 per cent. — Monetary Interviews.

[3] The Governor of the Bank of France is the authority for the statement that

was for the most part stable. Stretches of three to five years without a change were common, while during one period the rate remained at 3 per cent for seven years (May 25, 1900, to March 21, 1907). Such stability would seem to preclude the possibility of considering Bank discount rates an important link in the mechanism of adjustment for the international accounts.

CHART 13

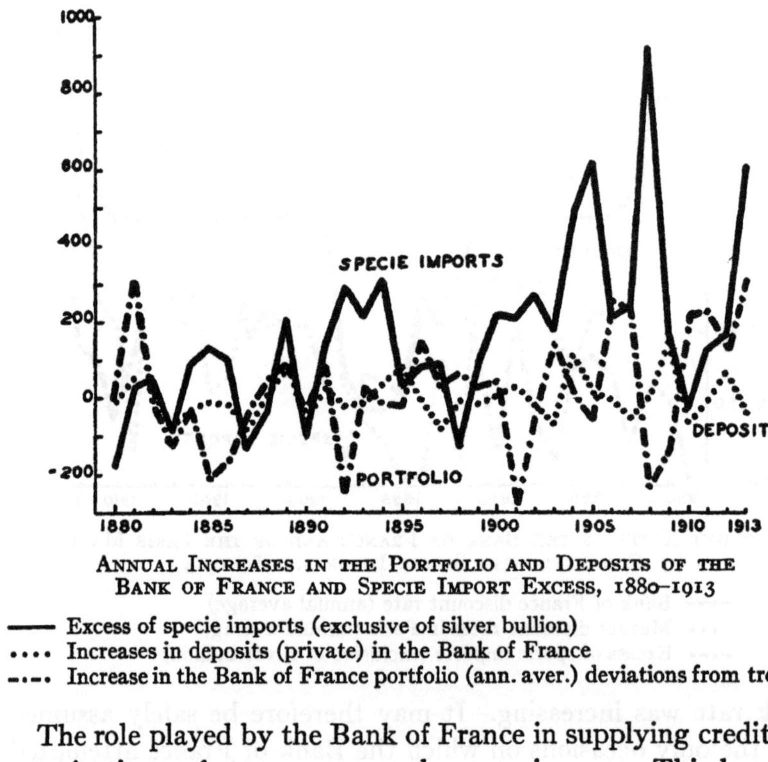

Annual Increases in the Portfolio and Deposits of the Bank of France and Specie Import Excess, 1880–1913

—— Excess of specie imports (exclusive of silver bullion)
.... Increases in deposits (private) in the Bank of France
-.-. Increase in the Bank of France portfolio (ann. aver.) deviations from trend

The role played by the Bank of France in supplying credit, except in times of stress, was purely a passive one. This becomes apparent when the movements of its discounts are compared with those of specie imports. The movements are plotted on Chart 13

the Bank never resorted to market operations to influence credit expansion or contraction.

Q. Does the Bank of France sometimes take steps to maintain the bank rate by the purchase of bills in the market or otherwise?

A. No, never. Such measures would appear to us to be absolutely contrary to the mission of the Bank, which is to moderate, as much as possible, the conditions of credit. — Monetary Interviews.

TABLE 32

ANNUAL MAXIMUM AND MINIMUM PORTFOLIOS OF THE BANK OF FRANCE AND OF THE FOUR LARGE COMMERCIAL FRENCH BANKS, 1880–1913 [1]

(Millions of francs)

	Bank of France				Four Large Banks			
	Maximum		Minimum		Maximum		Minimum	
Year	Month	Amount	Month	Amount	Month	Amount	Month	Amount
1880	Nov.	1018	Apr.	579	....	....	....	....
1881	Oct.	1525	Mar.	917	....	....	....	....
1882	Feb.	1724	Sept.	891	....	....	....	....
1883	Jan.	1248	June	896	....	....	....	....
1884	Feb.	1351	Sept.	798	....	....	....	....
1885	Jan.	1116	Sept.	583	....	....	....	....
1886	May	1125	Sept.	414	....	....	....	....
1887	Jan.	792	Sept.	430	....	....	....	....
1888	Oct.	816	June	495	....	....	....	....
1889	Apr.	1076	Sept.	491	....	....	....	....
1890	Nov.	1059	Sept.	493	....	....	....	....
1891	Jan.	1437	Sept.	533	....	....	....	....
1892	Jan.	871	Sept.	410	Sept.	942	Dec.	842
1893	Jan.	802	Sept.	476	May	951	Jan.	832
1894	Apr.	1030	Sept.	360	Aug.	1026	Apr.	800
1895	July	1090	Mar.	367	Aug.	1021	Apr.	892
1896	Feb.	1016	Sept.	511	Nov.	1102	Feb.	880
1897	Jan.	1060	Aug.	535	May	1200	Jan.	1063
1898	Jan.	1115	Sept.	563	June	1293	Feb.	1158
1899	Jan.	1240	Sept.	585	July	1384	Dec.	1269
1900	Jan.	1422	Sept.	624	Aug.	1520	Jan.	1288
1901	Jan.	1106	Sept.	387	Aug.	1633	Jan.	1517
1902	Jan.	931	Aug.	393	May	1756	Oct.	1589
1903	Nov.	973	Aug.	452	May	1844	Jan.	1647
1904	Jan.	1045	Sept.	469	Sept.	2231	Jan.	1761
1905	Dec.	1023	Aug.	445	Aug.	2292	Dec.	2093
1906	Apr.	1346	Aug.	616	May	2524	Jan.	2108
1907	Jan.	1555	Aug.	848	June	2484	Jan.	2346
1908	Jan.	1624	Sept.	549	Aug.	2773	Jan.	2378
1909	Jan.	1533	Aug.	547	May	3091	Jan.	2849
1910	Oct.	1514	Sept.	749	Sept.	3172	Feb.	2986
1911	Nov.	1769	Aug.	944	Apr.	3355	Sept.	2958
1912	Mar.	2188	Aug.	1020	Nov.	3453	Jan.	3198
1913	Jan.	2303	Sept.	1334	Nov.	3776	Jan.	3416

[1] Crédit Lyonnais, Comptoir d'Escompte, Société Générale, Crédit Industriel et Commercial.
Source: G. Roulleau, Les règlements par effets de commerce (Paris, 1914).

above. They show an inverse relation in almost every year except the few in which the Bank rate was increased. This inverse relation is due to the fact that, with discounts in the commercial banks increasing every year, a decrease in specie imports, by decreasing the supply of available funds, forced the banks to turn to the Bank of France for some of the funds needed to meet the constantly increasing demand. Fluctuation in the demand for funds impinged mostly on the Bank of France, as evidenced, for example, by the fact that the difference between the annual maximum and minimum portfolios for the year was much greater in the Bank of France than in the commercial banks (see Table 32).

In contrast with the movements of portfolios of the Bank of France, the movements of deposits show no consistent relation to gold imports. There are many long stretches, however, when they show an inverse relation to discounts, probably indicating that in times when rediscounts were increased the other banks cut down their deposits to a bare minimum.[1] Loans on collateral, insignificant in quantity before 1895, show a movement in the later years corresponding to that of discounts. This was doubtless due to the same factors which influenced discounts.

We conclude from our examination of the movements of loans, deposits, discount rates, and reserve ratios that in normal times the Bank of France exercised no influence on the contraction or expansion of credit. If any connection, then, is to be found between French net gold flows and changes in purchasing power, it must be sought elsewhere than in the activities of the Bank of France.

[1] Deposits in the Bank of France bore little relation to loans. Loans on collateral, debited only when withdrawn, were taken almost wholly in cash. The movements of the reserve ratio and the percentage of bills discounted by the Bank of France show, as is to be expected, an almost perfect inverse correlation, indicating that discounts did not take the form of deposits. The deposits of the Bank of France, including private and Treasury deposits, covered a surprisingly small range of fluctuation from 1880 to 1913. The lowest average was 533 millions in 1884 and the highest 888 millions in 1882. When the sums kept on deposit by the treasurer were deducted — sums accounting for one-third to two-thirds of the total — the fluctuations were considerably reduced. (Chart 13.) Private individuals preferred to keep as little as possible of their funds in the Bank of France since commercial banks paid interest on deposits. Other banks used their surplus funds on the call markets ("reports") and kept in the Bank of France only enough funds to insure them adequate rediscounting privileges.

CHAPTER IX

PARIS MARKET RATES, BANK PORTFOLIOS, QUANTITY OF MONEY IN CIRCULATION

In considering the effect of specie movements on the discount rates we have so far confined our attention to the Bank of France rate, but market rates also must be examined, for the volume of credit may have been sensitive to these and they in turn may have been affected by the specie movements. Market rates were those rates at which the large commercial banks bought in the open market in Paris certain kinds of the best paper. These rates were much less important than the Bank rate, for most discounting in France was done at the Bank rate or at a rate slightly above or below it. Only a small part of the commercial paper — that owned by the very large business houses and by the better known private banks — was discounted at the published market rates.[1] Some paper, not considered quite so good as this prime paper, yet better than the bulk of commercial paper, was frequently discounted by the large commercial banks at a rate somewhat lower than the Bank rate but higher than the published market rate. The spread between the market rate and the Bank rate was not large even for prime paper because the Bank rate was usually low. The average spread over the whole period was little more than ½ per cent on the best paper, excluding years when the Bank rate was increased, at which times the spread was practically eliminated. It was much less than the spread between market and bank rates in either Germany or England. From 1890 to 1900, for illustration, the average spread in Berlin was .91 per cent, in London .81 per cent, while in Paris it was only .32 per cent. This narrow spread was partly responsible for the relative unimportance of the market rate. Nevertheless, the amount of business transacted at rates lower than the Bank rate was not wholly negligible, particularly when the market rate

[1] G. Roulleau, Les règlements par effets de commerce (Paris, 1914), Chap. IV.

dropped to 1 to 1½ per cent lower than the Bank rate, as it sometimes did (see Table 33, page 203).

Unlike the Bank rate the market rate was sensitive to movements of gold in and out of France. Chart 12, page 197, on which are plotted the movements of Paris market rates and of specie import balances, shows that in almost all years, except those in which the Bank rate changed, specie imports and the market rate of discount moved in opposite directions. Large specie imports coincided with relatively lower market rates. This is in accord with the explanation of the inverse relation found between the discounts of the Bank of France and specie movements. (See page 200.) When specie imports decreased, the continuously growing demand for hand to hand circulation caused the commercial banks to rediscount more paper at the Bank of France. Under such circumstances it is to be expected that the market rate would increase. The movement of the market rate was thus apparently strongly influenced by specie movements.

The important consideration, however, is the relation between the movement of market rates and the quantity of credit. Was the quantity of credit influenced by fluctuations in the market rates?

The amount of bills discounted by commercial banks steadily increased thruout the whole period; more and more use was being made of credit. For this upward trend in the use of credit, allowance has to be made in trying to discern annual movements that might have been induced by movements in the discount rate. The figures for the annual average portfolios when plotted resemble closely an exponential curve, and the trend lines fitted to the curve reveal an annual rate of increase of 4 per cent from 1880 to 1897, and just double that rate from 1897 on. The deviations from these trends are plotted together with movements of discount rates and specie imports on Chart 14, p. 204. From 1900 on, the movements of portfolios and of discount rates are in inverse relation, showing that discounts were large when market rates were low, and low when market rates were high. But the increase in commercial portfolios that appears with low market rates does not always represent an addition to the total quantity of bills dis-

TABLE 33

MARKET DISCOUNT RATES AT PARIS, LONDON, AND BERLIN, 1880–1913

Year	Paris[1] High	Paris[1] Low	Paris[1] Ave.	London[2] High	London[2] Low	London[2] Ave.	Berlin[3] High	Berlin[3] Low	Berlin[3] Ave.
1880	3.2	2.1	2.7	2.7	1.5	2.4	5.	1.9	3.4
1881	5.	3.	3.6	3.8	1.7	2.7	5.3	2.8	3.5
1882	5.	3.1	3.5	5.5	2.2	3.5	4.8	2.8	3.8
1883	3.3	2.5	2.5	3.7	2.1	3.	4.6	2.5	3.
1884	2.9	2.	2.5	4.1	1.1	2.2	3.8	2.1	2.9
1885	2.8	2.	2.5	4.1	.7	2.1	4.2	2.1	2.8
1886	2.8	1.	2.2	3.6	1.1	2.	4.5	1.1	2.1
1887	2.8	2.1	2.4	3.6	.8	2.3	3.8	1.5	2.3
1888	3.8	2.	2.7	4.3	1.1	2.3	4.	1.2	2.1
1889	4.2	2.	2.6	4.2	1.5	3.2	5.	1.2	2.5
1890	3.	2.2	2.6	4.7	1.7	3.7	5.5	2.6	3.7
1891	2.8	2.1	2.6	3.5	.7	1.5	4.2	2.2	3.
1892	2.6	1.	1.7	2.7	.7	1.3	4.2	1.2	1.8
1893	2.5	1.8	2.2	3.7	1.	1.6	4.8	1.2	3.1
1894	2.3	.7	1.6	2.1	.5	1.6	3.3	1.4	1.7
1895	3.	.8	1.6	1.5	.5	.8	3.8	1.1	2.
1896	2.	1.2	1.8	3.1	.5	1.5	4.8	2.	3.
1897	2.1	1.7	1.9	3.1	.8	1.8	4.7	2.2	3.
1898	3.	1.7	2.1	4.	.8	2.6	5.6	2.3	3.5
1899	4.5	2.7	2.9	7.	1.8	3.2	6.3	3.5	4.4
1900	4.5	2.5	3.1	5.5	2.3	3.7	5.6	3.6	4.4
1901	3.	1.5	2.4	4.5	2.1	3.2	4.1	2.1	3.
1902	3.	1.7	2.4	4.	2.4	2.9	3.6	1.5	2.1
1903	3.	2.2	2.7	4.2	2.1	3.4	3.8	1.8	3.
1904	2.9	1.1	2.1	3.5	1.8	2.7	4.2	2.2	3.1
1905	3.	1.1	2.1	4.1	1.7	2.6	5.3	1.7	2.8
1906	3.2	2.1	2.7	6.	2.8	4.	6.	3.1	4.
1907	4.	2.8	3.4	7.	3.	4.5	7.3	4.	5.1
1908	4.	1.2	2.2	5.	1.1	2.3	6.	2.1	3.5
1909	2.8	1.	1.7	4.8	1.2	2.3	4.6	1.7	2.8
1910	2.8	2.	2.4	4.7	1.8	3.1	4.7	2.7	3.5
1911	3.5	2.	2.6	4.1	1.8	2.9	5.	2.2	3.5
1912	4.1	2.6	3.1	5.1	2.6	3.6	6.	3.	4.2
1913	4.1	3.5	3.8	5.	3.5	4.3	6.	4.	4.9

[1] 3 mos. prime paper.
[2] 3 mos. bank paper.
[3] 2-3 mos. prime paper.
Sources: U. S. Document No. 578, 1910. Statistics for Great Britain, Germany, and France, 1867–1909. G. Roulleau, Les règlements par effets de commerce.

counted in France; in some years part of the increase was at the expense of the portfolio of the Bank of France. In the year 1901, for example, the portfolio in the Bank of France declined 280 millions from the previous year, whereas the increase in the portfolios of the four large commercial banks was only 180 millions. The actual situation was thus a decline in total discounts not-

CHART 14

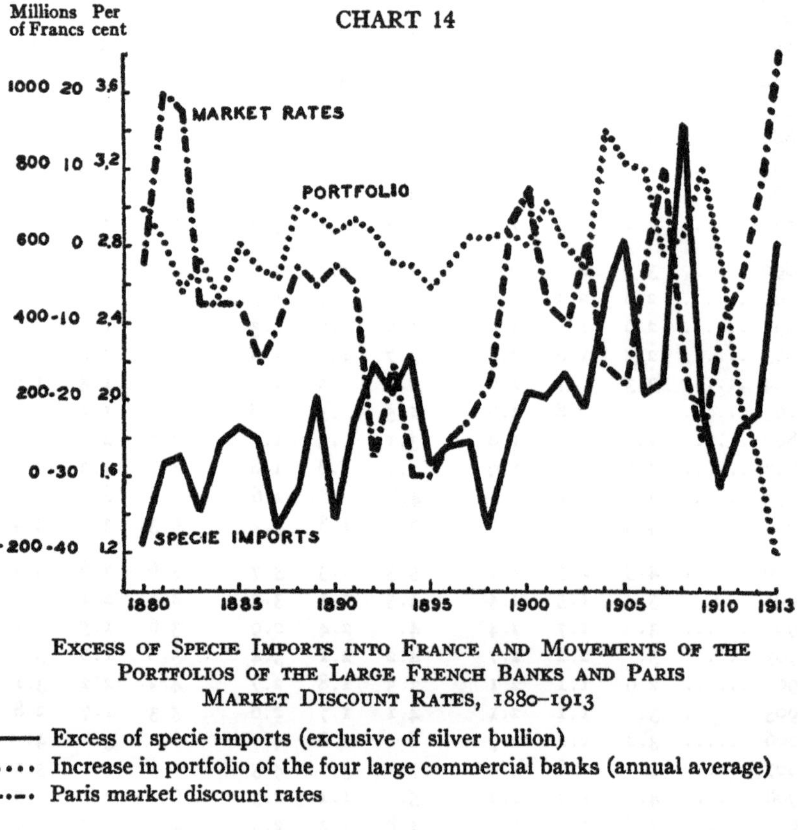

Excess of Specie Imports into France and Movements of the Portfolios of the Large French Banks and Paris Market Discount Rates, 1880–1913

—— Excess of specie imports (exclusive of silver bullion)
.... Increase in portfolio of the four large commercial banks (annual average)
-.-. Paris market discount rates

withstanding the low market rate. This, however, happened only seldom. The increases in the portfolios of the commercial banks usually represented in large part a net addition to the average portfolio of the previous year.

The movements of portfolios and market rates before 1900 are for the most part confused. From 1890 to 1896 they show, if anything, a positive correlation. The market rate during these years hovered around the extremely low rate of 1½ per cent; even the Bank rate remained at 2 per cent for three years.

On the whole the evidence of an inverse movement of market rates and discounts is not sufficient to remove doubts as to their relationship. Yet certainly after 1900, when commercial discounts in quantity were much more important than in the earlier decades, the inverse movement is too persistent to be overlooked. It is possible that the market rate may have been an important link in the chain connecting capital exports with merchandise movements. That is, the gold-flow-credit-price mechanism may have operated in France thru the market, instead of the Bank, rate. But it is difficult to believe, notwithstanding the apparent correlation after 1900, that the movements of market rates were the principal cause of credit movements. Market rates applied only to a small part of the discounts, and the spread between the Bank rate and the rate available to any but the very large business houses was ordinarily so slight that it seems unlikely that business activity in France could have been sufficiently sensitive to respond to its movements.

The difference in sensitivity between the French credit structure and that of England and of the United States is indicated by the fact that the relation of the movements of discount rates, portfolios, and gold movements in France is contrary to the relation existing prior to 1914 in the gold movements of the United States and England. In the case of these two countries it has been found, according to a recent study,[1] that gold, attracted by increasing discount rates, flowed in to replenish the specie reserves in the Central and New York banks, which had been depleted by an internal drain of specie. Notwithstanding an increased discount rate, the internal drain persisted, thereby necessitating further attempts of the central banks to secure reserves. This continued until a crisis was precipitated. During the ensuing depression gold flowed back to bank reserves and thence to foreign countries. In the case of France these movements appear to have been reversed. Large gold imports were concomitant

[1] W. E. Beach, International Gold Movements and the Business Cycle (Cambridge, 1929), thesis in the Harvard University library.

with low portfolios in the Bank of France, and the Bank discount rate, as we have noted, was increased only two or three times in the thirty-four years because of internal drain. In only one period — 1904 and 1905, years of expanding business — did large imports of gold occur at the same time as large increases in the number of bills discounted in the commercial banks, but during this period the Bank discount rate did not increase, and the market rate remained very low. In 1906, also a year of prosperity, gold imports declined and the market rate increased. In 1908, a year of mild depression in France, gold imports were enormous and discount rates low; while in 1909, 1910, and 1911, years of prosperity, gold imports were low and market rates rising. Again in 1891 and 1894, years of depression, gold imports were large and discount rates low, while in 1895 to 1899, years of prosperity, gold imports were low and interest rates rising. In almost every year from 1880 to 1913 gold movements of specie imports, discount rates, and portfolios were the reverse of those noted in the case of England and the United States.

The different relation of discount rates to gold movements in France demonstrates the relative insensitivity of the French credit structure. From 1902 to 1905 (inclusive) over one billion francs of gold coin and notes were absorbed into circulation, yet the Bank discount rate remained unchanged and the market rate decreased. In the next two years a billion more was absorbed. This time the Bank rate was increased, but not with the intent of attracting specie into Bank reserves; it was raised to prevent an efflux to countries with interest rates double that prevailing in France. The circulating medium was further augmented after 1900 by an increase in deposit banking; the number of checks issued in France almost doubled. But even this expansion of the effective circulating medium was not sufficient to reduce the ratio between total demand liabilities in France and the specie reserves in the Bank of France to the point where it was necessary to raise either the Bank or the market rate.

The huge sums of gold that poured into France apparently neither caused nor supported so great an expansion of credit as similar gold movements would have done in England, the United

States, or Germany. Much of the gold was absorbed into circulation. As has been noted, from 1901 to 1913 three billions of gold and one and one-half billions of notes were thus absorbed. Some of the gold may have been hoarded during this period, but the comments of various financial writers are to the effect that hoarding had declined.[1] There is no reason to suppose that the four and a half billion increase in money did not enter into hand to hand circulation; so large an addition is not surprising in view of the slight extent to which checks were used. The following replies by the head of Crédit Lyonnais to questions regarding the check-using habits of the French people indicate the relative unimportance of the check as a medium of payment.

Q. What proportion of the business of France is done by checks and what by actual money?

A. I do not know.

Q. I understand none of the farmers or peasants will use checks?

A. The use is extremely rare.

Q. How about your tradesmen all through the small towns, and the doctor and lawyer and professional men; would they draw the money out and pay their bills in cash?

A. Certainly; most of them.

Q. How about the pay rolls of manufacturers?

A. Always in money.

Q. How do you pay your own employees?

A. Always in money.[2]

Checks were used only for large transactions and only by the larger business houses. Each check issued was subject to a small tax; therefore the number of checks used in a year is known. The slight extent to which checks were drawn is shown by the table on page 334. From 1880 to 1913 the number of checks used in a year increased from only four to fifteen million. The value of these checks can be only estimated, since there are no published

[1] In the monetary interview with the head of Crédit Lyonnais the question of hoarding was raised.

Q. Do the French people hoard money as much as formerly?

A. No; it is becoming more the custom to put money in the banks. Thirty years ago they kept the money at home.

Q. The people are hoarding money less as banks and branches increase?

A. Yes. — Monetary Interviews, p. 245.

[2] Ibid., p. 248.

records except for checks cleared thru the Paris Clearing House. Roulleau in 1912 made inquiries at all the large banks as to the average value of checks. He concluded that the average sum was 5800 francs.[1] It is obvious that checks were used only for very large transactions, and therefore played a limited role in the circulating medium. In an attempt to ascertain the amount of checks which circulate daily, Roulleau also examined 1070 checks drawn on the Bank of France and classified them according to size and days elapsed between date drawn and date cashed. As regards size he concluded that in 1912 — in which year he estimated that 5 billion francs had been drawn — the daily average value of checks in existence was 320 millions. Compared to the 12 billions of money circulating in France this sum was relatively unimportant, even if allowance be made for the greater rapidity with which checks circulated.

Since hand to hand circulation played so important a part in the daily transactions, its annual fluctuations ought to be a rough index of the movements of total purchasing power in France. Monetary inquiries have been periodically conducted with the purpose of determining the amount of money in circulation in France. On the basis of the results of the various investigations, Rist arrived at the following estimates of money in circulation:[2]

(Millions of francs)

1878	8300	1897	7230
1885	8228	1903	8720
1891	6970	1909	10320

From these periodic figures, with the aid of other data, I have obtained a fairly accurate measure of the annual movements of coin and notes in circulation. The base for calculation was the estimate of the specie in circulation in 1903. The monthly excess of imports of gold coin, gold bullion, and silver money was added to the monthly increase or decrease in note issue. To this sum were added again the monthly diminutions of the specie reserves

[1] Op. cit., p. 57.

[2] C. Rist, La circulation monétaire française et le mouvement des prix, Rev. d'Écon. Pol., 1914, Vol. 28, p. 276.

TABLE 34

Ratio of Reserves to Deposits of the Important French Banks on December 31 of Each Year, 1888–1913

Year	Deposits of Four Banks[1] (Millions of francs)	Cash Reserves of Four Banks[2] (Millions of francs)	Ratio of Reserves to Deposits of Four Banks
1888	1315	100	7.6
1889	1219	121	10.
1890	1294	126	10.8
1891	1405	142	10.1
1892	1568	157	10.
1893	1489	146	9.8
1894	1741	166	9.5
1895	1626	197	12.1
1896	1851	202	10.9
1897	1989	211	10.6
1898	2107	260	12.3
1899	2229	256	11.
1900	2434	281	11.6
1901	2551	278	10.9
1902	2659	264	10.
1903	2919	251	8.6
1904	3604	300	8.3
1905	3538	388	10.4
1906	4059	384	9.4
1907	3688	324	8.8
1908	4164	353	6.1
1909	4371	331	7.6
1910	4782	363	7.6
1911	5002	502	10.
1912	5137	487	9.5
1913	5380	478	8.6

[1] Crédit Lyonnais, Comptoir National d'Escompte, Société Générale, Crédit Industriel et Commercial.

[2] Cash in banks and on deposit in the Bank of France.

of the Bank of France, the increases being subtracted. Deduction was made for the sums of gold used in the arts, and addition made for subsidiary coinage. Since France produced practically no gold, the figures obtained by these calculations ought to give the annual movements of circulating medium in France.[1] The figures are subject, of course, to errors arising from mistakes in the records of specie movements and in the inventory of the metallic stock in the base year 1903. These mistakes are unavoidable, but fortunately the latter source of error is not of consequence, since for our purpose it is the changes in monetary stock, not the absolute amounts, that signify. One further miscalculation creeps in. It has its source in the make-up of the cash in banks other than the Bank of France. We have noted that the banks did not distinguish between cash in their own vaults and sums deposited in the Bank of France. But the fluctuations in the "cash on hand and in the Bank of France" were not great. The annual movement of these holdings of the four large banks, tabulated on page 209, shows a fairly steady upward trend, — with the exception of the year 1908, — but in no year before 1903 was the annual fluctuation more than 20 millions, and in only one year thruout the period — 1911 — did it exceed 100 millions.[2] The error involved in ignoring the coin holdings, therefore, cannot be large.

The annual movements of the quantities of money outside the Bank of France, arrived at in the manner described above, are tabulated on page 211. The figures obtained for the years 1891 and 1909 agree fairly well with the estimate arrived at by Rist, but in the figure for 1885 there is a discrepancy of one billion francs. It is difficult to account for this great difference. From May 28, 1885, to April 22, 1891, the Bank of France reserves increased only about 400 millions. To offset this there was an increase in note issue of 300 millions, and a specie import excess of 150 millions. The coinage of silver and bronze during this period was negligible. Making an allowance of 200 million for gold used

[1] In order to make allowance for monthly fluctuations, the median of the monthly movements was taken as representative of the quantity in circulation during that year.

[2] These are figures for only the four largest banks, but these four banks received the bulk of the commercial deposits of the country.

TABLE 35

QUANTITY OF NOTES AND GOLD IN FRANCE OUTSIDE THE BANK OF FRANCE AND FRENCH "EXPORT" PRICE INDEX. DEVIATION FROM THE TREND

(Millions of francs)

Year	Quantity of Money[1]	Deviation from the Trend	Price Index[2]	Deviation from the Trend
1880	7240	−160	126	...
1881	7420	80	122	5.7
1882	7350	70	120	5.4
1883	7430	210	116	3.1
1884	7450	290	108	−2.8
1885	7280	180	104	−5.5
1886	6870	−170	103	−4.8
1887	6650	−330	99	−7.1
1888	6370	−550	99	−5.4
1889	6730	−130	102	−.7
1890	6770	−30	105	4.
1891	6930	190	102	2.7
1892	7040	360	100	2.4
1893	7450	90	102	6.
1894	7570	80	94	−.2
1895	7730	110	90	−2.5
1896	7880	130	90	−.8
1897	7820	−60	90	.5
1898	7780	−230	92	.3
1899	8000	−140	97	3.7
1900	8210	−60	100	5.
1901	8260	−140	97	.5
1902	8350	−180	96	−2.1
1903	8760	100	97	−2.7
1904	8850	60	96	−5.3
1905	9200	−30	98	−4.9
1906	9660	80	102	−2.5
1907	10100	170	111	5.
1908	10290	10	105	−2.7
1909	10530	−100	108	−1.3
1910	10760	−220	113	2.1
1911	11220	−110	115	2.5
1912	11620	−40	116	2.
1913	12300	270	116	.3

[1] Quantity of notes and gold in France outside the Bank of France. Annual average of monthly medians.

[2] Price in France of commodities subject to international competition.

in the arts,[1] the result is a decrease of money in circulation of 150 millions. The difference between Rist's estimate for 1885 and for 1891 is 1300 million francs; whereas according to the reasoning above it ought to be less than 200 millions. It is very unlikely that in so short a time a billion francs of specie could escape the trade statistics; yet Rist's estimate for 1885 is close to estimates made for that year by Soetbeer, Haupt, and De Foville. The difference of a billion francs is puzzling and there appears to be no reasonable explanation for it.

When the annual movements of cash outside the Bank of France were plotted, it was found that the best trend lines that could be fitted necessitated breaking up the series into three parts. On the chart, page 213, the deviations from these trends are plotted against the deviations from the trends found in the price series of French commodities entering into international trade. The movements of the curves are not unlike, but the correlation is low. There are periods of several years — 1898 to 1902, 1904 to 1908 — when the curves move together, but there are other years — 1897, 1912, and 1913 — when the movements are in opposite directions. In the last two years the increase in money and decrease in prices may be partly explained by the increased hoarding that occurred in those two years. For one period of eight years — 1882 to 1890 — the two curves move together with prices lagging one and two years behind the movements of money, but during the next five years money lags behind prices. The fact that these movements are deviations from trends, and that neither lends itself to a simple curve, makes comparisons less reliable; yet there appears to be enough similarity in the movements to warrant a withholding of judgment as to the connection between the movements of the quantity of money in circulation and wholesale prices in France.

The movements of circulating medium (deviations from the trend) were compared also with the movement of retail prices in France, an index based on prices of twenty-two commodities,

[1] In 1886 Soetbeer estimated this item for France at 21,000 kgs. per year. (Op. cit., p. 507.) This is higher than the officially recorded sums by several thousand kgs.

mostly foodstuffs,[1] unfortunately the only index in existence covering that period. The quantity of money in circulation appeared to follow this curve a little closer than it did the curve of wholesale prices, but here also the correlation is neither high enough nor low enough to warrant drawing definite conclusions as to their relation.

CHART 15

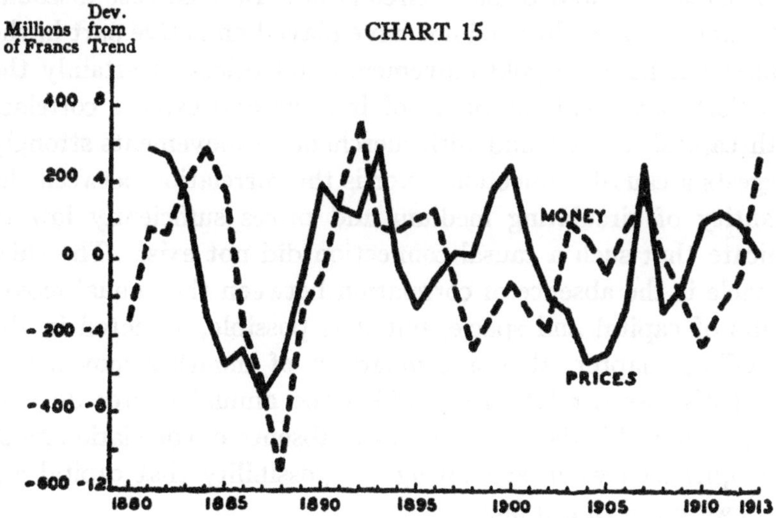

Annual Movements of Notes and Coin Outside the Bank of France and French "Export" Prices, 1880–1913

—— French "export" prices (deviations from trend)

- - - Quantity of money in France outside the Bank of France (deviations from trend)

It would appear, then, that the interrelations of specie flow, bank reserves, discount rates, bank portfolios, and prices yield no conclusive evidence as to the connection between French

[1] L. March has made a study of the cost of living for five grades of French workers, ranked according to income, for the years 1880 to 1910. In his Salaires et coût de l'existence à divers époques jusqu'en 1910 (Paris, 1911) the following commodities were selected and weighted according to the amount consumed by a household of four persons of each grade of worker: bread, meat, lard, fish, butter, eggs, sugar, salt, rice, macaroni, cheese, milk, potatoes, dry beans, cooking oil, vinegar, coffee, chocolate, petrole, charcoal, and coal. One of the series is for a well-to-do household of nine persons and includes in addition to the above items candles, gas, jam, pepper, tea, prunes, poultry, and delicatessen. All the series were combined for this study. See Table 59.

capital exports and prices. Lacking such evidence, the correlation which we noted between merchandise movements and capital exports cannot definitely be attributed to the influence of foreign investments on merchandise movements. Nevertheless, there is no evidence that disproves such a causal relationship. It is entirely possible that gold movements affected French prices thru their effect on hand to hand circulation. In such case discount rates and bank credit need not have played an active part in the connection between gold movements and prices. Certainly the fact that movements of prices of imports and exports correlate with capital exports and with merchandise movements strongly suggests a causal connection. Nor is the correlation between the quantity of circulating medium and prices sufficiently low to indicate that such a causal connection did not exist. The chief obstacle is the absence of correlation between the annual movements of capital and specie, but it is possible, as noted in the preceding chapter, that a comparison of monthly movements would disclose a relationship which the annual figures do not. Without monthly data, however, the absence of correlation must be emphasized when evaluating the possibility that capital exports were the causal factor.

We turn now to a consideration of another possible explanation of the correlation between capital exports and the movements of merchandise balances: the interpretation that merchandise movements caused the export of capital.

There are several means whereby merchandise movements may modify the flow of foreign investments. The direct linking of loans with exports — that is, the extension of book credit to facilitate exports — would bring about an increase in foreign investments. The foreign investments of France, however, as we have pointed out, seldom arose out of such transactions, so that the possibility of a direct linking of loans with merchandise exports may be ignored. Again, an increase in foreign investments may be brought about thru the effect of merchandise movements on exchange rates. Thus an increase of imports would tend to increase the rate of foreign exchange, thereby making foreign investments more expensive to the investor. An increase of $\frac{1}{4}$ to $\frac{1}{2}$ per cent in the price of a foreign bond caused by a rise in the rate of foreign exchange between countries on a gold standard may be sufficient to bring about speculative sales by bankers and exchange dealers. But it is hardly likely that so small an increase will cause an investor to change his mind on the choice of securities. Besides, even if such small changes were an element in the choice between foreign and domestic securities, they could not have influenced French purchases of foreign securities issued in France; French foreign holdings consisted in large part of securities issued in France and kept in France. Altogether it appears that the amount of long-time foreign investments influenced by exchange movements could not have been large.

Another possible means thru which foreign investments may be influenced by merchandise movements is the effect of merchandise movements on discount rates. An increase in merchandise imports may bring about an increased export (or decreased import) of gold. The loss of gold may cause discount rates to increase, and may thereby make domestic securities a little more attractive to the French investor than foreign securities. But the relationship between discount rates and long-term interest rates is not at all close. Examination of the monthly movements of discount rates on sixty-day bills and of the price of bonds shows no correlation to warrant the view that an increase in discount rates made the bonds more attractive to foreign buyers for investment purposes. Monthly movements of discount rates and stock prices do, however, show a negative correlation, tho not very marked. Whether the downward movements in the price of domestic stocks attracted significant quantities of foreign investments (not speculation funds) is very doubtful. In any case, the French merchandise and gold movements give no indication of the sequence of increased merchandise imports, decreased gold imports, increased discount rates. The sudden increases in imports which occurred in 1891, 1894, 1898, 1903, and 1911 because of poor domestic crops were not accompanied by a decrease of gold imports save in two instances, and in both the discount rate did not increase.

A third possibility is that crop failures may be responsible for a decline in foreign investments. By necessitating extra expenditure on additional food imports, they may check the rate of domestic savings. But the French figures offer no substantiation of this. In some of the years of poor harvests capital exports do show a decline, but in those years, except for 1903 and 1911, the per capita deposits in savings banks continued to increase. Again, during the years 1880–1886, when there were heavy imports of wine owing to the destruction of domestic crops, capital exports showed broad fluctuations. Notwithstanding, crop failures, particularly when they are serious, as in 1910,[1] curtail a country's purchasing power. Thus the host of small savers, who largely constituted the French investing class, must have found it necessary to spend a somewhat greater portion of their income on foodstuffs, and it is therefore quite likely that in certain years the suddenly increased imports due to crop failures caused foreign investments to be smaller than they otherwise would have been.[2]

There remains the final possibility that both foreign investments and merchandise movements were induced by the cyclical movement of business activity. During the upward phase of the business cycle all the familiar phenomena of prosperity appear, and among them increased investments. If the expanding domestic enterprise does not attract the additional funds, foreign investments increase. The industrial character of the lending country and the relative intensity of prosperity in other countries determine whether or not all the additional funds will be absorbed in domestic industries. There appears to be, however, no close correlation between capital exports and periods of prosperity. To be sure, French writers are not wholly in agreement as to which were the years of depression and which the years

[1] The extent of poor crops in France in that year is suggested by the fact that the potato and grape crops decreased 50 per cent.

[2] Many of the farmers doubtless had their net income increased during years of poor crops owing to the higher price obtained for their products, but the price rise in such years was usually not great enough to compensate for the diminished crop yield. In any case such gain in income was more than offset by the decreased income of other consumers who spent more on both domestic and imported foodstuffs.

of recovery.[1] The numerous indices of various aspects of industrial and financial activity presented in Aftalion's Les crises périodiques de surproduction do not appear to justify any one curve as representative of business activity. But it is possible to obtain a fair general picture of the French cyclical movements.

CHART 16

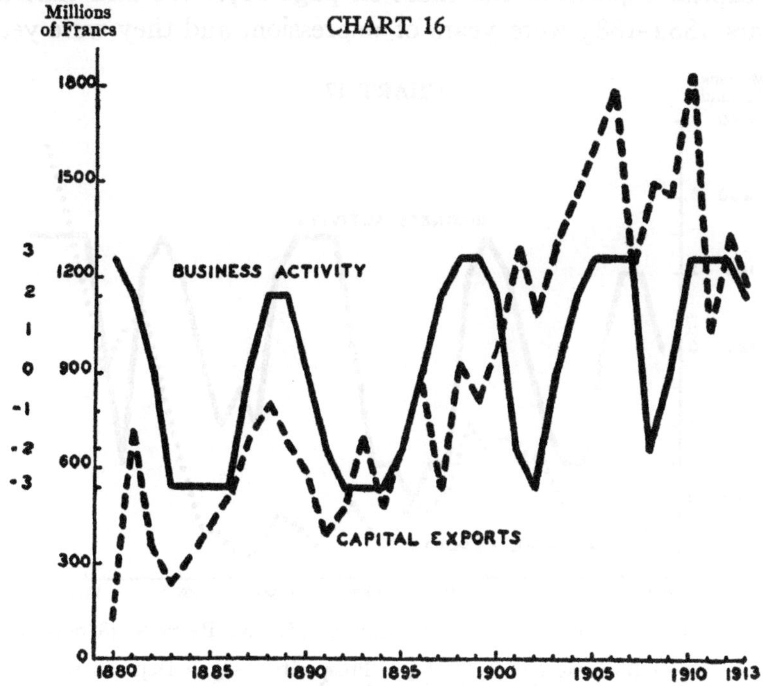

Capital Exports and French Business Activity, 1880–1913

—— Business activity

Depression = −3	Revival = +1
Mild depression = −2	Mild prosperity = +2
Recession = 0	Prosperity = +3

---- Capital exports

W. L. Thorp in his study Business Annals gives a conspectus of business fluctuations thruout the world.[2] In his study, based on an extensive examination of pertinent sources, he classifies the years according to the various phases of cyclical activity under the heads of depression, mild depression, revival, mild prosperity,

[1] See D. Bellet, Crises économiques (Paris, 1918), Chap. XI.

[2] W. L. Thorp, Business Annals, Chap. III.

prosperity, and recession. For the purpose of determining the relationship between capital exports and business activity, these rough classifications are sufficient. Given an ascending scale of values running from -3 for depression to $+3$ for prosperity, the curve of French business conditions is plotted against the curve of capital exports in the chart on page 217. We find that the years 1882–1885 were years of depression, and they were years

Millions of Pounds

CHART 17

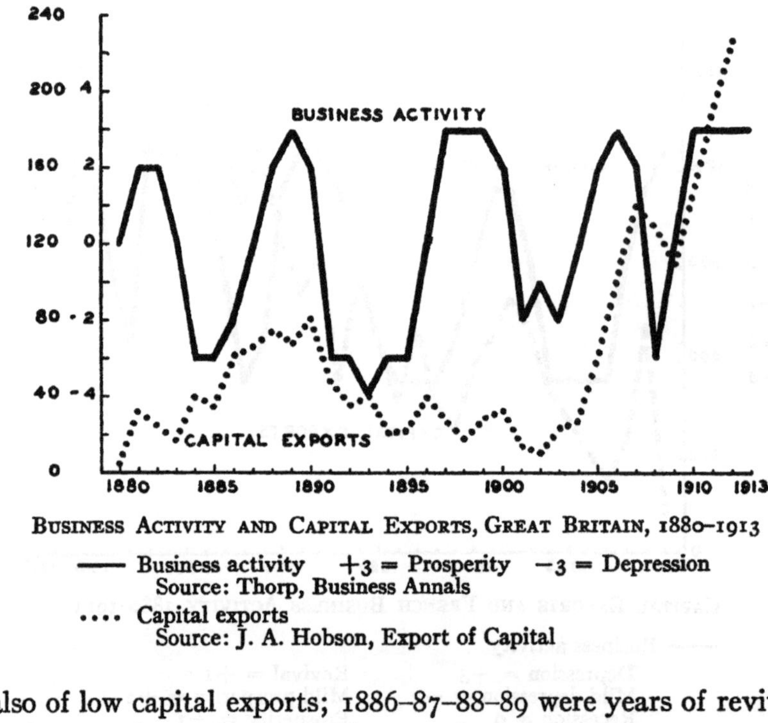

Business Activity and Capital Exports, Great Britain, 1880–1913

—— Business activity $+3$ = Prosperity -3 = Depression
Source: Thorp, Business Annals

.... Capital exports
Source: J. A. Hobson, Export of Capital

also of low capital exports; 1886–87–88–89 were years of revival and prosperity and years of increased capital exports; 1903–04–05–06 were years of prosperity and rapidly increasing exports; but the remaining years show no marked agreement.

A similar comparison of capital exports and business activity for Great Britain for the same period and for the United States for the years 1922–1930 appears above and on page 220. The data upon which both charts are based appear on pages 219 and 221. In the case of Great Britain there is discernible a positive correlation between the two for many of the years. In the years 1885–

TABLE 36

CAPITAL EXPORTS AND BUSINESS ACTIVITY. FRANCE AND GREAT BRITAIN, 1880–1913

Year	France: Business Activity[1]	France: Capital Exports (Millions of francs)	Great Britain: Business Activity[1]	Great Britain: Capital Exports[2] (Millions of pounds)
1880	3	120	0	4
1881	2	720	2	33
1882	0	350	2	24
1883	−3	235	0	17
1884	−3	325	−3	41
1885	−3	420	−3	34
1886	−3	500	−2	61
1887	0	700	0	66
1888	2	800	2	74
1889	2	685	3	68
1890	0	590	2	82
1891	−2	390	−3	48
1892	−3	490	−3	35
1893	−3	700	−4	40
1894	−3	485	−3	21
1895	−2	680	−3	22
1896	0	865	0	39
1897	2	545	3	27
1898	3	930	3	17
1899	3	810	3	28
1900	2	1000	2	31
1901	−2	1280	−2	13
1902	−3	1080	−1	11
1903	0	1300	−2	23
1904	2	1440	0	27
1905	3	1620	2	62
1906	3	1790	3	104
1907	3	1220	2	140
1908	−2	1500	−3	129
1909	0	1460	0	110
1910	3	1830	3	150
1911	3	1030	3	190
1912	3	1340	3	226
1913	2	1110	3	...

[1] 3 = Prosperity, −3 = Depression. Source: Thorp, Business Annals.

[2] Source: J. A. Hobson, Export of Capital.

1889, 1895, 1903–1906, 1909–1913 business activity was high or increasing and capital exports rose; in the years 1889–1895, 1900–1902, and 1907 business was depressed or receding, and capital exports declined. During the remaining ten scattered years the correlation is negative. In the United States, on the other hand, the correlation, such as it is, appears to be inverse. 1923, 1926,

CHART 18

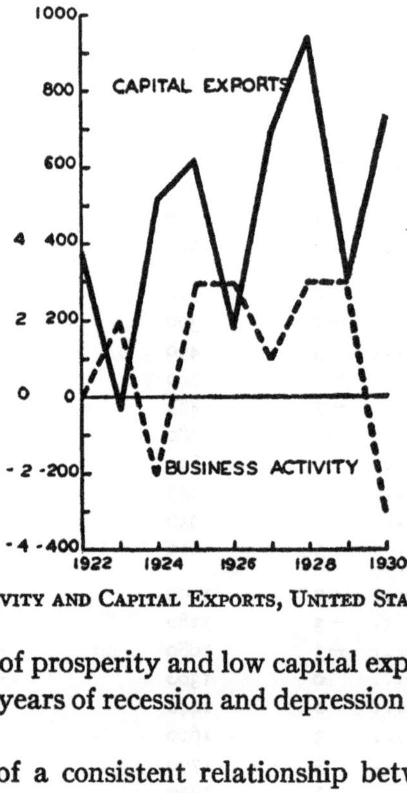

Business Activity and Capital Exports, United States, 1922–1930

1929 were years of prosperity and low capital exports, while 1924, 1927, 1930 were years of recession and depression and high capital exports.

The absence of a consistent relationship between capital exports and the state of business activity in these two principal lending countries makes it difficult to evaluate the significance of the lack of correlation between business cycles and capital exports in France. An absence of correlation does not necessarily mean an absence of causal relationship. There is reason to expect that the relationship between the two movements would differ according to the nature of domestic industry and the intensity of prosperity and depression. During a period of prosperity, expanding domestic industry absorbs additional funds. If the domestic industry is experiencing a more rapid rate of expansion than industries in the borrowing or other lending countries, it may attract so great a proportion of the additional funds as to cause capital exports to decline, or at least to prevent them from increasing. If, on the other hand, the rate of recession or the intensity of the depression is greater than that abroad, the domestic demand may decline so much that notwithstanding a decreased rate of saving there would be more capital available for export. Capital exports and cyclical movements of business activity

TABLE 37

Business Activity and Capital Exports of the United States, 1922–1930

	Business Activity	Capital Exports (Millions of dollars)		Business Activity	Capital Exports (Millions of dollars)
1922 ...	0	378	1927....	1	695
1923 ...	2	−33	1928....	3	944
1924 ...	−2	517	1929....	3	306
1925 ...	3	621	1930....	−3	733
1926 ...	3	181			

could hardly be similarly related in countries where the economic pattern is different, or even in the same country over many cycles because of the differing degrees of relative intensity experienced by any one country. In a country such as the United States or England, where there is a highly sensitive industrial life, we should expect capital exports to decline during periods of prosperity; whereas in a country such as pre-war France, with a rather sluggish industrial life, we should expect the contrary to be more often true. In any one of these countries, however, the relative intensity of prosperity or depression, differing as it does from cycle to cycle, could hardly be expected to have the same effect on capital exports. The figures for France serve neither to affirm nor to deny the relationship. For some years a positive correlation did exist, and the fact that for other years it did not may perhaps mean only that other forces were more powerful in those years.

The movement of capital exports is, however, only one of the factors to be considered. Even if capital exports were closely correlated with business activity, it would yet remain to be explained why merchandise import balances should coincide with the movements of business activity; that is, why exports during the upswing of the business cycle should increase more rapidly than imports. In the case of France a possible answer may be that other countries experienced greater intensity of both prosperity and depression. Those countries would consequently in times of prosperity increase their imports more rapidly than France would increase hers, and during periods of depression would decrease their imports more than would France. This, of course, would signify only if the cyclical movements in those countries coincided with the French cyclical movements. We find that England, Germany, and the United States, large importers of French products, all experienced more intense cyclical activity than did France. In England and in Germany the various phases of the cyclical movements, also, were in fairly close agreement with those in France, as the following table, taken from Professor Mitchell's study of business cycles,[1] shows.

1867–1925	Agreement in Phase	Partial Agreement	Opposition in Phase
France and England	54	34	12
France and Germany	46	42	12
France and United States	39	39	22
France and England, Germany, United States, and Austria	37	38	25

It is possible that during the few periods of world-wide prosperity, when France was extending her foreign investments, England, Germany, and the United States increased their purchases from France to a greater extent than France increased her imports. Such a concomitant movement of merchandise and foreign investments, however, means only that under certain conditions of growing world-wide prosperity the French export surplus increased. It does not satisfactorily explain why the increase in the merchandise export balances approximated in amplitude the

[1] W. C. Mitchell, Business Cycles, The Problem and Its Setting (New York, 1930), p. 428.

growth in capital exports. Some other factor or factors must have been operating to check exports or to stimulate imports when the export excess in the lending country (or the import excess in the borrowing country) was persistently exceeding the amount of capital exported. The correspondence in the amplitude of the two movements has occurred much too frequently in the international trade of the countries that have been examined to be called accidental. If the approximate equality of amplitudes is not accidental, then there must be a causal connection between them or between them and yet a third factor.

But the evidence in the case of France is confused and supports clearly neither one nor another explanation. For the most part merchandise movements appear to have been the dependent factor, but not invariably. Thus there are years in which sudden movements of merchandise caused by unusual crop conditions were the disturbing factor; once the price of the chief imports was heightened by a war and so modified the trade balance; once the imposition of high import duties caused imports to decline. But whether merchandise or capital movements were the causal factor, the question of the manner in which equilibrium was achieved still remains. It was with a view to discovering this mechanism that the monetary and banking phenomena were examined, but the results have proved chiefly negative. In trade with countries not on the gold standard, some approach to equilibrium was doubtless secured thru the effect of variations in exchange rates. Changes in demand schedules caused by transfers of purchasing power probably also served to aid adjustment, tho at times the direction of the flow of specie apparently caused demand schedules to move in such manner as to retard rather than promote adjustment. The relationship observed between sectional prices, capital exports, and merchandise movements suggests that sectional price changes likewise played some role; but the cause of the price movements is not revealed by the monetary and banking data, altho there are definite indications that changes in bank reserves and discount rates may be ruled out. The gold-flow-discount-credit-price sequence of the neo-classical theory appears to have been wholly absent.

CHAPTER X

BARTER TERMS OF TRADE

Any disequilibrium in the balance of payments modifies, according to the neo-classical theory, the terms under which a country exchanges its exports for its imports. Thus an increase in the export of capital causes specie to leave the lending country; prices and incomes in the lending country decline; and exports sell at lower prices, while imports are purchased at higher prices.[1] The outcome is a loss to the lending country in that its imports are obtained under less favorable terms of exchange. The sequence assumes, however, that the adjustment of equilibrium is brought about thru changes in sectional prices. But in so far as adjustment is effected thru changes in demand schedules, the loss does not necessarily occur; exports are sold not at lower prices, but at the same price or even at higher prices; while imports are purchased not at higher, and perhaps even at lower, prices.[2] In so far, again, as both capital exports and merchandise movements are concomitant effects of the cyclical movement of business activity, the terms of exchange also need not become less favorable to the lending country; under certain conditions they may even become more favorable.

The adjustment of the French balance of payments appears to have been brought about, as we have seen, in varying degrees thru the agency of all three forces: changes in sectional prices, changes in demand schedules, and changes in business activity. The extent, then, to which increases in capital exports worsened the terms at which France exchanged her exports for her imports must necessarily have been more limited than the neo-classical theory would lead us to expect. Moreover, altho the net barter terms of trade are proximately determined by price changes, the cause of those price changes varies, and the interpretation of the

[1] All these movements are, of course, relative.

[2] See Chap. I.

change in the terms of trade varies with the cause. In the following pages the terms under which France bartered her exports for her imports and the direction and extent to which those terms may have been influenced by the export of capital will be considered.

The terms of trade, or, to use the more expressive phrase coined by Professor Taussig, "the barter terms of trade," may be determined by a comparison of the physical volume of imports with the physical volume of exports, a comparison, that is, of quantities of silk, feathers, wine, and butter with quantities of coal, copper, raw wool, and coffee. At first thought such a comparison appears both meaningless and impossible. When, however, we compare the quantity of imports exchanged for a quantity of exports at a given time with the ratio of exchange at another time, the comparison becomes meaningful. Its significance lies in the quantitative *changes* of the ratios, the barter terms of trade, in other words, may become *more* or *less favorable* than they were at some other given time. The use of index numbers makes this measurement possible.

Barter terms of trade, as Professor Taussig has pointed out, are of two kinds, gross and net.[1] Gross barter terms of trade apply to the relation between the physical volume of a country's total exports and the physical volume of her total imports; net barter terms of trade apply only to the relation between the physical volume of goods imported and the physical volume of goods exported in payment for the imports. If merchandise imports and merchandise exports are the only items in the international accounts, the net and the gross barter terms of trade will be the same. If, however, other items such as capital exports or indemnity payments appear in the accounts, not all the goods sent are in payment for goods received; some of the goods are sent without any receipt of goods in exchange. In such case the gross and net barter terms of trade will differ.

To illustrate the distinction let it be assumed that France imports 5 billion francs of commodities. In order to pay for these,

[1] For a complete discussion of the meaning of these terms and of the method of measuring them see Professor Taussig's International Trade, particularly Chap. 21.

France sooner or later has to export 5 billion francs of commodities (or services, or specie). Gross and net barter terms of trade are in this case the same. Now let it be further assumed that France wishes to invest abroad a billion francs. She then has to export an additional billion francs of commodities, services, or specie in return for which she receives no imports. In a year or two, or even sooner in some cases, there will be interest and dividend payments due France as a result of those investments, but until then the exports are made without any commodities or services being received in exchange. The *gross* barter terms of trade are then the terms under which the physical quantity of total exports — representing 6 billion francs of monetary value — is exchanged for the physical quantity of total imports, represented by 5 billion francs of imports; the *net* barter terms of trade are the terms under which the physical quantity of imports into France — represented as before by the 5 billion francs — is exchanged for the physical quantity of *that part of the exports* which was necessary to pay for those imports, obviously represented by 5 billion francs.

In this chapter the gross barter terms of trade, that is, the terms at which France exchanged *all* her exports for her imports, will be considered.

To ascertain the gross barter terms of trade it is necessary to have a measure of the movements of the physical volume of trade. It can be obtained in two ways. The first is by means of a quantity index series for imports and for exports. Such a series may be constructed according to any one of the formulas customarily used in the measurement of quantity movements. For the import index a group of imported commodities is selected. The aggregate of their quantities, weighted by their price in the base year, or by an average price over several years, is then compared with similarly compiled aggregates of the quantities of the same commodities imported during the other years under survey. The series of aggregates reduced to relatives presumably reflects the movements of the quantities of all imports.

The second method of measuring the movements of physical volumes of trade is by the process of deflation. Given an import price index series and the money value of imports, the procedure is simple. After removing the difference in the total value of imports caused by changes in their price, there are left presumably the annual quantities of imports at the prices prevailing in the base year. That is, prices being kept the same as in the base year, changes in the total value of the imports presumably represent changes in the quantities of those imports. By reducing these aggregates to a series of relations, we have what purports to be an index series of the physical volume of imports.

The following figures for French imports in the years 1885, 1900, and 1913 illustrate the procedure by deflation.

Year	Recorded Value (Millions of francs)	Import Price Index	Estimated Value at 1900 Prices (Millions of francs)	Relative Physical Quantities (1900 = 100)
	(1)	(2)	(3)	(4)
1885	4255	96	4430	88
1900	4984	100	4984	100
1913	8884	122	7280	146

Column 1 gives the total money value of all the imports at the prices prevailing in the current year (i.e., imports of 1885 at prices prevailing in 1885, imports of 1900 at prices in 1900, etc.).

Column 3 gives the money values of those imports as they would be at prices prevailing in the year selected as the base — 1900 in this instance. Column 3 is obtained by dividing Column 1 (the total values at current prices) by Column 2 (the import price index).

Column 4 contains the total values in all years at the price prevailing in the base year reduced to relatives. These relatives thus measure the changes in totals due to changes in the quantities of imports.

Both methods of measuring quantity movements have disadvantages. In the method of deflation errors arise from changes in the kind and quality of commodities entering into international trade. The classifications in the trade statistics are at best crude. In spite of the constant refining, the total number of classes separately listed in the trade statistics of France was before the war less than 1500, — counting as two any item appearing in both imports and exports, — a number which represents only a small part of the total number of separate commodities that move in and out of France. Such items as electrical machinery, leather novelties, clocks, silk cravats, and stoneware utensils — items which count as one but include commodities of highly diverse qualities and types — are illustrative of many of the classes listed. An increase, then, in the recorded value of such an item as "electrical machinery containing coils of insulated metallic wire" may be due to higher prices of that type of machinery, or to more machinery at the same price, or to better or different types of machinery at higher prices. Deflation will give good results only if either of the first two causes is responsible for the rise in total value. If a change in the type of machinery is responsible for the rise in value, the result obtained by deflation will not adequately represent the quantitative change; and since a good part of manufactured goods is subject to this kind of change, the range of probable error increases. It is mitigated, however, to some extent by the fact that an increase in the recorded import value due to an improvement in quality of machinery is very similar to an increase in quantity in that more labor or material is commonly required for the production of a superior article. But the possibility of error resulting from changes in quality is not wholly eliminated because, clearly, there is no necessary equivalence between improvement in quality and increase in quantity.

Increases and decreases in the relative importance of commodities introduce a further source of error. The process of deflation assumes that the various commodities maintain their respective relative importance. In so far as they do not, the probable error is increased in range. In France the importance of some of the larger groups fluctuated not a little. For example, in the short space of ten years the food imports declined from 32 to 21 per cent of total imports, while the imports of raw materials increased from 52 to 65 per cent. But this source of error is somewhat reduced in this study by the fact that the price series used in the deflation is weighted by the average of quantities entering into the imports. The series is divided into two parts:

1880–1900 and 1900–1913. A different base is used in each, and the weights in each division are the average of the quantities in those years. Any change in importance as between the two periods is therefore reflected in the different weights. Finally, and this constitutes perhaps the most important source of error, the method of deflation assumes that the price series used adequately represent the actual price movements. In so far as they fail to do so, they lead to inaccurate results.

The other method of measuring quantity changes in imports and exports — by the construction of quantity index numbers from the original quantity data — has disadvantages somewhat akin to those mentioned above. The heterogeneity of commodities that fall under each official classification makes it necessary to eliminate a large share of the items listed. Raw materials, certain foodstuffs, and certain manufactured articles of a simple type are the only items that can be included in the index. The assumption is that the items selected are sufficiently representative of the entire list. Unfortunately manufactured articles are hardly represented at all. Furthermore, the list of items that can be selected is again narrowed by the many changes in classification that took place in the French trade schedule. Finally, the matter of changes in the relative importance of commodities constitutes a source of error here as in the method by deflation. But this last source of error is here diminished in importance by the use of separate average weights (according to value) for the different periods.

For this survey the index series for the physical volume of imports and exports have been constructed by both methods outlined above. The price series used in the index obtained by deflation are those especially constructed for the study.[1]

The import and export quantity series and the price series are each composed of two separate series, one from 1880 to 1900 and the other from 1900 to 1913. The weights used in each of the two periods are in the quantity series, the average of prices for that period, and in the price series, the average of quantities for that period. The source of the data is the annual issues of the Tableau

[1] A description of these price series will be found in the following chapter.

Générale du Commerce et de la Navigation, an official publication of the French Department of Commerce. The index numbers were constructed according to the formula $\frac{\Sigma Q_1 P_0}{\Sigma Q_0 P_0}$. The year 1900 is the base year in both series.

The articles included in the index series of 1880 to 1900 are as follows:

Imports: Wool, Cotton, jute, hemp, flax, silk, rubber, linseed, cotton seed, rape seed, coal, coke, petroleum, iron ore, pig iron bar iron, copper, lead, zinc, tin, cotton yarn, wool waste, mohair, horsehair, soda nitrate, copper sulphate, pyrites, potassium sulphate, ammonia sulphate, lead oxide, raw hides, kid skin, whalebone, catechu, mahogany, oak stavewood, oak timber, wheat, corn, oats, barley, rice, foreign sugar, colonial sugar, coffee, cocoa, alcohol, beer, wine, tobacco, butter, eggs, flour, olive oil, cod liver oil, saffron, pepper, chicory, figs, raisins, salt pork, dried cod.

Exports: Cotton, wool, wool carded or combed, wool waste, silk, silk floss, silk cocoons, woolen rags, jute bags, cotton yarn, silk thread, rubber, coal, iron ore, pig iron, steel rails, coke, turpentine, construction stone, zinc oxide, cream of tartar, sulphate of copper, oleic acid, stearic acid, caustic soda, linseed oil, buckwheat, rye, barley, flour, sugar, butter, margarine, alcohol, wine ordinary, wine Gironde, olive oil, colza oil, dried cod, eggs, potatoes, horses, poultry, fodder.

The series for 1900 to 1913 contains in the import index all articles contained in the 1880 to 1900 index (except raw hides) and in addition the following: cellulose, tallow, lime, borax, superphosphate of lime, manganese ore, building stone, nickel, cotton fabrics, plain silk cloth, black silk cloth, paper pulp, leather, beef, beans, lard, peanuts, cheese.

The export series for 1900 to 1913 contains all articles included in the export index of 1880 to 1900 and in addition: tallow, Swiss cheese, pork, beef, aluminum, cotton fabrics, superphosphate of lime, clay tiles.

These quantity index series are tabulated on pages 232, 233. In Chart 19, page 231, both sets of import and export quantity series are presented and contrasted. Considering all the possibilities of error in constructing a dependable quantity index for French imports and exports, the series obtained by the use of the two different methods are in fairly close accord. Before 1900 there are, however, discrepancies. For the imports the years 1880 to 1890, and for exports the years 1883, 1892, 1896, and 1907, show

CHART 19

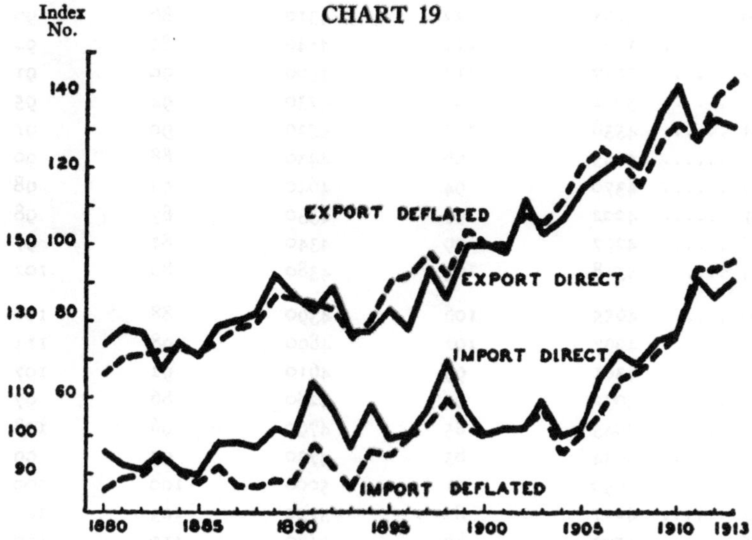

Comparison of Quantity Indices of French Exports and Imports Obtained by Direct Method and by Method of Deflation, 1880–1913 (Base 1900 = 100)

Upper Graph:
—— Export quantity index (direct method)
- - - Export quantity index (by method of deflation)

Lower Graph:
—— Import quantity index (direct method)
- - - Import quantity index (by method of deflation)

the greatest differences. But the differences are mostly in amplitude. In only a few years thruout the period are there serious differences in direction. The series between 1900 and 1913 are in closer accord, owing, doubtless, to the better price and quantity data for the later period.

The gross barter terms of trade are computed by dividing the

TABLE 38

INDEX OF QUANTITIES OF FRENCH IMPORTS, 1880–1913

(Millions of francs)

Year	1 Declared Value[1]	2 Import Price Index[2]	3 Estimated Value at 1900 Prices Col. 1 ÷ Col. 2	4 Col. 3 Reduced to Relatives (1900 = 100)	5 Quantity Index[3] (1900 = 100)
1880	5264	122	4310	86	96
1881	5081	114	4440	89	92
1882	5047	112	4500	90	91
1883	5021	106	4730	94	95
1884	4538	101	4520	90	91
1885	4255	96	4430	88	90
1886	4370	94	4640	92	98
1887	4202	97	4330	87	98
1888	4297	99	4340	87	97
1889	4518	103	4380	88	102
1890	4655	106	4390	88	100
1891	4997	102	4890	98	114
1892	4381	95	4610	92	107
1893	4032	94	4280	86	97
1894	4045	85	4790	96	108
1895	3934	83	4730	95	99
1896	4050	81	5000	100	100
1897	4227	82	5150	103	107
1898	4702	86	5470	110	120
1899	4703	93	5150	103	107
1900	4984	100	4980	100	100
1901	4639	91	5100	102	102
1902	4680	92	5080	102	102
1903	5081	96	5350	107	109
1904	4783	100	4780	95	100
1905	5100	102	5000	100	102
1906	5970	112	5330	106	115
1907	6587	114	5780	115	122
1908	5982	102	5860	117	119
1909	6631	108	6140	123	125
1910	7572	119	6360	127	127
1911	8489	118	7190	144	142
1912	8676	120	7230	144	137
1913	8884	122	7280	146	141

[1] Including corrections for probable underestimates.
[2] See pages 245 ff. for description.
[3] Weighted by average value 1800–1900 and 1900–1913. Indices obtained by the direct method.

TABLE 39

INDEX OF QUANTITIES OF FRENCH EXPORTS, 1880–1913

(Millions of francs)

Year	6 Declared Value[1]	7 Export Price Index[2]	8 Estimated Value at 1900 Prices Col. 6 ÷ Col. 7	9 Col. 8 Reduced to Relatives (1900 = 100)	10 Quantity Index[3] (1900 = 100)
1880	3960	126	3140	67	74
1881	4054	122	3320	70	78
1882	4081	120	3400	71	77
1883	3943	116	3400	72	67
1884	3689	108	3410	72	74
1885	3500	194	3360	71	71
1886	3678	103	3570	75	79
1887	3686	99	3740	79	80
1888	3696	99	3730	80	82
1889	4203	102	4120	87	92
1890	4280	105	4070	86	86
1891	4094	102	4010	85	83
1892	3930	100	3930	83	89
1893	3681	102	3610	76	77
1894	3538	94	3760	80	77
1895	3888	90	4320	91	83
1896	3933	90	4370	92	78
1897	4166	90	4630	98	94
1898	4024	92	4370	92	86
1899	4783	97	4930	104	100
1900	4739	100	4740	100	100
1901	4611	97	4750	100	98
1902	4881	96	5100	108	112
1903	4879	97	5030	106	103
1904	5104	96	5310	112	107
1905	5596	98	5650	121	115
1906	6030	102	5910	125	119
1907	6422	111	5790	122	123
1908	5795	105	5520	116	120
1909	6550	108	6060	128	134
1910	7136	113	6260	132	142
1911	6954	115	6050	127	128
1912	7669	116	6610	139	133
1913	7883	116	6800	143	131

[1] Including corrections for probable underestimates.
[2] See page 245 for description.
[3] Weighted by average value 1880–1900 and 1900–1913. Indices obtained by the direct method.

TABLE 40

GROSS BARTER TERMS OF TRADE FOR FRANCE, 1880–1913, ON THE BASIS OF OFFICIAL AND OF CORRECTED STATISTICS OF IMPORTS AND EXPORTS[1]

(Base 1900 = 100)

Year	1 Relatives of Imports at 1900 Prices[2]	2 Relatives of Exports at 1900 Prices[2]	3 Gross Barter Terms of Trade[2] Col. 2 ÷ Col. 1	4 Gross Barter Terms of Trade on Basis of Corrected Statistics
1880	86	66	77	78
1881	89	70	78	78
1882	90	72	80	79
1883	95	72	76	76
1884	90	72	80	80
1885	89	72	81	80
1886	93	75	81	81
1887	87	79	91	90
1888	87	79	91	92
1889	88	86	98	98
1890	88	86	98	97
1891	98	85	87	87
1892	92	83	90	90
1893	85	76	90	88
1894	95	79	83	83
1895	95	91	96	96
1896	100	92	92	92
1897	103	98	95	95
1898	110	92	83	84
1899	103	104	101	101
1900	100	100	100	100
1901	102	100	98	98
1902	103	107	104	106
1903	106	106	100	99
1904	96	112	116	118
1905	100	120	120	121
1906	107	125	117	118
1907	116	122	105	106
1908	117	116	99	99
1909	123	128	104	104
1910	128	133	104	104
1911	144	126	87	88
1912	145	140	96	96
1913	146	143	98	98

[1] Obtained by process of deflation.
[2] On the basis of official statistics (i. e. not including corrections).

TABLE 41

COMPARISON OF QUANTITY INDICES OF FRENCH EXPORTS AND IMPORTS DERIVED BY DIRECT METHOD AND BY METHOD OF DEFLATION, 1880–1913

(Base 1900 = 100)

Year	Import Series Direct	Import Series by Deflation	Export Series Direct	Export Series by Deflation
1880	96	86	74	66
1881	92	89	78	70
1882	91	90	77	71
1883	95	94	67	72
1884	91	90	74	72
1885	90	88	71	71
1886	98	92	79	75
1887	98	87	80	79
1888	97	87	82	80
1889	102	88	92	87
1890	100	88	86	86
1891	114	98	83	85
1892	107	92	89	83
1893	97	86	77	76
1894	108	96	77	80
1895	99	95	83	91
1896	100	100	78	92
1897	107	103	94	98
1898	120	110	86	92
1899	107	103	100	104
1900	100	100	100	100
1901	102	102	98	100
1902	102	102	116	108
1903	109	107	103	106
1904	100	95	107	112
1905	102	100	115	121
1906	115	106	119	125
1907	122	115	123	122
1908	119	117	120	116
1909	125	123	134	128
1910	127	127	142	132
1911	142	144	128	127
1912	137	144	133	139
1913	141	146	131	143

export quantity index by the import quantity index. In Chart 20 below the gross barter terms of trade computed from the two sets of quantity series are compared. It will be seen that they agree better than the quantity series themselves. Thruout the period the direction of change is the same in all years except 1881, 1887,

Index No.

CHART 20

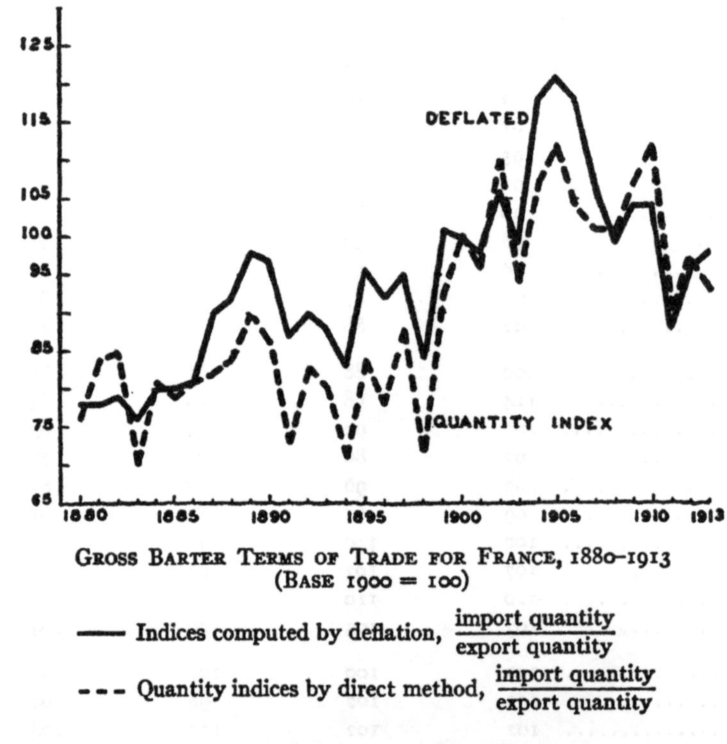

Gross Barter Terms of Trade for France, 1880–1913
(Base 1900 = 100)

—— Indices computed by deflation, $\frac{\text{import quantity}}{\text{export quantity}}$

- - - Quantity indices by direct method, $\frac{\text{import quantity}}{\text{export quantity}}$

1899, 1907, and 1913. This by no means proves the accuracy of both curves, — they may both err in the same direction, — but at any rate it gives no proof of inaccuracy. There appears no evidence that the two curves fail to represent fairly the quantity movements of imports and exports.

The gross barter terms of trade, it will be remembered, represent the ratio of the quantity of all merchandise exports to all merchandise imports, or rather the *changes* in those ratios.[1] When

[1] "Let it be premised that they (gross and net barter terms of trade) in no way indicate whether a country secures a large or a small share of the total gains which

the quantity of exports decreases relatively to the quantity of imports, the index of barter terms of trade drops; the terms become more favorable. Chart 21, on which the gross barter terms of trade are plotted, shows the terms to be more favorable before 1900 than after that year. True, the movement is not regular. The fluctuations are large; as explained elsewhere, there were sudden and irregular changes in imports (see Chapter VI). Nevertheless, there is discernible a less favorable trend between 1898 and 1910, the period which coincides, it must be noted, with the sustained increase of capital exports.

Gross barter terms of trade measure only quantities of goods. They do not, because of the difficulties of measurement, include services. This separation of goods and services is, of course, wholly arbitrary, for the transaction is in both cases the same. In the case of merchandise exports a Frenchman sends the products of his labor to a resident of another country, whereas in the case of tourist services, for example, the resident of the foreign country comes himself to France to get the products and consumes them, or the major portion of them, in France instead of at home. In each instance the products of French labor are consumed by residents of foreign countries. And in each instance the ratio of products exported to products imported may be greater or less at one time than at another.

In the case of France services were an important item in the international accounts, and allowance must be made for their omission from the gross barter terms of trade. If the annual amount of those services were also subject to little fluctuation, the omission of services would not affect the gross barter terms of trade. So far as these two conditions do not prevail, the significance of the figures for gross barter terms of trade, when based solely on commodity movements, is reduced. In the case of

the international barter brings to all concerned — to other countries with which it trades as well as to itself — and which are divided between them. They only indicate in which direction the accretion of gain is changing; whether the gain, whatever it be in a given year, is less or greater in that year than in previous years or in subsequent years. It is *changes*, and changes only, both in the net barter terms of trade and in the gross barter terms, which we are able to follow." — Taussig, op. cit., p. 249.

France, tourist services, the principal item in the category of services, grew steadily from 1880 to 1913. The omission of this item tends to make the gross barter terms of trade appear more favorable toward the end of the period and less favorable at the beginning of the period than would be the case if tourist services were included along with commodity exports. The error, however, is mitigated by the probable increase in the price of those services from 1900 on. Services were increasing in total money value, but they were increasing, almost certainly, in prices per unit as well; therefore the change in the physical volume was less marked than the change in total value. On the other hand, during a greater part of the period from 1880 to 1900 prices of tourist services (such as transportation charges, hotel bills, food, and other things) were less than they were in 1900; and this in like manner makes up in part for the decreased value of those services before 1900 as compared with the base year 1900.

When the curve of gross barter terms of trade is compared with the curve representing the merchandise balance of trade, the result is what would be expected. It will be observed that there is an inverse correlation between the gross barter terms of trade and the movement of merchandise balances. At every increase in the import excess there is a decrease in the index of the gross barter terms of trade; the terms become more favorable to France. In view of the omission of shipping services in the compilation of the gross barter terms of trade and their inclusion in the curve of merchandise balances,[1] the inverse correlation suggests that in the case of France the absence of at least those services does not introduce serious errors in the gross barter terms of trade.

The conclusions to be drawn from the movement of the gross barter terms of trade are comparatively simple, and of limited significance. Favorable or unfavorable gross barter terms of trade seem to imply that a country benefits more or less according to the direction in which the terms move. This may be true in so far as the change in terms has been proximately induced by relative changes in the price levels: as in the case of a capital exporting country, which may find its exports increasing relatively

[1] See p. 52.

to its imports because its price level is declining relatively to price levels in some other countries. To the extent that imports in this case cost more relatively to money incomes, the country is worse off. But if this is all that gross barter terms of trade indicate, then net barter terms of trade, as we shall see, are a better indicator of the phenomenon.

CHART 21

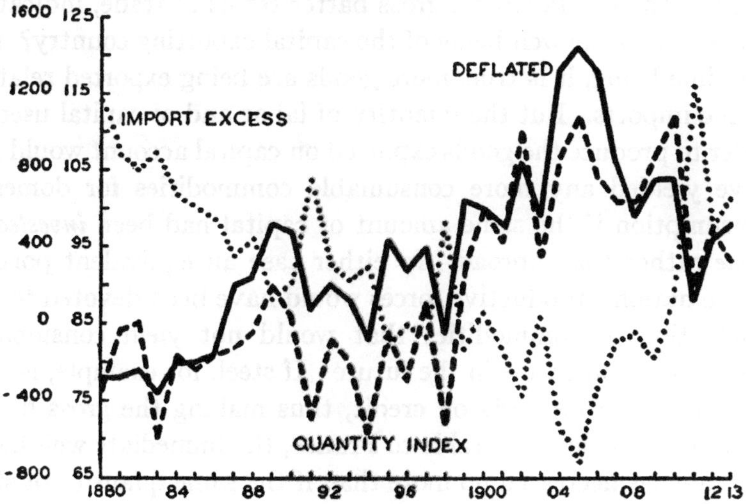

Gross Barter Terms of Trade and Merchandise Balance of Trade for France, 1880–1913

It may be said, however, that favorable or unfavorable gross barter terms of trade imply something more. They seem to suggest that a country having unfavorable terms — i.e. sending out more goods relative to the quantity of goods it is receiving — is, for the time, losing something. Writing of international loans, Professor Taussig says:

The people of Great Britain (the lending country) send merchandise to the United States (the borrowing country), and add to the tangible equipment of the Americans, or to their consumable goods, giving up for the time being some of their own possessions and adding to those of the Americans. But not only do *they give up something in this way — make a sacrifice, incur a loss, for the time being* — but they incur a further loss in that the barter terms of trade become less advantageous to them.[1]

[1] Italics not in the original.

It seems that Professor Pigou, as well as Professor Taussig, implies that *foreign*

The inference that there is a loss, tho only for the time being, appears to me to be unjustified. A movement towards more or towards less favorable terms is brought about most commonly by changes in the volume of foreign investments. An increase in foreign investments results in an increase in the export of goods or services relative to import of goods and services. In what way does this relative increase in the quantity of exports, which shows itself in the less favorable gross barter terms of trade, indicate a worsening of the well-being of the capital exporting country? For the time being, it is true, more goods are being exported relative to the imports. But the quantity of labor and of capital used in order to produce the goods exported on capital account would not have yielded any more consumable commodities for domestic consumption if the same amount of capital had been *invested at home* rather than abroad. In either case an equivalent portion of the nation's productive forces would have been devoted to the production of commodities that would not yield consumable goods until some time in the future. If steel, for example, is sent from France to Algeria on credit, thus making the gross barter terms of trade less favorable to France, the immediate well-being of France is decreased no more than if the same quantity of steel were used instead in the construction of a factory in France. In both instances there is merely a sacrifice of present consumption goods for future goods. Less favorable gross barter terms of trade due to increasing capital exports indicate merely that

investments deprive labor of goods because the country is exporting more without importing more. Pigou writes that in the event of a British loan to foreign countries "the volume of things immediately available in this country will be diminished. This is practically certain to involve a direct injury to labour, either *by making the things workpeople buy more expensive*, or by reducing the supply of tools and machinery that help them in production." — Economics of Welfare, rev. ed., p. 708. The italicized phrase (not italicized in the original) seems to imply that there is a decreased supply of goods for *labor*, and therefore they become more expensive. But had the investment been made at home, the same proportion of the productive factors would have been devoted to future utilities. It is true, of course, that labor may lose because of the increased domestic rate of interest that may result from foreign loans, but I fail to see how — aside from the interest factor which will be discussed in a later chapter — labor would necessarily have any more consumer's goods if production for the future were carried on by domestic investment. In either case the investor, not the worker, postpones consumption.

present utilities in increasing amounts are being exchanged for future *imported* utilities instead of for future utilities produced at home.[1]

Whether the investments are made at home or abroad, the immediate well-being of the investing country is being sacrificed for an expected increase of well-being in the future. The wisdom of devoting productive forces to future rather than to present utilities is not a problem of international trade. The question as to the wisdom of exchanging present for future goods exists whether capital is being exported and the gross barter terms of trade become less favorable or whether capital is being imported and the terms become more favorable. In either case the movement of terms cannot be interpreted as an indication that such movement is favorable or unfavorable to a country's well-being.

Nor can changes in the gross barter terms of trade that result from changes in the other items of the international accounts be so construed. Immigrant remittances, for example, may increase and thereby cause the gross barter terms of trade to become less favorable to the remitting country. But in this instance also the less favorable terms are not an indication of national loss. The residents of the remitting country would have had no more goods to consume had the immigrants elected to consume the products of their expenditures themselves instead of sending them abroad to their families. It may be that immigrant savings would have been larger in the absence of remittances abroad, but the question of possible loss accruing to the nation from decreased savings is a problem quite independent of international trade.

[1] There is, however, this important distinction between investment at home and investment abroad: namely, that the repercussions on the distribution of national income among the various classes of income receivers, or even on the total income, may differ according to the direction in which investments flow. This matter is discussed in Chapter XIII.

CHAPTER XI

BARTER TERMS OF TRADE, *continued*

THE modifications introduced by capital exports into the terms at which a country exchanges its exports for its imports appear not in the gross but in the net barter terms of trade. It will be recalled that net barter terms measure the physical volume of only those exports which serve to pay for a given volume of imports. Thus, when a country's imports are rising in price (in terms of gold) and its exports dropping in price, it has to give a larger quantity (not value) of its exported commodities in exchange for a given amount of imported commodities; the net barter terms of trade become less favorable to the importing country. In such case the increase in the quantity of exports will not yield a return at some time in the future; it constitutes a definitive loss in the sense that it has been necessary to export more goods in order to secure the same quantity of imports. The case of the country whose net barter terms of trade are becoming more unfavorable is somewhat analogous to that of the farmer whose agricultural products are decreasing in price while the tools and clothing he buys are increasing in price.

In order to compute the net barter terms of trade, separate series of prices for imports and for exports have to be secured. No such price series exist for France for the years 1880 to 1913. There is a price series for the years 1890 on (annual 1890 to 1900 and monthly after 1900), published by La Reforme Économique,[1] but this series cannot serve as an index of either imports or exports because it is based on prices of both imported and exported commodities. There is also another series covering the years 1880 on. It is an annual series, published by the Statistique Générale de la France, based before 1905 on the import price of

[1] For a description of this and other French index numbers see Index Numbers of Wholesale Prices in the United States and Foreign Countries, Bulletin of the United States Bureau of Labor Statistics (Washington, 1921), No. 284, pp. 203–216.

45 articles.[1] The prices were fixed by the Commission des Valeurs en Douane. After 1905 the index numbers were computed from the average yearly prices of the different articles in the interior markets of France. Purporting to be an index series of prices in France, it really is before 1905 a crude import index, since it was made of the prices of import articles.

More dependable than this undesigned import price index are two series of index numbers constructed independently by A. W. Flux and by A. De Foville.[2] These two series are both constructed according to a simple and ingenious method. The Department of Commerce publishes two sets of import and export figures: one a preliminary estimate, issued monthly, in which the prices of the preceding year are used in evaluating the commodities, the other a final estimate, made annually, embodying corrections of the preceding year's prices according to the officially ascertained prices for the year for which aggregates were being constructed. By comparing these two aggregates an index number is obtained which is a weighted arithmetic mean of the prices of the commodities entering into the section of the trade considered, the weights being determined by the relative importance in the trade of the different commodities. This link type of index has the disadvantage of being weighted differently each year because of the changing quantities of each commodity, and there are drawbacks in using it to compare the indices of years widely separated. Yet for comparison of consecutive years the link type of index is very useful. The series constructed by Flux goes down only as far as 1898, but a comparison of the two series shows them to be so nearly alike that the De Foville series can safely represent them both thruout the period. Both series are tabulated on page 244.

None of these series were considered adequate for the purpose in hand and so an attempt has been made to construct some price series that might more accurately reflect the price movements in

[1] See Annuaire Statistique de la France, Vols. 1904, p. 151, 1907, p. vii, and 1912, p. 223. These contain descriptions of changes made in the series.

[2] A. De Foville, Variations des prix en France de 1881 à 1910, Bull. de l'Inst. Inter. de Stat. (1912), Vol. 3, p. 220.

A. W. Flux, Price Movements in Foreign Trade of France, Royal Statistical Journal, 1900, Vol. 63, p. 481.

TABLE 42

FRENCH IMPORT AND EXPORT INDICES OF DE FOVILLE AND FLUX

Year	De Foville Base 1900 = 100 Export	De Foville Base 1900 = 100 Import	Flux Base 1893 = 100 Import	Flux 1893 = 101.1 Export
1880	...	...	...	...
1881	114.9	129.9	130.	113.3
1882	113.8	124.7	126.1	112.6
1883	111.5	126.	121.2	110.4
1884	108.1	115.6	116.4	106.4
1885	104.6	112.3	112.9	103.2
1886	103.4	111.7	112.2	101.6
1887	101.2	105.2	105.8	99.7
1888	102.3	106.5	107.2	100.8
1889	104.6	110.6	110.8	103.3
1890	105.8	110.4	111.1	104.5
1891	103.5	107.8	107.7	102.7
1892	101.2	101.9	102.2	99.8
1893	101.2	100.	100.	101.1
1894	95.4	93.5	93.5	94.6
1895	95.4	87.7	94.	94.2
1896	95.4	87.	93.	94.1
1897	93.1	85.7	92.1	92.2
1898	93.1	87.7	94.	92.3
1899	98.9	94.1		
1900	100.	100.		
1901	96.	92.8		
1902	96.6	92.2		
1903	98.3	95.4		
1904	97.7	94.8		
1905	100.	96.7		
1906	104.4	104.1		
1907	105.4	107.1		
1908	100.9	99.2		
1909	104.6	103.7		
1910	108.7	110.5		

exports and imports. Two separate series were constructed for imports, and two for exports. One pair (export and import) was based on the prices of import and export commodities as established by the Commission des Valeurs en Douane. These prices are, as explained above, simple averages of the prices of the preceding year. The classifications usually included many varieties of qualities and sizes, and according to the departmental assistant chief, there were no written instructions to the various commissions as to the method of obtaining the average price for the commodities included under each classification.[1]

The official evaluations established by the commission were used in one pair of series. The prices were weighted by the average of the quantities of that class imported or exported from 1880 to 1900 and from 1900 to 1913. These price series are a duplicate of the quantity series described on page 230. The articles, years, and source of data are the same. The weights in the case of the price data are the average of quantities imported or exported during the period. The formula according to which they are computed is $\frac{\Sigma P_1Q_0}{\Sigma P_0Q_0}$.

The second pair were based on the wholesale prices of specific articles — i.e. specific quality — as published in various trade and financial journals. Of the second pair only the import series was weighted, the weights being similar to those used in the first pair. The export price series contain many French commodities which are important in domestic trade but not important as exports. Their inclusion reduces the accuracy of the series as an index of the price movements of exports, but is necessitated by

[1] One of the assistant chiefs of the department, who was in charge of that particular work, stated in an interview with the writer that the price used for coffee, for instance, was an arithmetic average price of all coffees, each grade being weighted by the amount imported. He was not certain whether this method of averaging had been used from 1880 on, and ventured the opinion that each sub-group (there were a score or more, each group responsible for a particular class of articles, e.g., textiles, metals) had used the same method, altho there were no written instructions on that point. The original price data as used by the commission were not available, altho in some few cases the detailed prices computed by the chambers of commerce who assisted the commission were published in their respective annual and monthly publications.

the paucity of adequate export price data. Notwithstanding, the series appear to be less crude than the other export indices.

The years, base, and formula used in the import index series are the same as those described for the previous import series, but the articles included are not entirely the same. When the prices quoted include the import duty, the amount of such duty has been deducted if the duty was changed during the period covered by the index series. The articles included in the import index of 1880 to 1900 are as follows: wool, cotton, cotton yarn, flax, hemp, jute, silk, silk thread, worked silk, rubber, hides, petroleum, copper, lead, tin, zinc, iron ore, pig iron, bar iron, coal, oak timber, wheat, oats, barley, corn, rice, sugar, coffee, cocoa, tobacco, wine (beginning with 1890), beer, linseed, nitrate of soda, ammonia sulphate, copper sulphate, dried figs, raisins, cod liver oil. The import index for 1900 to 1913 includes those listed above and also the following: butter, eggs, ham, potassium sulphate, olive oil, saffron, pepper, peanuts, cheese, lard, tallow, sulphur, borax, superphosphate of lime.

The index of French domestic commodities entering into international trade and based on wholesale prices prevailing in French markets includes: coal, iron ore, pig iron, sheet iron, steel rails, zinc, turpentine, charcoal, kindling wood, tallow, candles, raw silk, worked silk, black crêpe silk, black satin, black soap, beef, lamb, mutton, pork, poultry, wheat, buckwheat, barley, rye, oats, corn, hay, straw, potatoes, vinegar, butter, eggs, wine, alcohol, sugar, flour, dried peas, lentils, colza oil.

In the years from 1890 to 1900, constituting a separate index, the articles enumerated above are included and also the following: wool yarn, cotton yarn, linen tissue, linen yarn, silk organzine, cotton cloth, muslin, flannel, stearic acid, oleic acid, glycerine, soda, carbonate, raw wool, raw cotton, sulphuric acid, raw hides.

In the index series for the years 1900 to 1913 the articles enumerated for the years 1880 to 1900 and 1890 to 1900 are included and also the following commodities: iron pipe, iron pillars, caustic soda, slate, superphosphate of lime, kaolin, cream of tartar, fish, vegetables, cheese, olive oil, margarine.

The combined series are tabulated on page 248. In Chart 22,

below, the import price indices of De Foville, the series based on market quotations, and the series based on the official evaluations are compared. The movement of the three series is very similar. The movement of the import series based on official valuations parallels very closely De Foville's series. This is to be expected since both are based on similar data. The weights are, of course, different, and De Foville's index includes the prices of all imports

CHART 22

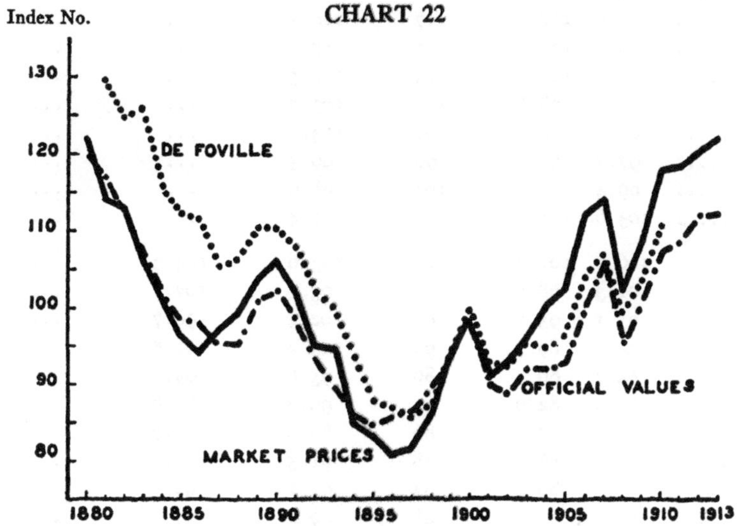

Comparison of Some Price Series of French Imports, 1880–1913
(Base 1900 = 100)

.... De Foville's index
—— Average of monthly market quotations (weighted)
-.-. Official annual evaluations (weighted)

whereas the series based on official evaluations includes only a relatively small number. Their concordance suggests that either series reflects the price movement of imports with a fair degree of accuracy. The series converge as they approach the base. This also is doubtless due to the fact that De Foville's indices are of the link type which are better for consecutive year comparisons than for comparisons of widely separated years. The series based on market quotations move in the same direction as the other series in all but a few years. In 1885, 1896, and 1902 the series move in

TABLE 43

FRENCH IMPORT AND EXPORT PRICES, 1880–1913

(Base 1900 = 100)

Year	Import 1	Import 2	Export 3	49 Commodities 1880–1913 4	77 Commodities 1890–1913 5	94 Commodities 1900–1913 6
1880	122.3	119.7	119	125.7	...	...
1881	114.3	116.8	118	122.2	...	...
1882	112.9	112.8	117	120.3	...	...
1883	106.1	106.5	111	115.9	...	...
1884	101.5	101.6	105	108.5	...	...
1885	96.2	98.6	101	103.7	...	...
1886	94.2	98.2	98	103.1	...	...
1887	97.2	95.3	96	99.5	...	...
1888	99.4	95.1	101	98.9	...	...
1889	103.6	101.	103	102.4	...	...
1890	106.2	102.2	106	103.6	104.9	...
1891	102.3	98.7	98	103.	102.3	...
1892	95.1	93.2	92	102.4	99.7	...
1893	94.5	89.7	97	105.2	101.8	...
1894	84.7	86.	86	95.6	94.	...
1895	83.3	84.9	87	90.8	89.6	...
1896	80.8	85.9	86	88.9	89.7	...
1897	81.6	86.4	88	91.5	89.6	...
1898	86.	89.4	93	95.2	92.	...
1899	93.5	92.7	98	99.2	97.2	...
1900	100.	100.	100	100.	100.	100.
1901	91.2	89.9	92	97.7	96.7	97.2
1902	92.	88.8	93	96.4	96.6	96.5
1903	96.	92.4	96	97.3	98.	97.2
1904	100.2	92.	98	93.6	96.7	96.6
1905	102.4	93.	101	100.8	98.6	98.1
1906	112.3	100.2	105	101.4	102.3	102.
1907	114.1	105.9	104	110.7	113.	110.8
1908	102.1	95.4	98	101.6	104.4	105.1
1909	108.6	101.	104	108.1	108.9	108.3
1910	117.7	107.3	106	112.7	114.1	113.2
1911	118.4	108.7	107	114.4	117.3	115.2
1912	120.4	112.3	107	116.	117.2	116.1
1913	122.	112.4	103	113.2	116.5	116.

[1] Import price weighted by the average quantity of imports. Source of prices, market quotations.
[2] Import prices weighted as above. Source of prices, official evaluation of imports.
[3] Export prices weighted as above. Source of prices, official evaluation.
[4, 5, 6] Export commodities "unweighted." Source of prices, domestic market quotations.

different directions, but the extent of these differences is not great enough to cast doubt on the utility of the series.

In Chart 23 below the series based on 45 commodities from 1880 to 1913, 17 commodities from 1890 to 1913, and 84 commodities from 1900 to 1913 are compared. They follow one another closely enough to show that the absence of a score or more of commodities from 1880 to 1890 does not make any significant difference in the series.

CHART 23

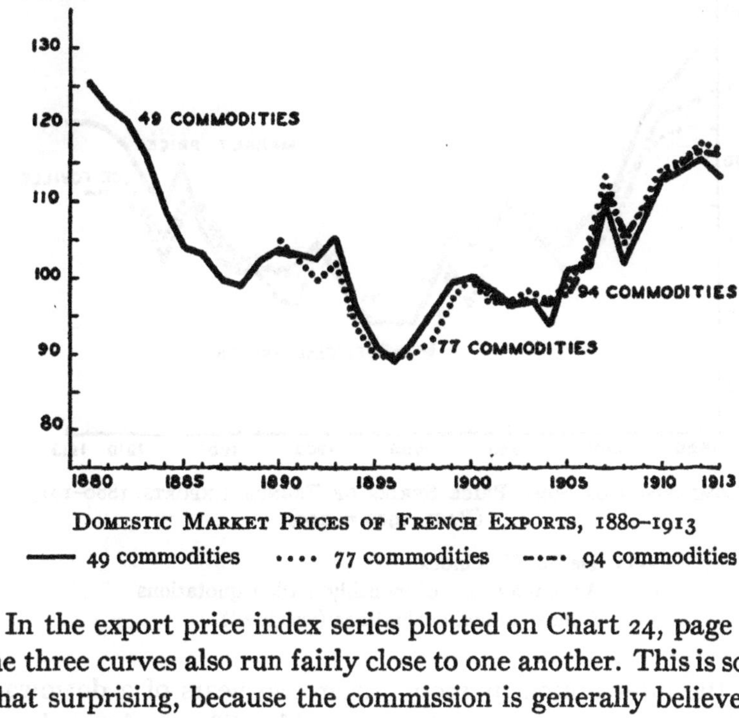

DOMESTIC MARKET PRICES OF FRENCH EXPORTS, 1880–1913

—— 49 commodities .... 77 commodities -.-. 94 commodities

In the export price index series plotted on Chart 24, page 250, the three curves also run fairly close to one another. This is somewhat surprising, because the commission is generally believed to have exercised less care on the collection of price data of exports than of imports and because the series are all weighted differently. In the years 1895, 1904, and 1907 there is a difference in direction of these two curves; but here again the difference is not sufficiently marked to invalidate the utility of any of the series.

From the index numbers based on market values the net barter terms of trade are computed by dividing the import price series by the export price series. When the index series rises, the net barter terms of trade become less favorable to France; when the series drops, the net barter terms of trade become more favorable to France. The result is tabulated on page 252 and presented in the Chart 25, page 251, where it is compared with gross barter terms of trade. It will be noted that the terms grew less favorable to France between 1886 and 1888, more favorable between 1891 and 1894, and continued to grow less favorable from 1897 to 1906,

CHART 24

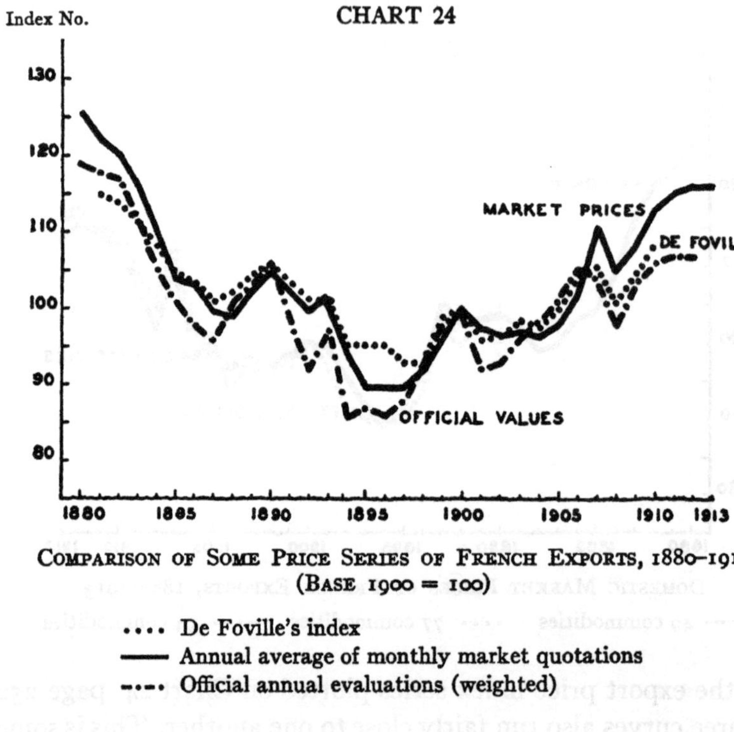

COMPARISON OF SOME PRICE SERIES OF FRENCH EXPORTS, 1880–1913
(BASE 1900 = 100)

.... De Foville's index
—— Annual average of monthly market quotations
-.-. Official annual evaluations (weighted)

with the interruption in 1900. After two years of a downward trend the terms again grew less favorable. The conformation of the curve follows that of the gross barter terms, but in the period before 1900 in a much modified form. The outstanding result is that the net barter terms of trade were less favorable after 1900 than before.

What is the significance of these oscillations in the net barter terms of trade? It will be remembered that when the curve rises France was giving an increasing physical volume of commodities in payment for a given amount of imports; the net barter terms of trade were becoming less favorable. This would happen when import and export prices were either both rising or both falling so long as import prices were rising more rapidly or falling more slowly than export prices. When the less favorable net barter terms of trade are proximately caused by import prices falling more slowly than export prices, the following is true: for every hundred francs (gold) France received for her exports she was

CHART 25

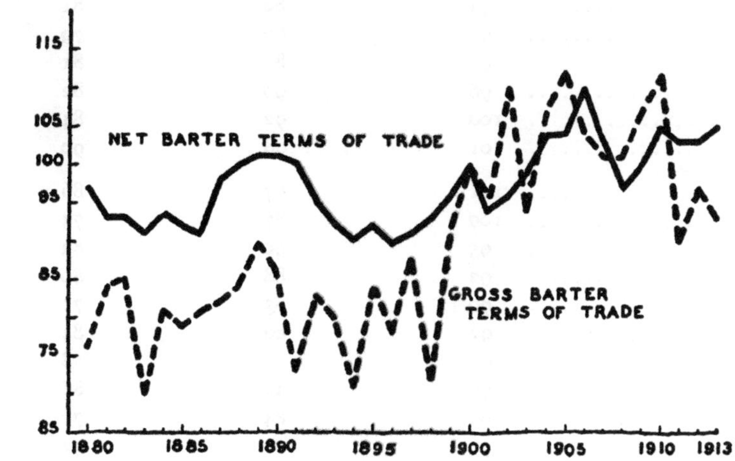

Gross and Net Barter Terms of Trade for France, 1880–1913
(Base 1900 = 100)

—— Net barter terms of trade (market prices)
---- Gross barter terms of trade (direct method)

giving more goods than she had been previously, while for every hundred francs she paid for her imports she was not receiving *as much more* as she was giving. When both import and export prices rise and the index of net barter terms also rises, the description of the change has to be set in different terms. Instead of giving more goods for every hundred francs received, France was giving less goods, but in return she not only received a decreased quantity of goods for every hundred francs paid out, but the decrease was greater in her imports than in her exports; the terms were becoming less favorable.

TABLE 44

ANNUAL NET AND GROSS BARTER TERMS OF TRADE FOR FRANCE, 1880–1913

Year	1 Net Barter Terms of Trade [1]	2 Gross Barter Terms of Trade [2] (Indirect Method)	3 Gross Barter Terms of Trade [3] (Direct Method)
1880	97	78	76
1881	93	78	84
1882	93	79	85
1883	91	76	70
1884	93	80	81
1885	92	80	79
1886	91	81	81
1887	98	90	82
1888	100	92	84
1889	101	98	90
1890	101	97	86
1891	100	87	73
1892	95	90	83
1893	92	88	80
1894	90	83	71
1895	92	96	84
1896	90	92	78
1897	90	95	88
1898	93	84	72
1899	96	101	92
1900	100	100	100
1901	94	98	96
1902	96	106	110
1903	99	99	94
1904	104	118	107
1905	104	121	112
1906	110	118	104
1907	103	106	101
1908	97	99	101
1909	100	104	107
1910	105	104	112
1911	103	88	90
1912	103	96	97
1913	105	98	93

1 Import price index divided by export price series.

2 Col. 9, Table 39, divided by Col. 4, Table 38.

3 Col. 10, Table 39, divided by Col. 5, Table 38.

Changes in net barter terms of trade are proximately due, of course, to changes in prices, but the causes of the price changes may vary, and the significance also. If imports are rising in price more rapidly than exports, the causes may proceed entirely from monetary and banking phenomena, or they may be due to an increased real cost of production of the important commodities imported. To illustrate: a country's imports may consist largely of certain foodstuffs or certain raw materials the real cost of producing which — let it be assumed — is increasing. Its exports, on the other hand, may consist largely of certain manufactured products the real costs of producing which are not increasing so much as those of imported foodstuffs, or not increasing at all. The result when converted into money terms would be an increase in the price of those foodstuffs or raw materials greater than the increase in the price of those manufactured products — or the increase in price might only be relative. The country importing mostly foodstuffs and exporting mostly manufactured articles would have to give an increased quantity of the products of its labor in exchange for a given quantity of imports. While the net barter terms of trade would be less favorable, they would be less favorable not for any reason connected with international trade or the international balance of payments, but solely because the real costs of production of foodstuffs had increased.[1]

On the other hand, the difference in price may be due not to an increase in the cost of the imported foodstuffs, but to a decrease in the real cost of production of the exported manufactured articles. In the instance of the absolute as well as relative increase in the cost of foodstuffs, the country whose net barter terms of trade are becoming less favorable is really worse off; it has to

[1] Keynes believed that the net barter terms of trade for England were growing less favorable after 1900 and claimed that this was due to the increased real cost of raw products, which constituted a very important part of English imports. He considered it to be evidence that the operation of the law of diminishing returns for raw products had set in. — Economic Journal, 1912, Vol. 22, p. 630.

Beveridge, discussing the above article, pointed out that the increasing relative cost of foods and raw materials may be not due to increasing real costs of raw materials but to the decreased real costs of manufactured goods. — Sir W. Beveridge, Keynes' Evidence for Overpopulation, Economica, February, 1924, p. 1.

expend greater effort to obtain the same quantity of imports. In the instance of only a relative increase in the costs of foodstuffs, it is neither better nor worse off (so far as international exchange of commodities is concerned); it gives more goods in return for the same quantity of imports as before, but the increased quantity of exports costs no more to produce than the smaller quantity did. It gains, of course, in its domestic consumption, by the decrease in the cost of production of those goods that it produces at a lower real cost. When the net barter terms of trade become less favorable because of the relative increase in real costs of production of imports, the consumers of those commodities get less of them in exchange for a given amount of their labor, but they do so whether they are in the importing or the exporting country. When, for example, copper rises in price relative to other commodities, all copper users, whether in the United States or France, get less of it in exchange for their products. If copper forms an important element in French imports, the net barter terms of trade would to that extent become less favorable. But the inference that France would thereby be worse off than the exporting country would be quite erroneous. The country exporting copper may experience as great a loss or even greater, depending entirely upon the amount of copper it consumes.

Thus, when the cause of a change in the net barter terms of trade is a change in the real costs of production, less favorable terms may not indicate that the country is worse off because of that change. Indeed, it is possible for a country to secure a larger share of the gain from the international exchange of goods even tho its net barter terms of trade are becoming less favorable. This may occur when the elasticity of the foreign demand for exports (whose real costs of production have decreased) is high and the reduction in the real costs of production is also high. Under such circumstances more exports would have to be sent out to pay for the given quantity of imports. But the real cost of production of the total larger quantity of exports might be less than the cost of the smaller quantity. In terms of money the total value of imports and of exports would be equal, yet the net barter terms of trade would have become more unfavorable because the index of imports would have declined less than that of exports. Notwithstanding the less favorable terms of trade, the exporting country would be better off for two reasons: (1) it would be obtaining its imports at a lower real cost, and (2) it would expend less in real costs for export commodities consumed at home.

An illustration of such a situation (in the form of a table) may serve to indicate the various effects of changes in the real costs of production on the net barter terms of trade and also the interpretation of those terms.

Let it be assumed that a country's exports consist chiefly of copper and imports chiefly of rubber. The following tabulation is assumed to indicate the conditions of trade before a radical change in the cost of production of copper occurs.

	Days' Labor	Wages per Day	Selling Price per Ton	Quantity Shipped Abroad (tons)	Total Value Exported	Total Labor Exported (mill. days)
Copper ..	10	$4	$40	1,000,000	$40,000,000	10
Rubber ..	20	2	40	1,000,000	40,000,000	20

Net barter terms of trade = 100

Now assume a 25 per cent decline in the real cost of production of copper and an elastic foreign demand for copper. The following situation represents the final outcome — the outcome after adjustment in the balance of payments has occurred.

	Days' Labor	Wages per Day	Selling Price per Ton	Quantity Shipped Abroad (tons)	Total Value Exported	Total Labor Exported (mill. days)
Copper ..	8	$4.25	$34	1,177,000	$40,000,000	8.9
Rubber ..	20	1.90	38	1,052,000	40,000,000	20.1

The final outcome shows the net barter terms of trade $\left(\frac{\text{import price}}{\text{export price}}\right)$ to have become less favorable. Formerly they were 100; in the final situation they are 112. Notwithstanding the less favorable net barter terms of trade, the copper producing country benefits by the change. It secures its imports at a lower real cost. It expends 8.9 million days' labor for 1,052,000 tons of rubber, whereas before it expended 10 million days' labor for 1,000,000 tons of rubber.

The reader will recognize the many combinations of given conditions possible: changes in relative elasticities of demand; changes in real costs of production; changes in the total value of the exported commodities, the real costs of producing which have changed; changes in the ratio of those commodities to other exports. Each set of conditions would result in different net barter terms of trade. The many possibilities have engaged the attention of some mathematically minded economists [1] who have usually worked out the possibilities of changes in reciprocal international demand and in real costs of production not in terms of money prices and money incomes, but in terms of barter.[2] It is hardly necessary to consider any more of the possibilities here. It is important only to note that when the cause of changes in the net barter terms of trade is changes in the real costs of production, the movement of the net barter terms of trade cannot by itself be interpreted as indicating that a country is worse or better off.

When, however, the relative price changes are a result not of changes in the real costs of production, but of monetary influences connected with international trade, the movement of net barter terms of trade has a quite different significance. A relative increase in import prices caused directly by monetary factors means that the importing country is receiving a smaller quantity of imports per unit of export, altho the *real cost* to the exporting country of producing those imports has not risen. The exporting country in this instance gains what the importing country loses. Nor does it matter — as it did when changes in relative prices were due to changes in real costs — whether the net barter terms of trade are growing less favorable because imports are rising or because exports are dropping in price. In either case the loss is the same, and in either case the loss is felt only by the consumers

[1] See, for illustration, F. Y. Edgeworth, The Pure Theory of International Trade, in Volume II of his collected papers.

[2] If the reader is interested in carrying out the possibilities to a greater degree of verisimilitude than the above illustration affords, he is referred to Taussig's International Trade, Part I, where the method of procedure is illustrated.

of imported commodities who are residents in the country whose net barter terms of trade are becoming less favorable; they are paying for those commodities a larger share of their income than they did when the net barter terms of trade were more favorable.

When the relative price changes are due to a rise or fall in the price levels, one of the contributory causes may very definitely be connected with the international movements of goods and capital. For illustration, a country which is investing more capital abroad than the sums due it from other countries has to transfer to foreign countries title to purchasing power. In so far as this transfer sets into motion forces which decrease domestic prices relative to foreign prices, less favorable net barter terms of trade for the capital exporting country will result; for a given quantity of imports the capital exporting country will have to send an increased quantity of exports, and this increased quantity of exports will represent an increase in *total* real costs, felt by all consumers of imported products. In this case less favorable net barter terms of trade indicate a definite loss to the community.

The question then arises as to what caused the changes in the French net barter terms of trade. Were the changes due to monetary factors, or were they a result of changes in real costs of production of French imports and exports? Further, is there any evidence that the worsening of the net barter terms of trade adversely affected the real income of the French people? [1]

A comparison of the curve of capital exports and the curve of net barter terms of trade shows the correlation to be not very high. In the years from 1894 to 1898 the movement is in opposite directions; capital exports increased, but the net barter terms grew more favorable. This unexpected movement of the net barter terms of trade may for part of that period perhaps be explained by the high tariff of 1892. It was pointed out in an earlier chapter that the effect of this high tariff was to check merchandise imports for several years. This caused specie imports to increase greatly in 1892, 1893, and 1894 (Table 4). Thus the transfer of

[1] Against the possible loss in real income to some Frenchmen from less favorable barter terms of trade is to be set the possible gain from higher interest rates induced by capital exports. See Chap. XIII.

purchasing power abroad brought about by increased foreign investments was to a certain extent offset by an increase in purchasing power in France due to heavy gold imports and to a concomitant increase in the domestic demand for domestic goods, caused by the considerably increased cost of imports.[1] As one French writer commenting on the effect of the high tariff graphically wrote, the French filled their strong boxes instead of their stomachs.[2] The increased domestic demand for commodities produced at home checked the fall of prices in France and thereby kept the net barter terms of trade from becoming less favorable.[3] It should be noted, however, that altho the curve shows the net barter terms of trade for France to be more favorable after 1892, France benefited from the more favorable terms only in so far as foreign goods continued to be imported. The effect of the tariff was to cause a decrease in the French consumption of some foreign goods. To the extent that domestic substitutes for the commodities effectively barred by the import duties were secured only at a higher cost, there arose a loss to offset the gain from the more favorable terms.[4]

The high duty may also explain why it was possible for the increased foreign investments to take the form of a merchandise export surplus notwithstanding a relatively increasing price of French exports. The high tariff served to decrease imports and to develop the surplus not so much by an increase in exports as by a decrease in imports. The quantity index of French imports declined from 114 in 1891 to 100 in 1896. It had leaped to 108 in 1894, but this change was due to poor domestic crops and was

[1] The increased duties on agricultural commodities varied from 10 to 25 per cent, and on industrial products 25 to 60 per cent.

[2] M. Dijol, Situation économique de la France sous le régime protectionniste de 1892 (Paris, 1910), p. 253.

[3] Commenting on a somewhat similar phenomenon observable in the net barter terms of trade of the United States, Professor Taussig writes: "Indeed, a protective system may be said to amount in substance to a conscious and deliberate determination to buy less of imports; and the less of imports a country demands, the more favorable are the barter terms for the imports which it continues to take." — Op. cit., p. 304.

[4] For discussion of this point see J. S. Mill, Principles of Political Economy, Bk. V, Chap. IV, Sec. 5; Chap. X, Sec. 1. Also F. W. Taussig, op. cit., Chap. 13.

not a reflection of a general increase in imports. In none of the other large countries during those years was there a similar checking of imports: the British import quantity index rose from 75 to 91; the United States from 55 to 63; and the German imports rose in value from 5127 to 5320 million francs, a rise which would doubtless reflect a much larger increase in quantities if due allowance were made for the sharp decline in import prices in those years. In fact, with the exception of Spain, France was the only country in Europe whose imports declined in total value from 1891 to 1897. It would seem, then, that the absence of a correlation between 1892 and 1898 is what should be expected; the incident would seem to strengthen rather than weaken the theory that an increase in capital exports normally serves to make the net barter terms of trade less favorable to the capital exporting country. On the other hand, the absence of correlation for several of the other years, for which no explanation serves, leaves the question of the relation of capital exports to net barter terms of trade in doubt.

Monetary and credit factors, in any case, were not the sole cause of changes in the net barter terms of trade. There were times when they were affected by changes in the cost of a few important commodities. In 1900, for example, because of the Boer War, coal increased 35 per cent, wool 22 per cent, and cotton 40 per cent. Their increased cost was almost wholly responsible for the rise in the French import price level; they formed 20 per cent of the French imports of that year. The net barter terms of trade again moved in a direction contrary to that of capital exports; in spite of decreased capital exports during that year, net barter terms of trade grew less favorable.

But even in normal times monetary and credit factors were not the sole cause of changes in the net barter terms of trade. The relative increase in the cost of producing raw materials was a contributory factor in causing the net barter terms of France to become less favorable. From 1880–1884 to 1909–1913 the *value* of per capita imports increased 54 per cent in France, only 32 per cent and 27 per cent in England and the United States respectively, while imports into Germany almost doubled. When, however, *physical volumes* of imports are compared (see Table 45 below), both England and the United States show a greater increase than France. England's 32 per cent increase in import values represents a 62 per cent increase in physical volume, whereas France's 54 per cent increase in value represents only a 36 per cent increase in physical volume. The United States duplicates England's experience, the increase of 27 per cent in value representing an increase of 45 per cent in physical volume. One

TABLE 45

INCREASE IN PER CAPITA VALUES AND QUANTITIES OF IMPORTS AND EXPORTS OF FRANCE, ENGLAND, GERMANY, AND THE UNITED STATES FROM THE AVERAGE OF YEARS 1880–1885 TO AVERAGE OF YEARS 1909–1913

	Value of Per Capita Imports			Value of Per Capita Exports		
	(Francs) Average 1880–1884	(Francs) Average 1909–1913	(%) Ratio of Increase	(Francs) Average 1880–1884	(Francs) Average 1909–1913	(%) Ratio of Increase
France	128	197	54	95	166	74
England.......	247	326	32	168	244	46
Germany	83	185	116	85	156	83
United States .	69	88	27	80	112	40

	Relatives of Quantities of Per Capita Imports and Exports (1900 = 100)					
	Imports			Exports		
	Average 1880–1884	Average 1909–1913	Ratio of Increase	Average 1880–1884	Average 1909–1913	Ratio of Increase
France	96	131	36	76	130	71
England.......	68	110	62	95	141	48
United States .	94	137	45	70	97	39

of the causes of this movement toward less favorable net barter terms of trade for France was that her imports during this period consisted of a large share of raw materials which had increased in price relative to other groups. Coal, raw wool, raw cotton, metals, and hides, all important French imports, rose in price relatively to manufactured commodities and foodstuffs. England, whose ratio of physical quantities to value of imports had increased much more than that of France, also imported these raw materials (except coal), but raw materials formed only 30 per cent of her total imports whereas they formed 47 per cent of French imports. Moreover, the proportion of raw materials imported into France was constantly growing — it reached 60 per cent in 1909–1913 — while the proportion imported into England did not change. It is therefore not surprising that the ratio of increase in physical quantities to the ratio of increase in value was larger in the case of English than in the case of French imports.

The relative increase in the cost of producing raw materials accentuated the effect of capital exports towards a worsening of the net barter terms of trade of France. How much of the change can be attributed to one cause or the other — how much to the changing costs of production and how much to foreign investments — it is obviously impossible to determine. In so far as the worsening in the net barter terms of trade was due to changing costs of production, there was no loss to the French consumer which was not felt by consumers of the same raw products thruout the world (except when the conditions of reciprocal demand helped to reduce the money incomes in France more or less than the money incomes in other countries). But in so far as the worsening was due to capital exports, less favorable barter terms of trade indicated a definite loss to the French consumer of imported commodities in that he paid a larger share of his income for *all* imported commodities altho only some of them were produced at higher real costs; and even those commanded a larger part of the French consumer's income than would have been the case had less capital been exported.

The preceding discussion has been confined to the influence exerted by capital exports on the net barter terms of trade thru changes in price levels caused by the transfers of purchasing power. There are, however, secondary effects induced by capital exports which once again influence the net barter terms of trade. These secondary effects may cause the terms to become either less or more favorable, according to the use made of the borrowed capital.[1] If the capital has been employed (in the borrowing country) to develop an industry producing commodities formerly imported, the effect may be decreased imports (into the borrowing

[1] The returning interest and dividend payments also affect the net barter terms of trade, but these returning payments are essentially the same as a reverse flow of capital and need no special discussion.

country), disturbed equilibrium in the international accounts, and an inward flow of specie. The net barter terms of trade may thus become still more favorable to the borrowing country. A similar final outcome might be reached if the borrowed capital were used to develop public works such as railways, harbors, highways, and power sources, for such expenditures usually operate to cut the costs of production of exportable commodities. If the foreign demand for those exports is very elastic, the total value of the exports would increase. The resultant disequilibrium would be followed by imports of specie, and — as in the previous case — the net barter terms of trade would become again more favorable to the borrowing country. If, however, the foreign demand for the borrowing country's exports is inelastic, the secondary effect on the net barter terms of trade would be the opposite; the terms would tend to become less favorable to the borrowing country.

The terms might also become less favorable to the borrowing country (as a secondary effect of foreign borrowing) if the borrowed funds were expended on such public works as would not operate to decrease the costs of production of exportable commodities (in the borrowing country), even tho they produced valuable utilities. In this class would fall expenditures on schools, playgrounds, some public buildings, some highways, armaments, sewage systems, and so forth. The loss of capital caused by the need to pay interest abroad on the foreign borrowing is in the case of such expenditures not supplanted by the savings that would have been produced had the borrowed funds been spent on railways, harbors, factories, and so forth. The net loss of capital (which to the borrowing country may be a wholly worth while price to pay for more schools, tho perhaps not for a better equipped army or more luxurious court) is increased by the additional cost of upkeep necessitated by the additional school buildings and so forth. The result would be a higher interest rate. This, in turn, would cause such commodities as are produced at home with relatively large amounts of capital to increase in price as compared with commodities produced with little capital and much labor. If the imports of the borrowing country consist chiefly of commodities made with much capital and little labor (e.g. machinery), and if its exports consist chiefly of goods made with much labor and little machinery (e.g. raw silk), then the price index of exports would decline relatively to imports. In such case, that is, the net barter terms of trade would become less favorable. If, on the other hand, the foreign demand for the borrowing country's exported raw materials was relatively elastic, the *final* outcome would be a flow of purchasing power into the borrowing country, and once again the net barter terms of trade would become more favorable, as when the loan was first consummated.

It is apparent, hence, that the adjustment of international accounts necessitated by capital exports may affect the net barter terms of trade in the borrowing country first favorably, then unfavorably, and then, perhaps, favorably again. Just what the primary, secondary, and tertiary effects of a loan may be on the net barter terms of trade depends on the size and purpose of the loan, the character of a country's imports and exports, and the elasticities of demand for these imports and exports. We cannot predict the final outcome on the net barter terms of trade in either country without knowing all the conditions stated above. Nor can we interpret intelligently changes in the net barter terms of trade without knowing the causes of those changes. The difficulty of predicting the effects of a loan on the net barter terms of trade, and the difficulty of interpreting the changes in the terms, should not, however, be confused with the attempt to ascertain the direction in which the terms moved. We may find that the terms became more or less favorable without being certain of the cause.

Evidence of the effect on incomes brought about by the movement of net barter terms of trade should be found in the movement of wages. Statistics of annual wage movements in France, however, for the period 1880 to 1913 are surprisingly meagre. The only annual wage movements that appear to have been published for more than a few years are the wages of workers in coal mines and in the beet sugar, the match, and the tobacco industries. Of these only the wages of coal miners continue thru all the years under study. A wage index based on so few series can hardly be used to represent the movement of wages in France.[1] There have been some very complete periodic official investigations of wages which give detailed wage data, covering most of the trades thruout France, for approximately every five years.[2] Their findings have been combined and results plotted on Chart 26 below with the indices of annual data mentioned above.

CHART 26

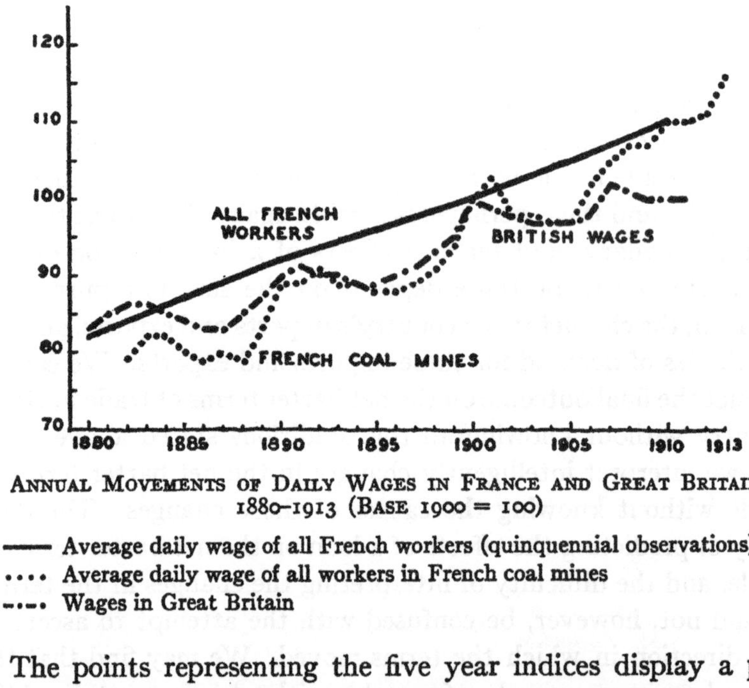

Annual Movements of Daily Wages in France and Great Britain, 1880–1913 (Base 1900 = 100)

—— Average daily wage of all French workers (quinquennial observations)
.... Average daily wage of all workers in French coal mines
-.-. Wages in Great Britain

The points representing the five year indices display a perfectly straight upward trend from 1880 to 1913, but the move-

[1] The wages published for the match industry are from 1890 to 1912, and for the tobacco industry from 1900 to 1913. Even the scanty annual data available lack dependability. The wages published are average daily wages of all workers in the industry. Separate classification is made for men, for women, and, in the beet sugar industry, for children, but the figures can be considered accurate only if it be assumed that the proportion of various grades of workers remained the same over the whole period. Such an assumption is risky for so prolonged a period.

[2] Office du travail, Salaires et durée de travail dans l'industrie française (Paris, 1907), 4 vols.; Bordereaux de salaires pour diverses catégories d'ouvriers en 1900 et 1901 (Paris, 1902).

L. March, Salaires et coût de l'existence à diverses époques jusqu'en 1910 (Paris, 1911).

TABLE 46

ANNUAL MOVEMENTS OF DAILY WAGES IN FRANCE AND GREAT BRITAIN, 1880–1913

(Base 1900 = 100)

Year	All Workers in Coal Mines	Average in Sugar, Tobacco, and Match Industries	34 Men's Trades Outside Paris	43 Trades in Paris	5 Women's Trades Outside Paris	Average for All Workers	Wages in Great Britain
1880	...	...	82	...	...	82	83
1881	...	102	...	...	...	...	85
1882	79	100	...	...	...	...	86
1883	82	104	...	...	...	...	86
1884	82	100	...	...	...	...	85
1885	80	95	85	...	...	...	84
1886	79	94	...	...	...	87	83
1887	80	95	...	...	...	...	83
1888	79	95	...	...	...	...	85
1889	83	94	...	...	...	...	87
1890	89	80	...	...	...	92	90
1891	89	81	...	...	...	...	91
1892	91	82	...	...	...	...	90
1893	89	84	...	...	...	...	90
1894	89	86	...	...	...	...	89
1895	88	89	...	...	...	96	89
1896	88	89	96	92	94	...	90
1897	89	91	...	...	...	...	91
1898	91	94	...	...	...	...	93
1899	94	97	...	...	...	...	95
1900	100	100	100	100	100	100	100
1901	103	101	...	...	...	...	99
1902	98	102	...	...	...	...	98
1903	98	103	...	...	...	...	97
1904	97	104	...	...	...	...	97
1905	97	105	...	...	...	105	97
1906	102	108	107	104	106	...	98
1907	105	110	...	...	...	...	102
1908	107	111	...	...	...	...	101
1909	107	113	...	...	...	...	100
1910	110	114	...	...	...	110	100
1911	110	115	113	104.5	114	...	100
1912	111	117					
1913	116						

Sources: Statistique de l'Industrie Minerale. Salaires et Coût de l'Existence.

ments of wages in the few industries for which there are annual data available are much more irregular. The sharp downward curve from 1883 to 1890 of wages in the sugar, tobacco, and match industries can be ignored, because it represents exclusively the movement in the beet sugar industry, the figures for the match industry not beginning before 1890 and those of the tobacco industry not before 1900. The drop is accentuated because in 1890 the wages in the match industry were much lower (in reference to 1900) than in the beet sugar industry (see Table 47). Other annual wage data in the iron and steel industry show movements which are more like the wages in the coal mines,[1] but annual wage figures in the "large industries" furnished by prefects from 1881 to 1887 show little movement in those years.[2] Altogether the annual wage data are quite unsatisfactory and the quinquennial data are useful only in depicting the trend of wages. The absence of all cyclical fluctuations makes the data of little use for comparison with annual data.

Professor Taussig in his discussion of the net barter terms of trade for Great Britain and Canada finds an inverse relation be-

[1] Average daily wage in the iron industry in France:

	Francs per Day		Francs per Day
1882	3.63	1890	3.32
1883	3.67	1891	3.48
1884	3.37	1892	3.16
1885	2.96	1893	3.23
1886	2.76	1894	3.18
1887	2.97	1895	3.24
1888	3.06	1896	3.39
1889	3.31		

L. Dechere, La productivité du travail et les salaires, Rev. d'Écon. Pol., April, 1899.

[2] Daily wages in the large industries:

	Paris		Departments	
	Men	Women	Men	Women
1881	5.27	2.67	3.54	1.76
1882	5.27	2.67	3.51	1.78
1883	5.33	2.68	3.55	1.80
1884	5.33	2.58	3.56	1.70
1885	5.45	2.66	3.58	1.77
1886	5.01	2.63	3.56	1.79
1887	5.02	2.65	3.57	1.78

A. Coste, Étude statistique sur les salaires des travailleurs et le revenu de la France (Paris, 1890).

TABLE 47

ANNUAL MOVEMENTS OF DAILY WAGES IN TOBACCO, MATCH, AND BEET SUGAR INDUSTRIES OF FRANCE, 1881–1912

(Base 1900 = 100)

	Beet Sugar Industry			Match[1] Industry		Tobacco[2] Industry	
Year	Men	Women	Children	Men	Women	Men	Women
1881 ..	102	95	105	...	...	60	...
1882 ..	100	95	106	...	...	63	...
1883 ..	104	96	106	...	...	...	...
1884 ..	100	91	103	...	...	...	...
1885 ..	95	90	99	...	...	...	...
1886 ..	94	91	100	...	...	...	...
1887 ..	95	89	99	...	...	...	...
1888 ..	95	91	102	...	...	...	...
1889 ..	94	84	87	...	...	...	...
1890 ..	94	84	88	67	60	...	...
1891 ..	95	86	94	67	63	...	...
1892 ..	94	84	90	70	63	...	...
1893 ..	95	85	88	74	70	...	...
1894 ..	95	84	90	78	75	...	...
1895 ..	95	86	91	78	81	96	90
1896 ..	96	88	93	83	87	...	...
1897 ..	96	89	91	87	91	...	...
1898 ..	97	89	92	91	94	...	...
1899 ..	99	98	99	95	96	...	...
1900 ..	100	100	100	100	100	100	100
1901 ..	102	102	101	102	103	101	101
1902 ..	102	104	102	102	105	103	105
1903 ..	102	102	100	102	107	105	108
1904 ..	103	101	99	104	108	107	111
1905 ..	104	104	103	104	109	107	111
1906 ..	106	108	104	107	111	112	115
1907 ..	108	108	104	107	115	115	120
1908 ..	108	110	101	109	117	118	122
1909 ..	111	114	104	109	117	119	124
1910 ..	112	118	106	110	119	121	127
1911 ..	115	117	111	110	120	122	127
1912 ..	117	119	117	111	120	124	124

Source: Bulletin de Statistique et de Legislation Comparée.

[1] State owned match factories. 10 hr. day to 1906 and 9 hr. since.

[2] State owned tobacco factories. 10 hr. day to 1906 and 9 hr. since.

tween the net barter terms and the money wages in those countries. But movement of the wages of French coal miners shows, if anything, the opposite. Nevertheless, no conclusions can be drawn from one wage series, particularly since it seems to move for many years independently of other wage movements. The paucity of French wage series makes comparisons of wage movements with net barter terms of trade impossible.

CHAPTER XII

ECONOMIC EFFECTS OF FRENCH CAPITAL EXPORTS

THE capital exports of France compel attention not so much because of their absolute quantity, which was large, but because they represent so great a part of the country's savings. Between the years 1880 and 1913 one-third to one-half of the savings of France was invested in foreign countries. The export of so much of a nation's savings provokes the question: what was the effect of this export of capital upon the welfare of France?

There is a tendency to dismiss the question on the ground that there is no difference between international and intranational movements of capital.[1] Capital moves, it is held, to that industry or place where the return is greatest, making due allowance, of course, for risk and marketability. The more freely capital moves, the more certain it is that the return will be greater. To hamper mobility is to interfere with the best use of capital. The effect of a free movement of capital from Paris to Lyons is increased production; the effect of a free movement of capital from Paris to Milan is the same — an increase in production.

On further thought it appears, however, that the matter can by no means be so readily dismissed. The existence of national

[1] E. W. Kemmerer in the introductory article of a symposium on foreign investments in the Annals of the Amer. Acad. of Pol. and Soc. Sci., November, 1916, writes: "The basic principles of foreign investments are essentially the same as those of home investments. The word *foreign* is a political term, but the word *investment* is an economic one, and the political boundaries do not obstruct the operation of economic law. Obviously there is not much difference in motive or in principle between the investment of a million dollars by a citizen of the United States in a paper factory in Ontario and one in New York. It is the likeness, therefore, rather than the difference that should be emphasized in comparing the principles of foreign investments with those of domestic." It is likely that Kemmerer was thinking of foreign investments only from the point of view of the individual; from that point of view his statement cannot be criticized. But the best good of the individual does not necessarily mean the best good of the nation. The quotation is given because Kemmerer's remarks express a widely held opinion with regard to the principles of foreign investments not from the individual but from the national point of view.

boundaries, of different national monetary, banking, and taxation systems; the varying degrees of mobility of the factors of production; different political and economic outlook and habits of saving and spending — all introduce elements which affect the situation. To ignore these differences is to overlook some consequences of major importance.

Even were we to admit that the gains from international movements of capital to the world as a whole are greater than the losses — and this is not to be granted without qualification — it is not alone with the gains of the world that we are here concerned. Rather are we primarily evaluating the effects of capital exports on the welfare of France. This purely national point of view needs no justification. It is national, not international, points of view that largely determine economic policies. One may wish it were not so; but to analyze economic problems without regard to national boundaries is naïve.

Even the nation is too large a unit; groups within the nation must be taken into consideration when weighing the effects of capital exports. Within the larger group there are land owners, wage earners, owners of capital, and business men, and it is quite possible that gains accruing to one class of income receivers may be obtained at the expense of another and larger group. Land owners may benefit at the expense of consumers; owners of capital at the expense of wage earners. Even within the same class of income receivers there are different groups each of which may be differently affected by capital movements. Bankers may benefit at the expense of manufacturers, exporters at the expense of importers, skilled labor at the expense of unskilled.

And not only does the effect of capital exports vary with each group; it varies also with the conditions surrounding each loan. Some foreign loans may be beneficial to both the borrowing and the lending country; some only to the lenders or to the borrowers; some to neither. They may be beneficial when made for one purpose and not when made for another. One can generalize on the effects only with so many qualifications as to vitiate the generalization; yet the statements commonly made about the effects of capital exports usually give no hint of such qualifications.

It has been commonly assumed that the effects of French capital exports were as follows:

1. That France received a higher return on her capital, since capital flowed out only in response to higher interest rates than could be obtained at home.

2. That the productivity of capital for the world was greater because capital flowed where it was most needed, and that consequently the lending nation as well as other nations benefited as consumers thru the cheapening of food, raw material, and transportation, and as producers thru expanded markets for their goods.

3. That the risk of investment was decreased thru geographical distribution of investments.

4. That foreign investments, by functioning as an international medium of exchange, protected France's gold reserves, and thereby her banking and (perhaps) price stability, from short-time fluctuations. Furthermore, that in times of stress foreign investments proved a very valuable liquid reserve.

These are the alleged effects. In the following pages we purpose to subject each of them to critical analysis.

The claim that France received a higher return on her capital invested abroad rests first of all on the assumption that the rate of return on foreign investments was greater than the rate of return on domestic investments. A comparison of the yields, however, from these two fields of investment offers evidence that casts some doubt on the validity of this assumption. The study of Decoudu in 1899, referred to in Chapter V, gives the exact rate of return on foreign and on domestic investments for all securities listed on the Bourse. At the market price of 1900 the yield on domestic securities was 3.23 per cent while on foreign securities it was 3.84 per cent — a difference of .61 per cent in favor of foreign securities.[1] But these rates of return, based as they are on prices current in 1900, do not indicate the gain to France from her foreign as compared with her domestic investments. It is with the

[1] The increase in favor of foreign securities would be somewhat higher if allowance were made for the inclusion of some low yield foreign bonds such as English consols, which in fact were held by the French only in small amounts.

rate of return to France as a whole that we are concerned. In the case of domestic investments this gain can be measured only on the basis of the price at which the securities were originally issued. In the case of foreign investments held by the French it is the price at which these securities were sold to Frenchmen that signifies.

The greater part of the foreign securities in the French portfolio was acquired, we find, at the rate of issue. Almost all the Russian loans were floated in France and remained there. The same is true of South American and Balkan investments. A large portion of Italian and Spanish securities were repurchased by those countries at periods when prevailing prices were higher than at the time of issue. The gain to France from the re-sale of these securities at prices higher than the issuing price probably made up in good part for the foreign securities that were acquired by France between the 80's and the 90's at prices higher than the price of issue. Also, as was noted in the discussion on interest, the foreign securities listed in 1900 included many conversions at the low yields current between 1889 and 1895. But these again were outweighed by the heavier conversion of domestic securities during that period. (See Table 15.) It is therefore at the price of issue, and not at the prevailing market price, that the yields of both the domestic and the foreign securities must be compared.

The yield on domestic securities in France in 1899 at the price of issue was 4.28 per cent; whereas the yield on foreign securities held by France in that year was, on the same basis, only 3.85 per cent. Instead of demonstrating an increased yield from foreign investments, a comparison of foreign and domestic investments according to the returns in 1899 — on the basis of the issuing price of securities — shows the opposite. This higher yield on domestic securities assumes that foreign investments were acquired at the price of issue. If more than the issuing price was paid, then the yield on foreign investments was still less. Since the price of foreign securities rose steadily from 1884 to 1896, it can reasonably be expected that any foreign securities acquired during that period at a price other than the issuing price were purchased at a price in excess of the price of issue. It is true that there were about 2 billions of French rentes repurchased during the 70's at prices higher than the price of issue, but there were also at least as many foreign securities repurchased in the 70's at the higher prices.

After 1899 both foreign and domestic securities were issued at higher yields, and the yield on foreign securities apparently was greater than that on domestic securities. I have been unable to find any study similar to Decoudu's for the later years, but it must be remembered that most of the 25 billions of foreign securities and the 50 billions of domestic securities continued to remain in France. To what extent the additional 20 billions of foreign securities increased the yield of the total foreign holdings is not known.[1]

This much, at all events, is clear. Even if the yields on the basis here used are not exactly representative of the whole period from 1880 to 1913, they are sufficiently close to cast serious doubts on the assumption that foreign investments returned a higher net yield than domestic. If the losses, defaults in payments, and reductions of debt service *before* 1914 are taken into account, the yield from foreign investments to France was even less. It is true that there were losses and defaults in domestic investments also, but there is this important difference as Keynes points out:[2] in the case of foreign loans, repudiation or failure leaves nothing to the lending country; whereas in the case of domestic repudiation, the tangible instruments of production do remain in the lending country. The loss to the French people when a Brazilian railroad built with French capital repudiates its debt is greater than when a domestic railroad does so. In the latter case the railroad remains in France; whereas in the former case it remains in Brazil. True, this criticism of foreign investments raised by Keynes is not wholly justified in all cases, nor must it be pushed too far.

[1] We have so far been comparing yields from domestic securities with yields from foreign securities in the situation as it existed between 1880 and 1913. But we are also interested in a comparison of rates that would have prevailed had less capital flowed abroad. Consideration of this aspect of the problem is postponed until later in the chapter.

[2] Foreign Investments and National Advantage, London Nation, August 9, 1924, p. 584.

The inability of a domestic enterprise to meet its interest payments also represents a definite loss to the French people in that the physical capital is less productive than it would have been if investment had been wise. A hundred million francs invested in a domestic industry which finds itself forever after able to pay only half its fixed charges (assuming its rates are not regulated) represents a loss of 50 million francs to the French people. Liquid capital once converted into fixed capital — capital goods — is valued on the basis of its earning power, and a diminution of earning power represents a loss of value as real in the instance of a domestic as of a foreign investment.

But it is only in the case of a privately operated and controlled industry that its earnings are a criterion of its value to the country, and it is only in such case that exception can be taken to Keynes' point of view. The default of a domestic public service corporation does not necessarily represent a loss to France equivalent to that sustained from a similar default in a foreign public service corporation. The domestic default may be due to a too low rate schedule, or to an excessive tax rate, or to poor financing, or to excessive overhead, or to any other cause which represents merely a transfer of wealth from one group of Frenchmen to another. In such case default entails only a slight loss to the French people as a whole; whereas the foreign default represents not transfer, but total loss. This difference between domestic and foreign defaults serves to strengthen the evidence against the assumption that between the years 1880 and 1913 the gain from foreign investments was greater than that from domestic investments.[1]

[1] Another source of loss or gain from foreign investments is change in price levels. From 1880 to 1896 there was a steady drop in prices and therefore France, whose foreign investments were largely in the form of fixed income bearing securities, was obtaining a larger real income as prices dropped, and — this is the important consideration — she obtained this increase in real income at the expense of the foreign borrower. France from 1880 to 1895 was simply in the position of a large creditor during a falling price level. Domestic borrowers, state railways, and industries, in so far as they had contracted to pay fixed sums, were also adversely affected because of dropping prices, but what they as debtors lost, other Frenchmen as creditors gained. In the case of domestic investments it was merely a transfer of real income from one group of Frenchmen to another; but in the case of foreign investments the

So far in our discussion of the comparative yields from foreign and domestic investments we have ignored the very important element of risk. Obviously, interest rates ought not to be compared without taking into consideration the amount of risk involved in the various types of investments. If the risk element in foreign investments is greater than in domestic, then the return ought to be proportionately greater; if it is less, then the return ought to be proportionately less. Now in the case of France during the period under discussion the yield on foreign investments, as we have seen, was probably no greater than on domestic investments. It might be supposed, therefore, that the risk element was equal in both cases. Subsequent events, however, hardly bear out this assumption. We know now that the loans to Russia and to other European countries were unwise. If we were to take into consideration events subsequent to 1913, it would be simple enough to conclude that French foreign investments were not profitable.[1] But we are interested in determining only whether they appeared profitable *under conditions prevailing before 1914*. We wish, in other words, to determine whether the yields reflected adequately the risk inherent in the type of foreign securities France purchased. We wish to test the validity of the assumption upon which rests the claim that foreign investments yield a greater return than domestic. The basis of the claim, it

real income was an addition to the country's income. From 1896 to 1914, however, the situation was reversed; prices were rising as rapidly on the whole as they had previously dropped. France, in her position as a creditor, was now losing, as before 1896 she had been gaining from the decline in prices. But during the period of dropping prices, French net foreign investments averaged 15 billions, whereas during the period of rising prices her net foreign investments averaged double that amount. Therefore France as a creditor nation lost from 1880 to 1913 much more than she gained from price movements. This fact, however, is not and cannot be a factor in determining whether or not foreign investments in the future are desirable unless the future trend of prices becomes predictable.

[1] During the war about 23 billions exclusive of war loans were lost to France — a sum equal to two-thirds of her net foreign investments. Russia, Turkey, Greece, Austria-Hungary, and the Balkans, and some South American countries suspended or repudiated their foreign debts. France may yet recover some of her loss, but the chance of her recovering a large part is rather slight. In any case there has already been a 15 year loss of income.

will be remembered, is that the investor selects that investment which gives him the greatest return, making due allowance for risk; therefore, if he selects foreign investments in preference to domestic, it must needs be because he gets a greater yield. The assumption underlying this claim is that the investor is a good judge of the risk involved in any investment. If he is, then it logically must follow that the interest rate adequately reflects the risk element in the investment; that is, it reflects the excess yield over the so-called riskless rate of interest on long-time investments, which presumably is determined by factors not primarily concerned with risk.[1]

From our comparison of the yields of foreign and domestic investments we have seen that in the opinion of the investor there was no greater risk involved in foreign than in domestic securities. Upon what evidence could the French investor have based his judgment? The given conditions surrounding loans vary. They vary with the borrower, with the purpose of the loan, with the time of the loan, — to mention only some of the factors, — and measurement of the risk involved in a particular loan is possible only with adequate information about it, and with a sufficient experience and a sufficient number of observations to ascertain the number of defaults to the number of payments under the given set of conditions. The French investor may have had ideas that certain investments involved vaguely more risk than a French rente or less risk than gold mining stock, but it is

[1] It is not to be assumed that the riskless rate of interest is independent of the quantity of investments involving risk. The supply of funds available for riskless investments is affected by the yields on risk bearing investments just as the supply for risk bearing securities is dependent in part on the yield for riskless investments. A decreased rate of return on riskless investments, due either to a decreased demand for capital for such investments or to an increased supply of capital seeking investments, will cause the yield on riskless investments to drop, and this movement in turn will tend to increase the amount of capital seeking investments with a somewhat higher yield. The demand and the supply of capital for investments of differing amounts of risk are somewhat interdependent. There do not exist, to adapt the term used in connection with wages, completely separated non-competing groups of capital each seeking a different level of risk, and each group accepting the price determined by changes in demand without in turn immediately affecting the supply of capital in that group.

extremely doubtful that he had sufficient information [1] or sufficient experience to be able to estimate the risk involved in a Spanish railroad or in a Turkish government bond.

Yet, it may be maintained, the judge of the risk element is not the investor but the experienced banker or underwriter, who studies the situation, and who demands on the part of his clients what he considers to be a just compensation for the risk. The investor merely chooses from a group of securities already selected by the banker those which best suit his purpose; no matter which he chooses, the yield will fairly reflect the risk involved. Such a point of view flatters the underwriters undeservedly. The price paid by the underwriters for loans is no doubt influenced by the risk which they feel is involved, but their estimate can scarcely be based on objective data sufficient to make possible quantitative measurement. Is it possible to determine that the chances of Russia, for illustration, meeting her obligations are 15 per cent greater than the chances of Denmark meeting hers? The underwriters may conclude that the likelihood is greater in Russia's case, but why 15 rather than 10 or 20 per cent? To put the question is to demonstrate the impossibility of answering it. The price underwriters will pay for a loan is dependent largely on how much they think they can sell the bonds to the public for, on the number of competitors for the loan, and on the need of the borrower. After deciding at what price and how much the public will absorb, they proceed to make the best bargain possible with the borrower. If they drive an excellent bargain because either competition is limited or the needs of the borrower are pressing, they by no means pass on the advantage gained to the investor.[2]

[1] That such information was not available even in the libraries is suggested by L. Guillaume, who said that no library in France possessed a complete collection of data necessary to pass judgment on the financial conditions of foreign states. Even if the information were available, it is wholly improbable that a prospective investor would have examined the books on finance and on the economic and political prospects of Turkey — say — as a prelude to determining whether or not he should invest in bonds of that country at a $4\frac{1}{2}$ per cent yield.

[2] The competition for foreign loans was limited in the nineteenth century. All countries except England, Belgium, United States, France, and the Scandinavian countries had little choice as to the conditions of the loan. The few large banking

When operating on a purely commission basis, they may be eager to have the price low so that the amount sold can be increased, but when the loan is underwritten at a certain price, which was usually the case, they sell it for as much as they can get and let the difference constitute their profit.[1] In the last analysis it is the reception of the issue by the public that determines the price — a reception influenced by the advice of the underwriters and by their publicity and sales program. But the public is hardly in a position to estimate the risk with any degree of accuracy; they either overestimate or underestimate it.

In France from 1880 to 1913 the risk was clearly underestimated. As Keynes wrote,[2] "Loans to foreign governments reached the utmost limit of magnitude and imprudence in France in the 20 years preceding the war. No investments have ever been made so foolish and so disastrous as the loans of France to Russia, and on a lesser scale to the Balkans, Austria, Mexico, and Brazil between 1900 and 1914. . . . To lend vast sums abroad for long periods of time without any possibility of legal redress if things go wrong is a crazy construction; especially in return for a trifling extra dividend." Analysis of the economic condition of Russia or of the Balkans in the 80's or 90's would never have resulted in loans to Russia at yields of 4.2 per cent; [3] yet in the next

houses divided the business amongst them at rates which were not competitively determined. — Jenks, The Migration of British Capital to 1875 (New York, 1927).

[1] According to E. Letailleur, writing under the pseudonym of "Lysis", the profits made by the issuing banks on loans of small states were enormous. Among the instances cited is the 5 per cent Bulgarian loan of 1902 which cost the Bank of Paris 86.3 million francs, and which was issued to the public at 95.4 million francs, leaving a profit to the issuing bank of 10½ per cent (Politique et finance d'avant guerre, p. 160). He also quotes the Russian Minister of Finance Kokowtseff as replying to objections raised in France against the security of the loans to Russia, "The French have nothing to complain of in view of the rate which was charged us for the loan; they have earned at least 17 per cent." (Ibid., p. 108. See p. 33 for other details.) Needless to say, the investor subscribed to the loans at prices yielding 5 per cent or less. This would be an illustration of one group, the bankers, profiting at the expense of other groups, the investors.

[2] Foreign investments and national advantages, London Nation, August 9, 1924, p. 584.

[3] The authors of Russian Debts and Russian Reconstruction, Paslovsky and Moulton, stated: "In the early 90's the Russian Government was definitely confronted with international bankruptcy." (P. 39.)

few years Russia successfully floated loans for billions of francs in France at rates of 4 per cent to 5 per cent.[1]

The absorption of these loans at such low yields was possible in France because there existed during the period before the war a definite bias in favor of foreign investments. This bias was created partly by political, partly by economic, and partly by psychological factors, but it was encouraged most of all by the peculiar structure of the French investment banking system. Before the nineteenth century investors in France were advised in financial matters by their notaries, in whom they had implicit confidence. But in the nineteenth century banks took over this advisory function.[2] All large loans were floated by one or other of several large banks, which had practically a monopoly over the flotations of issues by virtue of their great number of branches. The close co-operation between the few large banks centralized the control over issues of securities. The large private banking firms like Rothschilds, Vernes, Mallet, had been largely superseded as leaders in the underwriting field, and were forced to co-operate with the large banks, since the latter controlled most of the agencies thru which securities were sold. The placing of issues floated by their central office was a very important function of the branch banks. Indeed, it was the most important of their functions. The branches were not local banks in the sense that they attempted to satisfy local needs for means of payment. They gathered savings and in exchange distributed securities issued by their central office. The function of local banking was quite subsidiary to that of forming a channel for the distribution of their securities, and their profit was largely made by selling securities, not by conducting banking operations.[3] Each branch

[1] From 1906 to 1913 innumerable articles appeared under the pseudonym "Lysis" emphasizing the underestimation of the risk prevalent in foreign investments and accusing the bankers of being unscrupulous in their recommendations of certain foreign loans. L'Escroquerie russe is prophetic in its estimate of the impending risk in Russian investments.

[2] J. Montety, Les banques et la politique de placement à l'étranger de l'épargne (Paris, 1923). Also D. Yovovitch, Les valeurs mobilières étrangères à la Bourse de Paris (Paris, 1910).

[3] Domergue in La question des sociétés de crédit (Paris, 1910) describes the functioning of the hundreds of branch banks as follows: "The clients, wholly im-

was allotted a quota of securities to be sold, and the branch manager was interested in selling his quota. Whatever estimate was made of risk involved was made by the central office, not by the branch, and the central office was usually more concerned with profits than with educating the investor.

Far from offering sound advice to their clients on the merits of foreign issues, the banks furnished financial prospectuses of new issues which very frequently grossly exaggerated the security and assets of the borrower. This was particularly true in the case of foreign issues because of the absence of any legal requirement as to published information about the financial condition of the borrower. Misrepresentation became so rife that in 1907 a law was passed holding the issuing bank responsible for the accuracy of sums stated in the prospectus. This law, however, did not apply to foreign government or municipal loans.

And not only did the banks issue grossly biased information thru the prospectus, but they also paid for newspaper support. Part of their publicity program was paid newspaper propaganda appearing in the guise of disinterested comment.[1] According to Marinitsch,[2] of the twenty-five independent financial journals not owned directly by banks or financial agencies,[3] only two or three were thoroly honest in their comments on the new issues. The financial columns of even the large dailies, Marinitsch stated, were leased to financial writers who were privileged to conduct their columns with complete liberty. Their power to influence public opinion for or against new security issues was, obviously, considerable, and rendered their support valuable to underwriters. Kaufmann in describing the details of French flotation of secu-

pressed by the vastness of the banks, followed their advice assiduously. The central agency fixed in advance the amount of securities that each branch ought to place, and the manager of the branch, whose word was law with his client, went over his client's portfolio and made room for the new issue. During the period of flotation the central office issued daily lists to all branches stating the percentage of its quota reached by each branch. Every attempt was made by the managers to reach and pass their quota." Under such conditions it would be most surprising if the advice to investors would be unbiased.

[1] Kaufmann, Banques en France, Chap. 3, Sec. 3.

[2] La Bourse théorique et pratique (Paris, 1892), p. 294.

[3] There were in Paris in the 90's 186 financial sheets.

rities wrote that the first care of a bank directing the flotation of an issue was to establish the "budget of publicity" — that is, to fix the sum to be distributed to the press not for paid advertisements, but for securing favorable comments in the financial news columns. The expense of this type of publicity was, he estimated, from 1 to 1½ per cent of the nominal value of the issue. In the decade before the war, Kaufmann claimed that there spread a practice of giving newspaper editors certain subscription privileges which would increase in value in proportion to the success of the flotation.[1]

It was the large profits frequently available to bankers from foreign loans that led them to prefer and encourage foreign investments. In recommending French rentes or City of Paris bonds, there was little or no profit to be made, but in recommending a Bulgarian or Brazilian loan there was opportunity for big gains. The poorer the security of the borrower and the more pressing his need, the less particular is he apt to be, the less "shopping" around can he afford to do, and the more is he willing to pay to the underwriters.[2] The result was constant pressure on the French investor to buy those foreign securities which the banks were issuing. A consortium or a single bank took a foreign loan and pushed it; they no longer were impartial counselors to the investor.[3]

[1] The probability of co-operation between the issuing banks and the press at the expense of the investor is indicated by the following incident cited by Becque (op. cit., p. 99). About the 20th of December, 1911, the important dailies contained lengthy, laudatory articles on the wealth and prosperity of and opportunity for investment in Paraguay. The following week a foreign loan of that country was issued on the Paris and other markets. Later one learned that the country was engaged in civil war and that during the course of the year there had been no less than four revolutions, and further, that the interest payment on previous loans had not been paid for 10 years.

[2] The answer by the officials of the Crédit Lyonnais to the United States Monetary Commission in 1910 on this subject of underwriters' profits is significant. The question was: "Have you a fixed percentage of profit, or do you buy them as you can and sell them at a price satisfactory to yourselves?" The answer was: "Naturally the commission varies." — Interviews on the Banking and Currency Systems, United States Monetary Commission, 1910, Senate Document No. 405, p. 234.

[3] The effectiveness of their advice to investors may be judged from the following answers by the chief officials of the Crédit Lyonnais to the United States National Monetary Commission in 1910.

The investor was all the more ready to buy the foreign securities which the banks and the press were urging upon him because foreign government bonds were free from an annual tax. The only domestic bond that was equally free from taxes was the French rente, the price of which was usually very high, partly because of its greater safety and partly because of certain legal requirements as to bank and trust fund investments. The absence of this tax may have been a gain to the investor in that it increased the yield, but it was a loss to France if it induced a French investor to purchase a foreign security the increased risk of which was compensated for by its freedom from annual taxation.[1] Foreign corporate and municipal securities, tho not free from taxation, were no less attractive than foreign government bonds in that they offered great opportunity for evading

Q. Our information is that the Crédit Lyonnais always endeavors to have a certain class of securities which they can recommend to their depositors, and that their recommendation is practically equivalent to a sale, and that they sell an enormous amount of securities and at times undertake large issues. Can you state the largest issue that you have recently purchased?

A. There are two kinds of such operations; first, when the Crédit Lyonnais is alone interested in the operation; and second, when others of the Paris bankers are interested with us. The largest recent issue, in connection with other bankers, was the 5 per cent Russian loan of 1906 of 1,200,000,000 francs ($240,000,000). What is very important in our way of floating a loan is that the sales are made in small quantities; the transaction is completed in a very few days, and each of our customers buys only the number of bonds corresponding to his investment requirement.

Q. As a matter of fact, anything you recommend they will buy?

A. Yes, and even with a very large issue; the bonds do not remain long in the market, because in our country savings are very extended. Everyone saves his money. The small savings of France are the wealth of the country. By examining the balances of the accounts of our customers we can know whether they want to invest or not, and then we endeavor to have stocks and bonds to offer to them as they require them, but this is variable, and sometimes we might have a large issue, 40 to 50 millions of francs, taken by the public in four or five days.

[1] The impartiality of French bankers towards foreign investments is apparently doubted by E. Becque (op. cit., p. 209), who writes: "The truth is that financiers who were interested in making foreign loans successful or who wished to obtain the co-operation of French capital in advancing funds to foreign enterprises have gone out of their way to raise the spectre of tax on revenue; and the fears of the capitalists of our country are due in large part to that frame of mind which we have already spoken of and which, unfortunately, France is particularly guilty of, which consists in admiring everything that is far off while that about us is regarded with distrust."

taxes.[1] It will be remembered that tax evasion according to French estimates was as high as 50 per cent.

All these forces combined in creating in the mind of the French investor a definite bias in favor of foreign investments. He could not, consequently, weigh impartially foreign against domestic investment even had he possessed the information and the experience necessary to evaluate justly the comparative risk. The result was that he purchased foreign securities at a yield which he did not recognize as being low because he underestimated the risk. If, then, we add this element of underestimated risk to the apparent equality of the rate of return, it can hardly be said that the yield on foreign investments was greater than that on domestic. Therefore the assumption that France received a higher return on her capital because capital flowed out only in response to higher interest rates than could be obtained at home is of very doubtful validity; the investor as we have seen, was not an adequate judge of the relative yield inasmuch as yield must be measured not only by the rate but also by the risk.

The second alleged effect of French capital exports is that the productivity of capital for the world was increased in that capital flowed where it was most needed, and further, that France thereby benefited as a consumer thru the cheapening of foods and raw materials, and as producer thru expanding markets for her goods. The claim is based first on the assumption that the yield from her foreign investments was greater than from her domestic, and secondly that an increased real rate of interest always means increased productivity. The first assumption we have noted rests on doubtful grounds; the second assumption also appears to be open to question.

[1] The following quotation from a recent essay on French banking suggests that the opportunity for tax evasion thru foreign investment was not without its appeal to the French investor. "With regard to the possession of money, of personal or family capital, the Frenchman seems to experience a respect, an intense love, which justifies any sacrifice . . . and any deception. The middle class Frenchman, as the press shows clearly, lives in a state of perpetual disquietude concerning the evolution of social and fiscal laws. He makes a fetich of the secrecy of his business." — R. J. Lemoine, Banking System of France, contained in Foreign Banking Systems, edited by Willis and Beckhart (New York, 1929), p. 524.

It is quite true that an increased yield often reflects increased productivity; but this is not always the case. Some loans are not productive at all. When French loans to the Balkans serve merely to advance them in the race for armaments, and when loans to the Ottoman empire are used merely to increase the luxuriousness of court life, the funds can hardly be said to be productive in the sense in which that term is ordinarily used. Loans of this type need no special discussion; their case is obvious, and moreover, such loans formed only a part of French foreign investments.

It is the loans for presumably productive purposes that enter into our analysis. When such loans are made to private industry, the yield presumably measures productivity; the sum that private industry is willing to pay reflects its estimate of the productivity of the capital it borrows. The one who offers the highest price for the use of capital presumably will utilize it in a manner more productive than one not willing to pay so much. To hamper funds from going to the highest bidder would under these conditions interfere with the most productive use of capital. But the larger part of capital borrowed from France was borrowed not by private industry (foreign), but by governments and municipalities, and in such borrowing a new element is introduced which no longer makes possible so simple a measure of productivity. The state uses the borrowed funds for building roads, railways, public buildings, harbors, canals, and other public works, and the possibility of measuring the productivity of such expenditures by the same yardstick — earnings — disappears. There are no earnings. For illustration, Argentine built ports and harbors costing millions of francs, which she borrowed largely from France at 5 per cent interest. Since the utilities were not sold, there were no earnings. It is maintained, however, that the utilities produced by the harbors were worth at least 5 per cent. The willingness of Argentine to pay that 5 per cent indicates that in her opinion their productivity was worth at least that much; if it were not, 5 per cent would not have been offered. But this explanation is not sufficiently searching. The productivity of the harbors is impossible of objective measurement. It is measured not by earnings but by what the persons responsible for the expenditure think the harbors are worth to Argentine. And their opinion may be guided by considerations which are not at all such as guide private borrowers who calculate earnings.

Even when the service rendered by public works is charged for, the earnings are not always a measure of the productivity of the capital involved. Russia, for instance, borrowed great sums for her railroads. These roads operated under a continual deficit. The interest on the bonds was paid from treasury funds, which in turn were largely borrowed from France. If the earnings of the railway were to be a measure of its productivity, the capital invested, altho yielding a 4 per cent return to its holders, was not productive at all; it did not yield a return sufficient to pay even the fixed charges, let alone dividends. But Russia may have preferred for political or economic reasons to have low freight rates and to make up the deficit out of taxes. Or she may have been charging for transportation service as much, in a monopolistic sense, as the traffic could bear; in which case the road operated under a deficit because she could not obtain dividends no matter how high the rate. Or Russia may have built her roads partly for political and military considerations — these frequently played an important part in her decision to build harbors, railways, and roads — and she may therefore have expected the railroad to operate under a deficit. How can Russia's political ambitions in the East — say — be evaluated in terms of productivity against harbor improvement in France? To fall back as a measure of that productivity upon the willingness of Russia or France to pay in terms of money for the satisfaction of such differing desires is to strip the term productivity of the signification given it in the assumption we are considering.

That assumption, it will be remembered, was that capital exports increase productivity. If the term productivity is to be given its narrow, technical meaning, namely, the creation of utilities,—utility being defined as the capacity to satisfy a want,—then the willingness to pay must, from the very definition, logically measure productivity. But the thought implicit in the assumption that capital exports increase productivity is that capital exports increase *well-being*. If productivity does not have this implication, then it cannot be held that increased productivity is an advantage to be claimed for capital exports.

The difficulties which arise from the indeterminate meaning of productivity are illustrated by the following passage by Hobson in the preface of his book on capital exports:

> Whatever view be taken as to the social consequences of a high rate of interest, it is at any rate evident that the wealth of the world as a whole benefits if capital flows to those quarters where it is most needed provided always that it is not used for purposes of waste or destruction, such as war, or for the exploitation and the oppression of helpless savages.

It is within the phrase "where it is most needed" that the difficulty lies. Apparently the writer does not intend the phrase to imply the greatest want as measured by the willingness of the borrower to pay a higher price for capital, since he qualifies the phrase with "provided that." By so doing he abandons money payment as the criterion, and proceeds to examine the purpose for which the loan is to be used, thereby interpreting the term productivity in its broader sense — well-being. It is in this sense that the term productivity will be used in this discussion, since it is so used in the assumption we are questioning.

Let us return now to the measurement of the productivity of capital. The estimate of the utility derived from the use of capital is in each country based on considerations which cannot be compared. It may be that the predominant cause for the borrowing was political or military, or perhaps fiscal, necessitated by the difficulty of raising taxes. Russia, for illustration, did not until 1909 obtain funds to meet her heavy interest charges out of taxes. Before that date interest charges were met out of increased borrowing. France, on the other hand, met the charges on funds borrowed for public works out of taxes. If the French political leaders disliked to increase the tax rate more than the Russian Ministry of Finance disliked to borrow, then the latter could offer more for funds. But it is scarcely reasonable to conclude from such a situation that the funds spent in Russia were more productive than if they had been spent in France. Russia's higher successful offer for capital might be interpreted not as indicative of the ability to put that capital to greater use, but rather as a defect in the conduct of Russian government finance, or as the extreme dislike of the central government in France to expend funds on public works of a local nature.[1]

Nor is the fact that a foreign government outbids *private industry* for capital an indication that the productivity of the capital is greater when used by the foreign country. The price industry can pay for the capital it borrows is definitely limited by the productivity of that capital. It cannot afford, on the penalty of loss or failure, to pay more. Industry may and does err, and when it does, a definite, measurable loss results; but it cannot err by much because it has a fair idea of the market value of the services it produces. The situation of a government borrowing is different; the limit it can pay is conjectural at best, and is determined mainly by political factors. How can it be otherwise since the service to be produced — if it is a loan for productive and not consumption purposes — has usually no measurable market value? What, for example, is the value of good roads, harbors, sewage, schools? The value of those expenditures to the community is determined by a compromise of such a diversity of interests that if the amount paid for the capital used in their construction is a measure of the productivity of that capital, it is probably an unusual accident and not, as in the case of industrial loans, a normal result. With this government hit-or-miss estimate of productivity it would be indeed surprising if each country disposed of its capital to the best advantage.[2] Can it, then, be said

[1] Masse, a well-known French engineer, describes at length how the productive capacity of France was seriously curtailed by the insufficient development of canals, ports, rivers, and other public works (La production des richesses, Paris, 1925). He explains the inability of France to compete successfully with other governments for French funds to be spent on French public works by the lack of local autonomy in matters of expenditure. He implies definitely that a change in the political structure of France would have resulted in more funds being spent on public works.

[2] It is significant that in the report of the Liberal Industrial Inquiry in 1928, written by such competent economists as J. M. Keynes, W. T. Layton, H. D. Henderson, B. S. Rountree — to name only some of the Executive Committee responsible for the report — there is recognition of the lack of necessary equivalence between yield on foreign investments and welfare of the lending nation when the loans are to foreign governments and municipalities. It is proposed that some other

that the French loans to Russia, Turkey, Spain, Austria-Hungary, Greece, and the South American governments, which accounted for at least half of France's foreign investments, resulted in greater productivity for society as a whole than would have been the case had that capital remained at home?

Even if they did, the welfare of the world at large must still be deemed of secondary importance; from the point of view of France, her own welfare is paramount. To her the significant gains and losses are not those experienced by Russia or Turkey, but those experienced by France. Just what did *France* gain from her foreign investments? It is to a consideration of this question that we now turn.

means than a reliance upon the price offered for the use of capital be adopted to insure a proper development of domestic public works. The Executive Committee writes as follows: "Secondly, there is question of the right distribution of savings in the national interest between investment abroad and investment at home. So far as industrial, agricultural, and mining overseas enterprises are concerned, we think that the freedom of foreign investments has in the past greatly increased the national wealth and is increasing it now. We see no reason to do anything but encourage the trading, business, and pioneering private enterprise of British citizens abroad. We also think that in the Railway Age, the development of foreign and colonial railway systems abroad out of British capital, when British materials, British savings, and British engineering enterprise were opening up the world for the supply of food and raw materials, was greatly for the interest of this country as well as of the world. But we are more doubtful whether at the present time, the existing machinery for the investment necessarily preserves the correct balance between expenditure on Public Utilities at home and loans for similar purposes abroad to Government, Provinces, Municipalities, and other public bodies in foreign countries and in the Dominions. Our constructive proposals below will be based on the assumption that the development and expansion of transport facilities, public utilities, industries, housing, and agricultural equipment *at home* should be the first charge on the national savings, and that only the surplus, after the satisfaction of all reasonable domestic requirements under these headings, should be made available to public bodies abroad." — Report of the Liberal Industrial Inquiry, Britain's Industrial Future (London, 1928), Chap. IX, Sec. 1.

CHAPTER XIII

ECONOMIC EFFECTS OF CAPITAL EXPORTS (*continued*)

BEFORE entering upon a discussion of the far-reaching influence of capital exports upon the domestic economy of France, we shall briefly dispose of two minor alleged benefits. It is generally assumed that capital exports lessen the risk of investment thru geographical distribution. This certainly was not true of France. A wise distribution does indeed reduce the risk of loss, but it can scarcely be said that the foreign securities in the French portfolio reflected wise distribution. One-fourth of France's foreign holdings were concentrated in Russia, and the rest consisted of loans to countries whose financial stability was doubtful and political prospects unsettled. The French portfolio was thus especially vulnerable in case of any untoward economic or political events, and increased rather than decreased the risk of loss from investment.

The claim that capital exports provide protection to a country's gold reserves, thereby insuring freedom from credit and price fluctuations, is hardly applicable to the French situation. It is true that foreign securities sold abroad or employed as collateral to establish credits against which the banks can sell exchange may be used to meet temporary adverse movements of exchanges; they thereby obviate the necessity for shipping gold and help to protect the banking system from fluctuations in the gold reserve due to temporary movements in the exchange rates. This protection is sometimes advantageous. The constant movements of gold both ways between countries demonstrates, however, that the use of securities is not always the most expedient method of establishing credits abroad; and in any event it is not necessary for a country to acquire billions of foreign securities for that purpose. Moreover, securities so used should have the greatest stability and the highest standing, in which class the larger part of French foreign holdings could scarcely be said to belong; her domestic rentes would have served the purpose far better than her Russian, Italian, or Spanish bonds. In any case long-time securities are not used nearly so much as short-time prime paper; a central bank can and does more adequately protect its gold reserve from fluctuations by the possession of a goodly stock of foreign bills. But for France the necessity for protecting temporary fluctuations in her gold holdings was of very minor importance because of her huge and ever increasing stock of gold and the lack of sensitivity in her credit structure. As for providing a liquid reserve for times of national stress, it is noteworthy that in the greatest crisis, 1914–1918, over half of France's foreign holdings became unsalable except at a very great loss.[1]

So much for the alleged minor benefits France derived from her capital exports. We turn now to a consideration of the effects of these exports on the French domestic economy — on the national income, on the distribution of that income, on the terms of trade, and on the development of the domestic industry.

[1] Several French writers claim for France this additional advantage from foreign investments: they serve to equalize what would otherwise be an "unfavorable" balance of payments which would denude France of her gold. The income from foreign investments is assumed to make possible a constant excess of merchandise imports without the necessity of exporting gold in payment. It is difficult to understand why this is included as an advantage of foreign investments for any country, especially France. We have seen that France did not have a consistent excess of merchandise imports, and that the revenue due France from her foreign investments did not serve to pay for her imports but was reinvested abroad (except perhaps for the years from 1880 to 1886). But even were a lending country to be at the stage where she receives a constant excess of merchandise imports — paid for by the excess of revenue due her from her foreign investments over new foreign investments — is it to be claimed that this constant excess of imports would, were it not for the foreign investments, have to be paid for in gold? During the first period of a lending country's operations, assuming equilibrium in the other items in the balance of payments, an excess of exports of goods or services is created. When the interest payments equal the annual excess of export of capital, equilibrium between the exports and imports of goods and services is established; and when the annual interest payments exceed the annual exports of capital, an excess of imports appears. To hold that this excess of imports would cause a sustained outflow of gold if it were not for the capital exports is to confuse cause with effect. If there had been no sustained capital exports in the first place, a sustained excess of imports would not have appeared. See, for example, M. Arboux, op. cit., Chap. I, and E. Becque, op. cit., p. 85. The latter, in enumerating the advantages of capital exports writes that "the first and most essential advantage is that the large profits from foreign investments permit lending countries to pay for their excess of imports and to transform a debit balance of payments into a credit balance."

The possible sources of an increase in national income from capital exports are three: an increase due to the difference in the rate of return on foreign investments over the rate that would have prevailed had no capital been exported; a cheapening of imports as a result of improvements in foreign industry and agriculture made with the borrowed capital; a reduction in the costs of production of domestic goods because of an increase in the foreign demand for those goods with a consequent development of more and larger plants, leading to lower costs from "external" and "internal" economies.

In France the export of capital probably caused the rate of interest to go up; had no capital been exported, the additional half to one and a half billion francs would have so augmented the annual supply of capital available for domestic industry that the rate would have decreased. How great the decrease would have been depends upon the effect that a decline in interest rates would have had (1) upon the volume of domestic savings and (2) upon the domestic demand for capital in the absence of opportunity for foreign investment. It is generally held that a decrease in the rate of interest decreases the volume of savings, but the extent of such decrease — the significant problem — is a debatable point. In the case of France there is reason to believe that savings would have been less responsive to a downward movement of the interest rate than the savings of other lending countries. The saving habits of the French nation, famous in French literature and thruout economic writing, were so firmly established that a matter of an increase or decrease in the reward for saving would not have been nearly so important in France as in a country where the saving habit was less popular. The ambition of almost every Frenchman is to be a rentier.[1] He does not have the passion of the American to earn a great deal in order that he may spend a great deal; his psychology is to live on little in the present

[1] Neymarck, in an essay in 1910, wrote: "Neither in England nor in the United States is there such an army of people who put by small savings. There are nearly 10,000,000 electors. All, or nearly all, save their money with the intention of putting something by for their old age. . . . To sell his securities is a resolution he takes only in the case of absolute necessity." — French Savings and Their Influence upon the Bank of France and upon French Banks (Washington, 1910), p. 167.

so that he may live without working in the future. Every penny is husbanded, and when there is a surplus the Frenchman feels, as Guyot[1] says, "a great delight" in investing it. A decrease in the rate of interest under such conditions would, it has long since been pointed out, tend rather to increase than decrease the amount of savings, since the principal would have to be greater in order to yield the same income. In the 90's, when interest rates were declining to very low levels, there does not seem to have been any slackening in the rate of increase of French savings.[2] Nor does there seem to be any comment in the literature of the period with regard to increased spending or reduced savings due to the lowered interest rates; in fact the contrary is true. Neymarck, writing in 1893 on L'abaissement du taux de l'intérêt, ses causes, ses avantages, ses inconvénients,[3] does not mention either increased spending or decreased saving as resulting from the great decline in interest rates on investments. But he does write:

> The rentier must therefore work for a longer time in order to have the same amount of enjoyments as formerly. The head of the family must work, earn, and above all economize more in order to insure the same income so that he can give the same dowry to his children. The laborer, while setting aside the same sum, must work for a longer time in order to create for his old age an income equal to that which he obtained formerly.[4]

There is reason to believe, then, that in so far as savings depend upon willingness to save, the supply of capital would not have been seriously affected by a reduction in the interest rate.

A decrease in the supply price of capital may, however, have decreased the *capacity* for saving. Doubtless with a smaller money income the French rentier would have found it more difficult to save an equal amount. But to offset the decreased

[1] The Amount, Direction, and Nature of French Investments, Ann. of Am. Acad. of Pol. and Soc. Sc., 1916, Vol. 68, p. 37.

[2] Savings in all savings banks increased one billion francs from 1890 to 1899 and only 1200 millions from 1900 to 1909. (Table 54.) These may represent chiefly "rainy day" savings, which are least sensitive to interest rates; but much of the French investment in bonds was similarly motivated.

[3] Finances contemporaines, Vol. 6, p. 111.

[4] Ibid., p. 116.

saving capacity of this class of income receivers there was the increased saving capacity of those groups whose incomes are increased by lowered interest rates. Whether the increased capacity of the entrepreneur, the wage earner, and the landowner would have wholly compensated for the decreased saving capacity of the investor — very frequently the same person — cannot be determined; but the difference in savings cannot have been great.

Without serious reduction in the volume of savings and barring a change in the domestic demand schedule for capital, the rate of interest would have been somewhat lower than the rate that prevailed when capital was exported. But it is quite possible that the domestic demand schedule would not long have remained unchanged. The extra supply of capital seeking domestic employment at a rate somewhat lower might very well have brought about a complete change in the psychology of production — as will be pointed out later — which eventually would have caused the demand schedule to move to the right. For many years, however, the interest rate would have remained at a lower level than that prevailing under capital exports; that is the money income from investments was higher than it would have been had no capital been exported.

This larger money income accruing to the owners of capital accompanied a shift in the income of other groups: wage earners, landowners, and entrepreneurs. The effect on labor was a reduction in wages. We may apply the usual economic reasoning. The more limited the supply of any one of the agents of production in proportion to the others, the higher the price it can command for its services; where capital is scarce and labor plentiful, wages are lower and interest higher than where capital is plentiful and labor scarce. Since there was less capital, each unit of capital received a larger share of the combined product than it would have received had capital per laborer been greater.

The wage earner suffered also because of the worsening in the net barter terms of trade in so far as the more unfavorable terms were caused by capital exports.[1] Imported commodities con-

[1] See Chap. 12.

sumed a slightly larger portion of his income because of the effect of large exports of capital on relative price levels. The loss in real income was felt by all French consumers, but the laborer had no offsetting gain, as did the investor, from the higher interest rates induced by capital exports. The entrepreneur likewise suffered from capital exports; as consumer his imported commodities cost him more, and as producer his services received a smaller proportion of the total product because of the relatively greater scarcity of capital.

As in the case of the other factors of production, so with land: any change which causes capital to be less abundant relative to land will increase the relative economic importance of capital and decrease that of land. Moreover, in the case of agricultural land, economic rent is decreased not only because of its diminished economic importance as compared with capital, but also because capital exports to some extent increase the world supply of usable land.[1] Altho this additional cause for decrease in economic rent was a loss to the landlord, it represented no net loss to France. By supplying the capital to develop foreign agriculture, foreign mines, and so forth, the cost of producing certain commodities in foreign countries became cheaper, and France along with the rest of the world benefited as consumer of those commodities.[2]

This reduction in the cost of imports — arising not from more favorable net barter terms of trade, but from the reduced cost of

[1] The term *supply* is given here perhaps a slightly different meaning than is frequently accorded it. The supply of land as the term is here used is not to be measured by the world's surface. It refers only to land having exchange value. If land which is unproductive is made productive by improvement in the arts of transportation, the effect is an increase in the supply of land. Regarded in this sense, the supply of land is by no means fixed.

[2] Pigou in his Economics of Welfare, rev. ed., Part IV, Chap. III, Sec. 7, expresses the opinion that the injury to labor caused by capital exports would in the long run be offset by an increase in the aggregate income. The increase would come from the compounding of the extra interest earned abroad on foreign investments and from the cheapening of those raw materials and foodstuffs consumed by workmen in the lending countries, a cheapening that results from better exploitation of foreign sources of supply. This was doubtless true of England, because her investments yielded rich returns and her capital was largely used for exploitation of foreign resources. (See footnote p. 296.) But as indicated in the pages above, this was hardly true of France.

production abroad — is one of the considerable advantages claimed for foreign investments. But it must be kept in mind that this reduction would have accrued to France no matter which country's capital developed foreign lands. From the point of view of France only commodities cheapened by *her* exported capital and consumed by *her* can be claimed as a gain from French foreign investments.[1] And in any case only a part of French exported capital was used for purposes that resulted in the reduction of the cost of French imports. The French capital loaned to foreign governments for their military purposes resulted in no reduction, while the capital loaned for foreign municipal improvements reduced it only in a very tenuous fashion if at all.[2] Nor, it must be noted, was the gain to France from the decrease in the cost of some of her imports a net gain. Domestic goods and services would also have been produced more cheaply had more capital been used at home.[3] To be sure, if the bulk of the French

[1] It may be replied that if every country adopted this attitude, the rich natural resources of much of the world would remain undeveloped. This argument would in all probability bear little weight in the determination of national policy. Moreover, it need not necessarily be true. Capital exports may have been desirable for Great Britain, Holland, or the United States, and yet for reasons peculiar to France unwise for her.

[2] It is noteworthy that from those countries which received most French capital, Russia excepted, exports to France declined heavily, as follows:

Imports into France

(Millions of francs)

	Average 1880–1884	Average 1905–1909	Change from 1880–1884 to 1905–1909 (Per cent)
Russia	240	27	10
Turkey	130	105	−20
Italy	400	150	−62
Spain	350	170	−50
Austria-Hungary	120	74	−63
Roumania	55	44	−20

These declines over a period of thirty years by no means prove that the cost of production of the imports from those countries had not been reduced, but they strongly suggest that the gain accruing to France from those reduced costs was not great.

[3] With regard to agricultural machinery Clapham concluded that "those machines which are the typical products of application of nineteenth century metallurgy and engineering to agriculture, had not even conquered the larger French holdings in 1892, if statistics are at all trustworthy." He mentions, too, that the cultivator was short of capital. — Op. cit., p. 171.

capital invested abroad had served to develop rich natural resources, as did much of the British foreign investments,[1] there would be less doubt about the gains to France from the reduced cost of imports. Some French capital did, indeed, flow to Brazil, Argentine, Java, Malacca, and similar spots, which yielded some return to the French consumer in the shape of reduced cost of rubber, coffee, hides, and so forth; but much more went to Turkey, Russia, Austria-Hungary, Roumania, and Spain, where the supposed increase in the productivity of the capital resulted in dubious gains to the French people.

The export of French capital resulted, then, in only a slight reduction in the cost of French imports. The decrease in the domestic costs of production arising from the possibility of increased economies from a larger scale of production in the exporting industries was even more doubtful. The export of capital resulted at first in a shift to the right of foreign demand schedules and also in an increase in demand — in the market sense — for French products. The increased demand for certain French products necessitated an increased production and resulted in some of the economies accompanying an increased scale of production. Here again the gains were not net gains. The increase in the foreign demand for French commodities was not an additional demand; it was only a substitute demand. The transfer in purchasing power abroad which causes an increased foreign demand for French goods and services decreases at the same time a domestic demand. There is no reason to expect more opportunity for reducing cost in exporting industries than in domestic.[2] Moreover, from the French point of view the saving from the reduced cost of goods consumed at home accrues wholly to the French

[1] In 1914 Sir G. Paish stated: "In the aggregate, Great Britain has supplied the world outside these islands with nearly £600 million for the construction of railways in the last seven years (out of a total so supplied by her of upwards of £1100 million), and all of the money has been placed in countries upon which we depend for our supplies of food and raw material." — The Export of Capital and the Cost of Living, Manchester Statistical Society, February, 1914, p. 78. Cited by Pigou, op. cit., p. 621.

[2] An increase in the foreign demand for French goods may be greater than the decreases in the domestic demand if the increased exports result in building up a foreign demand for French products.

people, whereas a reduction in the cost of export goods — unless produced under conditions of monopoly — benefits the French people only to the extent that those commodities are consumed at home.[1]

It must be remembered that the possibility of the savings we have been considering presupposes that an export of capital takes place thru an increase of exports. But it is also possible for the export surplus to appear with the aid of a decrease in imports, as apparently happened from 1892 to 1897 when there was a decline in the physical quantity of French imports altho every other European country (except Spain) showed an increase in those years. In such case there were no economies of this kind in the export industries, whereas there *may* have been the reverse effect in the domestic industries. Whether the purchasing power in France was transferred thru an increase in exports or a decrease in imports, or both, the irregularity of the movement of French capital exports introduced *additional* elements of maladjustment into French industrial life, and these helped to reduce any gains that may have accrued from the economies of larger scale production.

The probable gains to France from her capital exports, as we have seen, could not have been very great, and they are rendered even less significant by the strong probability that the huge volume of French capital exports adversely affected the tenor of the domestic industry. During the period under survey, while other leading countries of the world were undergoing a great industrial expansion, French industry remained apathetic. Many a French writer observing the industrial progress of neighboring Germany was emphatic in his condemnation of French industrial

[1] An additional consideration is that the reduction in cost may have been so considerable — a likely assumption in view of the nature of the small scale production of many French exports — that, notwithstanding increased sales, the total value of French exports decreased and the net barter terms of trade became still more unfavorable. We are obviously dealing here only with probabilities; yet they cannot be ignored if we are attempting an evaluation of the effects of foreign investments. It were better to admit that the effects of foreign investments on the terms of trade can be determined only after a careful examination of the use of each loan as well as of the total situation than to assume a result which may be the very opposite of the actual one.

unprogressiveness. Truchy expressed the prevailing impatience with the sluggish development of French agriculture and industry in the following words:[1]

> Our horizon is limited and our ideal mediocre. We risk little, we earn little. . . . In these quiet paths where the sons are led by the fathers and where in their turn they will lead their own children, we shall perhaps find happiness; but most assuredly those are not the paths that modern peoples tread in their march to greatness and a historic role.

Again, Masse in the introductory chapter to his lengthy volume on the production of wealth in France wrote:[2]

> Let us note that even at this moment France is content to live from hand to mouth, to create new capital by savings. She leaves her powers of production partially unfertile and idle . . . improving neither machinery nor methods. She employs her capital to make fertile the labor of other nations. . . . She desires only to continue her lazy role of banker to the world.

This stagnation of French industry was due in the opinion of many French writers to the inability of domestic interests to secure capital because of the strong bias for foreign investments. In an address to bankers one of these writers dramatically expressed the lack of capital for domestic use as follows:[3]

> While [French] gold flows over the entire world, business, industry, agriculture vegetate at home, languishing in a consumption, and do not find the capital necessary for their development, and these two facts — financial prosperity, poverty of credit — equally incontestable and uncontested, but in appearance contradictory and irreconcilable, face each other in a sort of paradoxical antithesis thrown in defiance at the good sense of the public.

M. Cawes, President of the Société d'Économie Politique, in a paper before that society in 1900 also stressed the difficulty which the French entrepreneur was meeting. His statement was "Be

[1] Étude sur le commerce de la France, Rev. d'Écon. Pol., 1904, p. 564.

[2] Op. cit., p. 4.

[3] H. Michel, cited in Becque, op. cit., p. 203.

It must be noted that some writers, notably Neymarck, were of the opinion that the stagnation of French industry was due not to the inability of industry to secure capital, but to the inability of capital to find business opportunities in France. He ascribed this state of affairs to the lack of real financiers, to the highly critical attitude of the government and the press towards big business in France, and to the constant threat of increased fiscal burdens on income. — Les gros magasins des capitaux, op. cit., Vol. 3, p. 506.

you Greek, Chinese, or Brazilian, it is often said, the Crédit Lyonnais will make you huge advances; but if you are French, you will get nothing." Raffolovich,[1] too, blamed foreign investments for the lack of capital for domestic industry.

> Financiers [he said] inclined to place German securities at home assert at the same time our industrial powerlessness and our financial power: the pessimism of our great banks in respect to our industry has almost taken the form of a dogma. . . . The truth is simple: the great banks hope to continue their activity as issuers of foreign paper by placing at home German securities which yield them large profits; nothing but their immediate interests motivate them.

The opinion of others, again, was that the foreign investments drew capital away not only from industry but also from very much needed public works, an opinion that is thus summarized by M. Arboux:[2]

> While France exports billions, she has done nothing for herself. While she has given the most complete tools to countries which soon turn about and compete with France in the sale of the products of those tools, she has not progressed in her own production methods. France has created harbors for Argentine, bored isthmuses in two hemispheres, established canals from the Baltic to the Black Sea, yet important public works remain to be accomplished on her own soil. Havre and Marseilles are not equipped to maintain their commercial position; canals are urgently needed in the east and southeast. With the money that we have sown in distant enterprises we could have realized ten times over our great national projects whose future even now seems chimerical.

Doubtless the apparently greater yield of foreign securities was even more appealing to the French investors because of their lack of confidence in domestic enterprise. The French attitude toward French ventures is well expressed in the remark attributed to a French officer who had spent twenty years abroad. When asked why he invested his savings abroad rather than in France, he replied, "I don't mind risking my skin for France, but I must keep my sous protected."[3]

[1] Le Marché Financier, 1910–11, p. 6.

[2] Op. cit., p. 110. The author of the above quotation is not in sympathy with the writers who place the blame for this state of affairs on the export of capital. He feels it is due to the lack of French business ability.

[3] Cited by Guillaume, op. cit.

It seems very probable that the bias for foreign investments, in large part artificially created by the powerful French commercial banks, was responsible for this lack of confidence in domestic enterprise. It is possible that the French attitude toward experimentation, toward new ventures, new methods, would have been different had French capital more eagerly sought opportunities for domestic investment. To be sure, to an aggressive, enterprising commercial spirit foreign competition for capital is of secondary importance; capital is eagerly sought after, coaxed into domestic channels by ambitious entrepreneurs. But lacking that spirit, French industry may have needed the special encouragement that a large supply of capital seeking domestic employment would have provided.[1] Once having gathered momentum, the whole psychology of production might have changed. Improvements, larger scale production, greater profits, might have ushered in a tendency toward industrial expansion similar to that of Germany during those years.

[1] It is significant that such expansion in the use of machinery as did occur in France came at a time of very low interest rates and most abundant capital. J. H. Clapham, after reviewing the statistics on the spread of machinery in France, wrote: "It might easily be argued that an 'industrial revolution' began in France somewhere about the year 1895. All the power used in French industry in 1890 would only have driven a few squadrons of the capital ships in 1920." — The Economic Development of France and Germany 1815–1914 (Cambridge, 1923), p. 240.

CHAPTER XIV

CONCLUSION

It has been generally supposed that the huge foreign investments of France yielded a net revenue large enough to make possible a continuous excess of imports. Contrary to this belief the balance sheet of French international accounts for the years 1880 to 1913 shows that the total net revenue due France from her foreign investments was no greater than the total exports of capital for the same period; France had not yet reached that stage of lending maturity when income from foreign investments exceeds capital exports. It is therefore evident that the persistent excess of imports which, according to the official figures, France enjoyed could not have been brought about — as French writers commonly stated — by her foreign investments. Nor was the import excess so large as the official figures indicate. After due allowance for the relative undervaluation of exports and after making comparable the statistics of exports and imports by correction for shipping and insurance costs, the movement of merchandise balances presents a quite different picture from that based on the official figures. Instead of the recorded constant excess of imports, in twelve of the thirty-four years under survey France had an excess of merchandise exports, and in several of the remaining years her import excess was very small. The departures from the trend toward an excess of exports after 1889 were of short duration and were chiefly the result of greatly increased food imports necessitated by unusually poor domestic harvests. Even the import excess of the period 1880 to 1886 was in large part due to the widespread destruction of domestic vineyards and the consequent extraordinary imports of wine. A curve representing the corrected merchandise balance of trade with these fluctuations eliminated would show an excess of imports in only a few years, and for the period as a whole a sizeable excess of exports. Such excess of imports as did occur was paid for not by the revenue from the French foreign investments but by the expenditures of foreign tourists in France, a revenue which looms very large in the international accounts and amounts during the thirty-four years to more than thirteen billion francs. The receipts from this source were sufficient to pay not only for the excess of merchandise imports but also for the large excess (six and a half billion francs) of specie imports.

Tho the totals of capital exports and net revenue from foreign investments over the period as a whole were not far apart, for any one year during most of the period they differed considerably, thereby raising the question of the mechanism for adjustment of the disequilibrium caused by changes in the volume of capital exports. We found by comparing the movements of capital exports with the partial balances that there existed a correlation between merchandise movements and capital exports high enough to suggest that the adjustment of disequilibrium occurred thru movements of merchandise. In attempting to trace the connection between the two it was necessary first to examine all the possible means thru which capital exports can influence or be influenced by merchandise movements, and then to evaluate the potency of the various means in the case of France.

We concluded that in the French trade with countries on a gold standard the movements of exchange rates were a negligible factor in checking or stimulating merchandise movements. In trade with countries not on a gold standard the movements of exchange rates were doubtless important. France exported little to such countries, but she obtained over one-fourth of her imports from them, and the wide fluctuation in exchange rates on those countries made a significant difference to the French importers.

We found also that countries which borrowed funds from France, unlike the countries which borrowed from England in the nineteenth century and from the United States in the twentieth, did not spend any appreciable portion of the loans in the lending country. The linking of French loans directly to her exports — the efforts of the French government notwithstanding — was definitely a negligible factor in the French merchandise movements. Changes in the volume of French exports to the borrowing countries played at best only a minor role in the adjustment.

Shifts in demand schedules were doubtless a more effective medium. No substantiation of this view could be found in the French trade statistics, but actual substantiation would in any case be impossible because fluctuations in prices as a causal factor in merchandise movements could not be excluded; it would be impossible to determine what proportion of the changes in the volume of merchandise imports and exports was due to changes in demand schedules and what proportion to changes in sectional prices. But the likelihood that changes in demand schedules induced chiefly by gold flows were a factor in the adjustment is, as we have seen from the general reasoning, fairly strong.

The influence of sectional price changes as a force in the adjustment does not in the case of France appear to have played so prominent a role as is presupposed by the neo-classical doctrine. Nevertheless, the indications are that they were a factor. Examination of the movements of sectional price changes and movements of the physical volume of merchandise reveals a relationship in accord with the orthodox sequence. Relative increases in the price of imports were accompanied by declines in the physical quantities, and relative decreases in price by increases in physical quantities. The changes continued until, in a large number of cases, there was a rough approximation between the changes in the values of the merchandise balances and the capital exports. No causal connection between the two movements, however, could be found in the movements of specie imports, bank reserves, discount rates, and changes in the volume of credit and money. Specie imports, as we have shown, affected bank reserves only thru the reserves of the Bank of France, all other banks keeping negligible amounts of specie in their vaults. Fluctuations in these reserves exerted only a slight influence on the volume of credit or note circulation. There was no trace of the gold-reserve-discount rate-volume-of-credit sequence held by the neo-classical theory to be the necessary chain connecting disequilibrium in the balance of payments with sectional price changes. The Bank of France discount rate, the rate at which the bulk of loans was made, moved so seldom and within such narrow limits that it could not have played an active role in the control of credit. Together with increases in the gold premium the Bank rate served to check outward movements of gold when there was danger of any large efflux; they were intended not to curtail credit at home but to prevent short-time funds from being drawn to foreign markets when very high rates prevailed. It was the avowed policy of the Bank of France to interfere as little as possible with the price at which business men could borrow short-time funds, and as a result of this policy — a policy made feasible by large and growing gold reserves and by a relatively undeveloped system of deposit banking — the stability of the Bank rate rendered it a purely passive factor in the control of credit. Tho the market rate was much less stable and appears to have been sensitive to specie imports, it applied to only a small proportion of the commercial loans, and was consequently a minor factor in controlling the expansion of credit.

It is certain that gold exerted no such influence on prices thru the medium of changes in bank reserves and discount rates as the orthodox theory presupposes; yet it is entirely possible that gold movements affected French prices without the aid of changes in discount rates or in the volume of credit. The great importance of the use of specie as a medium of payment in France makes such a connection between specie movements and prices possible even when discount rates and bank reserves remain passive factors. But no clear evidence on the problem of the relationship of the quantity of money in circulation to prices is revealed by the comparison between the fluctuations in the quantity of specie and notes outside the Bank of France and the movement of prices. Moreover, even if such a relationship were revealed, the absence of correlation between the annual movements of capital and specie renders dubious the interpretation that changes in sectional price levels were induced by capital movements. And in this instance the lack of monthly figures is not likely to be of sufficient importance to invalidate comparisons on an annual basis, for the price structure in France would not have been so sensitive to monthly movements as to the cumulative effect of a group of net monthly movements. Altogether analysis of French banking and monetary movements appears to show no definite relationships upon which can be based a satisfactory explanation of the connection between French capital exports and movements of sectional prices.

The possibility that merchandise movements influenced the volume of French capital exports cannot be wholly dismissed. In certain of the years the increased domestic expenditure on imported foodstuffs caused by serious crop failures may have curtailed the rate of savings and so affected capital exports; and bumper crops, again, may have served to increase both food and capital exports. On this point, again, the figures yield no definite evidence; the movements of capital exports show no consistent relationship with years of large or small food imports induced by poor or bumper crops. Nevertheless, in those years in which food imports were high owing to poor domestic crops and capital exports low, it is quite possible that the poor crops may have been one of the factors causing the decline in capital exports. The absence of any constant relationship may, as has been pointed out, mean only that other factors affecting capital exports were more influential in some years than in others.

The possibility that both capital exports and merchandise movements were concomitant effects of changes in business activity exists, but its potency is a matter of doubt. In certain of the years it is probable that both movements were accelerated or checked by business conditions, but the absence of any correlation between phases of business activity and capital exports suggests that cyclical movements of business activity were not an important factor in the positive correlation noted between capital exports and merchandise movements.

The evidence obtained from the analysis of French banking, monetary, merchandise, and price movements suggests the conclusion that no one force was alone instrumental in effecting adjustment of the disequilibrium in the French balance of payments. And it seems very doubtful to me that any one force is ever alone responsible for effecting a balance. Many forces making for adjustment are always involved, and each operates with a varying degree of effectiveness according to the particular situation. The specie-flow-price mechanism is doubtless one of the forces, but there seems to be no justification for assuming that it is the sole or even the dominant means of adjustment. It is my opinion that nothing in the experience of France, the United States, or Canada verifies the claim that the specie-flow-price mechanism of the neo-classical theory is the all-important means of adjustment.

The neo-classical theory is not the complete explanation. The theory fails in that it explains what happens only under certain given conditions seldom found. It expounds a sequence of changes which undisturbed would in time bring about adjustment, but which seldom, if ever, operates unchecked by the frictions and rapid changes characteristic of modern economic conditions. By ignoring some of these forces and minimizing others, the neo-classical exposition exaggerates the effectiveness of gold flows and sectional price changes as a means for establishing equilibrium in international accounts. A comprehensive theory should include the following factors:

1. Movements of exchange rates. These, as we have pointed out, are ineffectual in trade between two countries on a gold standard. They assume, however, an importance when one of the trading countries is not on a gold standard, for in such case the movements of exchange rates are no longer confined within the narrow limits of the gold points, and the resulting fluctuations cause significant changes in the price of goods to the importer. Too frequently the effectiveness of this medium is overlooked when considering the international account of a country on a gold standard. There is no reason to regard the exchange rates of such a country as fluctuating only between the gold points. The United States and France, for example, altho on a gold standard, trade extensively with countries not on a gold standard. Fluctuations in exchange rates may not be a factor in French trade with the United States, but they become an important factor in their trade with countries on a paper, silver, and (to a less extent) on a gold exchange standard.

The proponents of the orthodox theory of international trade are fully aware of the difference in the mechanism of adjustment among countries all on the gold standard and among countries not all on the gold standard. Yet their explanation of the mechanism for adjustment seldom makes allowance for the fact that rarely, if ever, does any country trade only with countries on a gold standard. For purposes of theoretic explanation it may be found convenient to assume that trading countries fall into two general classes — those on the gold standard and those not on the gold standard — and to distinguish between the different mechanisms that operate in each class. The actual situation with every important country, however, is that a significant portion of either its imports or its exports comes from or goes to countries not on the gold standard. Adjustment, therefore, is always aided by the movements of those exchanges which fluctuate between regions more widely separated than the gold points (or rather the gold regions).

2. Changes in demand schedules induced by transfers of purchasing power. Large transfers of purchasing power without gold shipments are becoming increasingly possible thru the growing practice of keeping foreign balances in the leading countries. The total of such foreign balances is large enough to permit of a considerable degree of fluctuation; and the increases and decreases, tho usually of temporary nature, immediately cause changes in demand schedules, which in turn modify the movements of imports and exports.

The efficacy of this modifying influence is enhanced by the rapidity with which it begins to operate. The modification of merchandise movements thru price changes brought about by transfers of purchasing power is usually much slower. It is slower, first, because a change in demand does not ordinarily cause an immediate occurrence of price changes; competition, custom, contracts, and unused plant capacity tend to render sluggish the response of price to a five or even ten per cent change in demand. Secondly, even when price changes do occur, the effect on the volume of purchases or sales abroad is apt to be small unless the price change is considerable. The elasticity of foreign demand for most exportable commodities is slight when a price change of five per cent or so is in question. Contracts, specialized brands, patents, transportation and credit considerations, most favored nation relations, trade secrets, special skills, good will, custom, all reduce the sensitivity of imports and exports to small price changes. This is not true of certain homogeneous products, like sugar and silver, but the total value of such goods entering into international trade is small as compared with the total trade. The effect, therefore, of gold or credit movements on demand in the market sense is not apt to be so rapid nor, for a time, so strong as the effect on demand in the schedule sense, for any fluctuation in total purchasing power brings about a corresponding change in purchases before much time has elapsed; and, as outlined in an earlier chapter, changes in purchases modify the balance of trade in varying degrees according to the circumstances. Moreover, an increase in the volume of imports resulting from increased demand schedules means more goods at the same price; whereas an increase in the volume of imports resulting from a decline in the price of imported commodities means more goods at lower prices. In one case an increase in the total value of imports must ensue; in the other the total value of imports will increase only if the domestic demand for foreign commodities has, within the immediate range of current price, an elasticity greater than unity. Because of these considerations it is entirely possible that a movement of gold or short-time balances will modify the trade balance, and perhaps, at times, bring about equilibrium thru changes in demand schedules before prices have had time both to change and to modify merchandise movements.

3. Changes in sectional prices induced by a flow of specie. Altho this means will always correct the disequilibrium if given sufficient time, its action is sometimes so slow that other forces effect the adjustment before the influence of specie flows makes itself felt on the volume of credit. Whether the specie flows serve to inaugurate an expansion or contraction of credit or only to sustain the movement already in progress is, I believe, not significant; so long as the expansion or contraction of credit is controlled by specie reserves, the remoteness of the control is of secondary importance. It is important to note that the movements of specie

may at the same time be of compensatory as well as correctional nature. They compensate for the minor disequilibrium which is the frequent accompaniment of short-time movements of capital and at times they are even large enough to compensate for a major disequilibrium; they are correctional in that their movements, either thru their effect on credit or on demand schedules, are an aid to the adjustment of a major disequilibrium.

4. Fluctuations in the rate of capital exports. Disequilibrium caused by sudden increases or decreases in the merchandise balance may be partially corrected by capital exports when the cause of merchandise movements is an exceptional crop condition in either the lending or the borrowing country. France, for example, may suddenly increase her imports because of extensive crop failures, and the disequilibrium so caused might be partially adjusted by a decline in the rate of capital exports, the decline in the rate of capital exports being in turn a result of the decrease in savings caused by the agricultural failures. In this way the very factor which gives rise to disequilibrium also provides partial correction without recourse to any of the previously mentioned means of adjustment. In the same manner a bumper crop or a newly developed important item of export may give rise to both increasing exports and increased capital exports. It must be noted, however, that the correction in such cases would only in rare accidental instances be complete, since there is no reason why the amplitude of both movements should be the same unless there be a causal connection between capital and merchandise movements.

5. The cyclical movement of business activity. As in the case of unusual crop conditions so in the case of changing business conditions disequilibrium may be caused and partially corrected by increasing or decreasing business activity. A rapidly developing country may, for example, be increasing its imports and thereby introducing disequilibrium. But it may also be borrowing abroad in order to aid the domestic expansion, and the borrowed funds will serve to partially correct the disequilibrium. Or a country having a large excess of exports brought about by capital exports may during a period of rapid business expansion con-

sume more of its domestic commodities and thus cause exports to be curtailed (thru the medium of rapidly rising export prices). The resulting disequilibrium (the appearance or intensification of an unfavorable balance of payments caused by a decreased export surplus while the rate of foreign lending continues) may in such case be partially corrected by a decrease in the export of capital, the decrease in capital exports being caused by a greatly increased demand for capital at home. We have then both a decline in imports and a decline in capital exports occurring at approximately the same time even tho there be no causal connection between them; both movements are the result of changes in business conditions. These cases are only a few of the many possible combinations which may give rise at approximately the same time to a disequilibrium in the balance of payments and to a partial correction of that disequilibrium without calling into play any other medium of adjustment. In all such cases, as in the case of unusual crop conditions, additional corrective forces are necessary to complete the adjustment, since, to repeat, the amplitude of the two movements would only accidentally be the same.

It must be emphasized that all these influences function at the same time, but with varying degrees of effectiveness. Different monetary and banking systems, different money habits, discount policies, the nature of the country's economy, its type of exports and imports, all cause differences in the relative effectiveness of each of the methods. Moreover, each of these means of adjustment even in the same country will change with changing phases of the business cycle. To stress the importance of any one means to the exclusion of the others is never warranted, but to hold one or two to be more important than the others with a particular country and during a particular period is reasonable. Inductive studies may help to reveal under what conditions each of these means gains or loses in potency relatively to the others. But to secure conclusive evidence on this score, the country and the period studied must be one for which there is a body of highly detailed accurate monthly data of all movements having any significant connection with the items in the international accounts. Several countries are at present collecting such data, and inductive studies of the contemporary period ought to throw much light on the relative importance of the various means of adjusting the international accounts.

The French experience in the matter of capital exports leads to the conclusion that the orthodox attitude towards unrestricted capital exports is open to criticism; the assumption that capital exports benefit both the lending country and the world at large is not unassailable. Examination of the conditions under which French foreign investments were made has clearly shown that the French investor consistently underestimated the risk inherent in the type of foreign securities that France acquired from 1880 to 1913. Thus, altho the rate of return on foreign investments was equal to that on domestic, the real yield was less, since equal returns imply equal risk. The productivity, if measured by yield, was thus no greater on the foreign investments. But in any case the productivity of French foreign investments cannot be measured by the rate of return because the bulk of French loans was made to governments and municipalities whose expenditures were on projects the productivity of which was impossible of measurement. The productivity, then, of French capital was not necessarily greater merely because it flowed out in response to offers of higher interest rates. But even if it had been greater, foreign investments cannot be lightly assumed to have been profitable to France — tho events subsequent to 1913 be disregarded. They may have increased the incomes of investors, or at least prevented them from falling; and they doubtless reduced the cost of certain French imports and increased the scale of French production in certain industries; but it is questionable whether these gains compensated for the loss to the French consumer from the unfavorable net barter terms of trade, to the wage earner and the entrepreneur from the reduction in wages, and to France as a whole from the withdrawal of huge sums from domestic employment.

The study of French foreign investments supports, in my opinion, the growing belief that capital exports are not always beneficial to the exporting country and that some measure of intelligent control of the volume and direction of foreign investments is desirable. It may well be that the foreign investments of the United States in the past decade have in the main added to the national as well as to the world income while not reducing the real income of the American wage earner, but there is no certainty that continued unrestricted exports of capital will yield similar benefits. The ramifications of exporting a large portion of a country's savings are too complex and the consequences too important to permit the continuance of capital exports without making some attempt at evaluating their effects on the well-being of the country at large.

APPENDIX

APPENDIX

TABLE 48

Various Estimates of French Domestic and Foreign Investments

(Billions of francs)

Year	Total in French Portfolio	Total Foreign Investments	Author
1870	...	12–14	Say [1]
1880	...	12–15	Leroy-Beaulieu [2]
1880	55.9	15	Théry [3]
1887	...	18.5	De Foville [4]
1887	80	20	Neymarck [5]
1888	67–70	10–12	Coste [6]
1890	...	20	Neymarck [5]
1890	78	20	Théry [3]
1896	...	26	Levy [7]
1898	93.9	26	Pougnet [8]
1898	...	20	Renou [9]
1898	...	22	Salefranque [10]
1899	93.7	27	Théry [3]
1900	94	26	Decoudu [11]
1900	95–97	26.9	Neymarck [5]
1902	...	30	Official Investigation [12]
1902	100	25–27	Neymarck [5]
1904	100–103	27–30	Neymarck [5]
1906	100	27.6	De Lavergne [13]
1906	100–105	20–32	Neymarck [5]
1907	...	37	Théry [14]
1908	106–110	32–35	Neymarck [5]
1908	...	38	Théry [15]
1909	...	40	Crammond [16]
1910	105–110	38–40	Neymarck [5]
1910	...	37	Becque [17]
1912	106–110	40–42	Neymarck [5]
1912	...	40	Guyot [18]
1913	...	45	Meynial [19]
1914	...	50	Martin [20]

NOTES TO TABLE

1 Léon Say, Rapport sur le paiement de l'indemnité de guerre (Paris, 1874), p. 70.

2 P. Leroy-Beaulieu, Économiste Français, October 23, 1880.

3 E. Théry, Les valeurs mobilières en France, Congrès des valeurs mobilières (1900), Vol. 2, Report No. 42.

In this article he estimated the amount of foreign securities held in France by applying an estimated ratio of foreign to domestic securities to the known quantity of domestic securities after having deducted 10 per cent for domestic securities held abroad. This percentage he accepted without comment from Neymarck. The ratio of foreign to domestic securities he estimated from correspondence with banks to be 31 per cent. The results he obtained for the years 1850, 1860, 1880, 1890, and 1899 are as follows:

(Millions of francs)

Year	Total French Securities	French Securities Held Abroad	French Securities in French Portfolio	Foreign Securities in French Portfolio	Total Securities in French Portfolio
1850........	7.3	.7	6.6	2.5	9.1
1860........	23.1	2.3	20.8	10	30.8
1880........	45.4	4.5	40.9	15	55.9
1890........	59.6	5.9	53.6	20	73.6
1899........	66.3	6.6	59.8	27	86.8

The estimates for the years 1850 and 1860 he admits to be mere guesses. See p. 94 for further discussion.

[4] A. de Foville, Économiste Français, August 4, 1888, p. 131.

Estimated foreign securities subject to a tax of 2 billions and not subject to tax at 16½. This latter figure he obtained by estimating the new credit balance since 1877. The figure of 2 billions taxed is too high because the income is capitalized at too low a rate, and the 16½ billions is also too high because of excessive estimates of credit due France annually on account of non-commercial items.

[5] A. Neymarck, Bull. de l'Inst. Int. de Stat., Vols. VI, IX, (2), XI (2), XII, XIII (2), XIII (3), XIV (2), XIV (3), XVII, XVIII (2), XIX (2), XX (2).

Finances Contemporaines (Paris, 1910), Vol. 7.

Neymarck has made independent estimates for the years 1887, 1890, 1896, 1900, 1902, 1906, 1908, 1910, and 1912. He has used all sources and every care in compiling his data. The differences between his estimates and the ones used for this study are due principally to difference in point of view as to the amount of French securities held abroad. His use of market price in estimating his value of securities outstanding also accounts for differences, since for this study it has been sometimes necessary to modify those figures according to the spread between issuing price and market price. For example, for 1890 both Neymarck and Théry estimated foreign investments at 20 billions as against 18 billions used in this study. Their estimates are based on market values. A glance at the following table showing the course of some of the principal foreign bonds will explain the difference between the two estimates.

	1883	1888	1890*
4% Gold Austrian	84	86.7	96.6
Unified Egypt	316	419	487
4% Spanish	55.7	74.1	77
4% Hungarian	75.7	79.9	95
3% Portuguese	52	58	58.4
5% Roumanian	90.5	90.5	101.5
4% Russian	79.5	84.7	96.9

* Raffolovich, Le Marché Financier, Vol. 1893-4, p. 474.

The difference in market price over purchase price of Russian bonds alone — of which France held over 5 billion francs — would account for one-half billion francs. Spanish, Egyptian, Austrian, and Hungarian bonds also rose greatly in price. The bonds were not necessarily purchased at the lowest prices, but they were purchased at lower prices than prevailed in 1890.

[6] A. Coste, Discussion du memoire de M. Neymarck sur les valeurs mobilières, Jour. de la Soc. de Stat. de Paris, July, 1888, p. 235.

[7] R. G. Levy, Revue des Deux Mondes, March 15, 1897.

His estimate of 26 billions includes the following geographical distribution:

Russia	7	Hungary	.4
Spain	5	Argentine	.5
Italy	1.5	China	.5
Austria-Hungary	2	Brazil	.5
Turkey	2.5	United States.............	.5
Egypt	1.7	Other.....................	4

Total 26 billions

His estimate of investments in Spain is 3 billion francs too much and that of Turkey at least 1 billion too high.

[8] M. Pougnet, Valeurs étrangères et fonds d'état étrangères (Paris, 1900).

Like R. G. Levy, he overestimated the amounts of Turkish and Spanish government bonds held by the French in 1896.

[9] Renou, Les valeurs étrangères (Paris, 1907).

Estimate of 20 billions arrived at on the basis of taxation data. He accepted estimates of fraud known to exist in registration of domestic securities, and assumed that at least the same amount of fraud existed in declaration of foreign securities. His estimate is too low if for no other reason than that the tax evasion on foreign securities was much greater than on domestic securities.

[10] L. Salefranque, Les valeurs mobilières dans la fortune privée en France, Congrès international des valeurs mobilières (Paris, 1900).

[11] M. Decoudu, Les valeurs mobilières admises à la côte officielle de la Bourse de Paris, Congrès des valeurs mobilières (Paris, 1900), Vol. 2, Report No. 44.

He accepted Théry's estimate of 30 per cent as the percentage of foreign securities in the French portfolio, and Neymarck's estimate of 10 per cent as the percentage of French securities held abroad, and applied that percentage to totals of securities listed on the Bourse. The article contains a complete list of securities listed on the Bourse, with nominal price, price of issue, market price, and dividend or interest paid in 1899. The totals of the various classes are listed on page 106.

[12] Official Investigation of 1900, Bull. de Stat. et de Leg. Comp., October, 1902, p. 450.

This report has been severely criticized as inaccurate by De Foville and by Leroy-Beaulieu (see p. 72), but it is useful as indicating the relative geographical distribution of investments, which was as follows:

(Millions of francs)

Europe					
Russia	6,960	Belgium	600	Germany	80
Spain	2,970	Switzerland	405	Monaco	150
Austria-Hungary	2,800	Luxembourg	660	Roumania	430
Turkey	1,800	Holland	200	Bulgaria	40
Italy	1,400	Denmark	330	Serbia	200
England	1,000	Norway	290	Greece	280
Portugal	900	Sweden	120		
Total Europe					21012
Asia		Africa		No. America	
Turkey	350	Egypt	1436	United States	600
China	650	Tunis	512	Canada	138
Japan	20	British Africa	1592	Mexico	300
		Congo	70		
				Total	1038
Total	1120	Total	3693		
				Total World	29855

[13] A. de Lavergne and L. P. Henry, La richesse de la France (Paris, 1908), Chap. I.

Their estimate of 27.6 billions for 1907 was made as follows:

Foreign government securities subject to stamp tax up to December 31, 1906	25.178
Deduction for securities amortized	2.5
	22.678
Deduction for foreign government securities resold to foreign countries	2
	20.678
Deduction for difference between real and nominal value of foreign government securities	2
	18.678
Non-government securities subject to transfer tax in 1896	5.562
Foreign securities subject only to stamp tax au comptant	1.5
	25.740

This estimate is open to serious doubt because this tax data cannot be used to give correct results. The transfer tax includes an annual tax on only bearer securities; "Nominative" securities tax includes conversions, and the stamp duties take no account of the mass of such securities bought and sold after having been issued. The estimate of only 20 billions of foreign government securities is much lower than other estimates. Only two years later Neymarck estimated that Russian bonds made up 16.3 per cent of total investments, and other government bonds 65.3 per cent, making a total of 82 per cent for foreign government securities. These are not subject to revenue taxation. Therefore the securities so taxed would represent about 18 per cent. In 1906 the revenue taxed was 263 millions. If this revenue is capitalized at 5 per cent, the total amount of government securities alone is 27 billion francs.

[14] E. Théry, Le progrès économique de la France (Paris, 1903), p. 307.

[15] E. Théry, Fortune publique de la France (Paris, 1911), p. 197.

[16] E. Crammond, Journal of Royal Statistical Society, September, 1909, p. 483.

[17] E. Becque, L'Internationalisation des capitaux (Montpellier, 1912), Chap. II. The estimate of 37 billions for 1910, based mostly on taxation data, is as follows:

Foreign government bonds	26.5
Securities abonnés	6.6
Securities non abonnés	1.8
Securities evading taxes	2
Total	36.8

The values of the above securities are market values at 1910. From 1906 to 1913 the prices of fixed income securities dropped 10 per cent, and over three-fourths of foreign securities held by France were in this form. Many of these securities were purchased during the period of 1888 to 1902 when higher prices prevailed.

[18] Y. Guyot, The Amount, Direction, and Nature of French Investments, Annals of Am. Acad. of Pol. and Soc. Sci., 1916, Vol. 68, p. 37.

[19] P. Meynial, Créances et dettes internationales (Paris, 1926), Chap. II.

[20] G. Martin, La situation financière de la France, 1914–1924, p. 100.

TABLE 49

MONTHLY MOVEMENTS OF SPECIE RESERVES, NOTE ISSUE AND DISCOUNT RATE OF THE BANK OF FRANCE; SPECIE IMPORTS AND EXPORTS OF FRANCE (EXCLUSIVE OF SILVER BULLION); GOLD PREMIUM AT PARIS 1880–1913

Date		Excess of Specie Imports [1] (Millions of francs)	Gold Premium at Paris [2] (per 1000 francs)	Specie Reserve of Bank of France [3] (Millions of francs)	Note Circulation [4] (Millions of francs)	Bank of France Discount Rates (Per cent)
1880	Jan.	...	1.47	1980	2321	3
	Feb.	...	1	2043	2251	3
	Mar.	...	.45	2091	2211	3
	Apr.	...	4.39	2039	2265	2.5
	May	...	3.42	2044	2258	2.5
	June	...	4.81	2048	2242	2.5
	July	...	4.5	2017	2304	2.5
	Aug.	...	4.69	2019	2233	2.5
	Sept.	...	5.84	1962	2346	2.5
	Oct.	...	6	1821	2357	3.5
	Nov.	...	4.22	1777	2400	3.5
	Dec.	...	5	1786	2476	3.5
1881	Jan.	...	3.36	1760	2524	3.5
	Feb.	...	4.91	1764	2477	3.5
	Mar.	...	4.38	1825	2524	3.5
	Apr.	...	5.53	1824	2539	3.5
	May	...	4.09	1856	2515	3.5
	June	...	3.73	1890	2596	3.5
	July	...	3.62	1874	2600	3.5
	Aug.	...	2.5	1862	2520	4
	Sept.	...	4.82	1838	2602	4
	Oct.	...	5.5	1801	2705	5
	Nov.	...	5.5	1809	2748	5
	Dec.	...	4.48	1817	2778	5

[1] Exclusive of silver bullion.
[2] Monthly average of daily quotations at Bourse de Paris.
[3] 1880–1888 — last week in the month. 1889–1913 — average of weekly figures.
[4] Last week of the month.

TABLE 49 (*Continued*)

	Date	Excess of Specie Imports (Millions of francs)	Gold Premium at Paris (per 1000 francs)	Specie Reserve of Bank of France (Millions of francs)	Note Circulation (Millions of francs)	Bank of France Discount Rates (Per cent)
1882	Jan.	...	2.65	1836	2852	5
	Feb.	...	2.5	1958	2775	4.5
	Mar.	...	1.5	2001	2666	4
	Apr.	...	.5	2031	2673	3.5
	May	...	.5	2071	2657	3.5
	June	...	.5	2133	2672	3.5
	July	...	.5	2137	2686	3.5
	Aug.	...	.5	2149	2740	3.5
	Sept.	...	.5	2133	2666	3.5
	Oct.	...	.5	2089	2726	3.5
	Nov.	...	.5	2061	2864	3.5
	Dec.	...	.5	2055	2790	3.5
1883	Jan.	...	.5	2033	2899	3.5
	Feb.	...	.5	2075	2803	3
	Mar.	...	.5	2051	2829	3
	Apr.	...	.5	2045	2859	3
	May	...	.5	2059	2988	3
	June	...	.66	2055	2900	3
	July	...	.75	2029	2980	3
	Aug.	...	.75	2014	2955	3
	Sept.	...	1.84	2003	2928	3
	Oct.	...	1	1983	2995	3
	Nov.	...	1	1969	2943	3
	Dec.	...	1	1963	2946	3
1884	Jan.	...	1	1945	3162	3
	Feb.	...	1	1988	2974	3
	Mar.	...	1	2006	2897	3
	Apr.	...	1	2005	2947	3
	May	...	1	2034	2902	3
	June	12	1	2048	2867	3
	July	0	1	2060	2974	3
	Aug.	13	1	2080	2821	3
	Sept.	5	1	2080	2814	3
	Oct.	18	1	2080	2899	3
	Nov.	−5	3.18	2063	2864	3
	Dec.	−8	3.5	2048	2858	3

TABLE 49 (*Continued*)

	Date	Excess of Specie Imports (Millions of francs)	Gold Premium at Paris (per 1000 francs)	Specie Reserve of Bank of France (Millions of francs)	Note Circulation (Millions of francs)	Bank of France Discount Rates (Per cent)
1885	Jan.	−10	3.5	2028	2978	3
	Feb.	5	3.66	2041	2907	3
	Mar.	−8	4.26	2061	2865	3
	Apr.	77	5	2112	2924	3
	May	29	1.74	2163	2782	3
	June	7	.5	2234	2763	3
	July	19	.5	2241	2815	3
	Aug.	28	.5	2272	2719	3
	Sept.	13	.5	2280	2726	3
	Oct.	2	1.2	2242	2820	3
	Nov.	−25	1.5	2255	2797	3
	Dec.	−13	.57	2242	2918	3
1886	Jan.	−8	.5	2235	2901	3
	Feb.	18	.5	2284	2825	3
	Mar.	21	.5	2369	2813	3
	Apr.	67	.5	2424	2851	3
	May	86	.5	2524	2774	3
	June	31	.5	2513	2754	3
	July	0	.5	2483	2765	3
	Aug.	−7	1.59	2499	2697	3
	Sept.	−9	3	2506	2742	3
	Oct.	−6	3.55	2485	2726	3
	Nov.	−33	4.5	2459	2712	3
	Dec.	−64	5.83	2384	2790	3
1887	Jan.	−38	4.8	2352	2854	3
	Feb.	−6	6.12	2365	2755	3
	Mar.	−5	6.03	2346	2818	3
	Apr.	−8	4.36	2347	2752	3
	May	11	2.17	2374	2698	3
	June	4	.65	2390	2753	3
	July	4	2.08	2382	2685	3
	Aug.	0	3.46	2398	2557	3
	Sept.	−14	7.42	2374	2617	3
	Oct.	−20	6.46	2335	2654	3
	Nov.	−22	4.8	2331	2661	3
	Dec.	−52	5.72	2309	2726	3

TABLE 49 (*Continued*)

	Date	Excess of Specie Imports (Millions of francs)	Gold Premium at Paris (per 1000 francs)	Specie Reserve of Bank of France (Millions of francs)	Note Circulation (Millions of francs)	Bank of France Discount Rates (Per cent)
1888	Jan.	−7	4.11	2282	2801	3
	Feb.	10	2.74	2312	2742	2.5
	Mar.	−2	4.16	2313	2719	2.5
	Apr.	−41	3.93	2314	2733	2.5
	May	7	3.37	2333	2722	2.5
	June	14	2.48	2338	2596	2.5
	July	2	2.7	2328	2592	2.5
	Aug.	10	5.25	2326	2547	2.5
	Sept.	−14	6.88	2299	2545	3.5
	Oct.	−22	5.61	2249	2608	4.5
	Nov.	−3	3.9	2249	2623	4.5
	Dec.	−7	4.41	2249	2600	4.5
1889	Jan.	3	3.55	2230	2829	4
	Feb.	−6	3.02	2240	2786	3
	Mar.	1	3.67	2240	2851	3
	Apr.	10	2.22	2250	2869	3
	May	6	1.53	2270	2899	3
	June	79	.98	2350	2802	3
	July	97	1	2460	2843	3
	Aug.	22	1	2550	2812	3
	Sept.	52	1.2	2590	2881	3
	Oct.	−12	1.5	2550	3123	3
	Nov.	−22	2.28	2540	3014	3
	Dec.	−12	3.62	2520	3003	3
1890	Jan.	−5	3	2495	3198	3
	Feb.	−4	2.72	2500	3109	3
	Mar.	8	1.98	2500	3025	3
	Apr.	9	1.38	2530	3042	3
	May	29	.5	2570	3006	3
	June	3	.5	2590	2989	3
	July	−2	1.07	2580	3088	3
	Aug.	−1	2.7	2580	2905	3
	Sept.	−31	1.65	2550	2948	3
	Oct.	−40	3.61	2460	3092	3
	Nov.	−66	5.64	2390	3061	3
	Dec.	−10	4.21	2370	3051	3

TABLE 49 (*Continued*)

	Date	Excess of Specie Imports (Millions of francs)	Gold Premium at Paris (per 1000 francs)	Specie Reserve of Bank of France (Millions of francs)	Note Circulation (Millions of francs)	Bank of France Discount Rates (Per cent)
1891	Jan.	6	3	2370	3173	3
	Feb.	78	3.6	2430	3133	3
	Mar.	−2	3.5	2460	3119	3
	Apr.	13	2.57	2480	3217	3
	May	32	3.18	2520	3045	3
	June	39	2.37	2580	3002	3
	July	37	3.75	2620	3051	3
	Aug.	−15	4.5	2630	2925	3
	Sept.	−42	6.5	2600	2950	3
	Oct.	−9	6.48	2570	3047	3
	Nov.	−6	3.54	2570	3016	3
	Dec.	2	2.05	2600	3194	3
1892	Jan.	15	1.97	2590	3136	3
	Feb.	18	1.76	2630	3066	3
	Mar.	15	1.18	2650	3166	3
	Apr.	30	.25	2710	3142	3
	May	50	.11	2800	3091	2.5
	June	66	0	2870	3211	2.5
	July	21	0	2910	3123	2.5
	Aug.	40	0	2960	3038	2.5
	Sept.	29	1.07	2970	3136	2.5
	Oct.	−5	1.91	2960	3213	2.5
	Nov.	−2	1.10	2955	3207	2.5
	Dec.	25	.5	2975	3298	2.5
1893	Jan.	6	.18	2870	3311	2.5
	Feb.	7	0	2860	3375	2.5
	Mar.	7	.4	2920	3478	2.5
	Apr.	139	.5	2940	3477	2.5
	May	36	1.12	2980	3414	2.5
	June	18	.98	2990	3450	2.5
	July	17	1	2990	3439	2.5
	Aug.	−31	6.42	2980	3471	2.5
	Sept.	−13	4.04	2960	3400	2.5
	Oct.	30	2.54	2960	3471	2.5
	Nov.	−2	1.78	2970	3558	2.5
	Dec.	5	1.5	2980	3478	2.5

TABLE 49 (*Continued*)

	Date	Excess of Specie Imports (Millions of francs)	Gold Premium at Paris (per 1000 francs)	Specie Reserve of Bank of France (Millions of francs)	Note Circulation (Millions of francs)	Bank of France Discount Rates (Per cent)
1894	Jan.	6	1.5	2960	3564	2.5
	Feb.	7	.12	2980	3484	2.5
	Mar.	7	0	2990	3453	2.5
	Apr.	18	0	3000	3470	2.5
	May	0	0	3040	3534	2.5
	June	20	0	3060	3397	2.5
	July	54	0	3100	3410	2.5
	Aug.	40	0	3160	3368	2.5
	Sept.	−10	0	3170	3377	2.5
	Oct.	32	0	3140	3452	2.5
	Nov.	82	0	3200	3500	2.5
	Dec.	52	0	3280	3481	2.5
1895	Jan.	62	0	3330	3749	2.5
	Feb.	46	0	3380	3675	2.5
	Mar.	30	0	3370	3574	2
	Apr.	−43	0	3300	3587	2
	May	4	0	3290	3546	2
	June	18	0	3300	3461	2
	July	15	0	3300	3423	2
	Aug.	6	0	3310	3340	2
	Sept.	−2	1.56	3290	3363	2
	Oct.	−61	1.5	3210	3627	2
	Nov.	−18	.5	3180	3506	2
	Dec.	−32	.04	3200	3484	2
1896	Jan.	1	0	3170	3681	2
	Feb.	11	0	3190	3575	2
	Mar.	18	0	3200	3577	2
	Apr.	−1	0	3195	3764	2
	May	27	0	3230	3581	2
	June	60	0	3280	3544	2
	July	54	0	3300	3579	2
	Aug.	20	.52	3320	3456	2
	Sept.	−101	1.57	3260	3491	2
	Oct.	−42	1.87	3190	3625	2
	Nov.	−28	2.98	3160	3601	2
	Dec.	−130	3	3160	3838	2

TABLE 49 (*Continued*)

Date		Excess of Specie Imports (Millions of francs)	Gold Premium at Paris (per 1000 francs)	Specie Reserve of Bank of France (Millions of francs)	Note Circulation (Millions of francs)	Bank of France Discount Rates (Per cent)
1897	Jan.	6	2.02	3130	3756	2
	Feb.	9	.79	3140	3664	2
	Mar.	7	0	3140	3624	2
	Apr.	−19	0	3140	3721	2
	May	13	0	3200	3635	2
	June	55	0	3220	3594	2
	July	23	0	3240	3613	2
	Aug.	−2	.11	3260	3544	2
	Sept.	48	1.88	3220	3760	2
	Oct.	−41	1.3	3170	3726	2
	Nov.	−26	1.5	3170	3691	2
	Dec.	6	2.3	3170	3809	2
1898	Jan.	16	2.36	3140	3784	2
	Feb.	10	1.43	3140	3711	2
	Mar.	18	3.94	3090	3832	2
	Apr.	1	4.98	3070	3711	2
	May	−90	3.5	3090	3652	2
	June	−29	3.72	3110	3703	2
	July	8	2.08	3110	3580	2
	Aug.	−41	2.56	3130	3480	2
	Sept.	3	4.8	3120	3591	2
	Oct.	−24	6.09	3080	3696	3
	Nov.	−2	6.62	3060	3717	3
	Dec.	−12	5.42	3040	3810	3
1899	Jan.	35	1.19	3010	3855	3
	Feb.	11	.21	3020	3798	3
	Mar.	3	.84	3010	3820	3
	Apr.	−5	.75	3020	3781	3
	May	16	1	3030	3701	3
	June	4	.61	3080	3758	3
	July	33	.76	3120	3722	3
	Aug.	0	.5	3125	3795	3
	Sept.	34	1.03	3115	3755	3
	Oct.	−20	3.62	3080	3858	3
	Nov.	−23	3.22	3060	4043	3
	Dec.	9	4.86	3050	3983	3.5

TABLE 49 (*Continued*)

Date		Excess of Specie Imports (Millions of francs)	Gold Premium at Paris (per 1000 francs)	Specie Reserve of Bank of France (Millions of francs)	Note Circulation (Millions of francs)	Bank of France Discount Rates (Per cent)
1900	Jan.	46	2.19	3030	4046	4
	Feb.	−13	.5	3050	3974	3.5
	Mar.	−4	.3	3070	3986	3.5
	Apr.	10	.5	3075	4010	3.5
	May	18	.07	3120	4106	3
	June	33	0	3220	3945	3
	July	63	0	3300	3972	3
	Aug.	60	0	3350	3955	3
	Sept.	−9	0	3385	3947	3
	Oct.	−6	.11	3400	4022	3
	Nov.	−7	0	3420	4090	3
	Dec.	28	0	3440	4180	3
1901	Jan.	43	0	3440	4446	3
	Feb.	6	0	3480	4332	3
	Mar.	38	0	3470	4170	3
	Apr.	−13	0	3510	4179	3
	May	18	0	3550	4031	3
	June	22	0	3580	3956	3
	July	41	0	3560	3966	3
	Aug.	−14	0	3570	3907	3
	Sept.	−42	1.41	3520	3956	3
	Oct.	18	.89	2470	4215	3
	Nov.	50	0	3530	4061	3
	Dec.	62	0	3560	4072	3
1902	Jan.	13	0	3550	4254	3
	Feb.	27	0	3590	4154	3
	Mar.	21	0	3630	4113	3
	Apr.	40	0	3670	4121	2
	May	3	0	3680	4084	3
	June	8	0	3690	4041	3
	July	33	0	3700	4215	3
	Aug.	45	0	3730	4004	3
	Sept.	−6	0	3720	4060	3
	Oct.	8	0	3670	4278	3
	Nov.	4	0	3640	4250	3
	Dec.	0	0	3650	4304	3

TABLE 49 (*Continued*)

	Date	Excess of Specie Imports (Millions of francs)	Gold Premium at Paris (per 1000 francs)	Specie Reserve of Bank of France (Millions of francs)	Note Circulation (Millions of francs)	Bank of France Discount Rates (Per cent)
1903	Jan.	13	0	3600	4426	3
	Feb.	31	0	3610	4330	3
	Mar.	12	0	3620	4273	3
	Apr.	3	0	3600	4480	3
	May	6	0	3600	4285	3
	June	40	0	3630	4225	3
	July	99	0	3650	4283	3
	Aug.	11	0	3680	4120	3
	Sept.	−36	0	3650	4137	3
	Oct.	−4	0	3550	4290	3
	Nov.	4	.72	3500	4217	3
	Dec.	−21	.69	3490	4491	3
1904	Jan.	10	0	3450	4358	3
	Feb.	−12	0	3450	4271	3
	Mar.	25	0	3460	4427	3
	Apr.	36	0	3510	4294	3
	May	266	0	3650	4167	3
	June	129	0	3910	4313	3
	July	−10	0	3860	4191	3
	Aug.	−22	0	3820	4106	3
	Sept.	−24	0	3770	4266	3
	Oct.	6	0	3710	4290	3
	Nov.	46	0	3750	4252	3
	Dec.	23	0	3760	4325	3
1905	Jan.	36	0	3770	4369	3
	Feb.	76	0	3860	4308	3
	Mar.	90	0	3890	4374	3
	Apr.	32	0	3870	4358	3
	May	9	0	3930	4296	3
	June	98	0	3980	4356	3
	July	76	0	4020	4311	3
	Aug.	48	0	4060	4430	3
	Sept.	155	0	4070	4377	3
	Oct.	−12	0	4020	4476	3
	Nov.	5	0	3990	4649	3
	Dec.	9	0	3970	4566	3

TABLE 49 (*Continued*)

	Date	Excess of Specie Imports (Millions of francs)	Gold Premium at Paris (per 1000 francs)	Specie Reserve of Bank of France (Millions of francs)	Note Circulation (Millions of francs)	Bank of France Discount Rates (Per cent)
1906	Jan.	56	0	3920	4721	3
	Feb.	28	0	3910	4666	3
	Mar.	80	0	3960	4704	3
	Apr.	89	0	4000	4710	3
	May	−27	0	4020	4772	3
	June	9	0	4010	4554	3
	July	13	0	3990	4510	3
	Aug.	11	0	3980	4499	3
	Sept.	−1	0	3940	4503	3
	Oct.	4	0	3850	4607	3
	Nov.	−19	0	3800	4707	3
	Dec.	−21	0	3730	4714	3
1907	Jan.	−2	0	3640	5026	3
	Feb.	1	0	3630	4929	3
	Mar.	−26	0	3600	4744	3.5
	Apr.	3	0	3570	4750	3.5
	May	35	0	3600	4754	3.5
	June	68	0	3690	4670	3.5
	July	25	0	3780	4695	3.5
	Aug.	14	0	3770	4618	3.5
	Sept.	26	0	3750	4685	3.5
	Oct.	41	0	3720	5053	3.5
	Nov.	−32	0	3650	4818	4
	Dec.	3	0	3620	4800	4
1908	Jan.	14	0	3590	4949	3.5
	Feb.	66	0	3660	4786	3
	Mar.	41	0	3670	4724	3
	Apr.	73	0	3700	4992	3
	May	159	0	3880	4751	3
	June	114	0	4030	4691	3
	July	61	0	4080	4797	3
	Aug.	49	0	4130	4661	3
	Sept.	59	0	4130	4748	3
	Oct.	138	0	4150	4905	3
	Nov.	93	0	4230	4886	3
	Dec.	17	0	4330	4934	3

TABLE 49 (*Continued*)

Date		Excess of Specie Imports (Millions of francs)	Gold Premium at Paris (per 1000 francs)	Specie Reserve of Bank of France (Millions of francs)	Note Circulation (Millions of francs)	Bank of France Discount Rates (Per cent)
1909	Jan.	110	0	4519	4994	3
	Feb.	33	0	4527	4933	3
	Mar.	−5	0	4491	4965	3
	Apr.	28	0	4503	5124	3
	May	51	0	4574	5028	3
	June	57	0	4607	4961	3
	July	1	0	4600	5001	3
	Aug.	7	0	4607	4874	3
	Sept.	−47	0	4534	5224	3
	Oct.	−20	0	4516	5141	3
	Nov.	−27	0	4460	5094	3
	Dec.	−39	0	4400	5140	3
1910	Jan.	26	0	4366	5290	3
	Feb.	12	0	4344	5183	3
	Mar.	−26	0	4333	5342	3
	Apr.	−1	0	4313	5190	3
	May	−27	0	4289	5071	3
	June	−38	0	4287	5236	3
	July	−27	0	4272	5037	3
	Aug.	−7	0	4281	4922	3
	Sept.	10	0	4227	5165	3
	Oct.	17	0	4191	5256	3
	Nov.	−1	0	4146	5167	3
	Dec.	−1	0	4118	5152	3
1911	Jan.	15	0	4080	5302	3
	Feb.	14	0	4070	5188	3
	Mar.	0	0	4070	5239	3
	Apr.	18	0	4070	5160	3
	May	−46	0	4080	5038	3
	June	7	0	4065	5126	3
	July	−24	0	4050	5025	3
	Aug.	−5	0	4030	5202	3
	Sept.	11	0	3970	5330	3.5
	Oct.	68	0	3910	5331	3.5
	Nov.	50	0	3970	5449	3.5
	Dec.	16	0	4010	5300	3.5

TABLE 49 (*Continued*)

	Date	Excess of Specie Imports (Millions of francs)	Gold Premium at Paris (per 1000 francs)	Specie Reserve of Bank of France (Millions of francs)	Note Circulation (Millions of francs)	Bank of France Discount Rates (Per cent)
1912	Jan.	17	0	3994	5321	3.5
	Feb.	6	0	4008	5462	3.5
	Mar.	61	0	4035	5232	3.5
	Apr.	−2	0	4033	5232	3.5
	May	8	0	4052	5235	3
	June	11	0	4065	5110	3
	July	27	0	4080	5088	3
	Aug.	−1	0	4090	5069	3
	Sept.	−5	0	4065	5185	3
	Oct.	28	1	4005	5655	3.5
	Nov.	3	1	3970	5466	4
	Dec.	10	1	3925	5584	4
1913	Jan.	0	1	3860	5884	4
	Feb.	2	1	3845	5787	4
	Mar.	43	1	3827	5590	4
	Apr.	20	1	3844	5610	4
	May	64	1	3865	5513	4
	June	29	1	3922	5398	4
	July	51	1	3955	5676	4
	Aug.	50	1	4032	5410	4
	Sept.	107	1	4025	5519	4
	Oct.	70	1	3100	5805	4
	Nov.	44	1	4140	5648	4
	Dec.	73	1	4165	5713	4

TABLE 50

Comparison of Annual Average Discount Rates of the Bank of France, Bank of England, Bank of the German Empire, Bank of Holland, and the National Bank of Belgium[1]

Year	Bank of France	Bank of England	Bank of Germany	Bank of Holland	National Bank of Belgium
1880	2.81	2.76	4.24	3	3.35
1881	3.84	3.48	4.42	3.72	4.08
1882	3.80	4.14	4.54	4.63	4.42
1883	3.08	3.58	4.05	3.64	3.60
1884	3	2.96	4	3.06	3.32
1885	3	2.92	4.12	2.58	3.28
1886	3	3.05	3.28	2.5	2.80
1887	3	3.34	3.41	2.5	3.10
1888	3.1	3.34	3.32	2.5	3.32
1889	3.16	3.55	3.67	2.5	3.58
1890	3	4.69	4.52	3.02	3.22
1891	3	3.35	3.80	3	3
1892	2.7	2.52	3.2	2.7	2.70
1893	2.5	3.06	4.07	3.48	2.83
1894	2.5	2.11	3.12	2.58	3
1895	2.1	2	3.14	2.54	2.60
1896	2	2.48	3.66	3.03	2.84
1897	2	2.64	3.81	3.13	3
1898	2.2	3.19	4.27	2.70	3.04
1899	3.06	3.75	5.04	3.58	3.92
1900	3.25	3.96	5.33	3.5	4.09
1901	3	3.72	4.10	3.23	3.28
1902	3	3.33	3.32	3.02	3
1903	3	3.75	3.84	3.5	3.17
1904	3	3.3	4.22	3.08	3
1905	3	3.01	3.82	2.7	3.17
1906	3	4.27	5.15	4.66	3.84
1907	3.45	4.92	6.03	4.84	4.95
1908	3.04	3	4.76	3.09	3.56
1909	3	3.1	3.93	2.91	3.11
1910	3	3.72	4.35	4.34	4.12
1911	3.13	3.47	4.40	3.56	4.16
1912	3.37	3.77	4.95	4	4.41
1913	4	4.77	5.88	4.65	5

[1] Average of weekly figures.

TABLE 51

RATIO OF BANK OF FRANCE RESERVES TO NOTE CIRCULATION AND DEPOSITS OF THE BANK OF FRANCE ON DECEMBER 31 OF EACH YEAR, 1888–1913

Year	Note Circulation (Millions of francs)	Total of Deposits and Note Liability (Millions of francs)	Specie Reserve (Millions of francs)	Ratio of Reserves to Note Circulation (Per cent)	Ratio of Reserves to Deposit and Note Liability (Per cent)
1888	2616	3346	2251	86	67
1889	3003	3735	2520	84	68
1890	3061	3671	2371	79	64
1891	3194	3934	2591	81	66
1892	3298	4048	2979	90	73
1893	3478	4055	2974	85	73
1894	3481	4226	3311	95	79
1895	3640	4481	3184	87	71
1896	3838	4681	3142	82	67
1897	3809	4642	3158	82	68
1898	3750	4503	3030	81	67
1899	3930	4781	3030	77	63
1900	4187	4912	3440	82	70
1901	4072	5061	3545	87	70
1902	4304	4869	3650	85	74
1903	4495	5110	3462	77	65
1904	4244	5038	3750	88	74
1905	4515	5534	3963	83	72
1906	4714	5599	3704	78	66
1907	4800	5547	3615	75	65
1908	5225	6010	4372	83	73
1909	5139	5959	4400	85	73
1910	5183	5976	4087	78	88
1911	5268	6237	3995	76	64
1912	5584	6523	3865	69	59
1913	5713	6752	4157	73	61

TABLE 52

RATIO OF RESERVES TO DEMAND LIABILITIES OF THE BANK OF FRANCE AND IMPORTANT FRENCH BANKS ON DECEMBER 31 OF EACH YEAR, 1888–1913

Year	(Millions of francs) Total Deposits of 4 Banks[1] and Bank of France	Total Reserves of the 4 Banks and Bank of France	Total Deposits and Note[2] Circulation	(Per cent) Ratio of Total Reserves to Total Deposits	Ratio of Reserves of Bank of France to Total Deposits[2]	Ratio of Reserves of Bank of France to Total Deposits and Note Circulation
1888	2045	2351	4661	115	110	48
1889	1951	2641	4956	135	130	50
1890	1914	2497	4965	130	124	47
1891	2145	2733	5339	127	121	48
1892	2318	3136	5616	135	128	52
1893	2066	3120	5544	151	144	53
1894	2486	3477	5967	139	133	55
1895	2467	3381	6107	133	129	52
1896	2694	3344	6532	124	116	47
1897	2822	3369	6631	119	111	47
1898	2860	3290	6610	115	105	45
1899	3080	3286	7010	106	98	43
1900	3159	3721	7346	118	109	46
1901	3540	3823	7612	107	100	46
1902	3224	3914	7528	121	113	48
1903	3534	3713	8029	105	98	43
1904	4398	4050	8642	92	85	43
1905	4557	4351	9072	95	82	41
1906	4944	4088	9658	82	75	39
1907	4435	3939	9235	88	67	39
1908	4949	4625	10174	93	88	42
1909	5191	4731	10330	91	84	43
1910	5575	4450	10758	79	73	37
1911	5971	4497	11239	75	66	35
1912	6076	4352	11660	71	63	33
1913	6619	4635	12332	70	62	33

[1] Crédit Lyonnais, Comptoir National d'Escompte, Société Générale, Crédit Industriel et Commercial.

[2] Including deposits and current accounts of four banks listed above and the Bank of France.

TABLE 53

NUMBER AND VALUE OF CHECKS USED ANNUALLY IN FRANCE, 1880–1913

Year	Number of Checks Issued in France (Millions)	Total Value of Checks Presented at Paris Clearing House (Billions of francs)	Total Transfers of the Bank of France (Billions of francs)
1880	4.3	3.2	65.4
1881	5.5	4	95.1
1882	4.5	4.5	77.7
1883	4.4	4.1	65
1884	4.4	4.2	62.8
1885	4.6	4.1	60.7
1886	4.7	3.9	71.1
1887	4.9	4.3	65.4
1888	4.9	4.6	73.7
1889	5.4	5.4	82.5
1890	5.3	5.1	86.6
1891	5.7	6	97.1
1892	5.7	4.8	74.9
1893	5.7	4.7	76.1
1894	6.7	5.3	92.3
1895	6.5	6.1	104.9
1896	7	7.3	85.2
1897	6.8	7.5	86.2
1898	7.2	8.5	93.5
1899	7.6	9.5	102.6
1900	7.9	10.6	102.4
1901	8.2	10.6	111.8
1902	8.7	9.9	120.2
1903	9.3	10.8	124.9
1904	9.4	11.8	152.8
1905	10.1	13.8	171.2
1906	10.5	17.8	189.3
1907	11.4	24.8	179.3
1908	11.7	26	170.2
1909	12	26.7	214.1
1910	13.3	29.6	245.8
1911	14.2	23.9	270.9
1912	14.9	34.7	319.7
1913	....	37.7	309.7

TABLE 54

DEPOSITS OF SAVINGS BANKS OF FRANCE, 1880–1913
(Millions of francs)

	Caisses d'Épargne Ordinaires [1]			Caisse Nationale d'Épargne [2]			
Year	Total Deposits December 31	Average per Pass Book	Average per Capita	Total Deposits December 31	Average per Pass Book	Average per Capita	Total Deposits of Both
1880	1280	333	34.1	...	...	...	1280
1881	1408	355	37.7	...	...	...	1408
1882	1755	396	46.4	47	225	1.2	1802
1883	1816	398	48	77	206	2	1893
1884	2022	425	53.2	115	213	3	2137
1885	2211	448	58	154	222	4	2365
1886	2314	454	60.5	191	225	4.9	2505
1887	2364	454	61.8	224	228	5.8	2588
1888	2495	465	65.2	267	236	6.9	2762
1889	2684	484	70	332	255	8.6	3016
1890	2912	505	76	413	274	10.7	3325
1891	3053	513	79.6	506	292	13.2	3559
1892	3227	527	84.1	616	312	16	3843
1893	3141	508	81.8	611	292	15.9	3752
1894	3287	519	85.5	691	303	17.9	3978
1895	3395	522	88.2	753	303	19.6	4148
1896	3382	510	87.8	785	292	20.3	4167
1897	3427	506	88.9	844	291	21	4271
1898	3400	494	87.9	875	283	22.6	4275
1899	3407	486	87.8	929	280	24	4336
1900	3264	459	83.2	1010	283	26	4274
1901	3349	462	86	1080	286	27.7	4429
1902	3283	449	84	1107	277	28.3	4390
1903	3188	435	81.4	1118	269	28.5	4306
1904	3246	437	82.7	1187	273	30.2	4423
1905	3377	446	86.1	1278	279	32.6	4655
1906	3434	448	87.5	1339	279	34.1	4773
1907	3543	454	90.3	1433	284	36.5	4976
1908	3689	466	94	1537	290	39.1	5226
1909	3833	472	97.6	1639	295	41.6	5472
1910	3933	474	100.2	1709	295	43.2	5642
1911	3908	465	98.7	1704	285	43	5612
1912	3947	463	99.6	1745	282	44.1	5690
1913	4011	463	101.3	1818	283	45.9	5829

[1] Over 2400 offices thruout France. Interest rate 1880–1890 3½–3¾ per cent, 1891–1892 3¼–3½ per cent, 1893–1895 3–3½ per cent, 1896– 2¾–3 per cent.

[2] Over 12,000 offices. Established in 1882. Interest rate 1882–1895 3 per cent, 1896– 2½ per cent.

TABLE 55

Wholesale and Retail Price Indices of Ten Consumption Commodities 1880–1909

(Base 1900 = 100)

Year	Wholesale[1] (1)	Semi-wholesale[2] (2)	Retail (3)[3]	Retail (4)[4]	Retail (5)[5]
1880	129	127	125	...	...
1881	126	122	...	...	...
1882	123	126	114	...	...
1883	122	121	120	...	...
1884	119	117	108	116	105
1885	117	110	109	...	...
1886	109	111	104	108	101
1887	105	105	97	104	103
1888	107	107	107	108	104
1889	111	105	108	...	...
1890	114	106	106	...	...
1891	107	109	107	...	...
1892	102	107	111	...	...
1893	100	102	107	...	...
1894	96	101	108	104	105
1895	92	97	99	100	99
1896	92	97	97	99	97
1897	96	100	97	96	98
1898	97	99	102	...	...
1899	96	100	103	99	101
1900	100	100	100	100	100
1901	104	100	102	103	106
1902	104	96	98	104	105
1903	103	97	97	105	106
1904	97	91	97	111	106
1905	100	86	97	111	106
1906	106	90	98	115	108
1907	112	96	98	112	110
1908	119	97	102	113	114
1909	119	94	104	110	109

Source: Salaires et coût de l'existence à diverses époques jusqu'en 1910. Paris, 1911, Chap. 1.

[1] Index of annual wholesale prices of bread, butter, cheese, potatoes, rice, cooking oil, ordinary wine, sugar, coal, edible oil.

[2] Index of price of above commodities paid by large public institutions.

[3] Index of price of above commodities at Railway Co-operative stores.

[4] Index of annual average price of white beans, Swiss cheese, olive oil, vinegar, salt, pepper, chicory, starch, candles, split peas at Railway Co-operative stores.

[5] Index of price of commodities in (4) at some retail groceries.

TABLE 56

ANNUAL PRICE INDICES OF TEN DOMESTIC COMMODITIES. PRICES AT PLACE OF EXTRACTION,[1] 1895–1913

(Base 1900 = 100)

Year	Index	Year	Index
1895	92.4	1905	97.4
1896	92.5	1906	98.1
1897	94	1907	95.8
1898	95.6	1908	95.4
1899	97.5	1909	99.3
1900	100	1910	98.8
1901	100.6	1911	101.9
1902	102.5	1912	104.7
1903	103.3	1913	106.3
1904	103.8		

[1] Building stone, roofing slate, sand and gravel, brick clay, limestone flux, marle, crushed rock, talc, flint sand, moulding plaster.

Source of prices: Statisque de l'Industrie Minerale de la France.

This index is "unweighted" and was constructed for this study.

TABLE 57

MONTHLY INDEX OF WHOLESALE PRICES IN FRANCE, 1900–1913. PUBLISHED BY LA RÉFORME ÉCONOMIQUE

(Base 1890 = 100)[1]

	1900	1901	1902	1903	1904	1905	1906
Jan.	102.8	98.8	93.4	95	97	95.2	100.8
Feb.	104.6	97.8	94.4	95.4	97.2	95.2	100.8
Mar.	103.6	95.8	94.8	96.6	96.6	94.8	101.2
Apr.	103.8	95.4	94.8	97	96.2	95.6	102.8
May	102.2	95.4	94.8	97.2	95	95.6	104.6
June	101.4	95.2	94.6	96.8	93.6	95.6	105
July	102	95.2	95	96	93.4	95.6	105.6
Aug.	102.6	96	95.4	94.6	94	95	106
Sept.	101.8	95.6	93.8	93.8	94.8	94.4	107.2
Oct.	102	95.2	93.4	94.2	95	96.2	109.6
Nov.	101.2	94.6	94.4	94.4	95.4	95.4	110.6
Dec.	100.6	93.6	94.6	96.4	95.6	99.4	110.4
	1907	**1908**	**1909**	**1910**	**1911**	**1912**	**1913**
Jan.	111.6	104.8	99.4	107	112.4	115.4	118.4
Feb.	112.6	104.2	99.4	106.6	114	116.4	117.8
Mar.	112.4	102.8	101.4	107	113.6	117.6	117.2
Apr.	111.8	101.2	102.2	107.4	113.6	119	116.8
May	112.2	100.8	102.6	106.6	114.2	120	116.2
June	112.6	99.8	102.4	105.6	113.8	120	115.2
July	113	99.4	102.2	106.8	112.2	118	114.2
Aug.	111	100.8	102.6	109.2	112.3	117.4	114.6
Sept.	111.2	100.8	103.6	109	115.2	117.4	116.6
Oct.	110.6	100	105.4	110	115.8	117.4	116.6
Nov.	108	100	106.2	111.1	115	117	115.6
Dec.	106	99.4	106.6	111	114.2	117	

SOURCE: La Réforme Économique.

[1] Annual indices go back to 1890. See Table 58.

TABLE 58

Comparison of "General Purpose" Annual Price Indices of France, Great Britain, Germany, United States, and the World

(Reduced to common base 1900 = 100)

Year	France (1)	France (2)	Germany (3)	Great Britain (4)	United States (5)	World (6)	World (7)
1880	121	...	113	117	117	...	117
1881	118	...	112	112	116	...	110
1882	115	...	112	111	119	...	112
1883	111	...	107	110	116	...	108
1884	102	...	101	101	109	...	102
1885	100	...	96	96	102	...	97
1886	96	...	89	92	101	...	93
1887	93	...	91	91	102	...	93
1888	97	...	93	94	104	...	97
1889	101	...	100	96	104	...	99
1890	101	97	98	96	102	...	100
1891	99	97	100	96	101	...	99
1892	96	92	93	91	95	...	95
1893	95	95	91	91	95	...	94
1894	87	87	85	84	86	...	87
1895	85	82	83	83	85	...	84
1896	83	80	82	81	81	...	83
1897	84	81	81	82	81	...	83
1898	86	86	82	86	84	...	87
1899	94	93	88	90	92	...	92
1900	100	100	100	100	100	100	100
1901	95	94	102	94	98	100	96
1902	94	92	91	93	102	102	96
1903	95	93	91	93	103	102	98
1904	94	93	90	94	102	101	98
1905	99	94	94	96	104	105	100
1906	105	103	99	103	111	109	107
1907	110	109	105	106	117	114	113
1908	102	98	99	97	111	109	105
1909	102	100	99	99	114	110	107
1910	109	105	103	104	119	113	112
1911	115	111	108	106	116	116	116
1912	119	115	...	113	122	122	...
1913	116	113	...	113	121	121	...

Col. 1. Published by Statistique Générale de la France in the Annuaire Statistique de la France. Prices until 1906 based on annual values of imports of 43 commodities fixed by the Commission des Valeurs en Douane. Since 1906 based on market prices in France of 45 commodities.
Col. 2. Published in La Réforme Économique beginning with 1890. Average of weekly market prices of 40 to 56 commodities.
Col. 3. Published in Hamburgs Handel und Schiffahrt. Based on import values of 28 commodities before 1888 and 42 since.
Col. 4. Sauerbeck's Index published in the Journal of the Royal Statistical Society.
Col. 5. Before 1890 Report to the Committee on Finance, March 3, 1893. Since 1890 U. S. Bureau of Labor series.
Col. 6. Coat's World Index. Published in Cost of Living Report, Vol. II. Board of Inquiry into Cost of Living. 1915.
Col. 7. Knibb's World Index. Prices, Price Indexes and Cost of Living in Australia. 1912.

TABLE 59

RELATIVE MOVEMENTS OF THE ANNUAL EXPENDITURE OF FRENCH WORKERS OF FIVE DIFFERENT RANKS OF INCOME, 1880–1910

(Base 1900 = 100)

Year	Very Low	Low	Medium	High	Very High	Average	Rich Household of 9 Persons
1880	117	115	115	115	114	115	109
1881	117	115	115	115	...	115	...
1882	116	115	114	113	113	114	108
1883	116	116	115	115	114	115	110
1884	109	109	108	108	107	108	105
1885	104	103	103	103	102	103	102
1886	100	103	99	99	99	100	99
1887	96	96	95	95	93	95	96
1888	101	100	100	100	99	100	98
1889	102	102	102	101	100	101	100
1890	105	104	99	104	103	103	105
1891	109	108	108	108	109	108	108
1892	107	106	107	106	105	106	105
1893	102	102	102	102	101	102	99
1894	105	106	106	106	106	106	101
1895	105	106	106	106	106	106	103
1896	100	102	102	101	103	102	100
1897	99	99	99	99	99	99	98
1898	106	105	105	105	104	105	102
1899	105	104	105	105	104	105	101
1900	100	100	100	100	100	100	100
1901	101	102	102	102	102	102	102
1902	103	103	104	103	104	101	102
1903	107	107	107	107	107	107	105
1904	106	104	103	104	103	104	102
1905	109	108	108	108	108	108	103
1906	110	109	109	109	109	109	102
1907	113	113	114	114	114	116	107
1908	115	115	115	115	115	115	109
1909	112	112	112	113	112	112	107
1910	119	117	119	119	119	118	111

SOURCE: Statistique Générale de la France. Salaires et coût de l'existence à diverses époques jusqu'en 1910. Paris, 1911.

TABLE 60

British Annual Export of Capital and British Barter Terms of Trade, 1880–1913

Year	British Export of Capital[1] (Thousands of Pounds)	Net Barter Terms of Trade[2] (1900 = 100)	Gross Barter Terms of Trade[2] (1900 = 100)
1880	4100	124	129
1881	33200	129	148
1882	24300	127	144
1883	16900	124	134
1884	41000	125	145
1885	33900	123	137
1886	61800	122	144
1887	66800	122	145
1888	74500	123	145
1889	68800	121	137
1890	82600	113	136
1891	48500	114	123
1892	35300	116	118
1893	40100	115	118
1894	21300	112	113
1895	22700	111	114
1896	39300	112	113
1897	27100	112	109
1898	17200	114	105
1899	27900	107	106
1900	31200	100	100
1901	13900	102	99
1902	11200	105	102
1903	23000	107	104
1904	27200	105	105
1905	62800	107	114
1906	104400	105	119
1907	140200	105	127
1908	129900	104	121
1909	110100	110	123
1910	150800	112	132
1911	192200	107	132
1912	226000	107	130
1913	....	103	130

[1] C. K. Hobson, The Export of Capital, Chap. 8.

[2] F. W. Taussig, International Trade, p. 412.

TABLE 61

PARIS MARKET DISCOUNT RATES, QUANTITY OF MONEY OUTSTANDING, AND PRICE SERIES OF LA RÉFORME ÉCONOMIQUE AND OF STATISTIQUE GÉNÉRALE DE LA FRANCE. QUARTERLY FIGURES, 1898–1913

Year		Quantity of Money[1] (Millions of francs)	Market Discount Rates[2] (Per cent)	Prices	
				La Réforme Économique[3]	Statistique Générale[4]
1898	1st	7896	1.88	...	...
	2nd	7786	1.88	...	...
	3d	7553	1.75	...	...
	4th	7650	2.75	...	...
1899	1st	7480	2.75	...	...
	2nd	7713	2.75	...	...
	3d	7765	2.75	...	...
	4th	8013	3	...	...
1900	1st	8093	3.75	101.2	...
	2nd	8073	3.25	100	...
	3d	7980	2.75	99.7	...
	4th	8036	2.75	98.8	...
1901	1st	8270	2.75	95.1	...
	2nd	7960	2.62	93.1	...
	3d	7870	1.88	93.3	...
	4th	8030	2.62	92.2	...
1902	1st	8210	2.5	91.8	94.6
	2nd	8080	2.12	92.3	95.1
	3d	8120	2.12	92.9	93.5
	4th	8400	2.75	91.8	92.4
1903	1st	8630	2.88	93.4	96.3
	2nd	8650	2.62	94.7	98
	3d	8570	2.5	92.5	94.9
	4th	8840	2.88	92.7	93.4
1904	1st	8880	2.75	94.6	94.6
	2nd	8800	2.12	92.6	93.4
	3d	8740	1.25	91.7	96.6
	4th	8970	2.38	93	95.4

[1] Bank of France notes and specie in France outside the Bank of France. Quarterly average of monthly figures.

[2] Market discount rates on prime paper at Paris. Quarterly average of weekly quotations.

[3] Price series of France published by La Réforme Économique. Quarterly average of monthly indices. Reduced to 1900 = 100.

[4] Quarterly price series of France published by the Statistique Générale de la France. 1902–1913.

TABLE 61 (*Continued*)

Year		Quantity of Money (Millions of francs)	Market Discount Rates (Per cent)	Prices	
				La Réforme Économique	Statistique Générale
1905	1st	9100	2.12	93	97
	2nd	9100	1.75	93.3	98.4
	3d	9230	1.75	92.7	98
	4th	9290	3	94.5	99.6
1906	1st	9590	2.75	98.5	100.8
	2nd	9620	2.62	101.6	103.2
	3d	9500	2.30	103.5	103.5
	4th	9810	3	106	107.7
1907	1st	10140	3	109.5	110
	2nd	9980	3.37	109.5	111.8
	3d	9880	3.37	109	109.2
	4th	10280	3.75	105.4	105.1
1908	1st	10280	2.75	101.1	102.2
	2nd	10310	2	98.2	100.4
	3d	10200	1.5	97.8	102.1
	4th	10500	2.12	97.2	98.9
1909	1st	10430	1.75	97.4	98.7
	2nd	10550	1.25	100	101.8
	3d	10560	1.5	100.3	102
	4th	10690	2.33	103.5	103.1
1910	1st	10920	2.5	104.3	106.2
	2nd	10740	2.25	104	108.9
	3d	10550	2.12	105.7	109.5
	4th	10830	2.75	108	107.6
1911	1st	10980	2.37	110.6	112.7
	2nd	10850	2	112	114.2
	3d	10720	2.5	110.5	111.8
	4th	11390	3.25	112.8	114.1
1912	1st	11400	3.12	113.7	116.6
	2nd	11290	3	116.7	119.7
	3d	11210	2.88	114.8	118.2
	4th	11800	3.88	114.3	116.7
1913	1st	12100	4	115	116.2
	2nd	12050	4	113.2	116.7
	3d	12230	3.75	113.8	115.1
	4th	12400	3.75	113	114.3

BIBLIOGRAPHY

BIBLIOGRAPHY

OFFICIAL

Administration des monnaies et médailles. Rapport au Ministre des Finances. (Annual.)

Commission Extra-Parlementaire de l'Impôt sur le Revenu. Rapport Général. Paris, 1895.

Direction de la Statistique Générale de la France. Annuaire Statistique de la France. (Annual.)

Direction générale des douanes. Tableau Générale du Commerce et de la Navigation. (Annual.)

—— Tarif des douanes de France.

—— Annales du Commerce Extérieur. (Annual.)

Ministère des affaires étrangères. La fortune française a l'étranger en 1902.

Ministère de l'agriculture. Statistique Agricole Annuelle.

Ministère des finances. Bulletin de Statistique et de Législation Comparée. (Monthly.)

Ministère des travaux publics, des postes et des télégraphes. Statistique de l'Industrie Minérale et des Appareils à Vapeur en France et en Algérie. (Annual.)

Ministère du travail et de la prévoyance sociale. Annuaire Statistique. (Annual.)

—— Bulletin de la Statistique Générale de la France. (Monthly.)

—— Renseignements sur l'industrie et les salaires de 1871 à 1900. (Annual.)

—— Salaires et coût de l'existence à diverses époques jusqu'en 1910.

—— Statistique internationale du mouvement de la population.

U. S. Bureau of Labor Statistics. Bulletin No. 284. 1921. Index Numbers of Wholesale Prices in the United States and Foreign Countries.

U. S. Department of Commerce, Bureau of Foreign and Domestic Commerce. Trade Information Bulletin No. 761. 1931. The Balance of International Payments of the United States in 1930.

U. S. National Monetary Commission. U. S. Senate Document No. 405. 1910. Interviews on the Banking and Currency Systems of England, Scotland, France, Germany, Switzerland, and Italy.

—— U. S. Document No. 578. 1910. Statistics for Great Britain, Germany, and France. 1867–1909.

PERIODICALS

L'Économiste Français. (Weekly.)

Le Marché Financier. (Monthly.)

La Réforme Économique. (Monthly.)

Journal de la Société de Statistique de Paris. (Annual.)

BOOKS AND ARTICLES

Allard, E. La statistique douanière internationale. Paris, 1908.

Angell, J. W. The Theory of International Prices. Cambridge, 1926.

—— Equilibrium in International Trade: The United States, 1919–26. Quarterly Journal of Economics. May, 1928.

Arboux, M. Les valeurs mobilières étrangères sur le marché français. Paris, 1913.

Arnauné, A. Le commerce extérieur et les tarifs de douane. Paris, 1911.

—— La monnaie, le crédit, et le change. Paris, 1894.

Asselin, O. Emigration from Belgium and France to Canada. Ottawa, 1911.

Augier, C., and Marvaud, A. La politique douanière de la France. Paris, 1911.

Baldy, E. Les banques d'affaires en France depuis 1900. Paris, 1922.

Bateman, A., and Fountain, H. The Import and Export Statistics of Various Countries. Bulletin de l'Institut International de Statistique. 1905.

Becker, H. Emprunts étrangers en France. Paris, 1880.

Becque, E. L'Internationalisation des capitaux. Montpellier, 1912.

Bellet, D. Crises économiques. Paris, 1918.

Beveridge, Sir W. Mr. Keynes' Evidence for Overpopulation. Economica. 1924.

Bodin, E. L'Encaisse métallique de la Banque de France. Rennes, 1925.

Carr, R. M. The Rôle of Price in the International Mechanism. Quarterly Journal of Economics. August, 1931.

Cassel, G. Foreign Investments. Chicago, 1928.

Casteignau-Caumont. Le régime fiscal des valeurs mobilières. Bordeaux, 1910.

Clapham, J. H. The Economic Development of France and Germany, 1815–1914. Cambridge, 1923.

Comdamain, H. Essai sur la conduite de la Banque de France aux époques de crise. Rennes, 1911.

Congrès international des valeurs mobilières. Rapport général. 5 vols. Paris, 1901.

Coste, A. Étude statistique sur les salaires des travailleurs et le revenu de la France. Paris, 1890.

—— Les bénéfices comparés du travail et du capital dans l'accroissement de la richesse depuis 50 ans. Journal de la Société de Statistique de Paris. November 18, 1896.

Dechere, L. La productivité du travail et les salaires. Revue d'Économie Politique. April, 1899.

Decoudu, M. Les valeurs mobilières admises à la côte officielle de la Bourse de Paris. Congrès des valeurs mobilières. Paris, 1900.

Dijol, M. Situation économique de la France sous le régime protectionniste de 1892. Paris, 1910.

Domergue, J. La question des sociétés de crédit. Paris, 1910.

Essars, P. des. Le papier et la monnaie dans la circulation. Journal de la Société de Statistique de Paris. 1896.
—— La vitesse de la circulation de la monnaie. Journal de la Société de Statistique de Paris. 1895.

Faure, F. Le mouvement international des capitaux. Revue d'Économie Internationale. October, 1911.
—— La Banque de France et le commerce extérieur. Paris, 1910.
—— Les budgets de la France depuis vingt ans (1868–1887). Paris, 1887.
Felsenhardt, W. La Banque de France de 1897 à nos jours. Bordeaux, 1922.
Ferrais, C. Examen des difficultés particulières que rencontre la statistique du mouvement des métaux dans le commerce international. Bulletin de l'Institut International de Statistique. 1887.
Flux, A. W. Price Movements in the Foreign Trade of France. Royal Statistical Journal. 1900.
Foville, A. de. Variations des prix en France de 1881 à 1910. Bulletin de l'Institut International de Statistique. 1912.
—— La Monnaie. Paris, 1907.
—— La fortune française à l'étranger. Revue Politique et Parlementaire. 1902.
—— La France économique. Paris, 1888.

Giffen, R. The Use of Import and Export Statistics. Economic Inquiries and Studies. London, 1904.
Gonnard, R. L'Émigration européen au XIXe siècle. Paris, 1906.
Guillaume, L. L'Épargne française et les valeurs mobilières étrangères. Paris, 1907.
Guilmard, E. L'Évasion fiscale. Paris, 1908.
Guyot, Y. Le commerce et les commerçants. Paris, 1909.
—— Lettres sur la politique coloniale. Paris, 1885.
—— The Amount, Direction, and Nature of French Investments. Annals of the American Academy of Political and Social Sciences. 1916.
—— Les capitaux et l'industrie française. Journal de la Société de Statisque de Paris. 1911.
—— Évaluation de la fortune privée en France d'après les éléments fiscaux. Bulletin de l'Institut International de Statistique. 1905.

Hobson, C. K. The Depreciation of British Home Investments. Economic Journal. June, 1912.
—— The Measurement of the Balance of Trade. Economica. 1921.
—— The Export of Capital. London, 1914.
Hooker, R. H. The Course of Prices at Home and Abroad. 1890–1910. Journal of the Royal Statistical Society. 1911.

Jenks, L. H. The Migration of British Capital to 1875. New York, 1927.

Kaufmann, M. E. La Banque en France. Paris, 1914.
Kemmerer, E. W. Theory of Foreign Investments. Annals of the American Academy of Political and Social Sciences. 1916.

Keynes, J. M. Foreign Investment and National Advantage. Nation (London). 1924.
—— The Transfer Problem. Economic Journal. 1929.
—— Return of Estimated Value of Foreign Trade of United Kingdom at Prices of 1900. Economic Journal. 1912.
Kreps, T. J. Import and Export Prices in the United States and the Terms of International Trade, 1880–1914. Quarterly Journal of Economics, 1926.

Lavergne, A. de, and Henry, L. P. La Richesse de la France. Paris, 1908.
League of Nations. Balance of Payments and Foreign Trade Balances, 1910–1923. Geneva, 1924.
Legrand, C. Les statistiques douanières. Mons, 1908.
Lescure, J. L'Épargne en France. Paris, 1914.
—— La puissance de l'épargne de la France et les placements étrangères. Revue Politique et Parlementaire. 1912.
Letailleur, E. Politique et finance d'avant guerre. Paris, 1920.
—— L'Escroquerie russe. Paris, 1906.
Levasseur, E. Aperçu des resultats de la statistique comparée du commerce extérieur. Journal de la Société de Statistique de Paris. 1906.
—— Histoire du commerce de la France. 2 vols. Paris, 1912.
—— Salariat et salaires. Paris, 1909.
—— Questions ouvrières et industrielles en France sous la Troisième République. Paris, 1908.
Levy, R. G. La fortune mobilière de la France à l'étranger. Revue des Deux Mondes. 1897.
—— Les grands marchés financiers. Revue Économique Internationale. 1905.
—— Psychologie des placements. Revue d'Économie Politique. 1905.
Lewis, C. The International Accounts. New York, 1927.
Liesse, A. Evolution of Credit and Banks in France. Washington, 1909.
—— La statistique, ses difficultés, ses resultats. Paris, 1912.
Loujon, M. Le fret d'exportation. La pénurie en France. Montpellier, 1923.

March, L. Salaires et coût de l'existence à diverses époques jusqu'en 1910. Paris, 1911.
Masse, R. La production des richesses. Paris, 1925.
Meynial, P. Créances et dettes internationales. Paris, 1926.
Montety, J. Les banques et la politique de placement à l'étranger de l'épargne nationale. Paris, 1923.
Moulton, H. G., and Lewis, C. The French Debt Problem. New York, 1926.
Mourre, C. D'Où vient la décadence économique de la France. Paris, 1899.

Neymarck, A. Finances contemporaines. 7 vols. Paris, 1911.
—— Le développement annuel de l'épargne française. Paris, 1906.
—— Les chemineaux de l'épargne. Journal de la Société de Statistique de Paris. 1911.

—— Les amortissements et les remboursements dans le cours du siècle. Journal de la Société de Statistique de Paris. April, 1910.
—— Une nouvelle évaluation. Paris, 1893.
Nogaro, B. Le rôle de la monnaie dans le commerce international et la théorie quantitative. Paris, 1904.
Nozelk, J. Une taxe sur la main-d'oeuvre étrangère. Revue Politique et Parlementaire. 1911.

Ohlin, B. Transfer Difficulties, Real and Imagined. Economic Journal. 1929.
—— A Rejoinder. Economic Journal. 1929.
—— The Reparations Problem. Index. April, 1928.

Paish, Sir G. Great Britain's Capital Investments in Other Lands. Journal of the Royal Statistical Society. 1909.
Pallain, G. Les douanes françaises. 2 vols. Paris, 1913.
Pallain, J. Les changes étrangers et les prix. Paris, 1905.
Paslovsky, L., and Moulton, H. G. Russian Debts and Russian Reconstruction. New York, 1924.
Patron, M. The Bank of France in Its Relation to National and International Credit. Washington, 1910.
Payen, E. Les étrangers en France. Économiste Français. 1910.
Petit, P. La dette publique de la Russie. Paris, 1912.
Pic, P. La main-d'oeuvre étrangère en France. Revue Économique Internationale. 1911.
Pirou, G. La main-d'oeuvre étrangère en France. Paris, 1916.
Pougnet, M. Valeurs étrangères et fonds d'état étrangers devant l'impôt. Paris, 1900.
Poujade, M. Étude sur les variations du taux de l'escompte en France et leurs consequences aux XIXe et XXe siècle. Paris, 1923.
Pupin, R. La richesse de la France devant la guerre. Paris, 1916.
—— Richesse privée et finances françaises. Paris, 1919.

Raffolovich, A. L'Exportation des capitaux. Journal d'Économistes. 1911.
Renou, M. Les valeurs étrangères. Leur rôle social et économique. Leur régime fiscal. Paris, 1906.
Rist, C. La circulation monétaire française et le mouvement des prix. Revue d'Économie Politique. 1914.
Rosendorff, R. Die Goldprämienpolitik der Banque de France und ihre deutschen Lobredner. Jahrbücher für Nationalökonomie und Statistik. 1901.
Roulleau, G. La production et les mouvements internationals des métaux précieux au début du XX siècle. Journal de la Société de Statistique de Paris. 1912.
—— Les règlements par effets de commerce. Paris, 1914.
Rozenraad, C. The International Money Market. Journal of the Royal Statistical Society. 1900.

Salefranque, L. Les valeurs mobilières dans la fortune privée en France. Congrès international des valeurs mobilières. Paris, 1900.
Say, L. Rapport sur le paiement de l'indemnité de guerre. Paris, 1874.
Schuller, J. La statistique douanière et ses méthodes. Paris, 1911.
Silverman, A. G. Some International Factors for Great Britain. The Review of Economic Statistics. August, 1931.
Soetbeer, A. Materials toward the Elucidation of the Economic Conditions Affecting the Precious Metals and the Question of Standards. Washington, 1887.
Stockbroker, A. The Depreciation of British Home Investment. Economic Journal. 1912.

Taussig, F. W. International Trade. New York, 1929.
—— The Change in Great Britain's Trade Terms after 1900. Economic Journal. 1925.
Théry, E. Fortune publique de la France. Paris, 1911.
—— Le progrès économique de la France. Paris, 1903.
—— Les problèmes économiques de la guerre. Paris, 1916.
—— Les valeurs mobilières en France. Congrès des valeurs mobilières. Vol. 2. Paris, 1900.
Thorp, W. L. Business Annals. New York, 1926.
Truchy, H. Étude sur le commerce de la France. Revue d'Économie Politique. Paris, 1904.

Vignon, L. La France en Algérie. Paris, 1893.
Viner, J. Canada's Balance of International Indebtedness, 1900–1913. Cambridge, 1924.
—— International Finance and Balance of Power Diplomacy, 1880–1914. Southwestern Political and Social Science Quarterly. March, 1929.

Wicksell, K. International Freight and Prices. Quarterly Journal of Economics. 1918.
Willis, H. P. A History of the Latin Monetary Union. Chicago, 1901.

Yovovitch, D. Les valeurs mobilières étrangères à la Bourse de Paris. Paris, 1910.

INDEX

INDEX

Bei Fragen zur Produktsicherheit wenden Sie sich bitte an:
If you have any questions regarding product safety,
please contact:

Walter de Gruyter GmbH
Genthiner Straße 13
10785 Berlin
productsafety@degruyterbrill.com